W9-CJT-022

THE GREAT FARINI

Shane Peacock and five generations of his ancestors have called the countryside just north of Port Hope, Ontario their home. In fact, his great-great grandfather lived a mere ten-minute horse ride from the Hunt's home near Canton. Peacock grew up in Kapuskasing and attended university in Peterborough and Toronto. His play *The Great Farini*, featuring a live high-wire walk, was recently produced by the 4th Line Theatre of Millbrook, Ontario. *Saturday Night* and various other magazines have published his writing, much of it about unusual people with unusual determination and desire: characters with character. H

The only excuse for making a useless thing
is that one admires it intensely.
Oscar Wilde

To live outside the law,
you must be honest.
Bob Dylan

The Great FARINI

THE HIGH-WIRE LIFE OF WILLIAM HUNT

Shane Peacock

Penguin Books

PENGUIN BOOKS
Published by the Penguin Group
Penguin Books Canada Ltd, 10 Alcorn Avenue,
Toronto, Ontario, Canada M4V 3B2
Penguin Books Ltd, 27 Wrights Lane, London W8 5TZ, England
Penguin Books USA Inc., 375 Hudson Street, New York,
New York 10014, U.S.A.
Penguin Books Australia Ltd, Ringwood, Victoria, Australia
Penguin Books (NZ) Ltd, 182–190 Wairau Road,
Auckland 10, New Zealand

Penguin Books Ltd, Registered Offices:
Harmondsworth, Middlesex, England

First published in Viking by Penguin Books Canada Limited, 1995
Published in Penguin Books, 1996
1 3 5 7 9 10 8 6 4 2

Manufactured in Canada

Canadian Cataloguing in Publication Data

Peacock, Shane
The great Farini: the high-wire life of William Hunt

ISBN 0-14-024360-7

1. Hunt, William, 1838-1928. 2. Eccentrics and eccentricities - Canada -
Biography. I. Title.

CT9991. H85P43 1996   971.04'092   C95-930002-3

The following are reprinted with permission:
Quotation from THE KALAHARI AND ITS LOST CITY by A.J. Clement
published by Longman Penguin South Africa, 1967.
Quotation from THE LOST WORLD OF THE KALAHARI by Laurens van der
Post published by Chatto and Windus, reprinted 1988.
Quotation from THUNDER ON THE BLAAUWBERG by Lawrence Green
published by Struik Publishers Ltd, 1966.
Quotation from I BROUGHT THE AGES HOME by C.T. Currelly
published by McGraw-Hill Ryerson, 1956.

Every effort has been made to contact or trace all copyright holders.
The publishers will be glad to make good any errors or omissions
brought to our attention in future editions.

*This book is dedicated to my father,
William Jackson Peacock, who usually
steers me in the right direction in spite
of my own better instincts.*

*And to my wife, Sophie Kneisel,
for her love and friendship;
without her* The Great Farini
would still be a dream.

INTRODUCTION

When I was a child my grandfather told me a wonderful story about a man who walked on a high wire over Niagara Falls. He told it as we sat on the sun-porch of our farm in the rolling hills of Hope Township in southern Ontario. It was the stirring legend of a country boy from just a few dirt roads away, and the unsinkable determination that pushed him to try his terrifying feat. My grandfather said that Farini Hunt, though forgotten by his countrymen, was one of the most extraordinary men who ever lived. He was absolutely right.

But years later I discovered he knew less than half the story. He didn't know that after Niagara, Farini had many more lives: in the palatial theatres of London, high in the air at Madison Square Garden and in the depths of the Kalahari Desert; Farini would be an inventor, an artist, a Svengali; he would be, as one amazed spectator called him, "the most versatile man in history."

Life in nineteenth-century Canada moved slowly, values were traditional and people were for the most part content. Excitement happened elsewhere. So why was William Hunt so different? What drove him like a demon through his life, and made him try so many reckless and sometimes unsavoury things?

He was born with enormous, but not unnatural energy, inherited from his physically vigorous and intelligent parents. They were shocked by his unbridled vitality, and told him it was evil. But he couldn't change what he was, so he dug in his heels. To live by his heart and his emotions, he thought, was to be honest; others were hypocritical, afraid of their own bodies and their passions. Fixated on this code of honesty, his life became an exploration of passion, an adventure story. He went out into the world beyond his repressed little farming community, looking for thrills.

But honesty is a dangerous thing. As the years went by, he became an almost amoral man, ready to try nearly anything, and ready to push others to dare the devil too. He created some of the most thrilling entertainment the world has ever seen, putting staid Victorians momentarily in touch with dangerous, almost-erotic sensations that sometimes alarmed them. Most of his shows were brilliant illusions, something he took great pleasure in, because he believed that people preferred illusion to truth. But he also made his shows look scientific, and morally upright, to prove to himself and ultimately to his father, that even though he had taken up the evil ways of a showman, he was still a respectable man.

By the end of his life, energy still flowing in him but the desperation long gone, he was a lighter, happier and even kinder personality, revelling in the honesty of children, chuckling at adults where he once sneered, apparently resigned to the idea that he would forever be considered eccentric and rebellious, if he were ever considered at all.

William Hunt had to invent Farini in order to be himself. And that was his greatest triumph. If it can be said that desire is the gasoline of life, then he had more fuel than anyone else, and if, in the end, the greatest thing about life is the experience of living it, then what a life he had.

It took nearly ten years to write and research his life. Investigating him was like exploring ten lives; his fame waxed and waned, he travelled in distant places and from time to time chose obscurity, and therefore disappeared from newspapers and other accounts for extended periods; and he told prodigious tall tales, which made the facts of his life blend with many extraordinary fictions. In telling his story it has been necessary to make certain educated speculations, and other times to even situate particular adventures in time-frames that seem unlikely: the reader is always, of course, informed whenever any such licence takes place.

To fully capture any human life is an impossible task and any such undertaking always leaves some aspects of a personality unexplored. The reader of Farini's life, for example, might be surprised to know that he was a man of great humour, in fact humour dominates his writings. Despite his deep-seated passions and his desire to live on the edge, he always felt that life was, in essence, comic, and that people, with all their puffed-up ideas of right and wrong, and long-winded views of their own nobility, were really always like children, full of unadulterated hopes and dreams and feelings, hilariously trying to play grown-up roles.

As my grandfather told me that fabulous story and I looked up the sideroad of our farm, trying to imagine walking in the air above the thundering green waters of Niagara, something must have touched me deeply. The story stayed in my mind, like the best of all bedtime tales. Farini: a genius, a devil, a hero, a Peter Pan; Houdini and Barnum and many more wrapped up in one; a man whose life was a book long before I wrote it.

PROLOGUE

It was December 1925. The reporter walked up the steep, snowy slope of Dorset Street in little Port Hope, looking for number 4 on one of the row houses. Finding it, he knocked. The door opened briskly.

Old Farini Hunt, dressed impeccably, snow-white hair and beard perfectly coiffed, took the young man's hand and squeezed it until it seemed it would break, then he led him on a brisk march down the hallway toward the living room. It was a sight to behold. What seemed like hundreds of brightly coloured paintings hung on the walls and sat on the floor, and the stuffed heads of exotic animals loomed above them; and there were strange photographs everywhere, of old circus people, sideshow freaks and a man on a wire high above a deep gorge; African trophies lay here and there: a Bushman's cape, a long sharp spear...and what looked disturbingly like two severed elephant's feet.

Turning to look into the old man's eyes he was surprised by what he saw. They were bright blue and anxious, ready, thought the young man, for anything. He glanced at his notes. They said Farini Hunt was eighty-seven years old.

The *Port Hope Times* wanted his life story, said the reporter; they had heard it was extraordinary, worth writing down. But he didn't say the other things he'd heard around town: that Farini Hunt had killed his first wife and had once kept a deformed child locked in his basement...that he was certifiably insane.

The old man smiled, as if he had a secret the young man would never know. He eyed him, suspiciously it seemed. Then he started to talk.

CHAPTER 1

Childhood:
Rebellion and Respectability

"I had natural, savage desires."
Farini; on his childhood

"Energy is eternal delight."
William Blake

Farini's ancestors thought they were respectable people, but they were renegades in their own way. His well-heeled great-grandfather Timothy Soper had even been a revolutionary, taking up arms against the king when the American War of Independence reached the frontier side of the Green Mountains of Vermont in the late 1770s. Then Timothy's son Leonard fell in love with Mary Marsh, the daughter of a prominent British Loyalist and enemy. The instant they married they were outcasts.

Abandoning their birthrights, the couple fled three hundred miles northward on horseback through dangerous territory to claim Loyalist land grants in the backwoods of Canada. At first they lived near the Bay of Quinte, but Leonard, six feet tall, swarthy and possessed of characteristic Soper restlessness, was soon on the move again, taking his little family by home-made sailboat up the northern shore of Lake Ontario further into the wilderness. Here in the new province of Upper Canada he came upon a place the Mississauga Indians called Cochingimink or Fat Fire Creek. Spotting a few log cabins recently raised in front of beautifully rolling hills covered with dense forest, they edged closer to shore. A few miles west they landed, and never left.

Soon other Sopers and Marshes joined their encampment in the woods and over the following decades built family dynasties in the land that stretched out around the village they called Port Britain. Leonard and his brother-in-law Samuel Marsh erected grist and sawmills, a tannery, distillery, blacksmith shop, hotel and tavern; they ran the justice system from their farmhouses, operated the schools and principal businesses; they were once again highly respectable people.

Despite forests full of plump animals and creeks so thick with Atlantic salmon that some pioneers fed them to their pigs, they lived bitterly hard lives, beset by constant sicknesses, terrible loneliness and bleak winters. In 1812 the Americans menaced them again and they marshalled themselves into ragged battalions ready to fight once more for their beliefs. But the following year disease proved an even greater foe when the "spotted fever" swept through Hope Township taking Mary Soper, one of her children and Samuel Marsh directly to heaven. The Sopers went on, uncomplaining, tough and ingenious to the core. More than a century later a friend of the family wrote, "[They] had wonderful physical strength and powers of endurance. Their ancestors must have been among the giants."

Alone with eight children, fifty-one-year-old Leonard wed his Loyalist neighbour's daughter Mary Odell. She gave him two new sons, David and Hiram; but their first child was a daughter named Hannah.

Growing up in the 1820s Hannah Soper learned that she was expected to follow the strict moral code that brought honour to the God-fearing Loyalist good names of her forebears. She was to attend Church of England services and not sway from practices of the past. By 1834, at the age of twenty, when she met a dark and handsome Englishman who had come to the adjoining Township of Hamilton to teach school, she was as educated and cultured as any woman within miles, and a prize for any ambitious young man.

Nineteen-year-old Thomas Wilkins Hunt was such a

man. He came from the centre of the world, but left London in the early 1830s because he sensed that life would some day be better on the periphery. In England the Hunts had been respectable enough (even related to titled people, T.W. claimed), educated members of the merchant class, full of new ideas about ascending in society through hard work and ingenuity, but young Thomas saw opportunities in spades in North America, a place where he could gain wealth and social standing even faster. Wanting both desperately, he sailed to Upper Canada, his sights set firmly on his future as a highly regarded businessman.

Undoubtedly he knew what a connection to the Soper family meant in Durham County, but he also saw strength and moral fibre in Hannah, someone who lived life with a sense of conviction; and she saw the same in him. On March 27, 1835 they were married at St. Mark's Church on hilly King Street in Port Hope. This union must have also pleased the Sopers: their new son-in-law was educated, self-sufficient and above all, Anglican.

Thomas's evident skills could have found him a place in William Marsh's rapidly expanding Hope Township business empire, but he was anxious to be on his own. He sensed the best place for him now was to the south-west, over the American border in Lockport, New York, where the Erie Canal and its commerce had, in just ten years, caused a village in the woods to grow into a burgeoning town of 5,000 with a railroad connecting it to nearby Buffalo and Niagara Falls.

When the spring of 1836 arrived, T.W. Hunt was established in the grocery business and had infant daughter Ann to support. The area was gaining a reputation as a major centre for shipping and fruit growing and it seemed the young Englishman had made an astute choice.

In December of the following year, just as Hannah was showing the early signs of another pregnancy, rebellion as earnest as her grandfather's burst onto the dirt streets of Canada. William Lyon Mackenzie alarmed Toronto's citizens to arms as he came down Yonge Street on horseback with eight hundred men. Turned back, Mackenzie fled the

country in the night, scurrying between friendly farmhouses, until he garrisoned himself and his little army on
Navy Island at Niagara Falls. Rumours of American
involvement kept Canada united against him, but the old
ways of the Loyalists, entrenched in their privileged and
undemocratic governments, were about to be dismantled,
and the rebels had struck the first blow. In Hope
Township the Sopers and Marshes stood by the Crown.

On June 10, 1838, with rebellion in the air and renegades nearby, Hannah Hunt gave birth to her first boy,
William Leonard. Thus Farini arrived, bringing a strange
and vibrant energy into the Hunt household and the world.

The Bible says that God demands a "broken and contrite
spirit" in us, and Thomas and Hannah requested nothing
less from their first-born son. But they should have known
as early as 1840, when they looked into the oval blue eyes
of their two-year-old toddler, that nothing like that would
ever be forthcoming from him. From the moment he
gained his balance he ran about recklessly, dark hair
dishevelled, showing little concern for injury, drawn naturally to any adventure he could find. Disciplining him
was nearly impossible, though the Lord knows they tried.
They believed fervently in not sparing the rod but it
seemed that the little boy actually gained strength from
their numerous beatings and loved to commit sins so that
he might not only gain the attention he craved, but test
his courage under parental duress. Crying was the real
transgression. Farini later recalled that he "took pleasure
in disobeying [their] commands."

He reached the age when he could get away from his
parents sooner than most and in no time was disappearing with great regularity. During these excursions he usually headed for water because it offered danger and
freedom and before he reached the age of four he swam
with uncommon ability. His exploits on land were numerous too, whether he was at the centre of snowball fights at
Eighteen Mile Creek where boys battled for possession of
the bridge, shamelessly shinnying up the liberty pole in

front of a distinguished 4th-of-July crowd to unfurl a
badly tangled Stars and Stripes, or secretly rising from
his sick bed to fall head-first into a well while playing
drop-the-carrot. Out in the countryside he often heard a
faint rumble in the distance: it was Niagara, thundering.

Hannah attempted to slow him down by declaring
swimming forbidden. But soon she would find him
upstream in the canal or outside of town in the creek. As
she stood angrily waiting on shore, he would pretend to
not see her and stay in the middle of the water until she
left. Soon she began sewing up his sleeves and collars so
he couldn't strip for swimming, but this he easily solved,
ripping his shirts open and having older school girls sew
them up again or plunging into the water with his shirt
on and running around in the sun until it dried. If he was
beaten, he would immediately return to the scene of the
crime as a point of honour.

Such behaviour gave him his first taste of infamy. The
town ladies began telling stories about him at tea, how
that Hunt child was an unholy terror, how he fought with
the other children and led them into mischief. It was a
reputation he would have in other towns and villages
throughout his youth, and, though he relished its atten-
tion-getting power, he deeply resented the judges who
accused him. He called them "croakers and grumblers,"
hypocrites who in their hearts desired his kind of fun but
for reasons of false propriety called it immoral: he was
merely honest and adventurous, exploiting the wonderful
energy God had given him.

Late in 1843 Thomas Hunt moved his family back to
Canada. Due to the success of his business, he had enough
capital to purchase a farm in Hope Township, and because
of the recent births of Thomas, Jr. and Myndert, three
growing boys to help him work it. His land was about seven
miles from Port Hope and Lake Ontario, just north-west of
the little village of Canton, a beautiful place nestled in a
dip in the hills with Smith's Creek running through its centre, and consisting of a few clustered buildings near a

church. The Hunts were nearly a mile and a half from the clearing, surrounded by forest, and in his first year Thomas was able to cultivate just ten acres. But despite this rather meagre start, Hannah's Loyalist connections ensured that they were included in the best of little Hope's society.

The family spent two and a half years here and Willie eventually tired of the isolation, but at first being in the wilderness was exciting. Every week day he walked two miles through the sometimes eerie forest with Ann to get to the log schoolhouse on Mr. Hawkins's property on the eastern edge of the village. And he did well at his lessons, though to no one's surprise he also scored high in floggings. At home, where the farm was quickly becoming a bigger operation, he was now responsible for some of the chores. His father, seldom pausing in his drive to get ahead, was cultivating nearly thirty acres by 1846, and had built a single-storey frame house, owned a horse, two oxen, three milk cows and several pigs. Soon he had more than doubled the value of the property.

In the autumn of that year Thomas started searching for a place where he could operate a successful general store. This time there was no need to leave Canada: the 1840s had been a time of tremendous growth and change. Though the population was still somewhat sparse out where he lived, closer to the lake, nearer the towns, immigrants from the British Isles were pouring in; and recent political changes had made Canada more democratic and opened up opportunities for adventurous small businessmen. This suited Thomas both commercially and politically. Despite his strict ways, he saw himself as part of a new breed.

He decided against purchasing a business in his wife's backyard in the Port Hope-Cobourg area and eyed a location on the main street of the village of Bowmanville. It was situated about twenty miles west along Kingston Road and all signs indicated it was ready to thrive.

The Hunt family had done well of late and looked forward to resuming town life. A fifth child, John Jackson, was on the way. Eight-year-old Willie had been easier to handle during these years in the country, but there was something in him that still worried his parents. Out in the woods there were fewer stuffy critics to agitate him and only nature to offer challenges, but soon there would be a whole menu of temptations. His energy was still extraordinary: he progressed quickly at school and was blessed with athletic talent, not only at sports, like cricket, but in everyday tests of strength or physical grace, like his remarkable skill for running along the top of rail fences without losing his balance.

He was also blessed with courage. Late one night the family was disturbed from their sleep by the frightened squeal of pigs. Thomas was away in Bowmanville making arrangements for moving and Hannah, left alone in the forest with her small children, immediately rose from her bed in a trembling state. Someone was in the barn! Going into her sons' room she roused the eldest and told him to run to the kitchen and get his father's shotgun. Willie, more than pleased by such a command, was dressed and holding the loaded weapon in minutes. Soon they were tip-toeing across the yard toward the pigpen where horrific squeals, mixed with growls, came out of the darkness. As they crept closer they heard brief pauses filled with deep breathing. They entered the barn and approached the storeroom: suddenly there was silence. Willie glanced through a crack in the storage door and saw two eyes like hot coals staring at him. Without thinking he thrust the gun into the opening and fired at the target. There was a painful howl, a heavy fall and then nothing. Immediately Hannah ran to the house for a lantern while Willie, fingers shaking, reloaded. When she returned, they slowly entered the storeroom. There, lying on the straw next to a bloodied pig, was a large bear with half his head blown away. Hannah picked up her son and kissed him.

Farini later said that he and his mother understood each other better after that. He also liked the idea that in the future no one would question his use of the gun. But the feat's biggest reward was the attention it gained for him at school. He was a hero, and everyone had to admit it.

CHAPTER 2

The Circus
Comes to Town

"The circus set my imagination wild."
Farini

"Genius is a habit that can be acquired."
Paul Valéry

In the quiet of another dreary summer morning a circus burst like an explosion on to the dirt road that ran through the centre of the village of Bowmanville. This was how they always came: suddenly, and in the eyes of the children, gloriously.

A few days earlier the advance agent, over-dressed and very Yankee, would be seen at a local hotel. Soon there would be a gaudy ad in the newspaper and a clown might appear out of the countryside and read an announcement near the town hall before plastering everything with handbills. But nothing prepared a little backwoods boy for the fantastic spectacle of the first appearance of the circus in his village on circus day. The faint sound of a brass band would be heard in the distance and the village would begin to stir, then people would move toward the main street, talking animatedly, and slowly the sounds would grow louder until...there it was, heading toward them past their familiar little stores, a pageant unlike anything they had ever seen, a circus in all its glory. Wonderfully painted wagons were pulled by long lines of horses, and acrobats, tightrope walkers, clowns, jugglers, equestrians, pretty ladies and exotic animals all danced on the main street like sprites from another world. In a life where a travelling fiddler or an itinerant evangelist could be a crowd-drawing sensation, the circus was an absolute marvel. Eight-year-old Willie Hunt saw one for the first time in Bowmanville and it transfixed him. It was what he had been waiting for since birth.

But these loud American shows weren't welcomed by everyone, in fact many respectable Canadians considered them low and immoral. Not only did they think the half-naked performers tempted people to feel emotions better left unexplored, but occasionally children ran away with the shows and brawls between circus people and village troublemakers were not uncommon. Thomas Hunt was among those striving for social position in Bowmanville, so the inside of the circus tent was declared out of bounds to his children.

But now the Hunts lived at the edge of a village, and the circus was difficult to avoid. Just a few months after their arrival, the Rockwell and Stone show visited, with its bull-fight pageant, English jousting tournament and genuine stars (like Levi J. North, the first man to somersault on a galloping horse). And over the next five years

King Street, Bowmanville, in the mid-19th century.

four more shows came to town. Willie viewed these wonders from afar, planning for the day when he would sneak into a big top and get closer to his dreams.

His parents anxiously pushed him in other directions. They had money, didn't need him on a farm, and dearly wanted him well educated, so they continued to send him to school on a regular basis. From 1846 to 1852 he attended a primitive one-room building in the village. An old place on cedar blocks, it had no ventilation, snow came in through the cracks in the walls, and a single stove "kept the children moderately warm." They sat along tiered rows of seats with their faces down, attention on their slates, or the master standing on the platform above them used his switch. Willie learned a great deal in that crude institution, but little that touched his restless young soul.

He roamed the dirt roads of the village like a real-life Canadian Tom Sawyer looking for adventure. The "unconventional" appealed to his imagination, illicit schemes filled his head. When the family moved it was hoped that unpolished little Willie would be left behind in the forest and a mature young Bill (as he now called himself) would grow up in Bowmanville, but his rebelliousness grew as he did and soon he was known as the "leader in all mischief." Criticism continued and his pride and self-righteousness swelled in response: in the schoolyard he vowed that "every boy [who]…fancied himself could have a fight without asking twice."

T.W. Hunt set up his general store on King Street and made it pay. He dressed well, was careful of the company he kept and tried to project the air of an English gentleman. Though a sombre member of the local Anglican church, he had a flourish to him, right down to the excessiveness of his flowery signature, while Hannah kept a lower profile and was more down-to-earth, but like all good United Empire Loyalists, was conscious of her heritage. The Hunts were soon considered by some to be a family who thought themselves a little better than others.

The village's strong upper-middle class, of which they were a part, were desperate to have manners and social positions like the "old country." Led by a coterie of young businessmen and their families, they worked to create a social hierarchy where none had ever existed. By their conduct, at the local barn raisings, communal bees, hunting expeditions or in their all-powerful churches where final judgements were cast, they struggled to establish names for themselves and gain positions of moral superiority. There was never any doubt that emotions like the ones which coursed through young Master Hunt the day he saw his first circus parade were decidedly unacceptable. And any adult condoning such feelings risked losing his respectability.

But despite such pretension, the village was really still a rough, frontier place and not without subversive passions. When Bill Hunt lay in bed at night, he could hear the horn blast of Weller's stage coach, a slow moving, inefficient vehicle that connected the community to the outside world, travelling on nearly impassable muddy roads, fending for itself in a wilderness where bandits prospered. Bowmanville made excellent liquor and its citizens consumed it at alarming rates. People with nothing to do at night staggered around the pigs and cows on the village streets and resorted to gambling in the upper rooms of the hotels, or fighting in taverns.

Thomas Hunt strictly forbade such things as drinking, gambling and profanity in his home, and ruled his family as if he were its lord. He even insisted his children remain silent in his presence at the dinner table. Farini's adjective for him was "imperious." Soon the lord had seven children, five boys and two girls (Mary was born in 1848 and James in 1851). Constantly alarmed at his eldest son's appetite for adventure, he prodded him to set his brothers a better example. But sneaking out of town to see Chief Waubakosh and his braves fishing in Lake Ontario or playing hooky from Sunday school skating on the mill pond easily gained precedence with Bill; and when he read stories in magazines, like those about David

Livingstone's adventures in the Kalahari Desert, he felt transported into a better world and the dreariness of Bible lessons or small-town business practices was amplified tenfold.

In 1851, the same year two more circuses came to Bowmanville (one making its entrance on to King Street with eight Syrian camels drawing its first wagon), Bill made the jump to the town's highly respectable new Grammar School. One of his teachers was a Trinity College educated Irishman named W.G. King, and next to Farini he may have been the strangest man ever to walk the streets of Bowmanville. He liked to wear his hat and gloves in class, used nicknames to address the students, and lived alone outside of town in a little village of buildings he had built, out of which he seldom ventured. On the rare occasions he wandered, he could be alarmingly reckless and spent much of his time drinking in taverns with disreputable men. It was rumoured that one reason for his perpetual glove-wearing was that he had badly mangled one of his hands smashing a bottle while in a drunken rage at a village inn. To no one's surprise Bill Hunt liked him, but they once met head-on with spectacular consequences.

On the first day of their infamous two-day battle Bill was serving as the class monitor, an occupation particularly odious to him. Out of a pin-drop silence there was a disturbance at the rear of the class and King, unable to see what had happened, asked Bill to do his duty and betray the perpetrator. The boy replied that he had no idea who it was, mainly because he had been doing his sums. When the furious teacher proceeded to give his class monitor, who was obviously not the criminal, an enormous number of lines to write out, the boy rose and, after excusing himself for what he was about to say, nonetheless said clearly that he thought the punishment severe considering he had done nothing. For this act of unconscionable insolence more lines were added.

The tired little boy came back to school the next day with his task complete, barely able to keep his eyes open.

Upon examining the copies the master detected a small error near the end and demanded that everything be done again. Bill Hunt rose to his feet once more: this time he refused. Mr. King was stunned. He rubbed his brow, removed his glasses and approached the boy. With lightning quickness he reached out, grabbed him by the hair, struck him repeatedly in the face, and then threw him to the floor. Lying there Bill could feel his temper soar: he could not be disgraced like this in front of his peers, and could not stomach the whole village hearing about it. All he had done was tell the truth. Bouncing onto his feet he rushed at his teacher, kicked his shins as hard as he could and struck him with a well-aimed head-butt to the midsection (or as Farini later put it, "into that region of the anatomy below which the canons of the prize ring have decreed it cowardly to strike"). His breath suddenly gone, the tutor fell against his desk and was immediately showered by ink bottles from a retreating Bill Hunt. The boy was out the door in a flash and running home.

Though he gained little support from his parents, a school trustee who liked him (and wished his boys had "as much stuffing in them") helped him get reinstated. This is Farini's explanation of the incident and its resolution, though one wonders if the facts have been altered a little and how a young boy in strict Upper Canadian society had the impudence, regardless of provocation, to engage in a brawl with his schoolmaster. Though he felt he was struggling under a suffocating hypocrisy, he was not always honourable himself, and his behaviour often bordered on juvenile delinquency. There was, and always would be, a dark side to him, characterised as evil not only by old "croakers" during his childhood but by some adult contemporaries in later life. His love of adventure would often grow out of control.

Meanwhile Thomas, doing well in business, purchased his own land in the village and built a house in the northeast part of town for his ever-expanding family (of eight— Edith May had been born *circa* 1852). One of the earliest brick homes in the village, it was constructed in the style

of an English cottage, and its red colour, four unusual
chimney stacks, large low windows and other peculiar features made it instantly recognizable. A unique and beautiful building, it announced the extent of its owner's
success in Canada and showed that Farini's father was
not without his own eccentricities.

Despite the fact that Bill turned thirteen in 1851, circuses
were still forbidden, and he nearly burst with anxiety over
the opportunity he was being denied. But during the week
of his fourteenth birthday in June of 1852 a show called
Pentland's Dramatic Equestrian came to Bowmanville
and he decided that his years of disappointment must
end. He *had* to see this performance, meet the stars and
find out what made them and their world so wonderful.
The circus, a realm of endless possibilities, seemed to be
calling him. Boldly, he plotted what had to be done.

The key to his plan was the fact that the show people
were staying at the Waverly House, a two-storey brick
hotel on the north side of King Street. Just a few steps
from the Hunts' general store, it was owned by family
friend Alphonso Hinds, and the cooperation of schoolmate
George Hinds would get Bill where he needed to go. He
rose from bed in the early morning darkness and tiptoed
out the door without waking his brothers. After descending the stairs he slipped past his parents' bedroom, eased
outside, and headed downtown. There were no gas lights
in the village yet, so when he got to King Street he picked
his way carefully along the wide wooden sidewalk, watch-
ful not to trip over the pigs which sometimes climbed up
onto the boards. He could wait here or with the bullfrogs
down on the mill pond at Barber's Creek.

When the sun finally rose, he crept over to the Waverly
House and met George at the door. They stole inside and
tried to be inconspicuous while they waited for a circus
star to appear. Meeting any of them would have been wonderful, but the boys knew they had really struck gold
when none other than Joe Pentland walked into the lobby.
Here before them was one of the greatest of all circus

stars, an acrobatic clown rivalled in his day by only the legendary Dan Rice.

Bill Hunt and George Hinds, like most village children, had heard of Pentland long before that morning. And despite the fact that he wore a flashy New York suit and his face was clean-shaven, without a touch of make-up, they knew him instantly. His heavy-lidded eyes and slightly turned-up mouth gave him a sly look and he exuded a presence that filled the room and left little doubt as to his identity. Bill loved his devilish cockiness, his worldliness and his graceful walk.

Joe Pentland was amused by the two country boys who came toward him. He had seen this many times before. In fact, there was a certain uniformity to these children, a particular look, which he recognized in the innkeeper's son. But when they stopped in front of him he sensed that the dark-haired one with the clear blue eyes was different: he was forceful, unusually intense, and did all the talking. His questions came fast and furious, and many were about performance techniques: of the acrobats, the strong-men, the trapeze artistes and the rope-walkers. Pentland allowed himself to be interviewed but couldn't resist having at least a little fun with the serious young rube. These hicks believed nearly anything you told them, if you told it well, so when the boy pressed him for the secret to his suppleness he spun him a straight-faced yarn. Get some fishworms, he told him, pack as many as you can into a jar, jam it shut, and let it roast in the sun until it has congealed into a useable lotion. Then rub it over your joints several times every day until you become as supple as a clown. The boy nodded solemnly.

Bill Hunt was beginning a day that would change his life. He not only met a famous show-business star and learned some of his secrets, but later, at great personal cost, sneaked into the big tent and actually saw the performance. From that day forward his life was infused with the bold spirit of the circus.

Illicitly watching Pentland's show that evening, Bill was shocked to see a drunken sailor stagger out of the

stands: it nearly made him jump to his feet. Everything
had been going so well—all the acts had been wonderful
and left him wanting more. But now, who was this fool? A
beautiful lady had been riding an elegant horse around
the ring, standing like a ballerina on its back, and casting
a rouge-cheeked smile at the stands. But when the disturbance occurred the crowd went silent. The drunk
tripped and fell to the ground as he approached the ring,
causing a few nervous laughs. He got up and in an embarrassed silence shouted, "I can ride that damn nag!" and
made for the horse. As the frightened lady jumped off, he
leapt at the circling animal, sailed cleanly over its back,
and landed nearly on his head on the ground. This time
quite a few people laughed. More attempts were made to
mount the beast and each time the man was foiled. Then
the band, apparently not spoilsports, entered the fray.
Finally the sailor seized the tail of the mighty steed and
somehow clumsily flipped himself up onto its back where
he clung, to the children's laughter, like a desperate man.
But then something strange happened: in the midst of
rotating uncontrollably on his back the drunk stood up
and executed a perfect flip! The crowd gasped. Again he
somersaulted, this time landing on the ground where in
two sweeps he pulled off his sailor's costume, revealing his
circus spangles and his identity...Joe Pentland.

Like many boys his age, Bill wondered if some of the
performers he saw at that first circus were superhuman.
But as he considered what he had seen, another feeling
came over him, one that was not as common: he felt
tricked, fooled the way Pentland had deceived the crowd.
People were not superhuman, and there were secrets to
such ostensibly marvellous deeds. (This sort of iconoclasm
came naturally to him, he who was constantly criticized
for being himself and was convinced that people preferred
illusions to truths.) He began analyzing the circus feats
and "immediately set [himself] a task to solve [them]." He
had often built home-made trapeze swings and tightropes
and tried them out for fun, but the day after he saw the
Pentland show he went to his father's stable to practise

somersaults as if he were on a mission, clear pictures of how those tricks were done etched in his memory.

A soft landing spot was of paramount importance, so he arranged some straw on a manure heap and started right in. Though he was the best gymnast in his school, he had never tried anything even remotely like the acrobats' brilliant tumbling tricks. His first attempt at their back somersault resulted in his landing on his head, which went down nearly a foot into the soft manure. Momentarily he lay there stunned, a sharp pain in his neck, but recovered his senses in a few seconds, got up, and went back to the other side of the heap to try the trick again. He had too much pride to give in and was too smart to make the same error twice; slowly, by examining his mistakes and performing the turn with attention to detail, he improved. He tried to see the somersault occurring in slow motion and then attempted to emulate it at high speed. It would later become Signor Farini's dictum that a performer should not consider the second and third parts of a move until he had mastered the first (forty-two years later a British newspaper would call him the world's best trainer of acrobats). Every morning before school he went to the stable and practised. Soon he showed unusual prowess.

A few days into his efforts his father came to the stable and eyed him with a serious look. He had been smelling a "terrible stench" and had found a burst bottle lying on the shed roof with some sort of thick oil oozing from it. He asked if William knew anything about it, and when told it was roasting fishworms, enquired further and soon the whole Pentland story came out. The governor didn't try to hold back his laughter; and then he berated William for his ignorance. He shook his head and went off to work, making his angry young son even more determined to succeed.

Within a week of Pentland's show, "P.T. Barnum's Colossal Museum and Menagerie" made its appearance in Canada West. Children watched in awe when it paraded into their little towns led by the "Car of Juggernaut," a massive vehicle drawn by ten Ceylonese elephants. Later, in the

large pavilion, you could see General Tom Thumb (twenty-
eight inches high and fifteen pounds) ride a baby elephant, and gaze at lions, tigers, Burmese bulls, a
strongman, and Mr. Nellis, the man with no arms who
could pick up a pistol with his toes and fire out bullet-hole
profiles on a target.

In the autumn of that year Bill began plotting something he thought was equally spectacular, unknowingly
set in motion by his unspectacular eleven-year-old brother
Tom. The basic skills the unassuming Tom displayed during acrobatic practice one day in the stable gave him an
idea. Surely he could find a few more boys with at least as
much athletic ability and put together his own circus right
there in town.

He quickly assessed the talents of his friends and gave
everyone something to do. Then he arranged with several
adult cricketers to use the booth on the Cricket Grounds
on a Saturday afternoon and found a lady who would help
them make tights and trunks. It was absolutely necessary
that the very existence of the show be kept from their parents so no posters were made and news was passed by
word of mouth until nearly every young person in town
was informed. Bill stayed away from home the entire day,
to avoid questions from Thomas and Hannah, and that
afternoon, with a company of artistes all fourteen years
old or younger and a capacity audience almost exclusively
the same age, the show commenced. First, a ragtag band
of two violins, an accordion, drum, tambourine, triangle
and trombone struck up "Camptown Races"...and then
encored it. Bill Hunt appeared first (of course) and displayed his new expertise on the trapeze. This was followed
by a jig, horizontal-bar feats by Bill and Tom, a clown act,
tumbling tricks by the Hinds brothers, and even the
enactment of *A Greenhorn From Vermont*. As a finale, all
the performers took their bows in a glorious walkaround.
The audience seemed entertained and Bill found six dollars in his hat.

But the evening show ended in catastrophe. Just as
Tom Hunt was about to step onto his short, low-strung

slack rope, shouts were heard near the entrance and instantly the booth was full of irate parents reaching for children who were rapidly deserting the premises. Tom spotted T.W. Hunt from the slack-rope platform and, suddenly seized with fear, leapt to the stage shouting, "Where's my trousers?!" Finding his pants, he pulled them on frantically, disappeared through the back door and ran off over the fields.

Bill was down at stage level and didn't know the reason for the disturbance until, as he later said, there "appear[ed] before me a dark object that looked very much like my father." Thomas seized his son and began shouting at him for this further disgrace he had brought upon the family. Then, unable to control himself, he pulled back his switch and began whipping William as hard as he could, screaming, "I'll give you circus!" Seeing this, a neighbourhood lady stepped toward them. "He ought to be whipped until he cannot stand!" she said, her face flushed red with anger. "Give it to him! You wicked, sinful boy, you are the ruin of all the boys in town!" Thomas stopped. He turned to the lady and informed her that William was no worse than the rest. The angry woman eyed Thomas. In a heated whisper she let him know that she had heard that he encouraged his son's well-known bad conduct, that any boy who acted like that should be locked up, and that her son had been an angel before he met Bill Hunt.

Farini stepped forward. "Then it is a pity he didn't die while he was so good," he said clearly. Instantly he felt the crack of his father's stick on the backs of his legs. "Hold your tongue," said Thomas sternly, "and don't argue with your elders! Now march!" With that, he shoved Bill forward, knocking him against the woman, who stepped aside as if touched by a leper and mumbled something about having him arrested.

He smiled to himself as he was roughly escorted home, refusing to be intimidated by authority or frightened by the prospect of a caning. Throughout his youth he had seldom been disciplined by his business-obsessed father and was surprised when this punishment came from him. He often resented his father's distance and this whipping was almost welcome: a kind of brutal closeness.

During these days events in their community were such that Thomas had less time to shape the morals of his children. In April 1852 Bowmanville's application for incorporation as a village was approved and elections were scheduled for December. Thomas considered himself a moral, organized man, and was critical of the anarchic state of things in the area, so he threw his hat into the electoral ring on the Reform ticket. Voting was public in the 1850s and political campaigns were never tame or slowly paced; violent intimidation was common. Thomas mounted the crude wooden hustings and spoke for what he believed in, and just before Christmas was elected as one of five men in the village's first government.

On January 17, 1853, Bowmanville council, consisting almost entirely of merchant friends, met for the first time in the Court House. Businessman David Fisher was elected reeve, but by far the most active official at the meeting and throughout the year was Thomas Wilkins Hunt. Jumping at his chance, he gave notice that he would soon draw up their first by-law, "for the prevention of vice, drunkenness, profane swearing, obscene language, and other species of immorality and indecency in the streets, or other public places, in this Corporation." Before long they took aim at the circus, passing a law "for regulating licensing of exhibitions of natural or artificial curiosities, Theatres, Circuses or other shows..." bringing young Bill Hunt and his show-business heroes into line and eliminating further amateur sawdust iniquities. The next generation was being told it had a well-defined place, governed by historical morals, and they were to keep to it. For Bill, with his mind set on unconventional ideas and goals, this would prove a difficult task.

In early October T.W. Hunt became reeve and led the community until the end of the year when he retired from politics altogether. The pressure to conform was especially great on his eldest son during this period. The reeve was also the chief convicting justice and T.W. cringed at the prospect of his son appearing before him for sentencing. But by his mid-teens Bill finally appeared to be maturing, becoming involved in things that were usually reserved for adults: going on hunting expeditions with the men (where he tried to outdo them), becoming an integral member of the highly ranked Bowmanville cricket team, and even playing in out-of-town matches with the senior squad. And he was one of the brightest students in the newly enlarged Grammar School.

He still did unusual things, however. In the spring of his fifteenth year when the dam at Barber's Creek over-flowed due to a late thaw and was on the verge of explod-ing, the many citizens who went down to the banks to watch the fireworks saw him give a chilling performance. There he was, leaping around on top of the dam, almost daring it to explode beneath him. "I courted peril because I loved it," he once said, "because the very thought of it fired my soul with ardour, because it was what others were afraid to face." The criticized bad boy desperately needed attention, and he was going to get it, one way or another.

By the summer of 1853 Bill was considered old enough to be making decisions about a career. The circus was really not a serious option, at least not to anyone with any sense. But he flirted with the idea, and each time a show came to town during the following years he found a way to get himself behind the scenes and mix with its rough-and-ready characters. One early morning he even went out into the countryside to meet a travelling circus as it approached Bowmanville in the darkness from the east. The Spalding and Rogers show was one of the most spec-tacular ever to come to the area, featuring the likes of James McFarland on the tightrope and Monsieur Le Thorn "the French Hercules."

But Bill was surprised by what he saw that morning on the far side of Soper's Creek. First there was an unsavoury man (the advance agent) with a long beard and diamond stick-pin, shouting orders and the name of the company's hotel in Bowmanville to the others with a sense of self-importance. Though he seemed slippery and untrustworthy, others looked much worse, very unlike the happy, carefree image he had of circus workers. The boss canvas man, for example, a tall rogue with black whiskers and a red nose, rode from one wagon to the next snapping his whip and swearing loudly, trying to rouse sleeping workers with a vulgarity that stunned Bill's young country soul. He thought momentarily of the things his father said about circus people. Most of these men, with their rotting teeth and filthy tongues, had looks of villainy that went right into him. And yet, in this atmosphere of danger and corruption there was something that thrilled him, something *so* alive.

When Bill returned to his stable gymnasium the day after he saw this show's performance, he had a whole new series of secrets to solve. Soon he was concentrating on rope-walking, an act which intrigued him because of its self-reliance and daring. He suffered numerous falls off his little low wire into the haystack, but they only fired his energy and it wasn't long before something magical happened. He discovered a key to his life, and called it "the balance." Out of the blue he was able to maintain his position on his home-made copper wire, and though he slipped to the hay a few more times, never again had a debilitating fear of falling. This sense of balance, apparently mysteriously obtained, was really the result of a slowly acquired confidence. "Courage," Farini loved to say, "is another word for confidence in oneself."

The strong-man he had seen at the circus had impressed him. The man seemed of ordinary build and yet could take the blows of eighteen-pound hammers smashed on the anvil on his chest, and pulled against two horses. At first he thought this man a marvel, but as he analyzed the act he came to understand that the strong-man was nothing more than an athletic technician, possessed of a few important facts. The first was that if you could learn to bear enough weight on your chest (the more the better) the thudding of hammers on this weight could do little damage. Bill practised with a feather pillow on his sternum and had Tom place a heavy stone on top of it: the stone was then dealt blows with a sledgehammer. Secondly, he discovered that if you constructed a wooden brace to go around your waist and developed your back and lower-body strength you could slip a rope through this brace and pull against ten horses if necessary, by arranging the rope inside so that the animals pulled against themselves.

To develop his muscles Bill found an old set of weigh scales in the stable and began exercising with fifty- and sixty-pound weights. Thus one of the country's first body-builders went to work on himself. Over the next few years, past his sixteenth birthday, his chest, arms and legs thickened; he exercised all year round, even sneaking his clubs indoors to his bedroom in the winter. He wanted a completely educated body, not just a muscular physique: before long he erected a pole at one end of the stable, hollowed out holes at eight-inch intervals and spent hours climbing up and down it by thrusting pegs into the holes. It was a rather strange pastime for a teenage boy, but he desperately wanted everything about himself to grow; he even believed that exercising was good for his brain. He seemed to be trying to prove something to someone, constantly practising for an adventurous future that was slowly forming in his mind. He kept working.

In his final year in Bowmanville he gave a few athletic exhibitions as an amateur act for benefits held at the Town Hall where he showed his new back somersault to the floor from the trapeze. His parents found these infrequent appearances less objectionable now; it was their (wishful) understanding that he was slowly becoming a more responsible adult and that gymnastics were now surely just a hobby.

By the autumn of 1854 Thomas had decided to move back to Hope Township and began selling his town property. Retiring to the country as a gentleman was a goal to which respectable people aspired and now he was sufficiently wealthy to do so and blessed with five able-bodied

sons to work his new farm. By April of the following year
he had purchased land in Hope and by the end of the
month the Hunts had left the town that had been their
home for nearly a decade.

The last months after Thomas's decision to move were
important ones for himself and his eldest son. It had been
firmly resolved that William would take an occupation,
and the arrival of Dr. Bradford Patterson in their neighbourhood put the finishing touches on an idea Thomas
had had for some time. He was impressed with his new
friend and so, it must be said, was his son. In fact, Bill
considered Patterson "a scholar, a gentleman...and a
great doctor"—the young medical man's liberal ways
inspired his respect and he did not feel the immediate
enmity toward him that he felt for many adults. So when
it was decided that he would become Patterson's apprentice, there was little resistance. Medicine actually
intrigued him—he thought it the "noblest science in the
world." Thomas and Hannah must have sunk to their
knees in gratitude when William appeared to accept this
honourable calling; but they should have known better.
There were breaks during his readings: "[I] always found
time to keep my muscles in good order," he said. "In the
back office I kept a set of clubs and when I was tired of
study had a go with them." Obviously, Bill Hunt wasn't
giving up on his dreams and, just like his muscles, Signor
Farini was still growing.

CHAPTER 3

Getting on
the High Wire

*"Life is on the wire,
the rest is just waiting."*
Karl Wallenda

The day they moved a hurricane struck Bowmanville, toppling church steeples, razing buildings, and propelling horses, buggies and even a few good citizens into the air. For a short time in Durham County that spring morning, it seemed that people could fly.

Bill had no such luck. He found himself ensconced in Thomas W. Hunt, Esq.'s new Hope Township farm, where he was expected to help plant crops, raise animals, study medicine and generally do his duty. When he stood on the slope of land in front of his father's big house on the north side of Kingston Road and looked out over the rolling hills and down toward the lake, he could see great tracts of property in all directions owned or controlled by his parents' relatives or friends. At seventeen he was finally home: surrounded by the respectability of his extended family. About a mile to the east the regal Marsh inn, with its huge park to the north stocked with deer, stood out like a castle in the country, announcing the Marshes and their relatives as special. William Marsh controlled one thousand acres in the area, a hotel in Port Hope and a fleet of schooners on the lake; he built schools to educate his many employees and exercised power over the powerful in

the township. When Bill Hunt visited his cousins or his
future brother-in-law (sister Ann did what was right a few
years later and married William Marsh, Jr.) at their big
sawmill next door or helped the men manoeuvre gigantic
pine masts (bound for the Royal Navy) along the gravel
roads behind teams of horses, he must have felt like
"someone," or more to the point, *almost* someone.

It would be clear to him now like never before that
there was a certain level of morality and accomplishment
expected of him. But he still dreamt about exotic places
beyond the farm lands and adventures foreign to the
expectations of his family.

Bradford Patterson's practice was flourishing in
Bowmanville and in January 1855 he began advertising
in the *Port Hope Guide*. He promised "at the solicitation
of his friends in Port Hope" to visit the Hetherington
Hotel on weekends once a month in order to help heal the
ill. At the bottom of the ad his references were listed, one
being "T.W. Hunt."

Bill had a busy spring and summer. There was a great
deal of work to be done settling into the new surroundings
and getting the land plowed and seeded; he was considered an adult now and, as the eldest son, was the man of
the family whenever his father was away. And of course
he was also obliged to study the books that Dr. Patterson
gave him and be ready once a month to ride into town for
his hands-on apprenticeship. Gymnastic practice was out
of the question for a while: his parents naïvely suspected
it was gone forever.

Port Hope, just twenty minutes away by horse and buggy,
exerted a strong influence on the countryside. Once the
little Fat Fire Creek of log cabins, it was now a thriving
town of nearly five thousand, its wharf busy with steamers and schooners (many built by William Marsh). Steep
Walton Street was lined with three- and four-storey brick
buildings and the *Guide* (perhaps surprisingly, Liberal)
was the most widely read newspaper in the region. With

the exception of its neighbour (and rival) Cobourg, it was
the largest town east of Toronto for more than one hundred miles. In 1856 two railroads were built through the
area: tracks were laid across Walton, a huge stone viaduct
rose high above the harbour and then the first steam
engine burst into town, a swift connection to the rest of
the world. It seemed that everything was suddenly going
faster in Canada.

But Bill was concerned that the pace of his own life had
peaked and was about to slow down. When he projected
his daily reality into the future, he saw himself curing
dyspeptic old ladies or administering to complaining
neighbourhood patients. And Mechanics' Institute lectures
at Town Hall about the gospels might interest others, but
it did little to light the fires of an anxious young man with
energy to burn. His late teens were like a pause in his life:
he put his back into his father's farm work and hoped for
something better.

He had almost no interest in religion or politics, highly
unusual for his time, and dated just a few girls (he
claimed one was the prettiest around, and during those
years became acquainted with the unconventional daughter of neighbourhood tailor William Osborne—she would
play an important role in his life), despite being a notorious lady-killer as an adult. What continued to arouse him
were spectacles: like a local appearance by magician
Signor Blitz; stories from the American wild west; or the
adventures of the rebel Garibaldi in the 1859 Italian War.
Nothing, however, could match the circus, even as he
approached his twenties.

Bigger and better shows came to the area during his
late teens and he made sure he saw them, despite the fact
that these "travelling pests and promoters of general
immorality" were just as reviled by the morally upright of
Port Hope as they had been in Bowmanville. The Hunts
continued to consider such things beneath them.
Education reigned supreme in their home, and contrary to
a commonly held, farming-community idea that boys were
more useful at the plow by the time they reached their

teens and girls should not be overly educated, their children stayed in school. The Hunts thought themselves of a class that should produce leading citizens, so even little Edith and Mary were expected to learn and show their breeding (as would their last child, a son born to forty-four-year-old Hannah in 1857). Thomas wanted his children to be strivers and thinkers. Not surprisingly, some neighbours considered that eccentric.

The cold, damp winters and hot, humid summers toughened the country people. Bill hardened with them and took on their uncomplaining nature, but was never really like them. The dull uniformity of their lives, which he despised, continued after the day's work and the choices for evening entertainment were both few and somewhat preordained. They wound down in front of the fire with a book, went to church or public-affairs meetings or visited neighbours. If they were a little daring they spent their time dancing, playing cards, betting at a local horse race in a field, or at a cricket match on a village pitch. And then there was Bill Hunt: dreaming of excitement, studying, and exercising on his homemade equipment. (Farini often said he trained and did some instructing at a local gymnasium in the 1850s, but there was no such facility in Port Hope. Later in life he also spoke of training at the University of Toronto, where he sometimes said he went to study medicine. This does not fit with other claims he made about taking his exams at Victoria College in Cobourg, though the fact that Victoria was later absorbed by the Toronto school may solve the discrepancy. Whatever formal gymnastic training he had was minimal.)

In those days he also began to pursue another pastime that would be a life-long passion, the art of invention. As would be expected, his ideas were rather odd, one of the first being a concept he drew up to allow locomotives to pass each other while travelling in opposite directions on the same track. It involved building a track up and over the length of each train to allow one to pass over the top of the other.

But the best invention of his youth was his first real high wire, which he raised right on the family farm. Their big house had once been a tavern (likely to catch the overflow from Marsh's) and had a spacious yard, necessary in previous years when stage coaches were left on the grounds, and had a brick stable capable of housing eight or more horses. The stable was about a hundred feet north-east of the house, two storeys high and the size of a small barn. Its roof became the apex of that first high wire, which he erected some time between the summer of 1855 and 1859, after he saw a woman ascend a rope from the ground to the top of a circus tent just before a show. Though it is difficult to be certain which circus that was, two unequivocal facts remain: he was inspired by a circus and *not* trained in one, and his first true high wire was home-made and ascension-style.

Bill's first problem was how to get his rope up to the roof and pull it taut. He enjoyed these kinds of technical dilemmas and had a talent for solving them. His first problem should have been his father, but Thomas's absence in England meant he had no effective opponent, no one to more than just question why a young adult, supposedly serious about a medical career, would want to construct a high wire in his barnyard in full view of the neighbours, and imitate the immoral ways of show-business people.

He had used smaller cords for short tightropes inside the barn over the years but now wanted to take several steps upward, as it were, and truly challenge himself. He could walk the lower ropes better than anyone in the township, and his weightlifting and trapeze exercising had made him supple and strong; his medical studies increased his interest in the health and potential of the human body and he treated himself like a specimen that needed constant fine-tuning. He was looking for something that could test his strengths and simultaneously impress others. So when he saw that female rope walker above him, applauded by an admiring crowd, a number of things crystallized for him. Now he was going to find a way to get his own rope up to the roof of the stable, walk it, and see if anyone else could muster the same courage and ingenuity.

During his teens amateur rope-walking was popular among young people, as a test of one's athleticism and bravery (and also because most adults frowned on it). In 1859 a kind of rope-walking mania swept through North America but its popularity had been building for several years. A Monsieur DeLave put a rope across expansive Great St. James Street in Montreal in May 1858 and walked on air between two third-storey windows. Five thousand people came to watch and as they gaped upward pickpockets prospered. In his "tight-fitting inexpressibles and jacket decorated with diamond-shaped ornaments," above a street jammed with moving buggies and pedestrians, DeLave slipped just once (and caught the rope) and finished to loud cheers. In the papers it was headlined, "Perilous Feat." Such news enthralled Bill: he liked the costume, the size of the audience, the danger and the applause; and above all he thought it devilishly clever. He didn't know then that within a couple of years he himself would tangle with this M. DeLave.

Surely, if someone could walk high above a Montreal street, it was a trifle to walk to the roof of your barn.

All he had was a rope. He used every penny he had to buy it and therefore had no pulley blocks for tightening or beams for support-columns: he had to invent the things he needed. First he took one end of the rope and tied it to the plate of the barn, which was just under the roof (nearly twenty feet high), and secured the other end to a log which he buried in the ground. When he stepped back to look at his high wire he was confronted with a disheartening sight: his rope sagged like an inverted rainbow. But soon a remedy occurred to him, and he went up the road to his cousins' place to borrow eight ship's scantlings (wooden poles). When he returned he tied them together in pairs, about six inches from their ends, sharpened the other ends and drove them into the ground, each a few feet apart. Wide at the bottom, and crossed in an "X" at

the top, each pair of scantlings now formed a crutch
at its apex, into which the
rope was laid. This was
done four times with gradu-
ally longer scantlings to
support the rope as it rose
toward the horizontal part
of the high wire. Bill could
pull the bottoms of the
scantlings together, like
scissors, and tighten his
rope as he pleased.

Now he needed a balance
pole. Professionals used
them and since he had
a formidable rope himself,
he found Thomas's axe, cut
down a small spruce tree
and tapered its ends with a
drawing knife.

All that remained was to try it.

*Farini's sketch of the high
rope he built to the roof of his
father's barn in the late 1850s.*

Archives of Ontario

Waking early the next morning anxious to get started, he
fetched the long pole from the woodshed and came out
onto the lawn. He looked up to see his high rope. It had
vanished. At first he thought someone had cut it down:
any number of old fogies along this road could have done
it. But as he approached the barn he could see that his
invention was lying on the ground, defeated by his own
miscalculation. The heavy morning dew had swelled the
rope until everything came crashing down. He made a
mental note to never leave it tight overnight.

He rounded up a few friends and some of his brothers
and with their help hoisted his rope back up and drew it
as taut as possible. He picked up his pole and came to the
foot of the high wire. He eyed its sharp climb, which rose
to a levelling-off point and went straight across some distance to the edge of the barn's roof: it looked like a steep

clothesline. If the truth were known, he really wasn't sure
if he could do this, and it was possible his reward would
be a broken neck. All around him his brothers and friends
watched anxiously.

Bill stepped onto the rope. Up he went: one step, two
steps, three…he swayed one way, leaned heavily the
other, and fell, landing on his feet. His spectators roared,
glad for a chance to mock their proud friend. Embarrassed, he stood back from the rope and pressed himself
against his pole, thinking. In his mind he watched the
woman aerialist ascend to the top of the circus tent: as she
moved slowly upward he zeroed in on her trunk, the mid-
point of balance, and examined the way she used the
pole…and there was the solution: she never moved the
pole vertically. The natural tendency was to pull it
upward at one end when you lost your balance, in order to
compensate, and that was exactly what he had done. But
the secret was to hold it parallel to the ground at all
times, only moving it horizontally, despite your feelings.
Let *it* balance *you*.

He stepped back onto the rope and felt it with his bare
foot. His friends laughed. Again: one step, then two,
three…four steps, five, six, seven: he walked steadily up
the rope to the level point. The sensation he felt up here
was breathtaking, and everyone on the ground below him
was deadly silent.

When he reached the level part he took a big confident
stride…and fell. Luckily he glanced off the rope as he
dropped and was able to grab it, and lowered himself
slowly to the ground, hand over hand down the decline.

Bill hadn't anticipated that the level part would be
more difficult than the incline and that was what had
thrown him, literally. As he sat down to check his bruises,
the other boys took turns at rope-walking, but none of
them seemed able to get beyond four or five steps, regardless of how many times they tried. They were too impatient and considered things like "guts" (something not all
of them had) and athletic ability to be the keys to their
prospective success. Not one of them thought thoroughly

about what he was doing, and they all fell. The best edged up close to the third shear and, unnerved by their perilous accomplishment, suffered heavy falls that finished their funambulistic careers.

In a week's time Bill could ascend the rope and go all the way to the barn roof with ease. Soon he was trying a few tricks, like hanging from the rope by his hands, and lying down on it and getting back up to a standing position. Of all the others only Tom had succeeded in getting to the last shear, where the rope levelled off, and he had fallen when he got there and landed hard on his head and shoulders. From that moment onward he steadfastly refused to place a foot on the rope. Bill thought his brother too cautious and went on trying new things that often put his untrained body into dangerous circumstances. One of his tricks was to descend the steep part walking forward, an ostensibly easy but actually difficult task. A little awed by his talent, the other boys came to watch him almost every day. Soon their numbers increased and their general feeling, not always spoken, was that Bill Hunt was doing something nearly miraculous. His love of showing-off came to the fore early as the crowds grew even larger. He dazzled them with his old trapeze tricks and displayed his strength by going hand-over-hand from one end of the rope to the other.

Soon he was trying headstands. The trick, carefully observed by him at circuses, was to lay your pole flat across the rope, grip it on either side, and then set the top part of your forehead down on the rope so that a triangle was formed. Holding the pole perfectly balanced, you then raised your feet slowly into the air. This feat took him "some months to perfect" and needed, as he said, "exquisite balance and constant practice." A hard ridge soon formed on his forehead.

Eventually he taught himself two particularly dangerous tricks. The first was to take a specially designed chair (with a couple of short sticks of wood fastened between its legs) up to the level part, set it on the rope and then...stand on it. The secret was to hold yourself perfectly

stiff from the hips down (Farini called it "a hard thing to
do"). His other supreme turn was one that would one day,
in an act of numbing recklessness, bring him glory, and
later cause terrible lifelong pain. This was the feat of carrying someone on his back. Surprisingly, he considered it
not overly difficult and claimed that as long as the performer had sufficient strength in his legs then the passenger's weight would actually press both of them to the rope.
Your partner had to sit nearly motionless as he clung to
your back and never attempt to help you, regardless of the
desperate nature of any problem you encountered. The
best passenger was a layman, ignorant of any kind of gymnastics and fully trusting in your capabilities. Tom, Jr.
refused to travel with him, so a neighbouring farmer's son
took the risk, and it seems his ignorance was magnificent.
Mary Osborne, a rebellious teenage girl from the neighbourhood (and a socially inferior family) may have also
climbed on his back once or twice. Her tomboyish ways
and unconcern for what others thought of her endeared
her to Bill and they became good friends, and possibly a
bit more. She was unafraid of both his high wire and his
reputation, and thrilled by his exploits.

The year 1859 was an eccentric year, tailor-made for
William Leonard Hunt. It had a bit of everything: people
who walked on water, others who crossed torrential rapids
on stilts, a local hanging, a glorious rebel war involving
someone named Farini, and of course, a mania for
tightropes and a man who actually walked one over
Niagara Falls.

   In early spring the *Port Hope Guide* and most every
newspaper in North America reported that Signor Gaspa
Morelli, real name Andrew Greenleaf, for a wager of
$1,000 had waded through the raging rapids at the edge
of the American Falls at Niagara on stilts. This incredible
feat had been accomplished in the early morning without
benefit of a crowd and the daring man had reputedly
spent the following day in bed in utter exhaustion. A story
circulated that he had been a stilt-walker with Barnum.

It was an adventure that boggled the mind: how could a human being last for a second at the brink of the Falls let alone successfully cross it? Apparently he could...if he were the invention of a prankster. The *Niagara Falls Gazette* (NY) commented a few weeks later, "The same fellow got a splendid view of the Falls by standing with one foot on Goat Island and the other in front of Saul Davis' shaving shop, on the Canada side." Of all the reactions to this fantastic story, Bill Hunt's was the most unusual, though he kept it to himself for many years...he wanted to try it.

Throughout that summer, balloons were all the rage, drawing crowds who were awed by the height to which they floated and thrilled by the danger of each ascension. Danger consistently drew the attention of the ostensibly moral men and women of the time: accidents at Niagara (and there were several in 1859), especially involving people swept over the falls, were of particular interest. But perhaps the most eccentric adventures of the year concerned men who actually walked on water. In Wisconsin a man claimed he could stroll across the entire width of Lake Michigan; at Oswego, New York, Mr. Gardner crossed and recrossed the Genesee; and in Toronto, Mr. Hickok brought out the press to see a promenade in his special shoes on the surface of the Don River. Bill Hunt thought this more than a little clever too, as later events will show.

As he approached his twenty-first birthday that summer, all he had been—a country boy from the Canadian backwoods, a medical student, an at-least-somewhat-respectable citizen—was about to die. A new persona was ready to surface. The greatest single impetus that created it came from the actions of a French acrobat. Late in June, Monsieur Blondin walked the greatest high wire in history, and the idea for Farini took root.

CHAPTER 4

Blondin's Challenge

"The King of the Tight Rope,
The Lord of the Hempen Realm,
The Emperor of All Manilla."
New York Times, February 23, 1897, on Blondin

B londin was a man held in such awe during his time that he seemed larger than life. He was the subject of children's stories and featured in three-dimensional "pop-up" books; and his name was a metaphor for the very concepts of balance and daring. It was said he walked on stilts on a tightrope, had cooked an omelette on a stove while up there, and once carried an eight-month-old lion across the wire in a wheelbarrow. To some he was foolhardy and reckless but to most he was a spectacular man talented in a nearly superhuman way.

Popular histories of his life say he first walked on a tightrope at the age of four, between two chairs in his parents' kitchen in the French town of Hesdin near Abbeville, and soon thereafter took to walking between stepladders. He had been born Jean François Gravelet on February 28, 1824, the son of a former soldier in Napoleon's army who had been nicknamed Blondin by his comrades due to his unusually fair hair. Little Jean was sent to Lyon as a child for one of two reasons: either to keep him from running away with circuses or to develop his gymnastic skills. Whatever the purpose, he was almost immediately enrolled at the École de Gymnase and his precocity is said to have so astounded his instructors that his professional debut as a rope-walker took place at age five, after only six months of training. Billed as "The Little Wonder," he was presented throughout Europe and even performed for royalty. The sight of this tiny child dancing with ease on a slender wire must have been one of the most extraordinary scenes in show-business history.

By the early 1850s his popularity was enormous in Europe and he was soon signed by William Niblo's agent and brought to America to perform with the famed French acrobat troupe the Ravel Family at Niblo's Garden in New York City. He made his American debut in the fall of 1851 (by then using his father's nickname) and soon became an attraction in the eastern states. When he first visited Niagara Falls, some time in 1858, he was either approaching the end of his time with the Ravels or had started his headlining appearances with the Martinetti Troupe, and shortly thereafter began pursuing a solo career.

Blondin was a short man (about 5'4") who packed 140 pounds onto a powerful, well-muscled physique. He is said to have had particularly "good shoulders and legs." His hair, of course, was blond, of medium length and well groomed, and his complexion was as fair as his moustache and the tuft of hair on his chin, while his eyes, characterized by an acquaintance as "keen and piercing" were also very light in hue. During his nearly decade-long residence in the United States (living in New York, Cincinnati and Niagara Falls) he learned to speak a broken English that helped him both in business and social life. Though friendly and courteous, his most striking personal traits were his self-possessed air and his immense confidence. Up on the wire he worked with an ease that seemed to defy good sense: in fact, there appears to have been a bravado about his performances, courageous, even reckless *tour de forces* that they were, featuring his extraordinary somersaulting and bizarre theatrics. He always denied that there was anything rash about what he did, claiming that every feat he tried was thought out beforehand and devoid of any real danger. But the audience's perspective was much different.

When Blondin first laid eyes on the falls at Niagara he was stunned by their "wonderful spectacle" and claimed that he instantly thought of walking above them. He liked to tell reporters that "...had a rope been at hand...I would have started at once..." Legend has it that the falls haunted him over the following months and then one night he had a dream that sealed his fate. "I stood by the great Falls, overpowered by its terrible sublimity," he said. "Suddenly my clothing dropped from my form as if by magic and before me, across the boiling flood, was stretched a silken cord as delicate as a thread of gossamer. I ventured upon the cord, and in a twinkling I had crossed the rushing torrent and was looking back upon the shore whence I started." Soon he and agent Harry Colcord were booked into a hotel in the village of Niagara Falls, New York.

During the last week of May in 1859 he made his move. "Several days ago," reported the June 4th *Niagara Falls Gazette*, "Mons. Blondin, the celebrated tight rope performer, called on us with his agent Mr. Colcord, and informed us of his intention, if sufficient inducements were offered, to extend a rope from the eastern point of Goat Island across the river to the Canada side, and to perform the wonderful feat of crossing on the same."

It was a truly bizarre announcement. Readers could barely imagine a tightrope big enough and long enough to reach over the mighty falls, let alone a man being able to rig it, and then *walk* it; that was almost beyond sane reasoning. It just wasn't possible: no human being had that kind of ability, or more importantly, courage. Slowly the announcement began appearing in newspapers internationally and was received variously with astonishment, scepticism and outright ridicule. The *New York Times* called him a fool and said he should be arrested, and in London he was considered a hoax, but at home the Niagara Falls paper stuck by him and recorded his preparations in detail. Many local citizens began intimating that the *Gazette* and area businesses had concocted the spectacular fiction of the Niagara Falls skywalker merely as a "sell" to draw crowds for the summer season.

Most of the news concerning Blondin throughout the
month of June seemed to confirm the critics' ideas. Before
two weeks had passed he changed locations, saying that
Mr. Porter, who owned Goat Island, had denied him access
and now he would put his rope over the gorge instead, at a
point halfway between the famous suspension bridge and
the two falls. Here the cliffs were nearly two hundred feet
high and the distance across, above an eddying current,
about one thousand feet. Mr. White of the Pleasure
Grounds on the American side gave him permission to
string his rope from his park. Then everyone waited for
the rope. And waited...and waited. It seemed things had
stalled. But finally, on June 22nd, after several false
reports that appeared to again give credence to doubts,
the cable arrived. It was announced that he would perform his feat on June 30th.

Despite eyewitness reports that earlier in the week
Blondin had (for maintenance purposes) walked out over
the edge of the cliffs on a minute 7/8" cord that was being
used to draw his large rope across, many feared a hoax
and on the day of the performance a crowd of only five to
eight thousand people appeared. And of those who did go
a good deal of their number were genuinely surprised to
find a rope in place, with guy wires, stretching like an
enormous spider-web over the river. It was a beautiful
warm day and "the Front," the Falls' Canadian-side carnival of commerce, was filled with brass bands, temperance people delivering sermons, freak-show presentations
and tents of curiosities. Blondin materialized on the
American side just before five o'clock, travelling in an
open barouche and wearing "white Turkish pantaloons, a
purple plush vest, a curled wig [and a] gaily decorated
skull cap." These he discarded, and dressed in only flesh-
coloured tights, shirt and hose, took up his thirty-eight-
foot balancing pole and stepped confidently up onto his
wire. The crowd, lining the banks of the river, is said to
have become instantly silent. He moved slowly at first and
the sensation (enjoyed by one and all, even if in a macabre
way) was of watching a man in a danger so perilous that

it was nearly unbearable. From the Canadian side he was,
at first, just a dot on a thread. But suddenly it seemed, in
just over fifteen minutes, he was all the way across! A
spontaneous roar erupted from the crowd as he set foot on
Canadian land, but he didn't spend much time revelling
in it because after a short rest, he was back up on his rope
returning to the United States, and made the trip in just
seven minutes. His performance featured him standing on
one foot, sitting down, drinking from a bottle he lowered
to the *Maid of the Mist* and leaping on his rope. When he
arrived on American soil safely the crowd crushed around
him, people reaching out to touch him, and he was borne
on the shoulders of his friends to his carriage.
Locomotives whistled and the bands played "Yankee
Doodle Dandy," but despite all the acclaim there was only
$250 (not even enough to pay for his $350 rope) in his coffers. Over the next few days his feat was reported
throughout Canada and the United States, but was met
with doubt in Europe. On July 1st it hit the Toronto newspapers and on the 2nd it appeared in the *Port Hope Guide*.
In Canada West, Niagara Falls and the eastern United
States the performance became "the principal topic of conversation" for the following week. One report called it "the
greatest feat of modern times."

Through the remaining months of that remarkably hot
summer Blondin gave a total of eight performances. He
had intended just three but when throngs of nearly 20,000
people came to see his second and third performances he
decided to continue. On the 4th of July he showed a holiday crowd how to walk backwards across a cable over
Niagara Falls and then how to survive the distance with
an opaque sack covering everything but the legs and feet;
and on July 14th a huge audience saw his unique showmanship surface when he pushed a groove-wheeled barrow
in front of himself and held a hat extended at arm's length
while crack pistol shooter "Captain Travis" (supposedly)
fired a bull's-eye through its brim from a steamer in the
gorge below. After a short absence he returned to Niagara
in August and gave his two greatest performances.

On the 3rd the streets of the village were as full as Broadway near Barnum's museum: some reports claim that by late afternoon the shores bulged with a crowd near or beyond 25,000. Blondin stunned them with a series of six headstands on the rope. He hung on by his hands, his feet, and then let go with one foot and literally held on by his toes! The *Niagara Falls Gazette* said "a sense of awe" could be felt by the spectators. On the 17th of August he was scheduled to carry a man on his back but few believed it would really happen, until he was spotted about to return from the Canadian side with his 145-pound manager (still wearing his boots) strapped to his back. (Unknown to the crowd, a rope had been tied to their waists so they could safely leap to either side of the cable if they fell.) Moving at a slow pace they stopped several times to rest on their crossing, Colcord standing behind Blondin on the cable clutching his shoulders. The great man was said to have been covered with perspiration and very fatigued when they touched land. The *Gazette* exclaimed that no one else on earth would "dare" try such a feat.

Three more performances, on August 24th and 31st, and September 8th, closed his season at the Falls. He walked with his hands and feet shackled in chains and with peach baskets tied to his feet; he carried a thirty-five-pound sheet-iron stove out to the mid-point and cooked and ate an omelette (dishes and cutlery included, of course); he crossed at night with roman candles on his pole (which went out and left him in darkness); and brought out a meal, a table and chair and had dinner. With the exception of a chair which slipped from his grasp and fell into the river, he never once made a false step and never seemed close to falling.

Blondin became an instant international celebrity. Children considered him a hero and reports of boys, small and not so small, falling from home-made tightropes were common that summer. Everywhere everyone seemed rope crazy.

In Rochester, New York in late July Monsieur DeLave

loudly announced his equality to the great one and by
August was drawing spectators (Blondin among them) to
watch a crossing on a rope extended over the Genesee
River. For a few weeks he publicly asked for a chance to
use the cable already stretched over the Niagara and
Colcord's refusal to let him do so (or DeLave's own reluctance to follow through on his boasts) caused an eruption
of bitterness between Rochester and Niagara Falls newspapers. For some reason the challenger seemed incapable
of setting up his own rope at the gorge. Was it a financial
or an engineering difficulty? Or was it fear of failure? More
finger-pointing occurred in August when some of Blondin's
guy lines were said to have been severed; and later, when
DeLave appeared in the area with Whitby and Company's
Metropolitan Circus, the *Niagara Falls Gazette* criticized
his performance as merely competent, lacking in daring
and stamina. In Rochester, a few weeks after Blondin's
final performance, DeLave made a stab at notoriety by also
attempting to carry a man on his back, but to the shock of
the crowd, he fell off his swaying rope, and he and his companion only escaped death by catching the cable with their
hands. Blondin reigned supreme, and unchallenged.

Niagara Falls enjoyed an unprecedented tourist season
in 1859. Perhaps Blondin's greatest accomplishment was
in somehow enhancing the attraction of one of the world's
natural wonders. He had arrived as a crank and was leaving as an acrobat held in awe by the public. His name was
now used in advertisements to indicate excellence and he
was imitated and revered by young people in schoolyards
across the continent. His feat was universally considered
to be singular: something nearly magical, beyond the
capabilities of other human beings. In fact, Blondin and
his supporters defied anyone else to try it.

Despite his success there were some who were angered
by his apotheosis. The *Rochester Union and Advertiser*, for
example, pointed out that he was only human and pleaded
for someone to prove it. "There are other men who can
walk that rope as well as he does, and he knows it; and we
hope that he will yet have his conceit taken out by a rival."

But who in the world would possibly have the talent, or more importantly, the courage, to attempt such a thing?

On a little farm in Hope Township, Bill Hunt was practising.

He was twenty-one now and just a few months from the examination that would get him recognized as a full-fledged doctor. There wasn't much work at home these days: much of his father's land was rented and the ten-acre lot they cultivated took only short tours of duty among the four older Hunt boys; so unlike neighbouring friends, they had time on their hands. Bill used it to the utmost, trying new tricks on his rope, lifting weights and working on his gymnastics; he read and studied. The summer months passed and the harvest began. Then one day during the first week of September he happened to ride into Port Hope and while wandering down the steep plank sidewalk on Walton Street was recognized by a man who was about to change his life.

Though Hugh Crea wasn't quite thirty years of age in the fall of 1859, as editor and publisher of the *Port Hope Guide* he held one of the most influential positions in Port Hope. He also happened to be the Secretary of the East Durham and Township of Hope Agricultural Societies, and in another month they would be presenting the "fall show." Crea was a man who never liked to do anything in a small way and it bothered him that once again the fair would consist of long days full of trite competitions for everything from prize steers and plows to the best raspberry jam. Tired of sitting through speeches and brass bands for the umpteenth time, he was looking for an idea with some drawing power. Such were his concerns that day in September when he saw Tom Hunt's eldest son walking, self-assuredly as always, down Walton Street near the *Guide* office. He had heard some strange things about this country lad and wondered if they were true.

That very week his paper ran a story entitled, "Rope Walking": "[it] is all the rage just now, and everybody able

to stand on his legs is trying his skill with a view of ultimately eclipsing Blondin or DeLave." Indeed many were
trying, but few were succeeding, and young men were suffering terrible injuries. Such feats were easier imagined
than accomplished, and only a few exceptional athletes
were making names for themselves; none could touch the
mighty Blondin.

Hugh Crea suddenly called out to Bill Hunt. The young
man was always conscious of his appearance and was
likely displaying himself a little that day, or maybe his
mind was in its usual high gear, thinking about wire-
walkers, water-walkers, medical books; for whatever reason, he didn't immediately respond. Crea came chugging
up to him, smiling broadly, his face betraying an inquiring
interest. He reached out and grabbed Bill's hand, shook it
vigorously and came to the point. Farini always remembered his opening gambit: "Youngster!" he said, "I hear
you do some very remarkable things on a high rope." It
was intended as a compliment, but Bill, less than a decade
younger than Crea, did not think himself a "youngster."
He was polite with the editor but took on a slightly toler-
ating air. For his part, Crea hardly noticed: he had too
much to say. He went right into his proposal, explaining
that he would like to see Bill performing on his rope and
if his prowess came even close to the stories people had
been telling him then he would, as sure as Bill Hunt was
standing there, make his fortune for him. Though Farini
always considered this day the "red-letter day" of his life,
at that moment one wouldn't have known it: the proud
young man with the dark good looks and agile brain and
body offered a cool reaction. He agreed to the proposition
and snapped that the demonstration (apparently a trifling
thing) could take place whenever the editor so desired. An
appointment was made for the Hunt farm on Tuesday,
September 13th. And so a small-town man of ephemeral
ideas lighted the fuse of an enormous personality.

"The day came," Farini later recalled, "and so did the
Editor and his party." Coming along Kingston Road in
their buggies they could see some of the neighbouring

farmers congregating in the barnyard in anticipation of a show. When everyone had settled, Bill slipped off his shoes, picked up his pole and started up the rope toward the peak of the barn. Though his friends knew what to expect the townsfolk were dubious to say the least, and not at all comforted when they actually saw him balancing on this little twine so high up in the air. Here they were, supposedly respected and responsible citizens, gathered around in an audience, perhaps about to watch a youngster break both his legs. They were glad his father was away: rope-walking wasn't exactly the Lord's work.

But what they saw astonished them: the Hunt boy walked the rope as though it were solid ground; he popped headstands and somersaults without hesitation, hung by his hands and his feet, took a chair up and stood on it and finally, as they watched in disbelief, lifted a neighbour onto his back and ascended and descended the rope like a delicate Samson. He worked with the seriousness of a scientist demonstrating an experiment. It was his moment and he knew it. He wasn't nervous; he didn't disappoint: he just went out and did it with a sureness that was amazing to see.

By the time he finished, any doubts Crea might have had had vanished and he took Bill aside. "You should be put before the public," Farini recalled him saying, "and I am the man to do it." Then he pointed up at the rope and said that if one could be rigged over Smith's Creek between two buildings in the centre of town, and someone could get up the nerve to walk it in front of a crowd, there would be a guaranteed one hundred dollars in it. He asked Bill what he said to that: the offer was meant to be tantalizing but contingent upon the young man's courage. Bill replied coolly: his fee was higher than that, and as for putting up the rope and the performance...those were simple matters. Crea smiled indulgently and shuffled his feet. He explained to his young acquaintance that he might not fully understand what was going on here: they weren't talking about a little slack wire in a barnyard: this would be four storeys high, above a rocky river with a crowd

looking on. The water and the height might make him
dizzy and he would undoubtedly be nervous. There was no
way anyone could know what it would be like, so perhaps
he should think about it more...because if he fell...

Farini later called Crea's comments insinuations. He
cut him off sharply, saying that such concerns were not
the business of the Agricultural Fair's directors. (Farini
would always feel demeaned when someone thought he
might not be capable of something, even if that something
was almost impossibly difficult.) "If I can do it at twenty
feet," he snapped, "then I doubt one hundred feet will
make any difference...those rocks aren't meant for me."
Crea was becoming excited. He had done his duty and
spoken truthfully, and still the young man was adamant.
He put it to him a final time: "Then you will do it?" Bill
snickered. Of course he would, but not for one hundred
dollars, a fee that would barely cover expenses. He then
proceeded to explain to the amused editor how the committee could make the whole scheme more profitable.
Crea's reaction to this was prescient: he called him "devilishly cute" like a showman, and then agreed to recon-
sider the terms and speak to him the following week.

The committee's excitement at what they had seen
must have greatly affected them because within a few
days they drove back to the Hunt farm with a sweetened
pot. The deal was struck. There would be two performances: one on October 1st to advertise the fair and
another on the 11th to close it, and in between he would
lecture on "Physical Culture" at the Town Hall and spice
it with feats of strength.

The editor had told him that his high-wire feat would not
be advertised if he had any hesitations whatsoever. No
such chance. By week's end his notices appeared and people began to talk. Then the rope went up. It looped across
Smith's Creek and swayed when the winds picked up. It
looked eerie at night, like a hangman's noose. The town
began to buzz.

CHAPTER 5

First Triumph...
and Departure

*"...we shall triumph with...energy,
and, if necessary, audacity."*
Signor Luigi Carlo Farini,
the dictator of Modena, Italy,
September 1859

Bill never considered using the Hunt name for his high-wire performances, that would have shamed the family beyond recovery. And so he began looking for the perfect replacement.

It was common for nineteenth-century performers to take a striking, foreign title: French or Spanish was nice, Italian was supreme. The most prominent news in the September 10, 1859 *Port Hope Guide* came from Italy, where the Austro-Italian War had just ended and Latin leaders were attempting to draw the peninsula together into a nation. The dashing Garibaldi was reviewing the army of Modena, and two articles mentioned the name of the new, unchallenged dictator of that state...a former physician named Signor Farini. He was a flashy leader given to dramatic utterances, but also an intellectual accomplished in several fields. And so, the very week that Bill Hunt agreed to his first professional rope-walking performance and went searching for a suitable stage-name, this Farini made his only significant appearance in world history, and in the Port Hope newspaper.

Some time between September 13 and 16, Bill began calling himself "Signor Farini." Later he added Guillermo

(William) as his first name and Antonio for his second.

That weekend readers of the Port Hope *Tri-Weekly Guide* found an unusual article on its third page:

> Niagara and Rochester have been immortalized by the rope walking feats of a Blondin and a DeLave. The mighty cataract has ceased to be one of the seven wonders of the world—Blondin reigns in its stead. The Genesee Falls, once attractive to strangers, is so no longer—DeLave with his tight rope feats has thrown it completely into the shade. Why shouldn't Port Hope have a little rope walking on its "own hook"? Echo answers "why"?
>
> We are in a position to announce that all the principal feats performed by Blondin at Niagara will be performed in the course of next week, in Port Hope, by Signor Farini who, in another column, challenges the Niagara champion.

The "challenge," really an advertisement, appeared beside a dressmaker's notice, but it was as bold and impudent as its author. "TO M. BLONDIN" it shouted, in thick black type that dominated the page:

TO M. BLONDIN !

THE undersigned challenges M. Blondin, as follows:—I will carry M. Blondin to the centre of his Cable across the Niagara River, he to carry me the rest of the distance across. Afterwards to start from either end, proceed to the centre, and down ropes to the deck of the *Maid of the Mist* below, returning the same way.

I offer this challenge in consequence of M. Blondin's repeated assertions that no man dare perform his feats.

SIGNOR FARINI.

Port Hope, Sept. 17, 1859.   v4-96   f

Port Hope Guide, September 17, 1859

One might have thought that an amateur from the country would have made his debut a modest affair. Why challenge the greatest daredevil in the world, and place such enormous pressure on yourself? What if Blondin did the inconceivable and accepted? It could, of course, be said that this was no more than an attempt to use Blondin's name to gain publicity, but Farini's personality and his actions during the following year indicate that he was in deadly earnest. No response was ever received, but if one had, he would have been at Niagara within days: he trusted his ability immensely and his well-developed pride gave him unusual fortitude. The last sentence of the challenge stands out. Blondin had claimed that no one would "dare," and Bill Hunt, desperate to prove himself, took it personally.

The advertisement appeared again on the 20th and word began to spread throughout the county and beyond. It turned up in the *Daily British Whig* in Kingston, the *Daily Globe* of Toronto ran it on their second page, and *The Examiner* (Peterborough) referred to it under the headline, "Fools Not All Dead Yet."

The fool now had a wise man's problem: inventing his own high wire and stringing it. The first part of the problem was solved by the Hunts' closeness to the Marsh family. He went to the harbour and secured the loan of a "set of blocks and falls" (the pulleys and hoisting-tackle ropes used in the rigging of a schooner), as well as the captain's unsolicited commitment to send two sailors to help him. Then all three went, at night or in the early morning, to the building where he would anchor his tightrope.

It was down at the foot of Walton Street, on the northwest side of the bridge, a four-storey brick structure occupied by the Craick and Gillespie Dry Goods company. As Farini looked up to its peaked roof and then down to the rocks at the bottom of the clear stream, the reality of his task was suddenly all too palpable. He could see across an open expanse of some two hundred feet to another four-storey brick building on the east side of the creek, the distance and height daunting: a fall would kill him, or cripple him for life. He climbed to the roof and looked down, and felt truly frightened. They went on with their task, attaching small guy lines to the main rope, hauling it up, passing it through trap doors in the two roofs and fastening it to the timbers that ran perpendicular under the roof beams. This way, it was reasoned, his weight, when pressing down on the rope, would pull sideways on the entire roof. When everything was secured he went home to the country to try to sleep.

Saturday October 1, 1859 was a favourable day for walking a high wire in Port Hope: unremarkable in temperature and wind speed. Signor Farini's "grand ascension" was to commence at four o'clock but several hours ahead of time the streets became noticeably busy and by three o'clock spectators were packed into any place that gave a good view of the rope.

Smith's Creek (now the Ganaraska River) flows through the town and into Lake Ontario at about 90 degrees and is the centre of a valley on whose basin and hills Port Hope was built. Walton Street bridge intersects it at the centre of town. People now filled the bridge, jammed northward on the east bank, stood shoulder to shoulder on the side of "Protestant Hill" (from which powerful old St. John's Anglican Church surveyed the realm) and covered the rooftops of every available building. To the west Walton "was one dense mass of spectators" all the way up its hill. The enormity of the crowd stunned Farini and his backers, for despite their boastful predictions, they hadn't anticipated such a throng. It was being said that many came to see him fall (and this kind of show drew that sort of spectator), but not everyone had such bloodthirsty motives. A typical Canadian curiosity had been put in motion after folks read in the *Guide* that Farini was a local man: they wanted to see if one of their own could do what the famous Blondin and other exotic people were doing in far-off places. In moments they would find out.

The *Guide* ran a long article entitled, "Rope Walking Today" on the morning of his debut. In addition to praising Mayor William Fraser for allowing the controversial performance to take place, they included a passage that sounded very much as though it came from Farini's own pen, embodying his brand of Victorian self-reliance:

> It seems a great feat to walk on the rope across the creek, but it in reality is not. It is as easy to walk at a height of seventy feet as at a height of seven. Of course at the former elevation a man must have nerve, or rather must be accustomed to being in high places. Signor Farini is in possession of every qualification necessary to the performance of the feat. He is a person of such great activity and muscular power that should he lose his balance—an event so improbable as almost to amount to an impossibility,—he would grasp the rope and proceed on his journey hand over hand.—By practice of gymnastics, for years, he has so developed his muscles that they never fail him.

The crowd that day was a mix of almost every sort of Upper Canadian: there were the many faces of farmers, children, merchants, city councillors and society ladies, as well as the hard-drinking young hooligans who came looking for brawls and other fun and wanted to see if Farini had any nerve. Tall black top hats, fancy and plain bonnets, and the caps of boys were thatched together in the solid mass below the rope. The *Guide* enjoyed "the presence of scores of those excruciatingly respectable people who had bored the Mayor almost to death to induce him to prevent Farini from fulfilling his promises. Somehow or other they had compounded with their respectability or their consciences, and stood their ground in the crowd manfully." Neither would those who gravely asserted that the young man's days were numbered give up their spots. By mid-afternoon thousands were waiting for Farini, eyes cast upward.

There is no record of how he felt during the hours before his debut and if he had been asked he likely would have said he felt no fear and was concentrating on doing his feats accurately. But one has to wonder. For some reason, he put on his costume a full hour before show time. As the crowd grew and reached overflowing, as it buzzed outside the building, his twenty-one-year-old heart must have been thumping.

When he finally came out of the trap door on the Craick and Gillespie building and they noticed him, a huge cheer went up which he later said, "nearly affected me." He was dressed in what the papers called the usual clothing of acrobats, namely his first silk tights. A group of muscular farmer friends then appeared on both roofs, ready to help him, and fend off anyone who might try to stop the show or touch his rope.

Signor Farini took the long balancing pole, which had just been handed up to him, and walked carefully down the roof to his rope. He slowly put one foot out over the brink and settled it onto the cord to get its feel. When his head had first popped up out of the trap door many in the crowd, apparently suddenly startled by the realization of what was before them, had begun shouting at him in almost desperate voices amidst the cheers to not go through with it. But when his first step came, they were collectively stilled. It was an eerie silence. This is a common reaction at high-wire performances, especially when they are death-defying. The empathy is almost palpable: spectators feel as though they too were up on the rope, and together in paralyzing fear, they attempt to ease the performer across. Farini said that when he glanced down he saw pain on the "old, sun-burnt faces."

He lifted his other foot off the roof and stood out on the rope, surrounded by the crowd's silence. The next few steps were slow, but he didn't shake...he kept going without pause...moving steadily until he was all the way to the centre, directly over the river. If he indeed had been nervous before, he seemed supremely confident now.

But suddenly there was an unforeseen problem.

Without warning the rope slipped under his weight and began to sway. The crowd felt themselves falling. Farini halted, steadied the rope with his powerful legs, and continued along the incline to the other building. People looked up at the bottoms of his feet and marvelled. It seemed like a dream: a man virtually suspended in midair, a fantasy in three dimensions. When he reached the building on the east side and got onto the roof safely, applause erupted from the crowd like thunder and rang up and down the street. As Bill Hunt revelled in it, on the ground people felt a sense of enormous relief, as though they too were safe now.

He had intended to return to the other side walking backwards but the loose rope made this feat treacherous. His friends warned him not to try it and he saw the sense in this, but refused to allow himself to be entirely frightened: he wanted to try something difficult. Casting his pole aside, he went back out over the rocks with only his arms for balance. This is difficult for a high-wire walker and can set him apart from amateurs. It seemed foolhardy for a beginner but he was determined to be uncompromising: an axiom maintained as much for business reasons as integrity. He felt so energized by the crowd's applause, he had the nerve to try nearly anything. Coming slowly to the centre, he let himself fall to the rope (causing a few screams), caught it with one arm and hung there, then pulled himself up, sat down, and held his arms away from the rope. Finally, he hung by his feet, his arms wide, stretched out toward Smith's Creek, his face looking down the banks toward Lake Ontario. Then, with the audience suitably awed, he returned to safety.

Farini claimed to have been hoisted onto the shoulders of his friends and carried to Town Hall, where his strongman routine and fitness lecture was to take place. This seems unlikely as no public notice of an exhibition of muscle after the October 1st walk is on record. In his early days he desperately wanted fame and his rousing account of being carried aloft by a big crowd to the hall and then performing to such masses that several shows were needed, the doors nearly broken in, and spectators seated on the stage, indicates how accommodating to that end his marvellous imagination could be. It is evident, however, that his professional rope-walking debut was an unqualified success and made him an instant local hero. Spectators were stunned by his skill, and indeed the dexterity he showed was amazing in such a young amateur. He seemed unnaturally stuck to the wire like a human fly. People wondered just exactly where he had come from and how he had learned to do such things.

Farini's account of his strong-man show, which actually took place six days later, is thorough. The imposing, box-like Town Hall sat next to the fairgrounds, about a five-minute walk toward the lake from the Walton Street bridge. In 1859 it still had a large lecture-ballroom with a stage and it was in this room that Farini performed, for an admission charge of twenty-five cents. He commenced with his lecture on "Physical Culture," using the knowledge he had gained from medical studies to describe how he had drastically increased his muscular power, and stressing the importance of a great deal of well-informed, intelligent exercise. On stage he was both showman and scientist, explaining that there was a way to teach yourself how to do almost any physical feat, and yet never revealing the secrets to his own tricks and deceptions. He was both a debunker and a humbug: he explained method, but always kept enough hidden to surprise his audience.

His first trick was the one he had learned as an adolescent in Bowmanville: he had a huge stone placed on his chest and allowed volunteers to smash it with sledgehammers. Then he did the rope-pull routine: more than a dozen sturdy men attempted to budge him as he planted himself and competed with them in an apparently hopelessly one-sided tug of war. He also lifted 160 pounds above his head with one arm; and it was during this feat that a large man, towering over him, appeared on the stage calling him a "boy" and insisting that he could easily lift the same dumb-bell. As the man struggled desperately to fulfil his boast, Farini sneaked behind him, picked him up, spun him around and dropped everything, weight and man, in a dizzy heap on the floor.

There is no doubt that Farini was an extraordinarily powerful man. At one of his strength exhibitions in 1860 he "threw a 60 lb. weight 23 feet, held out at arms length a 60 lb. weight on each little finger," and supported a 300-pound stone on his chest as he absorbed the sensational sledgehammer blows. It was said that he could dead-lift at least half a ton, making him temporarily one of the world's strongest men. His athletic prowess was astonishing and there likely never was, and may never be again, another great acrobat who also possessed such prodigious muscle.

His second Port Hope walk was scheduled for Tuesday October 11th, the last day of the County Fair, and he promised to display a new series of high-wire feats, "that have never been attempted by Blondin or DeLave" (a typical showman's boast, knowingly false). These included turning somersaults, walking blindfolded with a bag over his head, and carrying a man on his back.

The crowd that filled every open space within sight of the bridge that day is now legendary in the town's history. "Such a multitude was never before seen in Port Hope," said the *Guide*. They numbered "fully eight thousand," nearly twice the population of the entire town. When Farini took to his stage, people swarmed below him in all directions and the buildings and hills were completely covered. Farini boasted, "there have never been as many people there even for HRH Prince of Wales, and I don't suppose there ever will be as many again." He had a man with him this time, and a harness to strap him to his back, but Mayor Fraser anticipated this and intervened. The spectacle of Farini wantonly endangering the life of another before such a huge crowd was something he couldn't afford and the community could not allow. He was a first-term mayor, successful in the safety-first insurance world, and not amenable to such sky-high gambling. The *Guide* report said that when the mayor "interfered" Farini "divest[ed] himself of his rider," indicating that they were harnessed up and at the very brink of the precipice.

Now alone, the Signor walked out to the rope's centre

Walton Street, Port Hope in the nineteenth century.

acting purposely nonchalant, tied down his balancing pole, and stood on his head. He then "went through with a variety of daring and difficult feats." Hugh Crea was astounded by his friend: "He appeared to be as much at home on his lofty bridge as though he were on the sidewalk."

Signor Farini's debut was over. Port Hope had proved a propitious place for his entrance: not too large or worldly to deny him a chance and just provincial enough to be mightily impressed. But soon, sooner than he had planned, Port Hope would become too small for his ambition and his "immoral" ideas. His imminent departure would prove wrenching, and affect him for the rest of his life.

He claimed he "figured at several fairs that autumn," and tried to remain level-headed about his success as his fame spread throughout the county and friends and strangers became admirers overnight. Later in life he would maintain that he didn't give up medicine but kept studying throughout that October and prepared himself for the upcoming exam. (Hugh Crea thought his desire to be "showman and surgeon combined" would destroy the former career, and told him to be "an amuser not a poisoner of people.") If he did try an exam he did so either at Victoria College in Cobourg or at the University of Toronto, and at various moments in later life spoke of having attended one or the other. His claims about passing the exam and receiving his diploma may never be satisfactorily verified or denied: as a follower of the Eclectic medical practice he was not subject to the government-approved graduation process and instead would have been examined by a small board of Eclectic officials who, while not openly condemned by the government, were not yet entirely legitimized. Eclectics did not accept the general approach to medicine at the time which involved a great deal of bleeding of patients and the use of quasi-miracle medicines; instead, they believed in the use of nature's cures, like herbs and other organic antidotes, and rest. The Eclectic approach greatly influenced Farini's own philosophy throughout his life. It wasn't until several years later, long after Farini had left the country, that Eclectic doctors began getting justice. There are no records of their certifications prior to the 1860s and even Dr. Patterson doesn't appear in the Medical Register until 1867. It is possible that Farini never achieved his doctorate, though we have his own word that he did and during his show-business career often told journalists as much. Later in life he seems to have stopped making this claim, though this may be due to the fact that as an early Eclectic, he had lost his status. There is little doubt that he studied medicine for an extended period and did so with Bradford Patterson. His knowledge of human physiology and its strengths and weaknesses was thorough.

If October of 1859 was his coming-out month, then November was his month of departure. It was hastened by his father's return from England.

When Thomas stepped down from the train in Port Hope that November he was seething inside: on his way in from the east someone had told him about "Signor Farini." William had decided to be the one to meet the "governor" and as he drove the family buggy into town that day was anxious to tell his father of his success, but somewhere deep inside must have known that T.W. would be less than pleased. At first his father seemed merely distant. As they

travelled into the country Farini began to describe his performances to his stony-silent listener and, as was his wont,
grew excited and soon spoke with unbridled enthusiasm.
Without warning his father cut him off, slicing the air with
a loud tirade. Farini called it a thunderbolt, and characterized his father's speech this way: "That will do, I don't wish
to hear anymore. Why, you seem quite proud of having disgraced the whole family. I'm astonished and ashamed. This
is the way you pay me for all my pains in educating you.
Your amateur gymnastics for health has ended in our
mutual disgrace. Never mention the subject again in my
presence. My son a mountebank—it's too terrible!"

Farini was so shocked by his father's reaction that he
described himself as "petrified" by it: the invisible wall
that had been building between them since birth instantly
became an impenetrable barrier and they separated on
that day as fate had dictated.

The rest of the trip occurred in tense silence. Farini's
thoughts went from bewilderment to anger to righteousness. He asked himself how he had disgraced the family
or himself and couldn't see it. "I had wronged no one." He
would not be ashamed of what he had done. I did not feel
any more ungentlemanly than before—my education and
refinement was no less." He had not run off with a circus,
he was still studying medicine: all he had done was take
an opportunity to push his skill and courage to the utmost
of his ability. Rather than be false about his passions, hiding them like those around him, he had done what he
wanted to do and received what he so desperately needed:
some praise. Then his father had knocked him down.

Back at the farmhouse the excited family gathered around
the returning father, who opened his travelling chest and
distributed gifts to his sons and daughters. But when
every child, even little one-year-old Mannie, had received
something, there was nothing left for William. Standing
off from the family, Farini felt distant and alone.

"I slipped out unnoticed and then for the first time I felt
I was a mountebank, a nobody. I had been forgotten."

He trudged along the dirt of Kingston Road in the cool day fighting back his rising anger, but as he stalked forward his moodiness turned into pride. Suddenly what he called an independent spirit came over him and he decided right then and there in the open countryside that he had had enough: he would leave home and strike out alone in life, using his wits to fulfil his dreams. He would finally cast off the croakers and grumblers, his imperious father, and the fundamentalist preachers who railed against his feats from the pulpits that very month. "The circus is among the...exhibitions of this wicked world which is at enmity with God," an Upper Canadian clergyman had recently written. But Farini simply could not accept that the world was wicked: like the circus, it could be a place of wonder and possibility. So he threw away his so-called respectable career, and put provincial little Hope behind him for good. It had plagued and hounded his dreams for too long already.

Only his mother came to say goodbye at the Grand Trunk Railroad station in Port Hope. He had insisted that his father stay away and it is evident that pride was a family trait because Thomas was nowhere in sight. Hannah, the loyal wife, claimed that his father was too bitter but right, and that William had greatly disappointed him. Farini was now so frustrated with this attitude that he addressed his mother harshly: "If it pleases you I'll say he's right," he snarled. Then he refused her offer of money and prepared to leave, "...and my darling mother kissed her mountebank son" and warned him about the lowness of the people with whom he would associate. "I've a will of my own," replied Signor Farini, "and no one can lead me where I don't wish to go."

Then he left on the next train for Bowmanville. And so a twenty-one-year-old medical man from a respectable family ran away from home and headed for glory.

CHAPTER 6

Freedom

*"There's no reason why the devil should have
all the enjoyable things in life."*
Dan Rice

His old home town was the first stop on the tour which was the rest of his life. The minute he arrived he began planning a high-wire performance which was an entire show in itself, not just a presentation at a county fair. It took place on the eastern outskirts of town in an area where there were open fields: the rope was strung from the top of the Eastern House to the upper part of a tall elm tree across the road. This hotel was a three-storey brick building with a peaked roof, and had a large ballroom, billiard parlour, lawn-bowling green and good stables and sheds; in other words, a respectable place. Assistants were, of course, in great supply in his old stomping grounds and the rope went up quickly. The crowd which waited anxiously for him to appear was a little rowdy, a not uncommon characteristic of his audiences, though this one's unruliness was spurred on somewhat by the nearness of a bar. At one point two citizens allowed their excitement, or intoxication, to get them entangled in a well-attended fist fight. And up in the air the former town hellion's performance didn't disappoint either.

From Bowmanville he went on to several other fairs, his most memorable show taking place in Lindsay, some

thirty miles to the north, where he walked on a snowy
day, so cold that people had to attend bundled up in their
sleighs. He finished that walk without incident, despite a
slight numbness in his hands, which were exposed so he
could grasp the balance pole.

Farini's life from this point in December 1859 until he
materializes at the beginning of July 1860 in a spectacular high-wire performance back in Bowmanville is something of a mystery. Neither his whereabouts nor his
activities can be fully accounted for, and his own recollec-
tions, made much later in life and filled with inconsisten-
cies, are the only guide to solving the puzzle. He told of
journeys that covered a few thousand miles, and of working at several occupations in numerous locations. He filled
these seven months with exploits that would have taken
him at least two years. They are marvellous stories based
on real experiences, but misplaced in time and stretched.

He claimed he began wandering, disappearing into the
American wild west in search of the adventure that had
always been so close to his heart. At first he went to frontier Minnesota to live with his uncle's family. (Hannah
Soper Hunt's full brother David Soper moved there from
Port Britain some time between 1855 and 1858, lured by
the American government's offer of cheap land: he picked
a spot about twenty miles west of the Mississippi River
and a few miles north of the Iowa border, near the future
village of Riceford.)
    Farini started out by train, visited Detroit and Chicago
on his way, much impressed by these the first large cities
he had ever seen, and used his rope-walking earnings to
stay at their finest hotels. Then he made his way westward across Illinois to the Mississippi River, took a steamboat north to Minnesota, and got off near the village of
Brownsville, a place of crude timber buildings that
seemed to him to have been erected overnight.
Discovering he had missed the stagecoach he decided to
walk the twenty miles to his uncle's home, carrying his

seventy-five-pound carpetbag. He arrived at Riceford the next day and began a long stay. His adventures, of course, were numerous. He worked hard helping his uncle plant two hundred acres of wheat, rode the range shooting wildlife with a revolver and rifle, spent time making limestone, had a close encounter with a bear and a rattlesnake, helped his uncle build and operate a general store and played cards with a rich Norwegian landowner's family who liked to sit naked together in a hot tub. All the while he distinguished himself as a brave, moral (he makes much of his unique abstinence from liquor) and enterprising individual. Much had been made of the dangers of confrontations with Indians and outlaws before he left for the frontier, but surprisingly Farini never claimed to have experienced that sort of wild-west adventure. (His brother John was in Minnesota a short time later and told of being in a town where the Jesse James gang robbed a bank and was then pursued by a posse.)

Soon bored with life on the prairie, he decided to make his way east again in search of action. His disappointed uncle protested his departure, convinced that his skills would have made him a frontier millionaire. When he reached the Mississippi a near-plague of smallpox was decimating the area, so he had to sneak through the villages until he got down to the water, where he found an abandoned rowboat and floated southward away from danger. In a few days he arrived at Prairie du Chien, Wisconsin and heard that a floating circus run by the renowned American showman Dan Rice was docking at Galena to the south, readying itself for its Mississippi River season. This, of course, suited him perfectly.

By the late 1850s Dan Rice was one of the most famous men in North America, a friend of presidents and a wit and performer extraordinaire, his clever political and social jests almost household sayings. During the early part of his life he had been a noted jockey, trained-pig presenter, riverboat gambler and strong-man, but found his true calling as a clown. He established his own circus and for a short time competed with former ally, the Spalding and Rogers Floating Palace, in an acrimonious showboat rivalry. He would become so popular that he actually put himself forward for the Republican nomination for president in 1868, and was a confidante of Abraham Lincoln, made an honorary colonel by Zachary Taylor, created the One Horse Show (temporarily broke, he put on marvellous circuses using a single horse), was paid the astronomical salary of one thousand dollars per week in the 1860s and is considered by many to be the prototype for the character of Uncle Sam (Rice had the same beard and often performed in a stars-and-stripes costume). He danced, sang, performed dazzling feats of trick riding and loved to engage in repartee with his audiences. A sort of American court jester, he was more comedian and raconteur than painted clown. The quickness of his mind was legendary.

Though the duration and the dates of Farini's involvement with Rice are suspect (it is doubtful he was with him in early 1860), his stories of their association, told many times in his later years, are vivid. First, he remembered marching into Rice's office and boldly announcing himself. The older man was a little crusty, having just lost his bookkeeper, and met the young Canadian hick with a surly lack of patience. But Farini presented himself as capable of almost anything, whether it be performing or a desk job, the answer to all "Uncle Dan's" problems. Rice had seen this many times before but something in the young man's demeanor and the fact that the show happened to be short an employee won Farini a job.

And so he started out keeping Dan Rice's books. He said he found them in such disorder that he had to buy new ones and then, of course, proceeded to do such a wonderful job, impressing Rice with both his skills and his ethics, that he was given other jobs such as advance agent, ticket seller, and eventually when a performer was ill, several turns on the horizontal bar.

The stories he told of his six-month stay on the showboat were filled with violence and corruption, things he

said disturbed him. He spoke of Irish and black workers
doing most of the hard labour and hating each other, so
much that fights were commonplace; and of canvas bosses
who beat black employees so badly he often felt compelled
to intervene. Slavery was in its final days, its victims dirt-
poor and illiterate, gaining admittance to the circus only
if they stayed afterward to work for the cost of their tickets, and even then distrustful foremen often confiscated
their coats and hats until all the work was done.

Dan Rice himself wasn't spared contact with violence
and Farini told wild stories about him: killing a knife-
brandishing black man by hitting him over the head with
a spike and then heaving him unceremoniously into the
Mississippi; and later seeing Rice wheeling out the company's saluting cannon, and pointing it, loaded, at a group
of unruly, revolver-toting spectators. The circus would
float near a new location and send out its advance agents
to the prospective town or plantation, often accompanied
by "fakirs," professional swindlers who could take the rich
for thousands by gaining their confidence and drawing
them into scams, or rob common people of smaller sums
by sleight-of-hand money-changing tricks. At times Farini
was drawn into the dark side of circus life.

He was supposedly involved in a duel in a small town
in the south while working as an advance agent, caused
when a rude citizen, insisting that Farini was a "damn
Yankee," accused him of cheating at cards in a saloon and
threw wine in his face. Farini (of course innocent of all
charges) picked up his accuser and threw him across the
room where he landed on a table. As Farini put it, "...a
glass of wine has been thrown, a blow has been struck, or
to speak more correctly, a gentleman has been pitched
into the air much to the inconvenience of himself and
those whom he honoured with the weight of his descending body." He then reluctantly fought the duel, a unique
one in a pitch-black room where the combatants began
without weapons, their knives hanging from the ceiling.
His opponent cheated by hiding a knife in his boot and
throwing it at the wall where Farini had been standing.

But Farini had cleverly dropped to the floor as the room darkened. Soon he had the villain by the throat, knife at the ready, but spared his life. Another time, while selling tickets one day in Baton Rouge, Louisiana, a man suddenly pointed a gun at his head and demanded money. Farini, who always carried a revolver on the frontier, accidentally shot the man with one of the two guns kept close to the ticket seller. The victim was picked up and taken away, his fate unknown. As Farini told it, Mississippi showboat life was full of such accidents.

Eventually the Dan Rice Circus went to New Orleans where they stayed for a month. Farini liked this racy city, though his Canadian country sensibility was a little shocked by it doing "business openly on a Sunday." When the show headed north he decided to quit and brought his salary and Minnesota money home for a reconciliation with his parents in the spring of 1860. From April to June he apparently worked the farm in Hope Township, though later he claimed he took up residence in his native Lockport at that time to go into the employ of a merchant friend, to whose daughter he became engaged; other reports place him on tour in the Philadelphia and New York area. Whatever he did, and wherever he went, he was on the verge of the greatest adventure of his young life.

In April, Blondin announced his return to his Niagara high wire.

Signor Farini, youthful and impetuous, was about to take him on.

He claimed that the manager of the mercantile part of the business where he was employed at Lockport died early that summer and he was given the job. Shortly thereafter he went to Niagara to see Blondin walk and as he watched became aware that the spectators nearby were in awe of the man and his feats, thinking him "more than mortal." This kind of uninformed hero-worship always bothered Farini, reminding him of the adoration of the false gods of respectability that had tormented his childhood. Unable to hold himself back, he shouted out that *he* could outdo Blondin! There was silence and then laughter, and then sneers that wounded him to his very soul.

His pride bursting within him, he decided to act at any cost. Suddenly it didn't matter that Blondin was the greatest rope-walker in the world and he was a ten-month beginner, or that no other professional would dare attempt this staggering feat. He wasn't Bill Hunt any more, condemned and held down. Farini could do what he wanted to do: he would prove himself...finally.

He quit his job the same evening and announced his intention to walk the Niagara gorge on a high wire. His friends thought him insane and his fiancée vociferously agreed, prompting him to cut off their engagement and head for the Falls alone the very next day. There he asked hotel proprietors and railway people to sponsor his walks.

Such was his romantic account. Here is what is known for certain.

Signor Farini was in Bowmanville during the first week of July 1860 presenting a strong-man act in which he dead-lifted one thousand pounds. On Tuesday the 17th and a week later on the 24th he performed there again, walking a tightrope strung across King Street from the Town Hall to the Wellington block on the other side. With that famous Niagara tightrope now fixed in his mind he was anxious to give a stunning performance high above his old home town. At three o'clock on the 24th a huge cheer went up as Signor Farini appeared at the dome on top of the Town Hall dressed in circus tights. He went out and pushed everything to the limit, giving a bravura show full of daring acrobatic manoeuvres, a hang by the nape of his neck and even a stilt walk on the rope. The crowd responded with roars of approval.

But these walks were just warm-ups. They put him in shape for what was to come and proved his skills to the Niagara Falls businessmen whom he had been petitioning to support his crossing. Now it was at least conceivable to them that this youth had the stuff to try the Frenchman's near-impossible feat.

The next day he was on a steamboat excursion to the Falls. When he arrived he publicly challenged Blondin, but the great man met this with disdain, treating him like one more pretender seeking publicity. Unlike the others, Farini responded: within a single day he secured financial backing at the rate of six hundred dollars per walk and started making arrangements to have an enormous cable shipped to the Falls and strung from one shore of the gorge to the other. He would soon show Blondin, and everyone else, that *he* was no pretender.

During the last week of July he took up residence at the American Hotel on the New York side and began supervising the details for his debut. The first public notice of him appeared in the July 26th *Niagara Falls Gazette*, which announced him as "Mr. Farini, a professional tight rope performer...prospecting in these rope walking diggings."

The place chosen for his starting point was in the general vicinity of Blondin's first rope, in an area called White's Pleasure Grounds or the Ferry Grove. Farini was determined that his wire would be the longest ever put over the gorge, so he moved the spot for anchoring a few hundred feet closer to the Falls and decided to send the cable over to a place not far below the Clifton House Hotel on the Canadian side. This would make his high wire just over 1,800 feet long, significantly longer than Blondin's original and about twice as long as his present one, which was over the Whirlpool rapids nearly a mile and a half downstream. There were rumours that the legendary man had had a falling out with the White's Grounds proprietor and that was why he had moved. Farini's rope would be behind the Niagara House, not far from the outlet to the Hydraulic Canal, and it went out over two-hundred-foot cliffs, remarkable for their nearly perpendicular drop. He wanted things to look, and be, perilous in the extreme. By the first of August he had ordered his rope from Newman and Scoville of Buffalo and was beginning to enclose a large area at the Grove. On that same day Blondin performed, and Farini was a featured spectator.

That show was rather pedestrian for the master, containing somersaults, headstands, backwards walking, some photography and several tricks with a chair. He carried it off very well, of course, but Farini saw some faults, or at least he saw an opportunity to tell the press there were faults. Getting the ear of several writers, among them a reporter from the *New York Daily Tribune*, he went right after the icon, calling him a bungler for what he said was a clumsy and tentative chair routine. Farini proclaimed that, unlike Blondin, he would have stood on his head on the chair as it sat balancing on the cable. This kind of "stump" was not entirely discounted by the writers, a few of whom wrote openly of their concern that this rope-walking duel could get out of hand.

One of the curious aspects of the Blondin-Farini rivalry is that Blondin was actually out of town during the week Farini raised his cable and put his publicity into the papers and therefore didn't know if his opponent was really going to mount the challenge until a day or two before the duel began. Shortly after his August 1st walk the master went to Chillicothe, Ohio for a performance which nearly ended the rivalry before it had a chance to start: part way through his evening act one of his fireworks exploded and ignited the upper part of his clothing, forcing him to walk the rest of the way on fire, suffering burns on his arms and shoulders.

Farini's rope arrived about the 8th of August and soon he had the huge coils brought to the river's

FARINI
"HAMPION OF NIACARA

banks for the daunting task of getting it across the gorge. There was 2,000 feet of cable, about three inches in diameter, and 50,000 feet of 3/8" rope; it all weighed 4,500 pounds and cost five hundred dollars (paid for by the hotels). Many people doubted a cable of that size could be properly raised; it was too long, too heavy and would cause problems if it so much as touched the Niagara's fast current. He almost relished doubts like these: unravelling such engi-

New York Historical Society

neering problems came easy to his scientific mind and he dissected the difficulties and solved them with ease. First he had an old sailor smoothly splice the ropes together where necessary and then had a large coil of the lighter rope carried to each side of the river. This rope was then brought down the cliffs on either side to small boats. They started out on oblique courses (to offset the effect of the current) toward each other at the centre of the river, where the lighter ropes were fastened together. Heavier rope was then attached and drawn across by a pulley and large windlass on the Canadian side. Thicker and thicker rope was fastened and drawn over until finally they had the big cable hanging over the gorge. He anchored it to a huge tim- ber driven six feet into the ground on the American side and the axle of a railway car, four inches thick and made of iron, drilled into solid rock in Canada. Dozens of small guy lines were then run from the shorelines to the main rope in an attempt to give it some stability. The big cable drooped more than 50 feet but was up and ready to bear him across.

His first advertisement appeared in the *Niagara Falls Gazette* on the 10th, making much of the length of his rope and modestly calling him "This Most Celebrated Gymnast and Funambulist." It was signed "Frank Soper, Agent." His broadsides also started appearing on posts and walls throughout the towns.

As Farini and his friends were putting the finishing touches on his rope, trying to get it reasonably taut, a difficulty occurred which Farini, by his daring, turned into something very positive indeed. The large cable was still sagging far too much late one evening and there was concern that it would snap the smaller guy wires and bring everything down. Farini decided to go out onto one of the wires, described by the *Gazette* as "about the size of a man's finger," in order to attach more guys. They had been using a box lowered from a crane but problems with it left him no choice but to make this daring attempt. As he walked out, the big cable touched the water several times and jerked violently, but he kept walking, going in total about 150 feet out over the water and accomplishing his task. Those of his fellow workers and financial backers who saw this lost their doubts about him in an instant.

When Blondin returned to Niagara from Ohio on the 13th he must have been more than a little surprised to see the Ferry Grove completely enclosed and a huge cable drooping over the gorge. The papers were saying that the young man who had been challenging him two weeks before, so unknown but so full of fire, was going to cross it the day after tomorrow.

This Farini fellow was for real.

CHAPTER 7

Walking in the Niagara Sky

"I have never in my life known fear."
Farini

He awoke at dawn. Outside the window of his room at the American Hotel the little town of Niagara Falls was deathly silent. There was almost no wind and the sun was rising in a cloudless sky. Downstream from where he lay two high wires stretched across the Niagara's gigantic gorge, waiting in the quiet of the early morning. When the winds came up the huge ropes shivered but held, fixed in place by guy wires that ran out to them from the shoreline and looked from above like massive spiderwebs spun by something unearthly. In the distance the falls thundered like a steadily approaching danger.

Out in the country, and in the towns and cities, as far as a hundred miles away, thousands of people were rising from their beds, packing lunches and spyglasses, brushing top hats and Sunday bonnets, and getting ready to travel. As they boarded trains and steamboats, or rushed from the early chores to their carriages or wagons, they spoke excitedly about Blondin and Farini and their deadly tightropes. Everyone, it seemed, was going to the Falls.

But at home on the farm Thomas and Hannah Hunt were at breakfast around a quiet table with six of their children. They pretended not to think of their eldest son

73

and the horror of a high-wire act over the Niagara gorge. But they had read in the papers about Farini and what he had promised, and they knew William's word was his bond.

He always claimed to have nerves of steel and actually characterized himself as nonchalant and almost cavalier as his hour approached. A number of eyewitnesses agreed. One man who saw him that day recalled that he appeared "quite cool and smiled complacently" as he ascended the wooden platform next to his cable, and a reporter from the *Daily Globe* said that even at the last moment he still looked "like a person who possesses a very determined spirit." But as he rose that morning, his well-rehearsed bravado was undoubtedly fading. Someone else who saw him that day said that when he looked into Signor Farini's eyes, "it was very evident that he was...nervous."

As the morning passed, the streets on the American side stirred from silence; and likewise in British Canada the colours of an excited and growing crowd could soon be seen on the dusty roads that went through the villages, along the woods, and up past the hotels. By noon Niagara was really bustling, and within another hour, as the steamboats began arriving and docking up and down the river, and the trains came rumbling through the villages toward the depots, the whole place seemed to overflow with people. *The Gazette* estimated that nearly 10,000 spectators swarmed the banks that day.

Everywhere, in every face, anticipation reigned. It mixed with fear when they saw the size of the gorge, yawning like an enormous crack in the earth, so wide that it seemed capable of swallowing up mountains. And their fear grew when they saw the thin wires stretching out across that vast panorama. It was only then, up close to the edge, that they really grasped what they were about to see.

The rope-walkers' broadsides were plastered on nearly every available surface: on the walls of shops, in the taverns and even in places where they had to be stuck side by side. "The Most Daring Feat Ever Witnessed in the

World!" boasted Farini's. There was a constant buzz in the
hotels and rumours were spreading like fire. A Rochester
newspaper reported that Blondin and Farini had accidentally met, face to face at a Buffalo train station: everyone
was saying that a fight had started and Farini had decked
his famous opponent. Others doubted the story and
claimed a retraction would soon be in print. Such a dramatic scene struck the fancy of many spectators that day;
they wanted to believe it had happened.

But perhaps the hottest topic was speculation about
how Farini would die. Many said he would be the victim of
a spectacular fall and drop into the gorge the way all high-
wire walkers did in dreams: like a flailing bird shot from
the sky. And there were other doubts about him. There
were those who believed he was fictional, a joke of some
sort made up to sell the weekend to the tourists; and others who thought he wouldn't show at all. Some claimed he
was an Italian, though several people swore that he was a
professional just in from New York. But a few nodded
wisely and said knowingly that he was only a barely competent farmer's son from Canada West who was likely in
way over his head, scared stiff, and about to be humiliated.

Over on Falls Avenue, in a guest room at the American
Hotel in the Gluck Buildings, Bill Hunt was doing deep-
breathing exercises.

He claimed to have spent his final hours presiding over
the details of the performance: adjusting the rope, greeting people, checking ticket sales and arranging for more
seats near the Gas Works to accommodate the overflow
crowd; and it isn't inconceivable that he attended to these
things in a general way. It was in his personality to try to
be everything to everyone and seek complete control of his
ventures. But his mind that day was set tightly on the
task before him and that task was to get over the gorge on
the path of a single rope without killing himself.

The hour kept gaining on him.

In the streets the boys shouted his name and imitated
his fall, using the short walls near the banks as high

wires. Outside the fancy hotels, top hats and parasols came down from carriages and slid through the crowds toward the dining halls. Inside, business was booming. Immaculate black waiters served up notoriously bad food at tables meant to serve far fewer customers.

At 2:30 someone appeared in the dining-room doorway of the American Hotel and shouted, "Farini walks in ten minutes! Hurry!" It was a false alarm, but many lurched forward, afraid that a moment might be missed.

Upstairs in his room Farini started putting on his costume.

Some of the spectators who came to the Falls that summer compared the feelings they had watching the rope-walkers to sensations someone might experience at an execution. Like witnesses before a hanging they now gathered around Farini's cable. The rope inspired little confidence. In fact, its tattered, drooping appearance terrified most onlookers. It descended into the gorge at a sharp angle and looked crooked in places. Word was spreading that Blondin had taken one glance at it and whispered that nothing would ever induce him to put a single foot upon it.

At ten minutes to four Farini got into his carriage and was taken to the northern outskirts of Niagara Falls, making a direct line toward his cable. He was dressed in pink tights, blue shorts of merino wool bound with red, and light gum shoes nearly the colour of his fleshings. Pulled tightly over his thick hands to help him grip the balance pole was a pair of lilac kid gloves. The rush and sound in the streets was now reaching a climax and his buggy disappeared into it almost unnoticed.

Over on the Canadian bank the notorious "Front" was heating up. This stretch between Horseshoe Falls and the spot where Farini's rope was anchored had often been condemned by authorities for its scurrilous characters and questionable businesses. Today it was a veritable carnival, complete with sideshows, brass bands, menageries, dime museums and belting temperance sermons. Tourists and their hunters moved about in a dizzying swirl that made

the New York side look tame. And just as the clock struck
four, a far-off cheer went up on the American side in the
vicinity of the outlet to the hydraulic canal. It was inaudi-
ble to most, but those with spyglasses, who had been
watching men the size of ants tightening the guys of
Farini's rope, now saw that someone was picking up a balance pole and stepping out.

When he arrived and mounted the platform the people
in the enclosure strained to see him. What would Signor
Farini look like? They saw a young man, dark and handsome, almost Spanish in appearance. When they looked
closely at his features many noticed the eyes first: the
incongruity of their bright blue colour with the darkness
of his complexion and hair made them stand out like
sparks in his face. Farini had a shining mop of thick black
hair slicked back on the sides, a moustache, and young
whiskers that nearly touched at the chin. He was olive-
skinned, oval-eyed and square-faced. The only blemish in
his looks was a long, straight nose that turned up a little
too much at the tip. Farini was noticeably bigger than
Blondin, standing about five-feet-ten inches and weighing
close to 170 pounds. Though he had just an average-sized
frame, his thickly muscled body, showing through his
fleshings, belied any thought that he was a man of average strength. Ladies were unaccustomed to seeing the
outline of a man's chest, so the ones nearest the platform
looked closely at this well-developed specimen on display
in the sun before them.

He entered the enclosure bareheaded and without a
cape or coat and announced in a clear voice that he would
be ready momentarily, while on the banks near him several assistants frantically tried to tighten the guy lines
that were pulling the rope in wayward directions. Some of
his hotel backers and his cousin (and nominal agent)
Frank Soper stood anxiously near the rope.

When Signor Farini briefly turned toward the enclosure
while moving on the platform, a man in the crowd was
stunned to recognize him. "It's Bill Hunt!" he shouted, his
voice echoing in the gorge. "It's Bill Hunt, old Mr. Hunt's

boy from Bowmanville!"

"He is from Italy!" yelled Soper immediately, almost in reflex. And then added purposefully, "It is a fact."

Farini picked up his balance pole, gripped it in his palms-forward style and walked slowly to the edge of the platform. He glanced down to the point where the cable met the planks. Beneath him he saw the tops of the trees, and then the rocks, and then the water, green and distant. Seagulls swept by, more than a hundred feet below, their heads barely discernible. This was the moment when fear could take him. It was both his friend and his enemy. It was the gasoline for his fire. It had drawn the crowds and the money, and offered him fame. But fear could also kill him. A tremble now, or a hesitation, would drop him two hundred feet and bury him in the bottom of the river. He tried to put fear out of his mind. It wasn't helpful to be afraid, so he wouldn't be. He had asked for this. In fact, all his life he had been asking for it; now he had to face it. So out he went, head up, into thin air.

His first step was like one you might place on ice frozen over a deep lake—ice you feared was too thin. He reached his foot out over the gorge, tested the rope gingerly, and settled onto it slowly...then he lifted the other foot off the platform and drew it across the first to find the narrow surface beneath him. Now he was off the ground, standing high above the river, on his Niagara high wire!

He tried a second step. And nearly fell: everything, man and rope, swayed to one side...he stopped, too frightened to move, balancing precariously. The brass band that had played sprightly on his arrival grew quiet. The crowd seemed alarmed by his caution. They drew in their breath collectively and a tense silence pervaded. Slowly Farini began moving again at a shaky pace, noiselessly descending away from them into the huge expanse of the gorge. He seemed to be walking on air.

Almost instantly he had another problem.

The balance pole is the high-wire artiste's most important ally, but from the instant Farini saw his it worried him. It was all of forty feet long and weighed a hefty forty pounds. He wanted it over-sized so it would press him to the rope against Niagara's winds, but obviously the manufacturers had exceeded even his exaggerated measurements and now its enormous length and slender shape caused it to bend like a bow. About fifteen feet from the shore, high above the maple trees and rocky embankment, this pole and his guy wires almost betrayed him. The guy lines descended from positions along the shore on either side of the cable in what looked like a steep valley of ropes. As he walked slowly down into this valley the tips of the pole were actually lower than the guys and as soon as he came in contact with them the pole became entangled and he was forced to stop. It was a ghastly dilemma: unable to move forward or backward, balancing on a sagging cable with over 1,800 feet to the other shore, carrying a lead-weight pole that was now stuck in his own ropes.

An American reporter on the scene feared for Farini's life. "The odds seemed terribly against him at this moment. There was an outcry that he never would cross and for a few moments of sickening suspense, in which he struggled with his pole, we believe half the crowd expected to see him fall." Farini fought for his life with every ounce of his strength and kept his mind fixed on what had to be done. Sweat spread on his back and beads ran down his forehead and into his eyes. Then he reached inside himself and found what he needed. Locking his hips and holding his lower body rigid he tilted his upper torso sideways and slowly lifted the right side of the pole over the right guy and then carefully did the same with the left one before straightening himself and stepping forward to the next pair. He treated each set of guys similarly and slowly edged out over the gorge, steadfastly performing a strenuous and deadly feat. This part of his act was afterwards described by many onlookers as painful to watch.

Just beyond two hundred feet he tied the pole down (between guys and rope) and stretched out full-length on the cable. On each shore his friends ran along the banks to adjust the guys.

Blondin and his handlers had predicted that Signor
Farini could not actually do many of the things he claimed
he could do, and almost none that their man performed.
Breathing hard, hands sticky, the sweat continuing to roll
down from his hairline, Farini now prepared to show them
something. It was windier up here than he had expected
so he would have to do this trick perfectly. Gripping the
pole on either side of the rope he concentrated on the tripod he had to form. Suddenly the crowd saw Farini's head
go down to the cable and, as smoothly as Blondin, he
snapped up into a headstand. He "looked so cool about it"
said someone later. A burst of cheering came from the
American side. The duel had begun in earnest.

Lowering his legs he dropped them below the cable,
gripped it in his hands and stretched out until he was
entirely beneath it, hanging on by his fingers. With his
legs waving slightly in the wind he gauged the conditions
and then slowly released one hand and balanced it off at
an angle. Now he was hanging over the Niagara gorge by
the fingers of one hand. For Farini and his nervous spectators this was an intensely three-dimensional sight: he
seemed weirdly suspended above the chasm, striking in
its panoramic depth and width, like someone hanging
high in the air during a nightmare. He was a tiny creature floating inside an enormous background. Thrills went
through him unlike any he had experienced before, but he
struggled to think practically. Steadily he moved his free
arm upward in a semi-circle, gripped the thick manila and
pulled himself up. After the acrobatics mere walking was
easier and his pace quickened slightly as he headed across
the rope toward its middle section. Several times he
stopped to execute more manoeuvres: one time hanging by
a crooked elbow, another time by the bends of his knees
and finally, in a kind of *coup de grâce*, lowering himself
below the cable until he held on with just his feet. From
the shoreline he seemed to be hanging by his toes. When
he reached the flat stretch at the cable's centre and then
began walking up the rope, he moved faster, his strides
looking stronger and more assured.

In 1860 the only bridge at the Falls was two miles downstream. So when he crossed the gorge that day his view of one of the world's natural wonders was not only breathtaking but also unique: no human being had ever seen Niagara's thundering sheet of green water from such a perfect vantage point.

Back up the cable toward the trees on the Canadian side he came, now showing signs of fatigue on his sweating face. His difficulties at the beginning had forced him to be on the rope for too long. The first half had taken a full thirty minutes. Stepping forthrightly he accomplished the third quarter in five.

Soon the spectators on the Canadian side had such a good view of him that they could see the blue of his eyes. He came up the cable toward them struggling, his legs shaking slightly but his attitude tenacious. He seemed to be falling forward with each step as though there were a heavy weight pressing him down. He climbed the final few yards in near desperation until his foot finally touched wood...and safety. Forty minutes after starting out on the longest and most perilous high wire ever strung at Niagara Falls twenty-two-year-old Bill Hunt was alive and standing on Canadian soil. The huge crowd erupted in cheers. At that age he valued praise above almost anything: this was his "kind of glory." The shouts of Port Hope and Bowmanville people in the crowd touched him even in the intensity of the moment. He was just the second human being to do this and a righteousness swelled up inside him: he wished *all* his doubters could see him now.

Immediately a crush of people surrounded him and it was only with extra effort that his helpers got him away and took him up the road to the elegant confines of the Clifton House Hotel. By then he was exhausted by a performance he had found extremely taxing. And he had promised something extraordinary on the way back, something more difficult than anything he had tried on the way over; somewhere he had to find the strength to get it done.

After a drink, a short rest and some grooming he returned to his rope and mounted it again. It was now twenty minutes past five and the crowd had thinned slightly, losing some of its number to a rush downstream once his safe arrival was assured. Word had spread through the ranks that Blondin was approaching his cable more than a mile away near the suspension bridge and many had left in a hurry, anxious to see both men in a single day and make comparisons.

About an hour and a half earlier tourists on the grounds and in the balconies of the magnificent Clifton had been witnesses to a strange sight. It had come toward them along the dirt road on the Canadian bank and appeared to be a regal-looking man dressed in tights, sitting up tall in a buggy but shifted off to one side so that everyone could see something that looked like a stove, jammed into the narrow space beside him. Then they began to recognize the famous blond hair and imperial beard, set perfectly in place, shining in the sun. The sight of Blondin coming toward them in the distance and growing clearer as his horse approached stirred the crowd. He was trying to look indifferent, but was embarrassed and angry, and had approached the Front for hard business reasons only. It was getting on toward four o'clock, the weather was perfect, show-time was closing in, and yet almost no one had come to his enclosures a mile and a half downstream at the suspension bridge. From the whirlpool at Devil's Hole he had seen signs of activity near Farini's rope in the distance, so he had loaded up his stove (the one he would take out on his rope that afternoon in order to fry an omelette at mid-wire) and performed the humiliating chore of displaying himself and his apparatus, like a sandwich-board advertisement, to the masses. Blondin turned in front of the Clifton so that both he and his stove were visible to everyone and headed back downstream. Stealing a glance behind, he noticed that no one had followed him. Some day, he thought, Farini will pay for this.

But the person who was the object of the great man's scorn was flying now. He was revitalized by his rest and as soon as he leapt up onto the rope started back to the United States at a brisk pace, used to his work now. He walked "with a good deal of self-possession" said one Canadian-side spectator. A short distance out, eyes sparkling, he turned around and posed for a photographer on the near shore. At this moment a long cord could be seen hanging from the balance pole. It had not been there on the way over.

Turning again he walked quickly down the droop of his rope and arrived at the centre in a few minutes. Directly beneath him the *Maid of the Mist* was drawing into position, its deck full of spectators looking up. A friend of Farini's, publicized as doubting his next feat could be performed, stood in the crowd on the steamboat. His wager with the Signor had been talked about all week on the streets and in the taverns of the Niagara region.

Farini stopped, tied down his pole, and sat on it while he unfastened the cord. Letting it down quickly he soon had it touching the water, a distance from his high wire of more than one hundred feet. The steamer edged over to the cord and soon a thicker rope was tied on and drawn up to the cable. Moments later he was seen quickly descending the vertical rope, going hand over hand and feet first. (This last detail proved to be controversial because he had clearly advertised to descend head first. He later claimed that the rocking motion of the boat had caused the rope, held firmly on the deck, to whip back and forth, making a head-first trick more difficult than could have been anticipated. But some insisted he had never intended to perform the feat as advertised.) Arriving safely on the steamer he drank a glass of wine with his betting opponent and within ten minutes was ascending the rope at a much slower pace than his descent.

The jerking motion of the rope made the upward climb terribly difficult and at the halfway point, rapidly tiring, he signalled for the men on the steamer to let go of it. Now the jerking stopped and he was left "gently swaying backwards and forwards like a pendulum." All the time, he had to squeeze the rope in an unusually tight grip, and his hands were turning numb. He began considering a plan for falling: he had to release at the right moment and hit the water or he would crash into the steamer's deck. But before he resorted to anything desperate he tried an old gymnast's trick: wrapping the rope securely around a leg in order to rest his arms. Looking up, the distance to the cable seemed as daunting as the drop beneath him. He tried moving again, and despite his shaking limbs, was able to maintain a slow pace upward, hand over hand, climbing for dear life. Soon he was so close that his nose touched the cable. Desperate to move that inch, unsure he could, he heard nothing, not the crowd, the steamer or the falls, just the sound of his own breathing against the rope. Then, "using every particle of power left..." he raised one leg over the cable and used it to hoist his wilting frame onto the narrow walkway. Though he remembered a long, terrified pause here where he lay face down trying to revive himself, spectators noticed very little hesitation between his regaining the rope and the continuation of his walk. Once he was upright and feeling stronger his relief was enormous—no one had ever tried this feat, and part way up he must have thought that he had bitten off more than anyone could chew.

There was an almost perceptible sense of joy in his step as he walked quickly toward the American side, pausing only for a few acrobatics. Feeling stronger as he progressed, he picked up the sound of the brass bands on the shore and actually began to dance to the music as he walked. One reporter was charmed by this *pas seul*, coming as it did at the end of an "appalling hour's work."

Stepping off the cable he was immediately surrounded by a swarm of friends. Frank Soper and the others who gripped his hands at that moment were shocked by their feel: they were wet, cold as ice, and seemed tight, like bound wire. His friends wrapped him in an overcoat, lifted him in triumph, and moved him quickly through the crowd toward a carriage outside the enclosure. The cheering, which had started slowly as he neared the bank and reached a crescendo as he alighted on the ground, continued around him as he was rushed forward. His tights were soaked through with perspiration and his legs were slightly unsteady but he fought to hide any signs of exhaustion. Everywhere hats were raised to him and shouts of praise were sung out. "Bravo Farini!" cried one and "Bravo Canada! Canada forever!" sang another. Ironically, the bands played "Yankee Doodle."

Head above the crowd, he saw the admiring faces and felt a sense of vindication. He had risked his life in a terrible way but at this moment it seemed worth it.

He was stuffed into the waiting carriage, taken at a trot along the bank into town and up to the American Hotel, where they whisked him past a few gaping employees (who were glad to see him at least alive). The crowd buzzed as they either rushed northward to see the rest of Blondin's performance or walked back into town. Some excitedly compared Farini to Blondin while others scoffed at the idea but admitted that what they had seen that afternoon had sent chills down their spines. Inferior or not, this Farini was a man of skill and daring. The mighty Blondin just could be in for a fight.

Farini said that at the conclusion of his Niagara debut the horses were taken from the shafts of his carriage near the enclosure and he was pulled into town by a group of admirers as the band played "Hail the Conquering Hero Comes"; and at the hotel he was taken into the drawing room where a "grand reception" was held in his honour. No eyewitness account exists of men drawing him through the streets and he would have arrived at the hotel ahead of anyone who might have received him. The state of his fatigue and the sweat-soaked condition of his costume were probably such that he was taken to his room as soon as he arrived and only then, after a period of recovery, returned to the reception. It took the form of a ball (or "hop"), fashionable in Niagara at the time, and was highlighted in his opinion by his being introduced to "all the ladies, many of whom were the wives and daughters of

some of the most prominent men in America." They "over-
whelmed [him] with compliments which [he] received as
gracefully as [he] was able." Women and their attentions
were the dominant theme for him that evening, as they
would be on many future occasions. Meeting the Governor
of New York pleased him, but so did dancing with his wife;
when he spotted a beautiful southern belle he "commenced a flirtation, [making] a particularly nice speech
and trying to look very killing." Carrying on just one or
two affairs, "was impossible so I turned it into a general
one and enjoyed myself considerably." Possessed of a huge
appetite for the affections of women, he would always
revel in their admiration, engendered as it was by his athletic good looks and daring occupations.

His reviews began to appear in the papers over the next
few days. It would take some time for Europe to notice the
new rope-walker at Niagara Falls but Canadian and
American publications quickly got him into their columns.
Though few raved about him, most were at least somewhat impressed. The *Daily Globe* thought him "not quite
so active on the rope as Mons. Blondin, but he will no
doubt improve by practice." *The Daily Leader* (Toronto),
while declaring Blondin superior, also noted the disad-
vantages on Farini's side and therefore felt his first performance "must be regarded as good." The *Morning
Express* (Buffalo) liked him and thought him capable of
being Blondin's peer. Only *The Buffalo Daily Republic* was
all negative, calling him awkward and frightful to watch.
On the positive side the *Niagara Falls Gazette*, in their
lead story, claimed that he "achieved a success greater
than even his friends expected." Influenced by Farini's
own feelings, they shot back at his critics: "After all that
has been said, and hinted, and suggested, he has at once
proved his ability to travel on the giddy route, and set at
rest croaking." At home the *Port Hope Guide* called his
feats "daring" and proclaimed him now proven as "a formidable rival." A few days later the *New York Times* (who
mentioned him often that summer) proposed that he had
"dimmed the lustre of Blondin's name." But perhaps the

most perceptive analysis came from the *Buffalo Daily Courier*. While the writer understood Farini's shortcomings, he also grasped the magnitude of his accomplishment when all factors were considered. He saw what Farini was really after and in his summation gave it to him:

> The universal sentiment was, that he had displayed, under the circumstances, a nerve fully equal to that of Blondin. He does not appear, as yet, so much at home on the rope as the Frenchman. The transit with him seems fraught with far more imminent peril. But the fact that this is his first great feat, that the rope is much larger than Blondin's, vibrating also very much more, and that he wrought at such disadvantage with his pole and guys, entitled him beyond a question to the dubious fame which he covets. Henceforth there are two Blondins.

Blondin's performance that day had been, as usual, flawless. His first crossing was made with his feet strapped into peach baskets and his return featured the aforementioned stove. At the centre of his cable he had set up his kitchen and cooked omelettes as if it were Sunday morning at home. His rope was as tight as a guitar string and not much in excess of eight hundred feet in length, but his act, performed over the deadly whirlpool, was still extraordinary. All who saw him attested to the ease and flair with which he walked and several on the American side discovered that his omelettes were also not wanting in taste.

But Farini had whipped Blondin in a category of great importance: the Frenchman's crowd was perhaps the worst of his two seasons, his dotted sidelines embarrassing next to the throng a short distance upstream.

And Farini, to all reports, was still alive.

When dawn broke the next morning the Great Farini was tucked into his bed, fast asleep. He didn't rise until late and found himself sore from head to foot. But there was nothing planned and he spent a quiet, relaxing day receiving friends and reporters (the latter, said Farini, "drinking much wine"), and gathering in all the ticket stubs and money.

There had been enclosures with seats in both countries near the rope, seats near the platform and at the American Gas Works; people standing at the Ferry Grove in Canada, on the *Maid of the Mist*, on the balconies of the Clifton House, anywhere they could see on the banks, and even on the rocks in the gorge below. Each ticket was twenty-five cents and some (especially the ladies, said Farini) gave more. Though his stated income of fifteen thousand dollars for the walk is far too high and his claim that each railroad gave him one thousand dollars is doubtful, it is evident that he fared well that day and throughout the summer. In addition to his on-site money, he had financial support from several hotels. He probably made more in one outing than Blondin did in either of his two seasons. In his old age he told a friend that he earned six thousand dollars at Niagara that summer and thereby gave up any thought of returning to medicine. Blondin, on the other hand, had a hat passed for his benefit during his first season and was reduced to getting prominent people to explain his situation in the newspapers so that citizens of the Niagara area would support him.

Farini's fame grew with each day that first week and the newspapers scrambled to discover more about him. Curiously, he seems to have offered little help. For a man of obvious vanity this seemed a strange bit of modesty, but he may have sought anonymity to protect his family, or because he thought it beneath him (not respectable) to run off to the press praising himself, or perhaps he thought mystery a good policy. One paper speculated that he was in his mid-thirties, another twenty-seven. A Rochester man came forward with the information that Farini was really William Hunt, that his father had been in Lockport and Bowmanville, but now lived on a small farm seven miles outside of Port Hope, Canada West. He

let it be known that Willie Hunt had been of disreputable
character ever since boyhood (though he personally knew
of no major criminal charge that had ever been laid
against him). The *Daily Globe* claimed he was from
Cobourg and the *Lockport Daily Journal*, stating that
their town was "not to be sneezed at," boasted of his connection to them. At home in Port Hope, Hugh Crea of the
Guide sharpened his pen and set everyone straight—"The
Globe is mistaken," said he, "Farini is a Port Hoper, a real
live Canadian..." Crea also reproduced an article from the
Drummondville Reporter (Niagara Falls, C.W.) which confidently identified Farini as an Italian.

Blondin's camp thought Farini was a philistine, and
argued that his vertical rope act was nothing but a feat of
strength. Rope-walkers often consider themselves something more than craftsmen and this criticism was obviously intended to separate the artist from the circus
performer. The *Niagara Falls Gazette* defended him in an
article that analyzed the unique problems he encountered,
and why, in response to these difficulties, he had slightly
altered his program. Other papers followed suit and he
seemed forgiven for the adjustments.

The day after his first walk he was already planning a
second. He decided to give a performance on Friday, with
less than twenty-four hours notice to the public. This walk
was in response to the fact that a large railroad excursion
was to take place that day on the Great Western from
Canada West.

His pattern throughout that summer was to wait for
Blondin to announce a grand program of "inhuman" feats
and then proceed to advertise a kind of duplication of
these tricks for his own performance. In his role as iconoclast Farini usually parodied Blondin in some way, attacking a false god, using a satirical stance to make his point
that performers weren't gifted, but just courageous, well-
practised and inventive, three attributes available to anyone. However, Farini didn't stick to his plan of waiting for
Blondin's bills every time out. In fact, his second walk was

actually more a reaction to the criticism of his own first performance. As he would do on several other occasions, he performed that day in the persona of a comical character. This time it was "Mickey Free, the Irish Pedestrian." Free was a well-known Boston long-distance runner of the 1850s and '60s whose name often made the pages of America's biggest sporting and entertainment journal, *The New York Clipper*, and who once visited Port Hope to race local athletic legend "The Flying Tailor." Pedestrians were quite popular in Farini's earlier days and vied with bare-knuckle boxers and cricket players (and in 1859 and 1860 rope-walkers) for the attentions of the sporting fancy. Some had said Farini moved too slowly during his first walk, now he was going to show them that he could be a pedestrian on the rope if he so chose.

The large crowd that came to see him that Friday indeed saw a different Farini. It was a powerful performance, perilous in the extreme, on a cable raised several feet at each end so it would sway in the wind like a huge skipping rope. It seemed like a message to Blondin.

Stepping aggressively on to his wire he marched away into the gorge at a quick pace and didn't stop until he reached the other side. The entire trip took nine minutes, about a quarter of the time of his first walk and one of the fastest crossings in history. On his return he carried a pair of gymnast's rings out to the centre of the cable, fastened them down, and went through a series of manoeuvres high above the Niagara. At various moments he was seen turning somersaults, hanging by his hands, by one hand, his feet, and then to everyone's fright, by the arch of one foot! And later, just as he drew within 500 feet of the American shore an unusually strong gust of wind shot up the gorge and his loose rope snapped like an enormous whip: Farini tilted, fighting for balance. The crowd leaned forward, dead silent; then some actually cried out, as if in pain. He edged closer. At the 150-foot mark another violent gust nearly threw him into the gorge—this time he stopped and sat down to save his life. Amidst high-pitched screams and desperate offers of help, he kept cool. "All right!" he called out, then stood up slowly, and walked up the incline to safety. The applause was thunderous.

Farini's friends at the *Gazette* called it "...the greatest slack rope performance on record. [But] we never wish to see another such performance by any rope walker, for however safe the performer may consider himself—however much confidence he may have—there is no pleasure to the beholder."

But for many, Blondin was still the darling of the moment. During his first season the citizens of the Niagara region had presented him with a medal, though he had dropped it into the river while performing one of his strenuous manoeuvres. The first week of his second season he had another one made in Buffalo, and now all was right again, the hero was properly decorated. His Friday walk saw him get into some difficulty when he went out in smooth-bottomed wooden shoes and found, at about the halfway point, that they prevented him from ascending the second half because they gave him no traction. He was forced to take them off and finish shoeless.

While Blondin stumbled a little his young opponent seemed to be everywhere. After presenting two exhausting performances in three days he announced an "Exhibition of Muscle" and lecture at Grant's Hall, followed by two more Niagara ascensions and a rope-walk in Buffalo.

A good-sized, but not capacity crowd came to see him at the Hall. These exhibitions were the cerebral part of Farini's showmanship in his early days, full of physiological facts and his seminal ideas about fitness, his time to instruct and pontificate. He was to "lecture...on the general subject of muscle...[and] illustrate his theories and positions by performing various feats of strength requiring great power and much practice." The *Gazette* reported these feats were "truly astonishing [and]...those present were highly gratified."

The next morning Farini prepared himself for his third walk: he was going to cross enveloped in a sack. Whether or not he could actually do this was, as later events would

reveal, not entirely known to him. Blondin was not going
to perform that day so for the first and only time that season Farini had Niagara all to himself. (The only other
ascension discussed on the 22nd was to happen the next
day at Moffat's Grove amusement park on the northern
outskirts of Buffalo and involve a mysterious aerialist,
"Signor Rossini from Pufalora, a new competitor of
Blondin, just arrived from Italy, or some other furrin
part." His performance was to include the transportation
of a lady on his back. At the appointed hour he appeared
carrying a man dressed in drag, and proceeded to walk
along a rope that lay on the ground.)

The sack walk had been enhanced by Farini's boast
that he would show everyone "something new under the
sun." As it turned out, the sun was something he intended
to avoid. Blondin's trick was to pull a sack over his upper
body so he was blindfolded, but leave his feet free. Farini,
never one to just put in an appearance, decided his sack
would cover his head and his feet.

He liked to justify his recklessness by claiming that he
never did anything, however dangerous it looked to the
layman, that he hadn't practised or thought out thoroughly. But at Niagara in 1860 it is obvious that he was
pushing himself to the edge. Blondin, working on his taut
wire, never seemed close to danger, while Farini appeared
to court it nearly every time out. Had he fallen while
bound head to foot in a sack, he would have sunk helpless,
deep under the current of the river. What happened during the opening moments of this performance was either
a very clever circus ruse designed to terrorize the crowd
or, more likely, proof that this sack trick of his was nearly
impossible.

At a few minutes past four o'clock he appeared at his
grounds on the American side and mounted his platform.
As soon as he was ready his friends produced a baggy
sack, made of glazed cambric with two arm holes, and
pulled it over him from the bottom and tied it securely
behind his head. He moved forward resolutely (or as resolutely as is possible when bagged inside a sack) and felt

for the beginning of the cable. Then out he went over the tops of the trees, moving at a cautious but steady pace. Almost immediately he was in trouble. It was barely noticeable from the banks, but inside the darkness of the sack Farini could feel that he had almost no traction. After ten steps he was nearly sliding down the rope. He tried two more and then stopped. The cambric was so slippery that he was in danger of actually sliding off the rope and plunging downward. *The Buffalo Daily Republic* commented that it would have been "death to him to have attempted his feat in that condition."

Slowly the sack was seen edging its way back up the rope to the platform; for an agonizing minute it moved in reverse. Reaching the wood it regained solid footing and untied itself. Then Farini's face appeared, perspiring but decisive. Many thought he had given up, but his brain was in full gear, calculating how he had to adjust, not considering failure. He quickly removed his India-rubber shoes, instructed his friends to re-bag him and pulled the rubbers back on to his feet on the outside of the sack. Without hesitating he turned back to the rope, walked out on to it at a quick pace, and didn't stop until he was one-quarter of the way across. Soon he started off again, and didn't stop a second time until he reached mid-point. Here, bound and blindfolded by his sack, he stood on his head! One spectator said that the sight of Signor Farini on his head in the sack, spreading his feet for effect, "looked like a small sail spread to the breeze." And he felt that getting over the rope in about twenty-five minutes "...was very well for a blindfolded pedestrian."

The crowd responded loudly when they saw he had succeeded. Out at mid-wire, unaware of their reaction, he came down from his headstand, un-bagged himself and proceeded on his way.

This performance brought raves from the press. "He persists in travelling on a very slack rope," exclaimed the *Gazette*, "It is of course very unsteady, swayed by the least wind, or by his own motion. To every appearance he cares nothing about it, and seems to dare any kind of peril."

Blondin began searching in his extraordinary bag of dangerous tricks for something that could knock this pretender off his rope. He must have wondered how far the young man would go.... Now, there was one particular feat that scared the wits out of people, something many ropewalkers couldn't do, or at least wouldn't try. It required experience, nerve, and above all, inordinate strength. Blondin decided to rest for a week and then go for broke with this feat, and see if the country boy would dare try it.

The ads came out a full eight days before Blondin's performance. "The most extraordinary tight rope ascension on record!" they said. It was "universally pronounced by everyone, to be the most wonderful and extraordinary feat ever performed by any living man. Mons. Blondin is the only man in the world that ever performed the feat." And with this, Blondin promised that at four o'clock sharp on the announced day he would place a fully grown man on his back and walk the high wire over the Niagara gorge.

The papers thrilled to the news and waited for Farini's response. Perhaps this time it would be too much. After all, to live up to his claims he had to not only duplicate the feat but also go a little further.

Three days later Blondin got his answer.

CHAPTER 8

The Duel
Gets Dangerous

*"Nothing will put a period to the daredevilry of
Signor Farini but a dash headlong into the rapids."*
Buffalo Daily Courier, September 1860

"The Invincible Signor Farini!" shouted his broadside, "Will not be Outdone." He would surpass the Master, not only by virtue of the length and slackness of his cable but by the greater height and weight of the man he would carry and the fact that he would unload and reload his companion as he walked, turn around at mid-wire, cross beneath him and then take him back to the shore. It was an alarming proposition.

That same week the newspapers, a little shocked by the dangerous sack walk, began to show increased respect for Farini, as though they were coming around to the idea that he had inordinate courage. Not generally concerned about Blondin's safety, they feared Farini was a different sort of man, who would push himself to the limit and perhaps beyond, a formidable foe indeed. "Blondin has met a rival worthy of him," said the *Newark Daily Advertiser*. "DeLave and a host of others, though perhaps equal to the great originator of the rope-walking mania, have unfortunately failed to convince the public of the fact. Blondin has regarded them from his Niagara wire with supreme contempt. [But] one Signor Farini...has already outdone Blondin."

Their frightful challenge took place on a beautiful day at
Niagara, perhaps the best of the entire season, and the
green cataracts glistened in the sunlight. The people, who
came in droves, twenty-eight train-cars full from Buffalo
alone, and crowded steamers from Toronto and southern
Ontario, felt a tension in the air when they arrived.
Though some of Farini's fans now believed he was superior, others chose to watch from his enclosures because
they still felt he and his companion were more apt to fall.

Both artistes were scheduled to begin at four o'clock, but
Blondin got off to a quicker start and maintained his
advantage from then onward. After showing off a few stunning acrobatics on the rope (including dislocations of his
limbs), he moved quickly to the centre and lowered himself
to a short slack rope slung about twenty feet under his
cable. The very fact that he wanted to perform on this kind
of a wire indicated the pressure he was feeling from
Farini. On his new rope he stood on his head, lay face
down and imitated a swimmer (perhaps displaying a skill
he thought Farini would need), and then performed a startling series of a dozen or more lightning-fast somersaults.
Hoisting himself back onto the main cable, he walked
briskly to the Canadian side. After a pause, there was a
sudden stirring in the crowd and there he was again, on
the platform loading his little manager onto his back.

Harry M. Colcord had been Blondin's manager for about
two years, having met him in Boston during the Ravels
days. He was a seasoned show-business man, adept
enough that Blondin had sought him out when considering a solo career. Legend had it that Colcord had no idea
he would be the man on Blondin's back when they first
surprised much of the world with their hair-raising feat
the previous year. He had been much in favour of Blondin's
idea of keeping the identity of his passenger unknown, but
more than a little unnerved when it was revealed that *he*
would be the human baggage. However, the stories about
him being nearly paralyzed with fear are exaggerations:
he was well aware of what was called for, and of the flawless skill of his transporter, and public pronouncements to

the contrary, he had likely practised many times on Blondin's back. He was the perfect weight and height: slightly taller than the little monsieur and somewhere around 140 pounds, light for sure, but still heavier than Blondin, therefore appearing to be a substantial load.

Looking pale and rather drawn from a recent illness, Colcord climbed aboard. Blondin had two straps around his waist and horns that stuck out near his hips, into which Harry placed his thighs. Then he wrapped his arms around the muscular little neck and set his chin down on a shoulder. He was still wearing his felt hat and everyday clothes.

The great artiste now proceeded to show his mettle. He stepped onto his cable and walked calmly out over the whirlpool until he reached a point not far from mid-wire where he stopped and let Colcord down in order to rest. In a short while he was ready to move again, so he lifted his manager back up and started off at a steady pace and stopped only once more before he completed his fourteen-minute stroll. It was a magnificent performance, much better than even his 1859 walk, and the crowd was ecstatic.

Now it was time for the rookie.

Farini actually arrived at his platform at four o'clock, but problems with his swaying rope made it nearly five before he was ready to hoist up his man. He was wearing his regular circus tights but had discarded his usual rubber shoes in favour of moccasins covered with rosin, hoping they would keep him from slipping. Though he always claimed he had not met his passenger until that day (and their only practice was that morning in his hotel room where they tried out the harness), it is more than likely that he knew him well. This man, waiting in the enclosure, struck everyone as strangely unaffected by what was facing him. He was a curious man indeed.

Rowland McMullen was the son of a tailor from Port Hope. He was twenty-three years old and had a nineteen-year-old wife and two very small children to support. Why he ever consented to be part of this death-defying act, and further why he was so disarmingly cool about it from start to finish, is difficult to understand. Farini commented: "I never could quite fathom this man, never could make out whether he possessed real courage or whether he was proud of my belonging to the same town or whether he was seeking notoriety or not quite right in the upper stories or a damn fool. But I do know this, he had unlimited confidence in me."

Though it would not prove to be a perfect feat, McMullen was certainly a perfect passenger. This "insane individual," as one spectator called him, sat as calmly on Farini's back as a stuffed dummy and obeyed every instruction to the letter. He had been advertised as standing about five feet ten inches and weighing around 150 pounds, but for once Farini may have actually understated things because when McMullen placed his long legs into the truss-like harness and was carried across the platform to the edge with his feet almost touching the ground, it was obvious that the man on the Signor's back was all of that size, and maybe more.

As people in the enclosure watched them starting out, Farini's legs were noticeably shaking. An unnerved spectator shouted out that he had no right to endanger another's life. The Signor seemed to agree: after just a few steps he stopped and edged back to the platform. Was Farini giving up?

He let McMullen down, adjusted the harness, reloaded, and started out again, just as shaky as before. It was terrifying to watch. Farini picked his way so slowly and deliberately with his more than two-hundred-pound load (including balance pole) that each step seemed life-and-death and when they reached a point about fifty feet out the pole again became entangled in the guys. Farini halted. McMullen, apparently unconcerned, took off his hat and waved to his friends in the crowd. Then they executed a perilous dismount. Farini recalled: "I asked him to descend from my shoulders and stand on the rope. He replied that he would do so if he knew how, whereupon I instructed him to bear on my shoulders, to release one thigh from the stirrup at my hip, to carefully place his foot sideways on the rope and follow with the other and to stand motionless with his arms round my neck while I did the balancing for both." People on the shoreline noticed that the two were talking again. Farini remembered that at that moment McMullen said to him "... that we were not over the water yet, to which I returned the reassuring reply that if we fell we would be dashed to atoms on the stones."

They started walking step for step, McMullen behind with his hands on his pilot's shoulders, until they reached the quarter point where they sat down momentarily and then got up again and alternately walked and rode all the way to the centre. Here they sat for a longer rest, Farini motioning for the *Maid of the Mist* to come over and McMullen, amazed to see it looking the size of a toy beneath him, taking off his hat again and waving to the passengers. They discussed fear for a moment, Farini saying that his friend seemed to show none and McMullen replying that there was no need for it since his only job was to remain motionless. According to program, Farini lowered himself beneath the rope, passed McMullen and reappeared in front of him facing back toward the American side. Then he reloaded and started home, going a long way before stopping again. They performed their unloading act a few more times (now in part because Farini's feet were becoming sore) until they reached the point where the cable started rising steeply toward the shore. Here Farini steeled himself, loaded McMullen, and made a desperate attempt to climb the remaining distance, perspiring profusely and his legs quivering. People shouted that he looked unsteady, but slowly he made his way up the rope and finally reached the platform, his legs nearly buckling as he landed.

"Bravo Long Legs! Bravo tailor! Bravo Port Hope! Canada forever!" shouted the crowd as McMullen dismounted on to firm ground, pulled on his coat and accepted a glass of beer from a friend. He was as calm as ever. Farini claimed that the cheering was loud and seemed endless, but it was mostly from relief and in appreciation of a daring show, because as an attempt to exhibit more skill than Blondin it had been a failure.

He never questioned Blondin's greatness as an artist of the wire. "I...compliment him on being the cleverist tightrope dancer in the world...for as such he was superior to me who not having been brought up to the line of business (to become proficient at which one must almost live for years on a rope), never competed with him as regards the terpsichorean art." Farini's forte was terror, and inventiveness, which was why he carried a heavier, inexperienced man on a rope Blondin wouldn't dare try. In 1859 Blondin had taken thirty-five minutes to cross with Colcord and had unloaded him many times, but even then his artistry was evident. Farini, a restless young man of red-blooded emotions, had no time for such subtle impressions.

Both men gave evening performances the day of their passenger-walks. This was the first time they ascended their cables at night and these exhibitions were wonderful: ghostly ascensions in the soft glow of the moon. Blondin was noticed about eight o'clock that cool, clear evening driving down to the Suspension Bridge with a wheelbarrow full of fireworks in his wagon. Promptly, at half-past eight, he mounted his cable pushing the wheelbarrow and eerily vanished into the night. Spectators could only guess where he was as he made his way over the river in darkness, the sound of the falls in the background.

The Signor made his appearance carrying one of his earliest inventions attached to his pole: four paper lamps and a number of "Farini Candles." A match was put to the "candles" and he started out at a rapid pace, his body disappearing into the darkness, the row of lights glowing, bouncing perceptibly to his gait as they made their way across the river. A short distance out there was a loud *bang* like gunfire, so loud it was felt by people on the banks. They looked out and saw one of his candles completely enflamed, and his lamps still moving quickly through the air. Then there was another bang and another and another, until they could see Signor Farini, a great distance out, surrounded by fire. Before he reached the centre all the fireworks had gone out, and with only the light from his lamps, he proceeded the rest of the way at a rapid pace and landed on the Canadian side to cheers. Almost immediately he started back, this time without a light. People caught only glimpses of him in the moonlight. Suddenly, in a moment remembered by all who saw it, Blondin's firecrackers went off in the distance over a mile away, and for an instant, in the glow of a beautiful lunar bow, the daring artists silhouetted each other in the night.

Then it was time for a little humour. For his September 5th walk Farini the iconoclast was determined to take another rip at the superhuman Frenchman. He would show people that it wasn't just a rookie who could walk the Niagara gorge like the mighty Blondin, so could a lowly washerwoman, in fact, *she* could even carry her washing machine with her and do her laundry at mid-wire. Local businessmen Messrs. Philpot and Hinckley provided the apparatus while Farini supplied the woman: an Irish laundry worker named Biddy O'Flaherty. Like his earlier persona, Mickey Free, the Irish Pedestrian, this character's traits travelled with her onto the cable.

The tone of the performance was irreverent right from the start. His broadsides called him "Farini the Comical, the Inexhaustible" and his Biddy was described as a "Wonderful and Laughable" character. He promised that the washerwoman would clean handkerchiefs two hundred feet above the gorge and hang them out to dry, leaving them all night if she so chose, having no fear that they might be stolen. She also generously offered anyone the chance to come out and check her work, to see if it was thoroughly done.

It was an Empire Washing Machine with a large wooden tub at its base, a pole rising from its centre and two others going from bottom to top with a rope strung across from the uppermost tips. It was six feet high and weighed about one hundred pounds. Farini, dressed in dark leg tights, a high-collared woman's blouse and a lady's dainty hat, arrived at his cable at four o'clock and made a show of receiving several handkerchiefs from a

number of ladies. Then he lifted the washing machine
onto his back and strapped it over his shoulders and
around his waist. His heavy load adjusted, he picked up
his balance pole, stepped out onto the cable and walked
deliberately until he was nearly at mid-wire. Here he fastened his pole and the washing machine to the rope, took
a pail and a cord out of the tub, lowered them down to the
river and brought up some Niagara water for his chores.
It took Biddy several minutes to do her laundry and when
she was finished she wrang it out and tied each item to
the cross-ropes and uprights. Her job done, she went
through the tricky manoeuvre of getting the machine up
onto her back again and her pole into her hands. But this
she did without incident and soon was heading home
again, the hankies flapping wildly in the winds. The
ladies on the shoreline reported no dissatisfaction with
the quality of the washerwoman's work.

Then he readied himself for what he hoped would be an
eventful weekend: the heir to the throne of the British
Empire was coming to Niagara and the whole world
would be watching.

The visit of the Prince of Wales (later Edward VII) to
Canada and parts of the United States was an event of
enormous importance to its citizens. Newspapers followed
his every movement in the minutest detail, down to the
clothes he sported, the expressions he wore and the young
women with whom he danced at the numerous balls held
in his honour. Just nineteen, full of vigour, always interested in social gatherings, and about to embark on an
adventurous manhood, he was the perfect royal family
member to undertake the challenge of mixing with the
people of the colonies. In Port Hope, his arrival on
September 7th was greeted with near hysteria; huge
crowds flowed down Walton Street and went under a big
archway built entirely of branches and wreathes and
topped with the royal coat of arms. "Welcome Prince of
Wales" and "Let Commerce Flourish" it read and in the
Guide that week everything a merchant could sell was

offered with His Royal Highness's name attached. It was difficult for them to believe that he would actually speak to them and walk on the ground in their little town. "It will be a day long remembered by the inhabitants," wrote Hugh Crea.

Meanwhile, Farini was trying to get the Prince's attention. He put together a two-day program of four inventive performances that promised to be unprecedented, but his most controversial move involved a letter he supposedly penned about the Prince. Datelined "Niagara Falls, U.S.A., August 22, 1860," it appeared in the *Niagara Falls Gazette* a week later, and read:

To his Grace the Duke of Newcastle:
Dear Sir:—It is important that the Prince of Wales' entrance into the United States should produce a sensation worthy of the country and himself.

He will probably arrive among us by way of Niagara Falls, where the greatest natural phenomenon on this continent has been running over six thousand years in preparation for this event.

In order that the occasion may be fitly improved, I propose to take the heir apparent to the British throne across the Falls in a wheelbarrow, on a tight rope, free of expense. The progress of the trip shall be diversified by fireworks and various gymnastic feats, such as the occasion and the inclinations of the Prince of Wales may suggest. In this way thousands may see him arrive who would not have an opportunity if he came by railroad or any ordinary conveyance.

If it would please your Grace, I should be very happy to bring you over in the same way, and other members of the Prince's suite which he may designate. If any accident should happen by which his Highness or any members of his party should be precipitated into the gulf below, (of which, I assure you, there is little or no danger,) the money taken from the spectators shall be promptly refunded. Please submit this proposition to his Highness and favour me with a reply at your earliest convenience.

I am your Grace's most obedient and most humble servant,

FARINI

Neither the Prince nor the Duke of Newcastle (secretary of state for the colonies) responded, but the lack of a reply and even the presumptuous nature of the letter were not its biggest problems. First among its difficulties was the fact that it had already appeared, late in the previous week in the New York *Evening Post*, signed by none other than M. Blondin.

Which man authored the letter may never be known. Blondin has in his favour the great advantage of being the first to publish, although when the *The World* of New York reprinted it on August 27th they made a point of noting that "Not being familiar with the handwriting of M. Blondin, we cannot guaranty its genuineness." Also in Blondin's favour is the fact that he was identified with the wheelbarrow act at the heart of the proposal. But the letter's style is decidedly unlike his and bears Farini's erudite turn of phrase, sense of humour and iconoclasm. Whoever wrote it, it had the desired effect, connecting rope-walking to the heir to the British throne.

Fresh from greeting crowds of 50,000 in Toronto and 20,000 in London, His Royal Highness arrived in the early evening of September 14th, by steamer at the village of Chippewa, a couple of miles north of the Horseshoe Falls. After a short reception he was taken by carriage to his quarters at the Zimmerman estate which sat a few hundred yards off the river across the gorge from the American Falls and not far from the Clifton House Hotel. By the time he arrived Farini had finished both his performances for that day.

The next day dawned slightly windy, not the best for rope-walking. The prince was up early and seen playing with the Zimmerman children before he and his suite rode by horseback to visit the falls and the surrounding area. Signor Farini gave two performances that day. One at eleven o'clock when he lowered himself fifty feet below the cable, swung like a pendulum and leapt into the water, and was immediately plucked out by his friends. This "dreadfully frightening" feat necessitated his falling and resurfacing at precise spots in the river in order to avoid being sucked under the current. At four he performed a mile-long run on his cable, stopping three times to stand on his head.

There were reports that the prince did not see Farini that day and when he arrived at Blondin's enclosure some time after four o'clock noticed the young Canadian's rope in the distance and asked an aide what it was. "A path for another fool," was supposedly the response. But Farini always maintained Edward saw one of his shows and this claim makes sense. How could the prince have moved along the edge of the gorge on horseback, as he did several times that day, in the vicinity of the Clifton (from which spectators often watched Farini perform), and not have noticed the two-thousand-foot cable that dominated the gorge and the man running upon it to the cheers of a crowd? The prince was said to have arrived late for Blondin's performance, therefore his entourage moved directly past Farini's platform as his show began. The Frenchman and his camp had the ear of the mayor and the welcoming committee and had apparently thus secured the patronage of the British royal; perhaps with that went influence over press reports.

Blondin's performance, stretching over two hours during which Edward remained watching, has gone down in both show-business and Niagara Falls history. There is no doubt it was riveting. The prince, after turning down Blondin's offer to be a passenger, showed a good deal of concern and expressed his wish that the dangerous performance not be carried out, since much of it was arranged as a royal tribute. But Blondin took Colcord out on the cable and charmed the crowd, withstanding a wind that threatened to blow them into the gorge, and returned on stilts, falling once (perhaps on purpose) and landing on the rope. The prince was very impressed and said to

Blondin as he finished, "Thank God it's all over." He offered him his patronage if he came to England and in a few days sent him five hundred dollars.

Farini claimed that his own feats (which also included him carrying McMullen again) were more sensational, and he may have been right. But nevertheless Blondin's royal show is recorded as one of his great moments, helping to immortalize him. The man with the right connections, with the respectable friends, had triumphed.

After that, the season was essentially over. Blondin made his royal performance his last and Farini gave just one more. By the end of September he took down his cable, a five-day operation involving the numbering of every part of the huge apparatus, and by the first week of October was gone.

Farini had many triumphs at the Falls in the summer of 1860. And not all occurred on the wire. His days as a pursuer of women began in earnest during that first flush of fame. There was the attraction between himself and Governor Sprague's wife at the hotel ball; rumours that he was romantically involved with the wife of a hotel-proprietor friend; a fling with a woman named Louisa Montague (curiously, the real name of a famous nineteenth-century circus beauty queen) who approached him one day near his cable wondering if he were made of steel and gushing that his feats were too wonderful for her to understand (later he traced her to a brothel in Buffalo); breathless moments with famous singer Anna Bishop who wanted to be carried on his back over the gorge; and an unrequited affair with a young woman who fell hopelessly in love with him after he saved her from certain death by leaping into the rapids at the Cave of the Winds. Anxious for attention and vain, he treasured each encounter.

He also succeeded off the wire at the Falls as a businessman. In that department he bested Blondin with ease. Accounts vary as to what he made, from his own outrageous statements that he received ten thousand dollars his first day, more than four thousand another and was disappointed if he made less than one thousand per out-ing, to the *Guide*'s report that he was given six hundred per show and an old friend's recollection that he made six thousand dollars that summer. Blondin's need to pass the hat, go to the press for money and his concern about per-sonal debt exaggerate his situation: he realized some profit from his famous Niagara feats. But despite com-manding huge fees throughout the 1860s Blondin would often struggle with his finances and was even forced to return to the high wire late in life to avoid bankruptcy. Farini, the clever, self-made professional, was a much more calculating and versatile man: not only did he ensure a financial bonanza for himself before he even came to the Falls, he proceeded to make large sums of money throughout his life. Unlike his erstwhile rival, Farini's financial schemes, as well as his adventures, were never confined solely to a high wire.

But his greatest triumph wasn't romantic, financial or even acrobatic. He had gone to the Falls to compete with a man whom everyone said was a superman. No one, they had said, could do the things that the immortal Blondin did. Now, they knew different.

CHAPTER 9

Funambulist
for Hire

*"Farini...asserts his intention to,
'win, or break his neck.'"*
Buffalo Commercial Advertiser, September 1861,
on Farini's high-wire duel with DeLave

By October 1860 it was obvious that Abraham Lincoln was just weeks away from being elected president of the United States, and the "fire-eaters" of the South began laying plans for secession from the union. But Farini had other things on his mind: things that were much more important and not nearly so solemn as politics. He negotiated a deal to make two ascensions at a county fair in Springfield, Ohio in mid-October, apparently for four hundred dollars a day, and was telling every reporter who would listen that he would tour the South during the winter, go to Europe during the early spring and return to the Falls in the summer to astonish everyone by taking a lady out on the cable and carrying people across in a basket, all to be accomplished on a rope stretched directly over the falls, with a starting point on Goat Island.

Blondin decided shortly after his last ascension that he would not walk at the Falls again. By early November he had dissolved his partnership with Colcord and his Niagara house was put up for sale. He planned to tour the States for a few months and then go to Europe in the spring, possibly establishing his residence in Paris. But when he sailed the Atlantic in April, after triumphant per-

formances in Philadelphia, New York and Boston,
England was his destination. On June 1, 1861 Blondin
made his debut at the legendary Crystal Palace in London
and began the second great triumph of his career. He took
the city by storm, appearing in every paper and even
being eulogized by poets. He solicited volunteers for
tightrope passengers and the response was immense and
much publicized. People of all classes and physical types
were carried across, but a sensation at least as scandalous
as it was popular arose when he took his five-year-old
daughter over in a wheelbarrow: this nearly ended his
Palace appearances. But the shows went on, as well
attended as ever. Even Dickens came to see Blondin, and
put his poison pen to work:

> Here are ten thousand of us whom the train has poured
> from its cellular throat, driving up the passage of Crystal
> Palace like so many black peas up a pea-shooter. We have
> all but one object—to see a man walk on (or perhaps fall
> from) a rope a hundred feet high...bishops, lawyers,
> authors, fashionables [are here] to see a rope dancer ven-
> ture his life for one hundred pounds the half hour. Half
> London is here, eager for some dreadful accident...
> Everybody seems afraid that Blondin will fall before they
> are able to take their seats.

Of course, Blondin didn't fall. In fact, this run, coming
so soon after his two magnetic seasons at Niagara Falls
enshrined him forever as one of the immortals of show
business.

Meanwhile, Farini was off on a series of high-wire adventures of his own, working his way across America, living
the life of a roguish bachelor, blissfully unconcerned about
Blondin and all his big doings and the new high-flying
agent who like so many others was taking the little
Frenchman for a financial ride.

Springfield, Ohio was a town of about 7,000 people an
hour west of Columbus and their excitement at having

Blondin's great rival in their midst was evident from the moment he arrived. "The Signor Has Come!" said the local paper, which published five articles about him before he even set foot on the wire, and called him "the greatest rope-walker living...the Champion of the World." They also remarked on his intelligence and good breeding, as if these traits were unique in a circus personality. An "accomplished scholar and a cultivated gentleman," they called him, formerly the proprietor of a gymnasium at a Canadian university, who often lectured about physical fitness. These things were of course true...in a manner of speaking.

Despite similar gushing welcomes for his Ohio shows, like in Dayton where the *Dayton Daily Empire* exclaimed "Wouldn't a positive announcement [of his appearance here] bring a crowd of people to Dayton!" and his ever-increasing brilliance on the rope (he now walked in peach baskets and did a stunning rings routine, once in the pouring rain), this tour did not draw huge crowds or thrust him into the spotlight. But he didn't care: adventure was what he was after. And he got almost more than he could handle in little Hamilton, Ohio when the rope, attached to trees, suddenly slipped and vibrated violently: he bounced into the air, but landed safely, later commenting that he had felt like an arrow launched by an enormous bow. Next he went to Cincinnati and by mid-November was continuing his march southward as he arrived in Louisville, Kentucky.

Just as he was entering this neither-Northern-nor-Southern, slave-holding state, Lincoln ascended to leadership and war clouds stirred. Generally Kentucky viewed his election with horror, though they were badly split on the major questions of the day. It was an intriguing place to be at election time. If Farini took a side in the political fray, his sympathies lay with the Democrats, who were soft on the slavery question in order to keep the peace. His arrival in Louisville and preparations for a performance were followed by the *Daily Democrat*, which said about Old Abe's election: "The evil days so long dreaded, are at last upon us." Farini had other issues to consider: a female reporter from the area, pretty and intelligent, was in love with him. "I was very much flattered and paid her considerable attention, but not being a covetous man nor wishing to monopolize so much beauty and genius I unselfishly left her to shed the bright rays of her talent on more deserving mortals." This seems like a euphemistic description of a love-'em-and-leave-'em affair. Such were his concerns as news of the nation's dissolution raged in the Kentucky air.

After a smashing show at the Louisville Theater he was moving again, plunging southward into the heart of rebel country, heading for the adventurers' magnet at the mouth of the Mississippi. New Orleans was one of the great American cities on the eve of the Civil War, not just in terms of size (it had 168,000 citizens, putting it in the top half-dozen), but also because of its reputation for culture, pleasure-seeking and lawlessness. Its legendary French Quarter, opera houses, theatres, whore-houses and many gambling saloons attracted all sorts of people, who mingled with the gumbo of races already present, all searching for wealth and thrills. The circuses and entertainment people came in huge numbers during the November-to-April period and, like everyone else, left by spring, heading north away from diseases like yellow fever, which often swept through the delta, brought to its narrow, unpaved streets by bad sewage systems left open in the hot, humid air.

Farini arrived during the first week of December, for a much more extended visit than the previous year, one that showed him the many sides of New Orleans. He spent the first few weeks enjoying himself, a twenty-two-year-old adventurer on the loose. Free from his parents and his heritage, and his pockets full of money, he was determined to investigate everything, and there was no shortage of things to do. Two circuses played during the first two weeks of December. One was Nixon's Royal Circus at the St. Charles Theater, featuring two acts which had major influences on his career: the Hanlon Brothers, who with the Ravels were the great acrobats of the day, their acts filled with spectacular tumbling and innovative trapeze turns; and the equestrienne Mlle. Ella Zoyara who, it was rumoured, was actually a man, the public debate about "her" true gender eagerly encouraged by her promoters.

By the end of the year he tired of doing nothing and decided to put together a company using a number of artistes who were doing very much the same. He put up money for his enterprise and even had a theatre rented when, on January 9th, the first incident at Fort Sumter took place and civil war seemed imminent. Coupled with the signing of delegates to attend the state secession convention, this turned people's attention from the theatre to more pressing concerns. He saw his venture would make no financial sense. But now, ensconced at the posh St. Charles Hotel, he was nearly penniless, and considered how he might raise the money to get away. Within a few weeks Louisiana seceded, the Pelican flag of the state was raised to gun salutes and men were being recruited for the army. There was pressure on everyone to show their loyalty to the South—it was almost a prerequisite to survival in New Orleans by January 1861.

At the Academy of Music, despite good crowds (including one stirred by the awesome presence of the mighty John C. Heenan, bare-fisted boxing champion of the world), even the great Dan Rice felt the strain of the enormous political cloud hanging over the city. On the evening of the 26th a man levelled a revolver at Rice's band as they played "The Star Spangled Banner"; in moments guns came out throughout the theatre and only the great humourist's appearance, staring straight at his accusers as he spoke of his loyalty to the flag, calmed the situation. But within days he was gone, up the Mississippi, often playing "Dixie" at his shows to avoid catastrophes. For many years his actions that night in New Orleans were surrounded with controversy, many in the North claiming his speech was about loyalty indeed, but loyalty to the Confederacy. In fact, a few months later he was forced to turn a show cannon on a mob who came after him in Cincinnati, insisting that he was a traitor.

Farini had no such dilemma. His first instinct was survival, so he stuck the Confederacy badge, or "cockade," in his hat and made his way about town without interference. But time was running out and he knew he had to find a way out of New Orleans or be forced into the Southern army. His solution was to search out a saloon in the French Quarter and gamble his way to a two-hundred-dollar fortune, despite supposedly feeling morally unclean for doing it. He made more money still by explaining the flaw in a game to a high-rolling gambler. Soon he and the gambler opened a game of their own, but Farini claims he stopped as soon as he made two thousand dollars, enough to finance his escape out of town.

Since it was getting more difficult each day to get passage up the Mississippi, he decided to go by steamer to Cuba and sail from there to New York. It was February by the time he arrived in the big city and there was snow on the ground. Seven southern states had now left the Union, compromises to save the country were failing, Senator Spinola of New York had publicly announced that all traitors should be hanged from Blondin's rope, Jefferson Davis had just been acclaimed President of the new Confederacy and Lincoln was weeks from being inaugurated. Seeing the bustle of New York for the first time would have excited him anyway, but arriving in the midst of war fever made the city look as though it were positively swirling. Farini was, however, for the first time, determined to turn away from excitement. He took the next train out of town and headed for the quiet countryside of Hope Township. It was time to see if he could really go home.

Somehow Farini was able to be Bill Hunt again and live in the same house with his father for three months. Thomas turned much of the farm operation over to him, and in a few years would sell him all his land and begin plans to retire permanently to Port Hope. There were now just six other Hunt offspring at home: Myndert, age sixteen, lived with relatives near Detroit, and Ann had married William Marsh, Jr. the previous year and was living

in an impressive brick home a mile or so east of the Hunt
house on the south side of Kingston Road, their little
daughter Lucia next in the long line of Soper-Marsh
hybrids. Tom Hunt, Jr., nineteen, was working as a clerk,
while John, fifteen, Mary, thirteen, Jim, eleven, and
Edith, nine, all attended school, leaving just little Mannie,
age three, home with Hannah.

By April Bill was busying himself with crop-planting
and other chores. It must have been odd for farmers to see
the Great Farini behind the horse and plow or mending a
fence. Children were told who he was, though admonitions
were usually added about never growing up to be like
him: he was both an object of fascination and an outcast,
considered morally questionable and full of fancy airs.
Some laughed at his attempt at farming, but like most
things he tried, he did it well. By mid-April the Americans
were doing what they had been threatening to do for
nearly a decade: fighting a full-blown war, a bloody implo-
sion that would affect the lives of millions of people,
including young Bill Hunt. With excitement boiling over
in the cities and towns he had barnstormed through just
a few months earlier, the banality of his circumstances
became difficult to accept and before May even began he
was itching to escape. Living in Hope Township would
never work for him: the energy that had possessed him
since birth just wouldn't rest. He had to head out into the
world again after adventure. To warm up he thought he
would treat Port Hope to another taste of Signor Farini
and launch himself into the second phase of his career.

He designed and printed his broadsides and soon had
them in all the post offices in the region and many of the
hotels and taverns. The date set for his reappearance was
May 16th. A buzz went through the county: the great hero
was returning, coming home after conquering the world.
Hugh Crea gave him a build-up in the *Guide*: "Signor
Farini announced two grand ascensions for Thursday, the
16th...[and] the news soon got raised abroad through
Lindsay, Omemee, Manvers, Cavan and Hope and at every
fire-side the wonderful feats of the Signor were discussed

and arrangements to witness them made." Despite bad
weather—cool and windy, with intermittent drizzles—and
the fact that this was a busy time for farmers, a big crowd
came to Port Hope that day. It was a festive occasion, even
for school children: many years later an old man from Port
Hope recalled, "When Farini came to town, father always
declared a holiday."

The rope was strung on the south side of Walton Street
bridge this time. At two-thirty the mighty Farini appeared
like magic out of the trap door on the roof of Gillett's
Building and the crowd gave their native son a huge hero's
welcome. Their excitement at seeing him again was
increased by his spectacular appearance, arrayed not only
in acrobatic costume but also a large Indian chief's head-
dress of eagle feathers. It was another triumphant moment
for reprobate Bill Hunt; the *Guide* even made reference to
his evident sex appeal, noting that "the ladies, particularly
the young ladies [pronounced him] a fine looking fellow."

He went out quickly with his balance pole, walked to the
centre of the wet rope, presented his finely tuned gymnastic routine and stood on his head. After righting himself he
walked quickly over to the roof of Waddell's Block. He disappeared for a few moments and then returned, completely enveloped in a sack. He was forced to go slowly due
to the wind and at various points in the recrossing made
little progress, but persevered and made it to Gillett's without incident. Then he performed one of his greatest feats
to date: he walked out to the centre carrying wooden peach
baskets, sat down on his rope, removed his shoes, tied on
the baskets, and somehow regained his footing on the rope
and walked back to the rooftop. Crea loudly claimed that
Blondin could never do such a thing. In the evening he
walked before another big crowd, utilizing his fireworks
which he theatrically tossed into the creek so that he
might prance about "like a spectre" in total darkness.

Within two weeks he was gone. By the end of May the
Buffalo and Niagara newspapers were reporting that he
was in their midst, laying plans for spectacular crossings

of the Niagara, and some time during the first week of
June he swept into the offices of the *Lockport Daily
Journal*, telling all that he would walk the gorge without
a balance pole, a hitherto unattempted feat, and carry a
woman on his back to spice things up ("Ugh!" said the
newspaper). He produced a picture of the woman and
proudly showed it to the editor. This was the first
Madame Farini.

The fearless Mary Osborne, his old friend from the township, had decided to go on the road with him. Whether she
was ever actually married to him, was merely his professional "wife" or his live-in lover is not certain. They had
been close for a number of years and she had supported
him through thick and thin. Born in Prince Edward
Island, one of William Osborne's six daughters, she came
to Hope Township with her family in 1850 or '51, after
Mary's eldest sister wed an Island apprentice shipbuilder
named Henry Hacker. The Hackers lived in Port Hope
and the youngest Osborne girl stayed with them, but
Mary, her father and her three other sisters found a home
on property belonging to the Curtis family in the township. Mr. Osborne (apparently widowed) was employed as
a tailor, perhaps working for the Curtises or their rich relatives, the Marshes. Living across the road was the
socially conscious, eccentric Hunt family, and by far their
most intriguing member, at least to Mary, was the romantic eldest son. With his help she too learned to walk a high
wire and was one of the few township people not frightened by his feats and his desires. When he returned to
Hope in 1861 as a world-renowned gymnast, their friendship was renewed. They were just one year apart and
obviously both rather unconventional people. When he left
home again after his second Port Hope walk she went
with him and publicly took the name Farini.

On June 6th, just four days before Farini's twenty-third
birthday, Captain Joel Robinson performed a feat on the
Niagara River which has gone down as one of the most

spectacular events in Niagara history. And though it gained fame for the modest Robinson, it inadvertently clouded Farini's big plans for that season.

In May the financially troubled owner of the *Maid of the Mist* decided that he had to sell the well-known steamer. The boat's Montreal buyers insisted that it be delivered to them on Lake Ontario. Robinson, the ship's captain, offered (for five hundred dollars) to pilot the Maid from its dock near the falls through the Whirlpool rapids to Queenston, a trip considered virtually impossible. But off Robinson went, an engineer and a mechanic with him, tossed and pitched through Devil's Hole, taking on water by the gallon and having their smoke stack snapped off at the stem. But somehow they made it. Farini didn't join in the applause that greeted Robinson and echoed in the many newspaper accounts printed throughout North America, for the *Maid of the Mist* had been an integral part of his first Niagara performances (and the only boat capable of getting his big cable across) and would be sorely missed in 1861.

The same day as Robinson's trip, Farini's plans for his Niagara walks were published and a tentative debut date of July 4th was set. A week later both of Hollis White's banks at Niagara Falls, New York failed. Such was the state of the resort's economy as its tourist trade faded, ravaged by the absence of southerners and the many northern men who had enlisted, and the nation's lack of interest in vacationing as the war worsened. A big high-wire show at the Falls, where people had to be drawn from far and wide to make the event financially feasible, now seemed out of the question and Farini's date came and went without his appearance. Two further dates in early August were also cancelled, though spectators actually arrived at the Falls that week expecting to see him, some on the steamer *Maple Leaf* from the Bowmanville area. To replace this excitement he experimented with speed-boat racing, in a state-of-the-art yacht called the *Iron Duke* owned by a wealthy New York industrialist, storming the three miles across the raging current of the river above the Falls in slightly more than nine minutes.

Then he was ready to get back on his rope. He announced his revised plans: he would present weekly shows at Moffat's Grove, the pleasure grounds just north of Buffalo where he had given a few performances the previous year, and walk a rope eight hundred feet long and ninety feet high, running from a huge tree to a set of gigantic shears. The city papers revelled in his return, writing of "that easy and devil-may-care style peculiar to the Professor of nerve and muscle," calling him "the youngest and most daring of all performers on tight or slack rope," and gossiping that Blondin had been offered one thousand dollars to cross the gorge on Farini's Niagara slack wire and had declined.

He appeared in the Buffalo area throughout August and September, presenting a series of stunning performances, even defeating Monsieur DeLave in a head-to-head challenge in front of a big crowd. After a couple of years at the trade he seemed to be hitting his stride.

His most controversial Buffalo show occurred on August 21st. Maria Schmidt was just four years old, but during practice seemed very cool about being strapped tightly into the wheelbarrow and pushed along the wire with the muscular Mr. Farini Hunt smiling down at her and her father looking on approvingly from below. But a few days later, with a huge, rowdy crowd milling around, she immediately dissolved into tears when she was hauled up by the pulleys toward Mr. Farini, who looked very different now in his brightly coloured costume, full of adrenalin as he shouted instructions amidst the cheers and cat-calls and the sound of the band. The *Buffalo Commercial Advertiser* picks up the story:

As she proceeded up her cries became more violent, and shouts from the crowd of "Let her down," began to arise. Farini stood at the top, the while, shouting "Haul her up." There was great excitement for a time, but finally the crowd prevailed, and the little girl was landed on terra firma. We were very much pleased with the incident. They were rough-looking men and women who stood around, and they had come out on purpose to see the child wheeled across the rope. If she had gone up smiling and fearless, no opposition would have been made. But the child's cries touched the heart of the mob, and it does them honor that they did.

Not everyone agreed. Some thought the mob was motivated by less honourable desires: to try to cause a mini-riot by interfering with the performance (not uncommon shenanigans at a circus). It was pointed out by most every commentator that the wheelbarrow had a groove in its wheel to keep it glued to the rope and that the child was strapped into it so it was virtually impossible for her to fall, and additionally that the feat had been practised several times without incident, without fear on the child's part and with the approval of her father. Many felt that she was actually frightened by the crowd and *not* the prospect of the high-wire act. Even the *Advertiser* toned down its comments when it responded to criticism of its initial review. They insisted that they had no quarrel with Farini and that he had taken exemplary precautions to prevent an accident, but that the crowd could not have known this. They maintained that the crowd had acted nobly, but they admitted that that nobility was born out of ignorance.

Farini believed that, deep down, everyone wanted the thrills he was after, so he seldom balked at putting others' lives in danger, a disturbing tendency that would grow as the years passed. He was absolutely disgusted by the turn of events. The snob in him rose to the surface, as he railed internally at the stupidity of people who could not understand the very rudiments of what he was doing. He snapped up his wheelbarrow and raced across the rope, keeping his eyes averted from the ignorant mass below. He grabbed his chair and stomped out again, throwing it down on the rope and leaping onto it carelessly. Instantly the chair wobbled beneath him and tipped sideways, throwing him off balance. His plunging weight spun the chair around and sent it crashing to the ground, but even

in his anger his cool brain and physical talent saved him.
He merely let the chair go and splaying his legs, fell on
either side of the rope and gripped it as calmly as if he
had intended to conclude this way. The crowd seemed
more impressed by this than if he had succeeded. Still
angry, he righted himself, walked off the rope, hoisted a
man onto his back and stepped out to the centre and back
without pausing.

Another walk featured the debut of Signora Farini. The
Advertiser, perhaps a little sheepishly, proclaimed that the
crowd would "not interfere" this time and everyone was
assured that Mrs. Farini was a well-practised and willing
participant. The exciting prospect of seeing him carry "a
live woman" brought out another big crowd. They watched
him step out onto his rope with Mary on his back and
head toward his "crow's nest" in the tree. He had invented
a new apparatus for carrying her, a kind of side-saddle
made of leather, steel bands and stirrups that strapped
onto his shoulders and rendered her ride comfortable and
as safe as possible. She was described as "a pale and
rather interesting looking person of twenty-two years, or
thereabouts" and despite the poor condition of the rope
that day she performed her task without fear and was
cheered heartily when they reached the crow's nest and
she was lowered safely to the ground.

To conclude his Buffalo engagements Farini performed
three times at St. James Hall in mid-September, each
time on the same bill with DeLave. It was reported that
at his final show he actually went through with the astonishing feat of carrying two people simultaneously.

He and Mary left town on Sunday the 29th and were
rumoured to be headed for the National Horse Fair at
Kalamazoo, Michigan, en route to performances at the
State Fair in Detroit and theatres in Chicago. But
unknown to him at that moment, he was about to temporarily leave show business and plunge himself into the
bloody mess that was the American Civil War.

CHAPTER 10

Civil War Adventures

"He used to talk about the way men acted
under momentary strain."
C.T. Currelly, on Farini's feelings about war,
in *I Brought the Ages Home*

S ome time in early October of 1861 someone convinced
Farini to go to war. Who that someone was is debat-
able. Farini told two different stories: one was that an
American cousin who was a major in the Northern army
and a veteran of the Mexican war came to visit him (either
in Buffalo, in Hope where he had gone for a respite, or possibly in Detroit where he had many relatives), and his stories of military adventure excited Farini's mind past
resistance. When the cousin departed for Washington,
Farini went with him, not sure whether he would enlist or
just get closer to the action; his other story, told frequently
to C.T. Currelly in old age, was that a wealthy gentleman
in Buffalo, and Farini knew quite a few, asked him to take
his son's place in a Northern regiment for a substantial
fee. This was a common practice, called "substitution."

However he got there, he arrived in Washington some
time in late October. Soon he was introduced to Colonel
John McLeod Murphy, an engineer who had been with his
cousin in Mexico (under General McClellan). Murphy
commanded the 15th New York Engineers Regiment, just
brought back from duties near the front to Camp
Alexander at the Navy Yard on the Anacostia River. Here

121

they were instructed to find a way to transport large groups of soldiers across rivers, in preparation for McClellan's coming campaign in the peninsula east of the Confederate capital of Richmond. A salient trait of Murphy's personality was his ability to tell wonderful stories, especially about Mexican adventures, and Farini, recognizing a kindred soul, soon became a friend. For his part, Murphy was enchanted by the extraordinary young Signor, not just because of his fame and flamboyance, but also because of his inventive mind, evident almost from the moment he opened his mouth. Trained as a farmer and a doctor, one would have sworn upon hearing him attack a mechanical problem that he was an educated engineer. Before long, at Murphy's request, he was fixing his mind on McClellan's needs. What the Colonel wanted was an invention that would "make a stir." Farini obliged.

He retired to the yard, apparently with "carte blanche" from his superior, and in three weeks came back with two strange creations. Murphy approved them and they were readied for public demonstration. Military reviews and exhibitions were favoured by McClellan, the pompous "Young Napoleon" of the north, and therefore were frequent in the Washington area during late 1861. On November 26th on the Anacostia, President Lincoln, McClellan with his almost-royal suite (including the Comte de Paris, Prince de Joinville and John Jacob Astor), General Alexander, General Barnard and their ladies assembled to watch an exhibition that was all about river crossings. Farini always said he showed his inventions at an exhibition attended by these dignitaries, and claimed the demonstration was given a full-page spread in *Harpers' Weekly*; indeed it was featured in the press, though in *Frank Leslie's Illustrated Paper*.

When all the officials were assembled the engineers quickly laid a pontoon bridge across the river, to much approval from the audience. Then it was time for Farini. First he had his portable "skirmish rope bridge" put over, a device which could be carried up to a river bank, quickly brought over the river and then used to transport troops

much faster than the enemy could move. This too met
with approval, especially when he raced over the bridge
himself, firing his gun to give things "a little life," as he
put it. Then, in response to anticipated questions about
how the bridge would be anchored on the other shore, he
delivered his *coup de grâce*.

He would walk on water. Hardly a surprising idea for a
man of his ambition. For this he used "water skates,"
devices similar to the ones he had read about other eccentric men using a few years ago. His shoes were made of
zinc, shaped like tiny boats, with air-tight compartments
and exterior flanges (or "fins"), lightly hinged near the
bottom and attached to strings he held in his hands. With
this bizarre invention strapped to his feet he prepared to
head out across the river. But six-foot-four-inch Abraham
Lincoln, described by Farini as "the rail splitting lawyer
President," sitting nearby with his knees up higher than
his chin, tapped him on the shoulder. "Young man," he
said to Willie Hunt, "don't be afraid, if you should tip over
and get in head down, I'm long enough to wade you out."
With that Farini was off across the river.

He claimed his exhibition was a great success, impressing McClellan in particular, and though Colonel Murphy
was at first publicly credited, Farini was soon given his
due and subsequently offered a captaincy in the 15th New
York Engineers. He accepted, studied hard for his exams
and passed, though he spent much of his time afterward
in Washington, avoiding the embittered man (apparently
a New York alderman) over whom he had been promoted.
He did appear for dress parades and was reported to have
spent some time drilling his company in his own unique
fashion: training them to use a ladder he had invented,
make themselves fit on his portable gymnasium and
teaching them to make human pyramids so they could
scale walls without hesitation.

But the months passed without any real action, the reason Farini had become involved in the first place. He
always claimed that his heart was not really in the war
anyway but he thought it was a shame to both see the

union broken up and miss out on adventure. He was becoming addicted to danger and to thrills, and war provided both. As the weeks and then months passed without engaging the enemy, McClellan became the target of criticism from Lincoln, the government, the press and even the people, though his troops, including Farini (who always remained a staunch defender) loved him dearly. History would judge McClellan's reluctant nature harshly.

Soon Farini was sick of sitting around in Washington (Mary was likely there too—as restless as her husband), so he determined to get himself into some danger. He applied to join the Secret Service. "Here my adventurous nature would have full play," he said. In one of his first missions, dressed in civilian clothes, he swam the river near Aquia Creek and went south, overland through enemy territory toward Falmouth and Fredericksburg. This was likely in March, when Confederate General Joseph Johnston began evacuating the area in fear of a massive Federal invasion. Farini claimed he was one of the first Northerners in the area, entered the town unscathed, and (playing on American ignorance about Canadians) convinced southerners that he wasn't a "damn Yankee" but an Englishman. Reconnaissance work was common for him that month, he later said, including several more dangerous forays behind enemy lines, sometimes involving enlistment in the rebel forces and subsequent desertion (punishable by execution, often public shooting) to bring information back to the north.

He rejoined McClellan's army when they went down the Atlantic coast that April, disembarked and made for Richmond, stopping scant miles outside the capital. In late June and early July the Northern army was driven from the area by the brilliant leadership of Robert E. Lee in a series of brutal battles called "The Seven Days." These horrific struggles were fought in and around the Chickahominy River, often in the low-lying swamps of the area (which the engineers desperately tried to straddle with their pontoon bridges). Farini claimed he actually went into battle that week and was injured at an engagement he called "Chickahominy Swamps." He said his wound was a slight one, to a leg, though it obviously did not hinder him entirely as he also claimed to have fought in the Second Battle of Bull Run during the last two days of August as the Northern army pulled back toward Washington, frightened by Lee's northern thrust.

Bull Run was another loss for the North and weeks later, after the bloodiest engagement of a bloody war, at Antietam Creek, Maryland, where dead soldiers were so numerous on the field it was impossible to walk about without stepping on them, Lincoln had had enough, on two accounts. Though Antietam forced the withdrawal of Lee from Maryland and was not technically a loss for McClellan, his failure to crush the rebels while he had them completely outnumbered (a fact he constantly refused to recognize) gave Lincoln more evidence that he should fire him, and by the end of the first week of November he did. Simultaneously, the retreat of the rebels from the north allowed him to act with strength on another issue. He freed the slaves; or at least, he began an irreversible move in that direction. His Emancipation Proclamation, issued late in September, to become law on January 1, 1863, declared free all slaves held in states actively in rebellion. Lincoln's two controversial moves did not sit well with Farini, and by the time McClellan was gone, so was he.

Farini's decision *vis-à-vis* McClellan was understandable—many other soldiers felt similar loyalty to their chief—but his action concerning the slavery question seems more disturbing. And that was emphasized by a story he later told about being robbed by his black servant around this time and being especially embittered by it. And yet there were instances in his life, some already documented, when he was concerned about the treatment of black people. He had the typical attitude of his age about the superiority of white men, but compared to many of his contemporaries, could actually be open-minded. His objection to the Emancipation Proclamation was likely mostly political in nature. Many others from the north, four-square against slavery (as Farini most certainly was), had supported Stephen Douglas during the 1860 election and felt that Lincoln's uncompromising position led to an unneeded and ghastly war. The proclamation was sternly opposed by many Douglas Democrats as continued provocation of former allies when compromise and calm, to their way of thinking, should have been the order of the day. This would be precisely the spirit of George McClellan's 1864 platform in his run for the Presidency.

By early November Farini had left Washington and the war. The true nature of his exploits while connected to the Northern army may never be known. There is no ultimate proof of his stories, no military records for a Captain William L. Hunt or Farini in the 15th New York Engineers, although several newspapers reported his involvement, his inventions, his exhibition before Lincoln, etc.; and the following year the *Niagara Falls Gazette* referred to him as Captain Hunt. These things, coupled with his personal reminiscences about character quirks in Murphy, and other obviously first-hand accounts of other men (all real people situated in exactly the right place and time), are enough to verify at least some of his story, though his imagination may have gotten the best of him at times and stretched parts of his military career into the realm of fiction.

If he thought by quitting the war he would leave pain and tragedy behind, he was badly mistaken. Some time in mid-November he and Mary (Signora Farini) were steaming out of an east coast harbour, heading for Cuba. Anxious to resume his career, knowing that it was out of season for circuses in the north and that performing anywhere in the southern states was out of the question, he felt the best place to go was Havana. But as usual he was pushing things too hard: he should have waited, or spent more time working the act with Mary before starting out again, because this trip would prove to be the greatest mistake of his life and contain a moment of terror that would haunt him forever.

CHAPTER 11

Death and Resurrection

*"The history of William Hunt's life, from my knowledge
as given to me by my mother, was not the best."*
Mary Osborne's nephew, A.E. Hacker, 1948

"Desgracia!"
Diario de la Marina, Havana, Cuba, December 2, 1862

Cuba and its burgeoning Havana, close to the United States by boat and booming with tourism in the 1850s, had actually been an inviting spot for circus acts for a number of years prior to the American Civil War, despite its shortcomings. More than half the people on this Spanish-owned island were either slave or "coloured," and the constant threat of a violent revolution led by slaves or native Cubans seeking independence was kept in check by 40,000 Spanish troops and sometimes brutal governors. Like a sheen over this misery, things appeared to be prospering. Havana, with a quarter of a million people, had some of the world's most luxurious hotels, a university with an associated medical school, a botanical gardens, two main avenues "as wide as they were long," an Imperial Lottery that could net anyone as much as $180,000 and four theatres (the Tacon was larger than La Scala in Milan). And on nearly any given day you could go to the circus.

Signor and Signora Farini sailed into the city's nearly circular harbour in November 1862 and gazed at one of the most beautiful panoramas in the world, with its deep blue foreground, beige Spanish architecture, palm trees lining the shore, and lush green hills forming the background. Somewhere behind that gorgeous skyline, hidden just like the cruelties in Cuban life, was the city's bull-ring, Plaza de Toros de la Habana, a place Farini would soon want to forget.

Among notices for the Italian Opera at the Tacon and Chiarini's Circus, the *Diario de la Marina* of November 29th announced that Signor Farini had strung a rope from one side to the other of the bull-ring roof and on Sunday the 30th would cross it, amazing the crowd by standing on his head, hanging by his feet, walking in peach baskets and inside a sack, and going through manoeuvres with a chair. Curiously, there was no mention of his wife.

The Plaza de Toros was an impressive structure, with a sixty-foot-high circular wall and thirty thousand seats descending in tiers. The distance across the ring was said to be so extensive that two brass bands could play at either end without confusion. At ground level an eight-foot wall, strong and thick, barricaded the spectators from danger. The choice seats for the Farinis' show were two pesos each, but you could get a seat in the general section for sixty centavos on the shady side and fifty in the sun. And of course, children, soldiers and coloured people were allowed in at half-price.

Things started well: the Signor ascended to the top of the wall and made four passages, back and forth, without incident. Then Mrs. Farini appeared and he lifted her onto his back and started out on the long journey across the huge expanse. The introduction of a woman into a dangerous performance always frightened audiences, without a doubt the reason why there were so many such acts, and the crowd at the bull-ring that day was noticeably nervous, watching the pair moving slowly along the high wire, the gentleman's muscles showing through his tights and the lady looking fragile and feminine in her translucent dress. Out they went, sixty feet over the seats and down the incline across the ring, and then up again over the other seats toward their perch on the opposite wall. As they approached safety the crowd began to relax, and in a communal feeling of relief and admiration, a burst of spontaneous applause rose throughout the stadium. The Farinis were just four feet from the perch; they could almost touch it.

At that instant Mary made a deadly decision: she decided to wave. It was just a slight motion to the crowd, meant to be casual, but a rope-walker's cardinal sin: a jerking action that was unrehearsed. She loosened her grip on her husband's neck and in the instant her hands came up and her weight shifted, she was falling. She screamed as she tipped away from his back and felt herself dropping, head downward, shrieking for his help so loudly that the audience could hear each word. A sense of horror transfixed the crowd as Farini tried desperately, in the split second available to him, to save his dearest friend. In a lightning move he released the balance pole and shot his arm back, his hand searching for the descending body...and he caught her!

Gripping her dress in one fist he held on tightly and fell with her until the back of his knee hooked around the wire. The Great Farini had more than enough strength to hold a human being in the air with one arm and he tensed his powerful muscles to meet the need. But the dress, that beautiful dress of light fabric, tore in an agonizing, ripping sound as her full weight pulled downward against it...and she was gone, spiralling away from him as he clutched at thin air, her piercing scream now mixing with screams from the crowd. Farini hung there, looking straight at Mary as she dropped. She hit the seats with a sickening thud, her head crashing against them and her body flopping sideways. For an instant she rose, staggering like a clubbed animal, and then collapsed.

Confusion reigned in the bull-ring, but she was soon gathered up, blood pouring from a horrible wound in her skull. Those who helped her were convinced she was dying, but she was still breathing so they took her to a house in the wealthy part of the city. The best doctors were sent for and the next day they actually thought she was doing better, though privately they were convinced she had suffered terrible injuries to her brain and would never recover her mental faculties if she lived.

Two days later she was still alive and a report circulated that she might be recovering, but soon she regressed and each day throughout that week the worst was feared. Finally, at six o'clock Friday morning, December 5th, she died.

One can only imagine Farini's feelings. Despite the many accomplishments of the last few years, and the terrors he had faced without flinching, and all the bravado he displayed in public, mustered from decades of feeling that he had something to prove to the world, his twenty-four-year-old soul must have been shaken to its very foundations. He had always considered himself invulnerable: a kind of magic shield had protected him, even when he pushed himself beyond the reasonable bounds of safety. Now, as his father had warned him, tragedy had struck. He was sitting alone in that house in Havana, people whispering in Spanish all around him as they came to pay their respects; it was three weeks before Christmas and in a bed across the room his disfigured friend, a farm-girl from home, lay white and breathless.

It was said that some of the biggest personalities in Havana came to console Signor Farini. Likely they were stars of the entertainment world and a number of wealthy, respectable people, a class of citizen to whom Farini gravitated wherever he went; like his father he craved status, and because of his father's criticisms he needed it. Young ladies from the Lladeros, Vega and Junco families all in the company of their mothers, helped soothe the dying Madame Farini, and when she breathed her last it was announced by Signor Francesco Castanos that he would donate a plot in the general cemetery, so that she might be buried without difficulties on Saturday afternoon. A horse and buggy, and other funeral amenities were also donated, as Havanans rallied around the devastated young man.

A few days after the funeral he circulated a letter to the press. In it he wrote of his loneliness and expressed his deepest thanks to the "charitable men and holy women" who had come to his aid. He called the afternoon of November 30th "unforgettable," the day when he had lost someone "who in the world was my dear wife." Proclaiming that his heart was theirs forever, he signed the letter Guillermo Farini, the first-known appearance of the first name he would carry for the rest of his life.

On Sunday the 14th, in an act that would have horrified his parents, he did something else that indicated the depths of his sorrow and the impression the kindness of his hosts had made upon him. He was baptised and accepted into the Roman Catholic Church. The service took place at the Iglesia de Guadelupe and was a major social event in Havana, attracting a crowd so large it could barely squeeze into the church, as well as a great deal of press coverage. His godparents were First Lieutenant D. Antonio Lladeros and his wife and it was reported that he "kept" his name. (When his godfather's name is considered, along with the signature on his public letter, it might be speculated that this was when he took his full name: Guillermo Antonio Farini.) After the one-hour service in which a short mass was said and the baptismal candidate was said to look "pleased and satisfied," the guests left the church in a procession of a dozen or more hansoms and made their way to the Lladeros home. Here 250 people enjoyed a sumptuous banquet and applauded when the President of San Vincente de Paul Church conference gave the new Catholic two medals.

Farini stayed in Havana for a long time after the death of his wife. He had an extraordinary faculty for picking up languages and was fluent in as many as seven (and probably capable in a few more) by the time he died: this period in Cuba may have been the beginning of his linguistic endeavours. Later in December it was announced that portraits of Signor and Signora Farini were available at various Havana photography shops and in the second week of January 1863 the great Cuban circus impresario Chiarini informed the press that he would stage a benefit at which the distraught rope-walker would perform. This shows the indefatigable Farini spirit, pushing himself to get back on the wire.

The benefit took place at Chiarini's massive new 2,500-seat indoor theatre on January 16th and featured two of the circus greats of the time: the equestrienne Madame Loyalle and her male counterpart James Robinson. Farini's performance was understandably tentative. He was the beneficiary of two more shows in January and on February 1st, returned the favour by headlining the circus again.

All of these benefits, and a report that $15,000 to $20,000 was to be raised for him by subscription after his wife died, indicates that there was some concern about his finances. Freshly released from a year's stint in the U.S. Army he may have come to Havana without much money and the death of his performing partner may have temporarily put his career in jeopardy. There was also a rumour in the city that the couple had a small child and the money raised was to be for its benefit. If they did have an infant, then there are only two possibilities concerning its fate: either it died soon after its mother, or it was a little boy they had adopted expressly for the purpose of one day incorporating him into their act. Less than two years later a child billed as "Alphonse" worked a few dates in Farini's act and in the mid-1860s a boy protégé would begin to emerge as a star of the Flying Farinis. That boy, under Farini's guidance, would eventually achieve international fame, performing before royalty and headlining the greatest circuses in the world. But his story, a bizarre one to say the least, is still a few years away. If there was a child left with Farini in Cuba, then there is no certainty that he was this future international celebrity.

For now, Farini moved on, for all intents and purposes alone again.

Though it is difficult to be certain where he went, there is some evidence that some time in February he embarked on a six-month journey to South America, Mexico and the west coast of the United States. After his tragedy, this was preferable to going back to the big cities of the eastern states or home to Hope Township. He needed to get away.

In his old age Farini became a storyteller. He was well suited to it: knowledgeable about everything, possessed of one of history's great imaginations and psychologically in need of self-promotion. But whenever he told his life story, the death of his wife was never touched upon, instead he liked to recount how he left the army some time in the early 1860s and was immediately afflicted with a kind of wanderlust. He told one reporter he "...went to California... Old Mexico, Central America, Venezuelas, Brazil and Chile." Bearing in mind his Havana tragedy, these statements conjure up the image of a rather lost young man "wandering" across two continents searching for himself. He probably travelled wherever his heart took him, not working strictly as a professional performer, just giving occasional ascensions whenever he ran out of money: a kind of hired gun in a dangerous business, in the land and time of hired guns.

Though he would have travelled through romantic places like Rio de Janeiro, Buenos Aires and Santiago and had the opportunity to perform in luxurious theatres where ladies were known to peer at circus performers through silver opera glasses, there was also a good deal of hardship in such a trip. Most of the travelling was by sea where shipwrecks and seasickness were common and on land where few railways existed: crossing the tail of the Andes to get to Chile, for example, meant an arduous ride on the back of a mule. Sanitation was poor in most places, poverty rampant and yellow fever abounded, inflicting its dreaded and often fatal "black vomit" most readily on foreigners. Many circus performers lost their lives on such trips. But Farini was in a reckless mood, now not worried in the least about others' judgements of his lifestyle, desperately needing adventure, anonymous in a place distant from Mary's death and that strict Anglo-Saxon world he had left so long ago.

It would have taken him about four months to get around South America and back up through Mexico to the

California coast; his most probable destination was San Francisco.

San Francisco was America's first prominent west-coast city, having exploded into the big time due to the late forties' gold rush. Farini saw a bustling metropolis in 1863, filled with dandies, cowboys and adventurers, and a thriving entertainment scene, with beautiful theatres, an opera house and visiting stars. That very summer the exotic Adah Isaacs Menken made her west-coast debut in the play "Mazeppa," causing as big a sensation as any performer has ever created anywhere. In this play her famously voluptuous body was clad in skimpy clothing (critics liked to say she was nude) as she bounced seductively around the stage hanging sideways with legs splayed, strapped to a galloping horse. Many other big stars and circuses came through the area. Signor Cristoforo Buono Core, the "Great Italian Salamander" or "Fire King" who walked through fire and kindled great interest wherever he went, appeared there in June 1863 and Professor Simmons, the "King of Conjurors" performed a few months later; both men would be connected with Farini's career the very next year.

Later in life Farini wrote a short story about a romantic liaison that took place in San Francisco and continued in Mexico. There is a Colonel, a beautiful young lady and a duel involved, elements all very fitting when the gold-rush city is one's background.

From the Bay area Farini would have been able to go only a short distance east by rail and then would have had to cross the great western plains by stagecoach. In 1863 this was still a hazardous adventure, as being attacked by Indians or wild animals was not uncommon. One only needs to read the account of Sir Richard Francis Burton (the British adventurer who had many characteristics in common with Farini), who took the same stagecoach route a few years earlier and shaved his head to make himself a less attractive target for scalping. This was the land of real cowboys, sheriffs and outlaws, many toting six-guns.

As Kansas and Missouri drew near, so did the railroads,

and Farini's trip from there to Buffalo passed much quicker. By the end of July he was back in the Niagara area and very much himself again, evidenced by the plan he was developing for his next feat. He notified the public that he was considering walking through the rapids at the top of one of the falls, on steel stilts. So bizarre was this feat that the New York *Sunday Mercury* published his contemplations, with an exclamation point. The fact that he didn't follow through with his plan did not mean he gave up on it, as later events would show.

Then he went home. The reunion on the front porch of his parents' farmhouse must have been difficult. He was now an ancient twenty-five-year-old, grizzled by his war experiences, the loss of his wife and a six-month trip which had taken him more places and shown him more things than Hope Township residents would see or possibly even hear about in their lifetimes. He took a few weeks off and went hunting with friends. Whether he avoided the nearby Osborne family or commiserated with them is unknown. As the days passed he again saw how irretrievably different he was from the people with whom he had grown up: to him they lived false lives, afraid to explore their passions. He felt the itch to move again, to get away from little Hope. If the horrific death of his wife had been a message from God to slow down, then he was ignoring it. He was hooked on excitement.

He left before Christmas came, going to visit friends in Niagara Falls before heading down to the United States to resume his career in as big a way as possible. Toward that end he paid a visit to the *Gazette* offices some time around December 20th. A few days later they told the public that Captain Hunt, better known as Signor Farini, had been to see them. Apparently they asked him what he considered his occupation to be.

He replied with a single word: "pangymnastikonaero-stationist."

CHAPTER 12

Pangymnastikonaerostationist

*"The feats...were truly wonderful—bordering on
the horrible—do not fail to see them tonight."*
Chicago Evening Journal, March 25, 1865,
on the Farini-Simmons show

T he fad for using long names in show business in the
early 1860s began with the Hanlon Brothers and
their creation, in late 1861, of the "zampillaerostation," a
variation on Leotard's "flying trapeze." Leotard was a
gifted French acrobat whose brief but brilliant career was
highlighted by his transformation of one of the most basic
gymnastic acts (the stationary performance on rings or a
high bar) into a death-defying thrill act in which he used
several trapeze bars instead of one, leaping and swinging
from one to the other. He gave the world the name (leotards) for thin tights and the song, "The Man on the
Flying Trapeze," and often crossed paths with Farini. The
Hanlons, immensely talented themselves, thought that if
their act were not totally original then they could at least
find an original name for it. Thus, the zampillaerostation
(performed of course, by a zampillaerostateur).

Soon there was talk of prestipedestrioptimism, basili-
conthaumaturgists and salamandrogymnasticoaeron
entertainments, making mere funambulism seem down-
right simple. The first had something to do with foot
races, the second was the name the magician Simmons,
Farini's soon-to-be colleague, gave to himself, and the

third was the act of the aforementioned Signor Core, the Fire King, who would be appearing with Farini in the summer of 1864.

What an opportunity these "chain-cable" names presented to a mind like Farini's: his pangymnastikonaerostationist and the later, amended, duopangymnastikon-aerostationist were the longest names of all. And soon he would create another tongue-twister for one of his gymnastic feats, the wonderful and indecipherable: perilosco-palanquisayre.

Until this point in his career he had essentially been just a rope-walker, though he occasionally did his strongman act, the physical-fitness lecture, and showed off his gymnastic skills at mid-wire. But his restless brain was pushing him to expand his repertoire: and from this year onward he began experimenting with different feats, starting an adventure in show-business history that would take him nearly thirty years to exhaust and bring spectators around the world an array of startling performances. His new act was everything its huge title suggested: a series of stationary and moving high-wire and gymnastic feats. It wouldn't be a simple thrill act as in earlier days, but an exhibition of the skills of a scientifically trained acrobat in a whole range of serious athletic endeavours. As well as being good theatre, it addressed his need to show off his intelligence and appear more respectable.

His journey into the States brought him to New York by June 1864. The last time he'd been here war fever was gripping the city and he had rushed in and out on his way home from the South, but this time he stayed much longer and the mood, almost exactly a year after victory at the Battle of Gettysburg and in the early days of Sherman's hellish march through the Confederacy, was much different. A sense of optimism was in the air. Well over a million people now lived in New York and it was the centre of most everything in North America, including the entertainment industry. Dozens of newspapers and magazines, led by Horace Greely's *New York Daily Tribune*, not only

influenced the New York area but much of the country.
And the theatre and circus business had their own papers,
like *The New York Clipper* and the *Sunday Mercury*. The
city's many opulent theatres were filled daily; on any
given night spectators might have a choice between seeing the voluptuous Menken on her steed, the legendary
tragedian Edwin Booth in his own theatre, Blondin on the
high wire at posh Niblo's Garden or Dan Rice with one of
his many circuses. And on July 1st at a new building
called the Hippotheatron, down on 14th Street near 4th
Avenue and the Academy of Music you could see a
"Cluster of Stars," and one of the marquee acts was a
troupe called the Farini Brothers.

The Hippotheatron had been opened on February 8th of
that year, the first permanent structure in the United
States built solely for the circus. Made almost entirely of
corrugated iron, 75 feet high where it touched the cupola
at its peak, 110 feet in diameter and fronted with a beautiful Italian portico, it was an imposing structure from the
outside, but inside it was nearly surreal: a pale pink
groundwork flecked with blue and gold lay under an
unusually large ring; there were two huge entrances opposite each other like ramps for gladiators, 2,000 seats rising in tiers and a 9-foot-tall, 40-foot-diameter chandelier
hanging high above the ring. When the chandelier was
glowing and the circle of lights that were attached to the
building's main posts were at full power, the variety of
light playing off the iron on the domed ceiling created a
magical backdrop for the high-speed entertainment below.

At the end of May, Spaulding and Rogers Ocean Circus
finished their run and the building closed for a month
before reopening with a collection of stars management
hoped would draw big crowds. In addition to the Farinis,
the two other headliners were Monsieur Louis Verrecke, a
superlative Belgian trapeze artiste who had been a sensation on the east coast the previous year with his original,
hair-raising feat of hanging from a swinging trapeze solely
by the nape of his neck as he played on a snare drum, and
Signor Core, the "Salamandrine Hero of the Universe"

who presented his "Carbohydrogyn Ordeal, in which he will stand, whilst Saturated With Inflammable Fluid in the midst of One Thousand Flaming Jets of Gas."

As for the Farini Brothers, there were apparently three of them: the Signor, "the Hero of Niagara, in his New Acts—the Marvellous Bars in the Air, the Goliath Swing, Giant Leap, and Novel Wire-Funabulism"; Carlo Farini, "the Herculean Gymnast and Great Indian Club Swinger, using clubs weighing 50 lbs. each"; and Enrico Farini, "the Athlete of the Arena, in Novel Acts of Strength and Grace." Carlo and Enrico also performed something called the "Wild Cossack Athletes." Exactly who these "brothers" were is difficult to know. This was one of very few performances. The mischievous Farini loved deception and it is possible that two of the siblings were none other than the Signor himself.

He performed alone early in his career but was now beginning his days as a manager and teacher, something for which he was well suited. His protégé(s) had obviously been taught very Farini-like tricks of strength and agility, in Carlo's case, even bringing weights on stage for a kind of strong-man exhibition. Farini's own act still centred around funambulism but now, as he was careful to point out, he walked on an actual wire (and he claimed he was the only performer doing so), one less than the width of a finger. The "Bars in the Air" showed off his substantial gymnastic skills and the Goliath Swing and Giant Leap incorporated both his power and suppleness. The title "Herculean Gymnast," which he had given to Carlo, was an apt description of Farini's unique skills at this time.

The Salamandrogymnasticoaeron entertainment stayed for about a week in New York, appearing right through another emotional 4th of July, and being "greeted nightly by unbounded applause." Then they went their separate ways: Verrecke to various dates in the States; Core to more fire-defying moments before large crowds, until two years later he publicly burned to death while performing in France; and Signor Farini, whom the *New York Daily News* had just dubbed, "the prince of acrobats and balancers," to

Niagara Falls, with one of history's most bizarre ideas prodding his imagination.

Back when Bill Hunt was twenty years old, that strange newspaper article about someone performing the impossible feat of walking along the edge of the American Falls on stilts had caught his and just about everybody else's imagination. Not long afterward another reporter discovered a legend about natives doing something similar. He found the story in a letter two friends had exchanged in 1750. It claimed that twelve years earlier:

...two Iroquois Indians, fishing above the Falls, were cast on to the island. It was seven days before their condition became known. The Commandant, when he came to the spot, ordered poles to be made pointed with iron. Two Indians determined to walk to the island by the help of these poles, to save the other poor creatures, or perish in the attempt. They took leave of their friends as if going to certain death. Each had two such poles in his hands, to set against the bottom to keep them steady. So they went, and got to the island, and having given poles to the Indians there, they all returned safely to the main land. Those two Indians, who, in the above mentioned manner, were first brought to the island, are yet alive. The Indians go to the island now to kill deer, but if the King of France were to give me all Canada I would not.

If this legend is true, then such perilous walks were not continued, since there were no reports in the 1850s from elderly Niagara residents that the Iroquois had walked the rapids at any time during anyone's memory. The only other story of a human being making it out into the rapids is verifiable. Joel Robinson, the same fearless gentleman who took the Maid of the Mist through the whirlpool, apparently walked into the water at the top of the Falls some time around the Blondin-Farini duels just to prove that it was possible. He took with him an iron-pointed staff to steady himself and albeit only went a short distance out, but nevertheless there he stood for a few minutes before retreating back to the shore. A marvellous photograph preserved his feat for posterity.

In mid-July 1864 Signor Farini arrived at Niagara and gave notice that he was thinking about trying the impossible. What he was considering wasn't a stroll along the narrow hundred-yard-plus route a third of a mile up the river in calmer rapids as the Iroquois tried, or edging out a short distance and then coming back like Robinson; he wanted the fantasy itself...walking along the brink of Niagara Falls. A New York sporting journal commented, "To accomplish such a feat requires considerable nerve, and if he succeeds in crossing safely he will have accomplished one of the most daring feats ever attempted in this country."

It must be remembered that the rapids and the falls at Niagara were very different in 1864 than they are in the twentieth century. Today six million cubic feet of water pour over the two falls every minute and the rapids reach a speed of about forty-two miles an hour near the crest, and yet, in the middle part of the nineteenth century, before the diversions for hydro-electric power, the falls and their rapids not only had more volume but were faster and much louder. Even though Niagara still empties the greatest volume of water over its cliffs of any cataract on the earth, experts claim that the spectacle is now but a shadow of what it once was.

It was into the teeth of this cascading mass of thunder that Farini proposed to go.

At first his public statements seemed a bit tentative. For example, he told a reporter on the 27th that he "would attempt the passage of the rapids to Goat Island on stilts if satisfactory arrangements could be made," and added that if it did not seem possible to try this feat he would present another kind of performance. He had been at the Falls for more than a week by then, making trips back and forth across the rapids (via the bridge) analyzing the water's speed, depth and bedrock, and trying to figure out just exactly how or if this feat might be accomplished. It is likely that by the 27th he had made a few short trips out into the rapids, toying with the idea of starting from Goat Island and crossing back to the shore, testing the effectiveness of his "steel stilts" and seeing if a pike pole would be useful. The stilts were another of his inventions and not entirely made of steel. They were about six feet long and made of ash poles fastened into two shafts of steel, which were pointed at the bottom to stick into the riverbed. His lower legs and feet were strapped to the wood. Most of the stilts would be beneath the surface of the rapids (which were at least five feet deep) and at a distance he would appear to be walking on water. He delayed a definite announcement not only because he wasn't sure if the feat was possible, but also to make it financially feasible and gauge public interest. For two weeks he continued studying, practising and modifying, starting his rehearsals before 5 a.m. so that few saw what he was doing.

Then early Monday morning, August 8th, the incredible happened.

There were many opinions about what he really did that day. Here, as nearly as can be ascertained from a comparison of all accounts, is what actually took place.

By the evening of the 7th Farini was convinced the feat was possible and he knew exactly how he was going to do it. The crossing would take place on the 15th, but first he would perform a dress rehearsal at dawn on the 8th.

In the dark hours of that morning he dressed himself in his circus tights in his room at his old friend Fulton's International Hotel near the American shore, gathered up his strange-looking stilts and headed out into the darkness with a few assistants and a group of friends. They took the bridge over to Goat Island and went through the woods until they were right next to the Falls, close to a place called Point View. Farini strapped himself into his stilts, picked up his pike pole and stepped carefully into the raging water.

It was a terrible, exhilarating moment: as he glanced over his left shoulder he could see out over the brink to a drop that looked as though it had no bottom and a vast expanse of sky. His plan was to always keep close to land during this perilous opening stretch, when he was but a stone's throw from the edge. Fifty or more shaky steps brought him across Bridal Veil, the little waterfall created by the nearness of tiny Luna Island to the shore. Now the roar of the Falls was so thunderous that a shout at the top of his lungs would not have been heard by his assistants on land. He headed north-west along the coast of Luna keeping within a safe distance of its shore until he reached the northern tip where he carefully turned and crossed toward larger Robinson's Island. He set each stilt down slowly, edging its point into the bedrock, bracing his powerful legs against the force of the water. He came within twenty feet of Robinson's and started going past its northernmost point. He had now gone about seven hundred feet, more than half the distance across, and there was nothing but open water between himself and the American shoreline. It was a daunting stretch to cross, without land nearby, but he was now far from the brink and hoped from here he could race to safety.

The preparations for this dress rehearsal, complete with inevitable little problems, had taken him a bit longer than usual, so now the sun was starting to come up and there were a few early risers near the shore. What they saw when they looked out across the American cataract looked like a dream: a man walking on water in the rapids of Niagara Falls!

Then suddenly, the man seemed in desperate trouble.

Just north of Robinson's Island he had taken a careful step with a stilt and plunged the pointed steel tip deep into a crevice in the bedrock. Then he took a step with the other stilt, but when he tried to lift the first one it wouldn't move. He tried again...it wouldn't budge. For long, agonizing minutes he tried to wrest it free, but the steel tip seemed permanently lodged in the rock in the middle of the rapids, and he with it. Finally, with no other alternative, he tried a desperate pull, using all his body weight. He threw himself off balance, swaying backward, forward...and then fell face down into the rapids.

Never, during any of his feats, had he been this close to death. He saw nothing but a blur, the water pounded in his ears and the world began to spin. Summoning all his strength he frantically snapped the jammed stilt off, then did the same with the other, desperate to free himself. But the instant he was loose the water picked him up...and shot him toward the edge! Below the surface he drove a foot into the rocks and dug the pike pole in. Like an enraged murderer the rapids pulled him, trying to rip him out and sweep him over the brink.

He looked up and saw Robinson's Island; it was fifty feet away in the mist. He decided his only chance was to make for it.

How long he struggled in the rapids is hard to know, but it was at least half an hour and may have been as long as two hours. How any human being could survive for this long in Niagara's rapids is difficult to fathom. It took enormous strength and presence of mind, an indomitable will to survive. Years earlier a man named Avery had been marooned on a rock almost at the spot where Farini was now stuck. He had eventually let go and gone to his death. Many human beings had fallen into the rapids over the years—none had survived.

Farini took a step toward the island, tensing his big leg muscles, now well submerged under the water. He drove the pike pole into the river bottom. Slowly he worked his way back to his destination. On the shoreline the excitement was intense: women were screaming, hotel guests were running toward the rapids, and others were shouting encouragement, scampering along the shoreline as if it might help the man in the rapids, give him the momentum he needed. Some headed for the bridge to get a better view of another Niagara execution.

But Farini wasn't giving up. The Niagara was no different than his parents or his classmates or Mr. King or the old croaking grumblers back home who said he would never do well, that his thirst for excitement was a curse.

But after struggling to within fifteen feet of Robinson's Island he was completely exhausted. The strength to take one more step or even hold himself upright in the current was gone. He looked downstream at the island...and threw himself headfirst into the water. The rapids took him like a rag doll, sucking him toward the precipice, smashing him against rocks, his head thudding into stone. His eyes searched frantically for the island...and suddenly there it was, bouncing around in his sightline, going past him as he went toward the edge. At the last moment he reached one weary arm up, felt the branch of an over-hanging bush rush by his hand, and made a desperate grasping motion. He caught it!

His legs and trunk whipped past the bush but he held on for dear life. Hanging here fifty yards from the edge he tried to calm himself, hoping his grip and the branch would hold. Then he reached for a final burst of energy and tried to pull himself ashore. Slowly he was able to get partially onto land. With another pull he dragged himself to safety.

But safe for how long?

He lay there face down on the ground, his whole frame heaving, unable to hear the shouts of the people watching him. Finally he lifted himself, staggered over to a log and sat down. As the shock slowly left him and the adrenalin subsided, his injuries starting making themselves known. One leg was nearly numb, but it was his throbbing arm that really worried him: he clutched it and pressed on it, rocking back and forth. As he rocked he reminded himself that he had to clear his mind and think. He hoped his friends on the shoreline were doing the same. He had just walked across a little stretch of land that no human being had ever set a foot upon. How in God's name was he going to get off alive?

He sat a long time, desperate to know if his friends had any ideas.

As word went out from Niagara that Farini was marooned on Robinson's Island, more people started com-ing to the spot. Soon there was a huge crowd, covering every vantage point on the shorelines and jamming the bridge upstream. Most were frightened by what they saw, but many were fascinated, and of course there were young

rowdies who took the opportunity to shout catcalls. The
newspaper reporters came in droves to this editor's
dream. Farini was still stranded when they went to press
in the evening, so they all reported the story as a cata-
strophe-in-progress; one paper even suggested that those
who didn't believe it and wanted to see for themselves
should run to the next train and get to the Falls. Not only
Buffalo, Rochester and Niagara papers followed his
predicament, but soon there was a front-page story
("Terrible Scene at Niagara Falls") in *The Daily Leader* of
Toronto, articles in nearly every Canadian city, and full
reports in the New York papers (some on front pages); and
slowly the story crept through the U.S. and into Europe.
The *Times* of London exclaimed he was in "A Perilous
Position.") Many assumed he was doomed: like the
Montreal Gazette whose headline "Fate of An Acrobat"
summed up their feelings. A slow and horrible death was
anticipated. Several spoke of starvation and the grotesque
spectacle of the huge crowd, some only eight hundred feet
away, watching Farini emaciate and expire, pound by
pound, everyone powerless to help.

But by the afternoon of that first "frightful" day, the
object of everyone's concern appeared about as unconcerned
as could be. *The World* (New York) said he sat on his log
like "patience on a monument, waiting for someone to build
a bridge or turn off the river." His wounds were feeling better and he was seen rising from his seat and moving
around, flexing his limbs. To everyone's astonishment, he
soon started exercising and before long he was standing on
his head. It was typical Farini: keep as cool as possible, use
your brains, get your body ready to meet the challenge.

All sorts of rumours were circulating about preparations
to save him. It was said that Robinson himself was building a boat to get him off and that all day his assistants had
been attempting to throw him a rope. The latter turned
out to be true, but their throws, made from Bath Island
(over which the bridge ran) were in vain. Finally, Farini's
"brother" decided that a desperate measure was needed, so
he tentatively waded out a short distance from the island

(apparently up past his waist in water) clutching a cord which was held firmly by others on land, until he came to a huge log that sat between Robinson's and the nearby paper-mill. From here he made several attempts to throw a sealed pail of food to Farini, and finally succeeded. But it was nearly nightfall by then and any rescue attempt would have to wait until the following day.

By noon August 10th the crowds had thinned considerably as interest began to wane, despite the fact that they were now being treated to the sight of Farini standing on his head on the topmost limb of the highest tree on the island. His assistants decided on a plan of action. They succeeded in getting another rope to him, attached a larger rope to it (the end of which they secured to a tree) and then waited for Farini, knowing that he knew what he had to do. A short while later the veritable "Robinson Crusoe" was seen coming their way using the rope as his support. It is known that he tied his end of the rope to a tree on Robinson's but it is unclear whether he walked on the rope or in the rapids. However he did it, in a short while he was on Bath Island and the ordeal was over. It was 5 p.m. when he reached safety: he had spent more than thirty-five hours in exile.

Controversy swirled around this feat almost from the moment it started. Many refused to believe it had happened, simply because they deemed it impossible. Others contended that he had not walked on stilts but had reached the island by other means and used his imprisonment there as a publicity stunt: he could have come off the island at any moment. These critics took to calling his adventure the "Farini Hoax" and went so far as to suggest that he had left the island in the dead of night and slept soundly at the International before going back out in the early morning. It was also said that he wasn't practising, as he claimed, but had failed in what was intended to be a very public presentation.

Farini was an expert at humbug, but it isn't likely that he was trying to fool people this time, at least not with the basic facts. He had told others he would give his first

performance on the 15th and since his August 8th walk
was commenced in the dark hours of the early morning,
one can hardly accuse him of lying about whether or not
this was a practice run. As to whether or not he used
stilts: several people, excluding his friends, saw him on
stilts in the midst of the rapids. Further, a greater number saw him struggling above Robinson's Island and making his desperate rush to grasp the branch that saved
him. And the idea that he came off the island (presumably
some time past midnight) and then went back out after a
short sleep is preposterous: getting to that island, whether
by boat, rope, stilts, on foot or any other means was very
close to impossible—he would hardly try it twice in one
night for the sake of a few hours of restless sleep. A few
days after his feat he issued a statement to the press,
signed by thirty-three witnesses, verifying his (albeit
slightly inflated) version of what had happened.

The only criticism which may be well founded is that he
might have been able to come off the island sooner than
he did, that once he and his cohorts had figured out how
a rescue could be made, they decided to milk the publicity
for all it was worth.

Farini of course attributed the criticisms to the echoes
of the old croakers: he had made a spectacle of himself in
a feat that had no point to it, of pure adventure and showmanship; that was nearly unforgivable. But Farini wasn't
pausing to worry about his critics: he was off to Ottawa,
with another extraordinary idea in mind.

When he arrived on August 19, 1864, Ottawa was only
nominally the capital of the two united British provinces
of Canada East and West. It would be slightly more than
a year before government members and officials reluctantly made their way from beautiful old Quebec City to
the rough, lumber town in the wilderness on the Ottawa
River. It had been such a surprising choice for the permanent capital (given the Montreal, Toronto, Quebec and
Kingston alternatives) that a legend evolved that Queen
Victoria chose it in a kind of pin-the-tail-on-the-donkey

trick: closing her eyes and sticking a pin on the map. In 1859 construction began on the Parliament buildings on a hill overlooking the river downstream from Chaudière Falls. They were plagued by cost overruns and delays and were far from finished when Farini hit town, though the exteriors were almost completed and their outlines were visible from a great distance. They were beautiful examples of Gothic revival architecture and the setting was truly spectacular. But the muddy lumber town of some 16,000 that surrounded it was anything but attractive. Its crisp northern air was often black with the smoke of ten sawmills, its Irish and French-Canadian lumbermen brawled constantly in the absence of a police force, lumber piles and sawdust were everywhere, and the incessant and irritating whine of the big saws provided a sort of soundtrack to daily activity.

Farini, now not an unwealthy fellow, booked himself into the town's most prestigious hotel, the Russell House, just a stone's throw from the construction site and soon to be a popular watering hole for prime ministers. He had come to Ottawa because it was in the news. A conference of British North American politicians was then convening in Charlottetown, Prince Edward Island to discuss the possibility of uniting all the British provinces into a single country named Canada. It was sensational news and made politics the chief topic on everyone's lips. Little Ottawa might soon be not just the capital of two Canadian provinces, but headquarters for a huge new nation. Farini saw an opportunity: a spectacular high-wire performance here would not go unnoticed nationally and even internationally. His first idea was to use the new buildings and the Rideau Canal, which cut into the land nearby, as backdrops for another daredevil crossing. It was announced on August 20th that his intention was to string a cable directly from Parliament Hill across the canal to Major's Hill on the other side. This proposed feat had the great advantage of an extraordinary setting but would not have been "death-defying" (unless he placed his rope extremely high). Within days he had a better plan: he would walk a little further upstream, across the Chaudière Falls. This had no difficulty meeting the requirements of defying death: if he fell in here the "Big Kettle" would take him to his maker in an instant.

Chaudière Falls was still a breathtaking sight in 1864. It went the full width of the opening on the Ottawa River between Chaudière Island and the island beside the (now Quebec) shoreline and dropped about thirty feet along an irregular edge, but what made it unique was the way it seemed to boil, like a kettle, after its water shot into the cauldron-shaped space at its feet. The rapids seemed to fight each other, spinning in circles and spiralling downward at several spots, creating an instant grave for any living thing that fell into its grasp. The Algonquins, who had named it for its boiling appearance, had to portage around it and always stopped on the way to offer prayers to the appropriate god. Champlain and other French explorers regarded it with awe.

Farini announced his ascension for September 9th, giving himself ample time to construct what would be a very difficult-to-raise cable. He had to put up a tower on the rocks on the north-east side of the falls and somehow get his huge rope over an unnavigable whirlpool. But before long, things were completed and the publicity build-up began.

Either because of the enormous amount of press he received for his Niagara stilt-walk or because he had chosen a perfect venue for this next performance, he became a star overnight in the Ottawa region and there was intense interest in his activities. A Blondin-like hero-worship swirled around him. The newspapers ran long articles, making much of his daring at Niagara and puffing about Ottawa's coup in attracting him. In addition to his own advertisements (one, likely written by him, included a doctored account of his stilt-walk from the *Niagara Falls Gazette*), private individuals used his name to sell their wares. It was understandable that the Russell House would do so or even the Royal Victoria Hotel, but a bookseller stretched things a bit with his ad: "Special

Announcement, Hurrah for the Great Canadian
Champion Tight Rope Performer, SIGNOR FARINI, Who
has not received a well assorted stock of Books,
Newspapers and Stationery, but CHARLES J. THOMAS
Has, and is selling off Cheap for Cash...." Politics even
crept into things: "The Government Question Settled!"
said one Farini ad, and "Next Session to be held in
Ottawa" said another (there were lingering doubts that
the nation's government would actually move to the lumber city). When citizens opened their papers during that
first week of September they saw Farini's name, often in
bold print, on nearly every page.

By the 7th, he had hoisted his wire from a platform
next to two sawmills on Chaudière Island, directly across
the foot of the "Devil's Punch Bowl" itself, just upstream
from the suspension bridge, and looped it through a tres-
tle on the rocks before running it to the shore. It was
reported to be 740 feet long and 120 feet high and 2 inches
thick. Anyone who had seen his magnificent cable spread
across the Niagara gorge knew that despite its gigantic
size, this shorter rope presented him with a more hazardous feat. He either walked it and was triumphant, or
slipped and died.

The site was perfect for spectating. There was a large
flat area on the Quebec side near the village of Hull just
south-east of the suspension bridge below the falls that
would hold the majority of people, many vantage points on
the Ottawa shoreline and space on the bridge itself; even
Parliament Hill, whose magnificent buildings would be
visible in outline about a mile from the rope, would afford
a distant view; and the wooden platform at the mills was
enclosed and fitted with seats for a few hundred specially
invited guests, each of whom would pay twenty-five cents
for the privilege of seeing death defied close up.

Farini was going to try nearly everything in his repertoire while over the Big Kettle and later that evening perform his new gymnastic routines and his old
stone-smashing feat (now the weight of the stone on his
chest was four hundred pounds) at the Theatre Royal,

before ending the festivities with a torch-light ascension over the Chaudière.

He would have been pleased to attract 4,000 people. But by three o'clock, when he appeared on the platform at the mills on the Ottawa side of his high wire, a throng estimated at anywhere from 12,000 to 15,000 awaited him. (About three-quarters of the entire population of the town; in the late twentieth century that percentage of Ottawa's citizens would total more than half a million.) They may have been drawn by the beautiful autumn weather, the danger of the feat, the free admission, or the half-price steam-car fares, but more than likely his greatest selling point was his burgeoning fame. And they would prove a responsive audience: applauding his appearance, groaning and shouting at his daredevilry and screaming at him when they were afraid he was going too far. A Quebec City scribe seemed impressed by the number of female spectators and commented that "outside of Quebec" he had never seen a "finer collection of the fair sex."

To begin things Signor Farini bowed flamboyantly to the roars that greeted him; then he stepped out sprightly onto the cable, impressing everyone with his nonchalance, and moved out to a point directly over the whirlpool. Here he stopped, tied down his pole and went through several manoeuvres, ending with a few one-armed hangs from the cable. Then he retraced his steps, backwards, until he was once again on the wooden stage. The cheers came in waves, but almost immediately he was off again, walking this time in baskets, frightening the spectators when his intentionally loose rope began to sway with gusts of wind. When he reached Hull the largest portion of the crowd was near him and they gave him a rousing cheer (as one reporter put it, drowning out the Chaudière). He unfastened his baskets and headed back, moving with a graceful, gliding motion, adding some artistry to the performance. At mid-wire he set down his pole again, stood bolt upright, and turning to his admirers, gave one and all an exaggerated salute. It was a marvellous scene: the thundering cauldron raging beneath an elegant man

*Ottawa about 1860, with Chaudière Falls in the foreground,
and soon-to-be Parliament Hill at centre.*

on a high wire, with a huge crowd looking on, and off in
the distance on a hill the evidence of a new nation about
to be born.

Farini then spiced things up with his sack walk, the
bag bunching up around his feet, giving the impression
with each step, that it would entangle him and drop him
into the falls. Another recrossing ended the performance
and the huge audience made its way back into town, a
number of them crowding around the Russell House seeking a glimpse of the daring hero.

When reporters inched near his place at the hotel dining hall they witnessed another performance. Signor
Farini had enormous presence. He dressed to the flam-
boyant nines, was physically attractive and possessed a
wagging tongue that could tell a story, true or false, as
well as anyone. The reporters were struck by the darkness
of his face: the piercing dark eyes, the perfectly slicked-
back black hair and the goatee and moustache now worn
in the imperial manner of Emperor Napoleon. His muscular frame bulged in his loud suit and he sat up straight
and moved quickly, his mind taking everything in.
Canadian men of that day generally dressed in sombre
clothing and were either clean-shaven or full-bearded;

they did little to attract attention. Farini was a tried-and-true dandy, who stood out in an instant. He told journalists he was twenty-three years old (just three years off), bragged about his feats and his travels, told of his doctor's degree and university education and informed one and all that he had a 46-inch chest and 18-inch biceps. But despite this braggadocio, his listeners were impressed with him and came away noting his "agreeable manners and considerable conversational powers." Expecting to meet an empty-headed mountebank, they were surprised to meet a man of extraordinary brain power.

With dinner over, he moved on to the Theatre Royal gymnastic exhibition and lecture, and at nine o'clock, with the town and the river blanketed by darkness, the night ascension began. During the day spectators had been kept off the suspension bridge, authorities fearing that the enormous weight would cause a tragedy, but at night it was harder to keep things under control and when Farini began performing in the glow of the torches on his balance pole, people started streaming on to the bridge. Officials kept trying to clear the area but the crowd grew until finally he was asked to cut short the exhibition to avoid an accident. He complied, not wishing to associate his triumphant Ottawa performances with a catastrophe.

On the 12th he left Ottawa and blew into Montreal on the tail-wind of a wonderful Chaudière outing and a full month of tremendous publicity.

In 1864 Montreal was by far the largest and most sophisticated city in Canada, the only place in the colony with any kind of international profile. One hundred thousand people lived in its environs, it boasted about a dozen newspapers, both French and English (people of British heritage were still slightly more numerous than French), and had a cosmopolitan air that set it apart. Most every major entertainment star of the 1860s played its theatres or pleasure gardens. Earlier that summer Farini had struck a deal with Monsieur Verrecke (the Belgian gymnast with the bizarre neck-hanging, drum-playing feat,

who had been on the same bill
with him in New York) to work
together in Montreal and
Quebec City. Farini's Niagara
adventure and his Ottawa sensation ensured that his name
would appear first in the bills
and he received the lion's share
of the reviews, quite an accomplishment considering that
Verrecke was one of the world's
premier acrobatic sensations.

New York Clipper, November 7, 1863

On the 19th Farini was seen parading around the
streets of the city in a circus van, dressed in his performing tights and accompanied by a full brass band. Later
that day and throughout the following week he performed
at Guilbault's Gardens on a rope seventy feet high. To add
flare to the proceedings he walked in a pink sack, danced
on the rope to a tune played by the British Grenadiers,
and once carried Monsieur Guilbault across on his back.
And part way through each show the muscular Verrecke
flew on to the scene, flinging himself between trapeze bars
set thirty feet apart and forty-five feet high, wowing the
crowds with his agility and daring, and performing his
neck-hang as his finale to great applause. On October 1st
a benefit was arranged for Verrecke at the Theatre Royal,
Montreal's premier entertainment place, and Farini put
in an appearance.

By the 2nd he was on his way back to Ottawa to fulfil a
promise he had made three weeks earlier. Perhaps still rid-
den with the guilt of his involvement with his wife's death
and remembering the comfort he had found through his
baptism into the Roman Catholic Church, he had sought
solace one day in Ottawa and had befriended a group of
nuns. In turn they asked him to visit their convent and
invited him to perform at some future date in aid of the
new General Hospital. Though Farini was at times a vain
and unscrupulous person, especially when it came to the
cut and thrust of show-business life, beneath the puffery

he was serious-minded and dedicated to his own code of ethics. On October 4th he gave a benefit for the hospital. It was typical of his mid-1860s indoor shows: he walked on a tiny wire (strung from the stage to the top of the theatre); he showed off on the horizontal bar, presenting his Chinese Turn, Fly Jack and Hand Balance; and had another huge stone smashed on his chest. There was only one significant difference from his recent indoor performances. A "wonderful boy" named Master Alphonse was announced as his assistant, the first appearance of a child protégé in a Farini act.

When he left after the benefit he carried with him a letter from the mayor and other prominent people. It recommended "SIGNOR FARINI to the citizens of other localities, as a first-class artist in gymnastic exercises, [and] also as a person of gentlemanly behaviour and address." Because he was desperate to appear respectable in a business that he feared wasn't, these sorts of recommendations would be constant throughout his career.

His next stop was Quebec City, where he and Verrecke and Alphonse performed to good crowds in both the English and French parts of town. Pickpockets, and some adverse publicity from the Anglo owners of a local newspaper, who looked down on showmen and were angered by the exaggerations in the self-penned articles he asked them to publish, marred these shows somewhat. Again, politics was in the air: future first Canadian prime minister, John A. Macdonald, his ally Georges-Etienne Cartier and erstwhile opponent George Brown were in town, further negotiating the foundations of Canada. Farini was prepared to carry any of them over the Montmorency Falls, a spectacular 250-foot cascade (higher than Niagara) situated at the junction of the St. Lawrence and Montmorency rivers nearby; but his first choice for passenger was the Governor-General, Viscount Charles Stanley Monck, and he said so publicly.

My Lord,—Will you accept of an engagement from me. I want you to get into a wheelbarrow at Montmorenci Falls,

where you are to allow me to wheel you over a tight rope.
I am to be blindfolded. Suppose you accept of ten thousand
dollars?

> Yours very humbly,
> M. Farini

It was said the Governor-General replied:

Monsieur,—I consent to your munificent offer. You must
have seats reserved for my Executive Council. I purpose to
invite Lord Lyons and suite, together with the New
Brunswick delegates. It is my desire that George Brown
should examine the rope before we ascend. Cartier has
undertaken to blindfold you. Believe me to be,

> Yours sincerely,
> Monck

But Farini never crossed the Montmorency, because he
was never given permission by the authorities. An anonymous Quebec citizen had told the press at the outset that
such a feat would run into difficulties: because the residents of the city were "not particularly partial to excitement." An editorial in *The Quebec Gazette* went much
further: "We consider such exhibitions as in the highest
degree improper and unfit to be countenanced by sober-
minded people, not to speak of Christian men... Such
feats we regard as a sort of foolhardy and impious daring,
which no one who has a proper regard for 'the precious
life,' can countenance; and we sincerely trust the
Christian public of Quebec will scrupulously abstain from
the sight, if Mons. Farini persists in his insane attempt."
Of course, the Christian public of Quebec would have
come out in droves. Several years later another rope-
walker crossed the Montmorency Falls without incident.

By early November he had taken his eastern Canadian
tour to the maritimes, showing at its larger urban centres.
Everywhere he was greeted with enthusiastic crowds,
impressing them with his intelligence as he lectured

about fitness, nutrition and physiology, trying hard to sound like a respectable man, even warning them to abstain from "tea, coffee, wine [and] strong drink"; and all the while thrilling himself in the air above their heads with sensations far more arousing and illicit than alcohol.

While he was in Fredericton rumours began circulating that he was planning to cross the Reversing Falls on the river near the Saint John harbour. Though this was never seriously considered, it elicited more shrill pronouncements. One commentator was fearful that young people would want to imitate Farini and "be launched unshrived into eternity," and shouted that if he made even a motion to perform at the falls the authorities should stop it.

On November 12th he arrived in Halifax, Nova Scotia for an extended visit that would gain him more fame, though not solely for what he did on stage. He was scheduled for four performances over three days at the Temperance Hall and opened to overflow crowds. Rave reviews claimed that Haligonians (who had seen their fair share of gymnasts) had never witnessed his like before. Prior to his first matinee show he even acquired the patronage of Sir James Hope, Naval Commander-in-Chief of British North America. Such associations pleased him immensely.

A rumour was circulating around town that Farini was going to present an exhibition on a big rope at the Horticultural Gardens. Instead...he got married.

This was indeed a mysterious marriage. Though there are no records of it and no evidence of the name of the bride, it was widely reported throughout Canada. Word began filtering out through the newspapers during the first few days of December that Signor Farini had had the good fortune to marry a Halifax heiress of property worth thirty thousand dollars. The lady apparently attended his performances in her city, and because of her extraordinary beauty and bearing Farini noticed her and sought an introduction. It was reported that they were instantly in love and were married in a private ceremony in a small

Nova Scotia town not far from the capital. She was said to be the daughter of a prominent Halifax citizen, now deceased, their name so distinguished that, every despatch claimed, it was unnecessary to name her. The news was spread in nearly every paper from the maritime provinces through to the west and even appeared in the *Niagara Falls Gazette* (though curiously, not in the Halifax papers). Journalists were charmed by the romance of it all, making much of the beauty of both the bride and the groom, gushing that it would have been difficult for the lady to have resisted the dashing young rope-walker's attractive physique: "Farini's mould is perfection itself," said one. It was a grand and exciting Canadian union.

It is tempting to speculate that this marriage never took place, that it was a particularly effective example of Farini's flair for publicity, especially when one considers the absence of appropriate records, the fact that her name was omitted from all accounts, the absence of a notice in the Halifax newspapers, and another Farini marriage, well documented, less than seven years later. But what of the preponderance of reports? And what of a journalist's observation, about three weeks later in the Kingston *Daily British Whig*, that Farini's wife was not only in their city but attended every performance he gave?

A two-week pause in his itinerary after he left Halifax also seems to point to something unusual occurring in his life. He turns up again on December 5th, now on a tour of Canada West with his "wife," in the little town of Brockville situated just over one hundred miles south-west of Montreal on the St. Lawrence River. Then he arrived in Kingston, played to appreciative crowds and left the next day on the train, going westward toward Port Hope.

If he indeed appeared at home with a new bride, it must have been an interesting reunion with his parents. Thomas and Hannah, both over fifty years old, presided over a maturing and dispersing family: Ann, now nearing thirty, was married with three children, Tom was in his early twenties and independently employed, and only five

others lived at home, among them twelve-year-old Edith
and little Mannie, the only real child left. He impressed his
brothers, who looked up to him and at times even called
him "Farini" rather than their father's formal "William";
even Thomas had to note his son's obvious financial gains.
He dressed elegantly, was heavily moustachioed and
exuded confidence. Most Port Hopers considered him outrageous.

By Boxing Day he was off again, heading out on the
Grand Trunk toward Toronto. Though Thomas and his
son hadn't seen each other for well over a year prior to
this meeting, and probably only a few times in the previous half decade, they must have gotten on reasonably well
because soon T.W. would begin selling his land to William,
at a price advantageous to both. Hannah, ever-loving,
couldn't have known as she bade her son farewell that
this was the last time she would ever see him.

Signor Farini went past Toronto to perform in Hamilton
and then returned to the bigger city. It was a very different place from the parochial, Anglican-Church-dominated
little town where Mackenzie staged his rebellion when
Hannah Hunt was pregnant with her first son, or even
the city he had known in his late teens. It was now the
centre of commercial activity for almost the entire
province, complete with a horse-drawn (rail) transit system, ethnic tensions, and rows of impressive new buildings, certainly not the least of which was St. Lawrence
Hall. Sitting on the city's main thoroughfare (King Street
East), and just north of City Hall, its beautiful carved
stone and cast iron exterior, and powerful Corinthian
columns at its entrance, gave it a majesty that no other
building in Toronto possessed. It housed a market, shops
and municipal offices but its crowning jewel was the
third-floor assembly hall. This Great Hall was a hundred
feet long, with gilt decorations, a beautiful plaster ceiling
and magnificent crystal chandeliers. It was the centre for
community happenings and international entertainments
and saw the likes of Jenny Lind and Adelina Patti per-

form within its walls. Then, just as 1865 peeked over the horizon, Farini came calling.

The public was told that seeing Farini was unlike seeing any other gymnast. *The Daily Leader*'s correspondent went to see if this loud boast was true and wrote an intriguing review of the first show on December 30th—it gave a clear picture of what it was like to see Signor Farini at the height of his athletic powers, with its description of his remarkable "coolness and self-possession" and his ability to absolutely terrorize his audience. The reporter watched as Farini built the tension to such a height that the crowd began rocking back and forth like metronomes. They might have been even more unnerved if they had known that while practising in the Great Hall prior to the show he had fallen and knocked himself cold when his head smacked the hard surface below. It had taken a good deal of time to bring him back to consciousness and yet there he was, giving a purposely dangerous performance that very evening. Terror was obviously one of the illicit emotions he wanted to explore.

He seems to have liked Toronto as much as they liked him, bringing the new year in and then staying for a while after his last appearance. He may have still been there two months later when a magician named Simmons came loudly into town. This man was to influence his life.

Hugh Washington Simmons was an Englishman, but had travelled all over the world displaying his magic. By 1863 he was in California and in the late summer, just after Farini was in town, performed at the Metropolitan Theater in San Francisco. In April of the following year he came to the large cities of the north-eastern United States, again near Farini, and then appeared in New York when Farini was readying himself for his big Hippotheatron opening. Later that year he went to New Brunswick and Nova Scotia, just like Farini, and could be found in the small towns in the vicinity of Halifax during the Signor's triumphant appearances there in mid November. Their closely connected itineraries continued into Toronto in early 1865.

Simmons became quite popular during his day, especially after he went to England in the late 1860s and
changed his name to Dr. Lynn. His place in the history of
magic is assured for reasons other than his proficiency,
which was not always of the highest order. In 1873 he
gained attention in a sensational competition with the
great J.N. Maskelyne at the Agricultural Hall in London,
later that year sold his Indian Box Mystery trick to
Barnum for $25,000 and while touring in the United
States, performing his trick of taking apart a human body
limb by limb and then reattaching everything, he tantalized the son of Rabbi Weiss. Young Eric found the inspiration for a career in magic from that performance, a
career he pursued using the stage name Harry Houdini.

But when Simmons and Farini briefly joined forces in
1865, Simmons was no Houdini. One of his great feats
was to cut off his head in front of the audience and tuck it
under his arm. A few months earlier in New York City he
had majestically unsheathed his gleaming blade and
sliced off his head to the anguish of the crowd...until he
fumbled it, dropped it on the floor and saw it smash into
a thousand pieces. The laughter nearly drove him out of
town. In Toronto his decapitation fared only slightly better and some of his other feats were considered poor imi-
tations of the renowned Davenport Brothers. He was also
capable of being a bit of a scoundrel: he cancelled his last
Toronto show, bills unpaid, and skedaddled north-west of
the city to the village of Weston with a chambermaid from
the Queen's Hotel. Though he claimed he wanted to marry
her, it was reported that her mother added a few lumps to
his oft-injured head by smacking him with a candlestick
and sending him packing.

Though Farini liked to associate with well-educated,
elegant people, a rogue like Simmons with his obvious
sense of adventure and weakness for what was magic
about life also interested him. They were a good match
and it is easy to see why they became colleagues. They
were about the same age, with large egos and abilities,
and even looked a little alike with their dark hair and

moustaches. They were also shameless self-promoters, capable of spinning fantastic yarns about themselves. But most importantly, they shared a quasi-scientific approach to life and its mysteries. Simmons always billed himself as an "anti-spiritualist," maintaining that he was merely an illusionist and his magic was the result of skilful tricks, *not* any kind of spiritual intervention. In an age when spiritualism was very much in vogue, this marked him as different. Just as Simmons debunked "magic" (lecturing so much about it he was known as the "talkee-talkee man"), Farini liked to explain the science behind his gymnastics (and de-mystify men like Blondin).

Farini was both intrigued by, and very opinionated about, the world of spiritualism and magic. He abhorred spiritualists, took great joy in letting the wind out of their sails and claimed he publicly debunked them on several occasions. A friend of his in his later years remembered:

Farini, who was a marvellous mechanic, told me that he had never been unable to detect the secrets of spiritualistic material that he had examined. In one case there was a cabinet, which was locked when everyone had satisfied himself that there was no other entrance, and which was so cleverly constructed that Farini could see no other method of getting into it. Farini managed to be the last one out, and as he left he sprinkled a package of tacks on the floor. The watchers were supposed to see a spirit face at the window of the cabinet. In a few minutes the spirit appeared, but almost immediately there was a series of little shrieks and the spirit departed, the medium explaining that there was someone in the audience uncongenial to the spirits.

He loved to attend seances: they were the perfect setting to decipher the tricks of someone else's trade. He claimed he was at one where a medium said she was going to douse the lights and then a spirit would play an accordion that had been placed under the group's table. Farini instantly inquired why the spirit couldn't do the same thing in the middle of the room with the gas lights on and was immediately asked by someone ("who wished to believe" in what was going on) if his intention was to break up the seance. Later the medium told everyone that a spirit was going to move about the room and touch each of them on the shoulder and, just so they would know it truly was a spirit, she would have her own hands bound. The instant the lights went out Farini rose from his seat, rushed across the room, and seized the spiritualist, who had undone her hands and was advancing toward the shoulder of one of her audience. He called such meetings "silly farces" and those who believed in them "dupes" and "idiots." He was fond of warning people to never believe something was supernatural just because they were unable to explain it. "People are easily humbugged by spiritualists," he once said, "on account of their credulity." This attitude is part of his conviction that people believed what they wanted to believe about life and not what was true, that they were easily susceptible to many kinds of illusions. Farini was a relentlessly rational man, more impressed by science than religion. Several times he sought out famous magicians to tour with (and years later, while managing a popular theatre in London, employed an ageing Dr. Lynn); they must have found him an intriguing partner.

One of Simmons's notices for his Toronto appearances made the interesting boast that he was about to go to Niagara Falls where he would get on the great Farini's back, and cross the cataract carrying his head under his arm. This never occurred, but in March they performed together at Smith and Nixon's Hall in the booming young city of Chicago and their show was an unqualified success. Simmons was billed as the great exposer of "the Davenport mystery and similar humbugs" and "Professor Farini," who incorporated a trapeze act into these dates, as the possesser of "more daring and nerve than any other living man." Emphasis was put on the macabre nature of their show and it certainly had a chilling effect. Here were

two dark-looking men who enjoyed frightening people:
performing decapitations, writing in blood on their arms
(a Simmons specialty), rope-walking with amateurs riding
piggyback, and trying headstands on chairs balanced precariously on a high wire. It took courage to even go to the
Farini-Simmons show and the more it curdled your blood,
the better it was. Farini's appetite for disturbing his audiences would continue unsatisfied for many decades.

The second show featured Farini carrying Simmons
across the wire as he exhibited feats of legerdemain. They
moved to Bryan Hall for the last shows, giving a benefit
for the Soldiers' Home of Chicago for Disabled Soldiers,
another example of Farini's charitable impulse, but also a
response to the true horrors he had witnessed during the
war. By April 1st they were finished at Chicago. Two
weeks later John Wilkes Booth, the youngest of a distinguished family of actors, and matinee idol to American
women, shot and killed Abraham Lincoln in a theatre in
Washington. The entertainment industry, plunged into
mourning like the rest of the nation, closed their theatres.
The great Edwin Booth temporarily retired from the
stage, despondent and frightened, and showmen everywhere wondered how a profession berated in the past for
its immorality would be affected by one of its own killing
the nation's great leader.

Farini kept moving. Over the following nine months he
continued to tour, but now he went international. He had
been telling the public for some time that Australia and
India were his eventual destinations for 1865, and he may
have even gone on to the Black Sea area and from there
to some of the capitals of Europe. By February of the following year he was in London, with his friends Verrecke
and Simmons not far away.

The rope-walking, multi-skilled-gymnast-and-lecturer
phase of his life was about to end. He would find enormous success in England and make it his second home
until the end of the century. His passion for thrills would
grow stronger...and darker.

CHAPTER 13

Flying in London

"Leicester Square is THE square of London. All roads lead to it, and out of it. ...To me Leicester Square, when I knew it, represented nothing but the Alhambra."
Thomas McDonald Rendle, *Swings and Roundabouts*, 1919

"The Flying Wonders, Farini and Father, A New Sensation!"
Alhambra advertisement in *The Times* of London, August 1866

In 1866 London was by far the largest city in the world. And in many ways it was the centre of the world, *the* place to be. If Farini thought that mighty New York was an eyeful, then London was an absolute fantasy: triple Gotham's size and bulging with more news and more stars and more kinds of entertainment than any place had ever had. Enthralled the instant he arrived, Farini set out to be part of it.

On its narrow streets, lined by ancient buildings, he saw people of every sort coming toward him in waves: the desperately poor from the sickening slums, the working class, civil servants, and elegant gentlemen with their ladies, everyone bustling forward, cramming every inch of sidewalk, stove-pipe hats set jauntily on heads, carriages and street trams in traffic jams and steam trains whistling in from the growing suburbs. Three million people lived in the London area.

In 1851 the world was invited to its doorstep so it could puff about its progress: the Great Exhibition was held in a huge, glass building in Hyde Park called the Crystal Palace and hundreds of thousands came to the celebration.

This beautiful symbol of the nation's achievements was not built on empty boasts: everything from population to citizens' rights to industry to railways to the size of the Empire had grown tremendously during the first half of Victoria's reign, and British pride was at an all-time high. Unrestrained optimism drove England through to the early seventies. Only then was the Victorian spirit beset by doubts, brought on by a slightly failing economy and dissenting voices criticising the naïve optimism, jingoism and the self-centred self-reliance of earlier days.

But in 1866, when Farini arrived, such doubts were still in the future. In politics, confident young lions like Disraeli and Gladstone were about to take to the stage; just off Oxford Street at the British Museum an unprepossessing man named Karl Marx devoured economic theory; out of town Charles Darwin created controversy; and in the House of Commons, John Stuart Mill, fought for new ideas like women's rights. In the parlours of those with reasonable capital Tennyson, Browning and George Eliot were read with pleasure, and Henry Mayhew's books awakened people to the horror of the city's underworld of poverty. Over it all rose the figure of Charles Dickens, who tirelessly walked the streets of his city, sometimes in the dead of night, taking the pulse of his time by speaking to the poor he found everywhere in rags. *Our Mutual Friend* was still fresh in the minds of Londoners when Farini came to town.

Dickens was a showman himself and one of his great passions was the theatre: in London he could get his fill, from the little amateur plays he loved to participate in, to the legitimate theatre in the classy West End, then dominated by such luminaries as Dickens's urbane friend William Charles Macready, an actor who was nearly ashamed of his trade. Young Henry Irving waited in the wings, about to electrify the city with his athletic, unrestrained acting and begin his long reign of the English stage. He would be the first knighted actor, bringing respectability to a disreputable profession.

The theatre was just a small part of the stunning array of entertainment in London. There were Handel Festivals at the Crystal Palace with orchestras numbering in the thousands, magnificent operas at Covent Garden, melodramas with on-stage horses, ballet, burlesque, opera bouffe, pantomime and farce; there were hundreds of popular singers, magic and spiritualist shows, menageries, low and high comedy, living curiosities, the circus and many more. Leotard, Menken, Sims Reeves, Anna Swan the Nova Scotia giantess, and the Christy Minstrels were some of the many stars of the day. Popular dandy George Leybourne, the one and only "Champagne Charlie," was like a symbol of the age, drawn by a team of white horses to the theatres, where he sang "The Man on the Flying Trapeze."

Prior to the mid-century the rich went to the lush theatres to see plays or opera, and the rich and everyone else went to the circus or to beer halls where songs were sung for the masses, or acrobats, animals and people with deformities performed. But by 1860 "low" entertainment began to grow by leaps and bounds, and soon there were new "music halls," some of them cavernous and soon to be legendary. The demand for action inside their doors was resounding. The circus, an indigenous invention first put together about a century earlier in the city, could set up for extended runs in London, or its stars found employment in variety shows in the theatres.

More sober themes, about the need for further social and political changes, were constantly debated in the clubs, pubs and on the pages of the city's dozens of journals, but the entertainment world and its celebrities intrigued Londoners like nothing else. Whether fascinated by a command performance at Buckingham Palace or Blondin with someone of renown on his back before 20,000 at the other palace, "of the people's pleasure," everyone wanted to know about everyone who was known.

Into the midst of all of this came Willie Hunt, the Great Farini.

He quickly learned how to play the entertainment game in London, teaching himself about its business and the value of connections and how to use them just as he had

169   Shane Peacock

taught himself how to walk a tightrope. In the tradition of
Londoner Samuel Smiles's *Self Help* (published in 1859, it
sold about a quarter of a million copies by the end of the
century) he was a self-made man. In this way he was typ-
ically Victorian and London was his home. Asa Briggs said
that the key words of the mid-Victorian period were
"thought," "work," and "progress," and few better describe
the code of William Leonard Hunt: they ruled his brain.
But his interest in sensation and adventure, which ruled
his soul, would many times get him in trouble with his
English contemporaries over the coming years.

He immediately sought good London connections, not
only to further his immediate career, but also to learn how
the impresario's game was played so one day he could pull
the strings. He quickly discovered that the best agent and
the most effective showman were, respectively, Andrew
Nimmo and E.T. Smith. The former was a veteran show-
business man who had been involved with things theatrical for nearly forty years by the time he met Signor
Farini. He liked to say that he knew every "star" (headlining performer) in the world and just a few months earlier had had another smashing success with Ethardo, the
Spiral Ascensionist. Ethardo was the great sensation in
London in 1866, performing his dangerous feat of balancing on a huge ball as he ascended and descended a steep
spiral that reached almost to the roof of the Crystal
Palace. Farini took a new act to Nimmo. The older man
immediately lent his worldwide reputation to "bringing
out" the Signor and his child-protégé "El Niño."

El Niño is the Spanish word for "the son" and can also
have a religious connotation when interpreted as "*the*
son," in other words, the Son of God. Fluent in Spanish,
Farini liked its exotic flair, and the fact that he adopted
this boy made it a natural. One also can't help but think
he liked the idea of presenting *his* son as *the* son, as in,
"you've seen the great man, now see the wonder he
fathered." There was probably a little theft involved too.
It was not uncommon for show people to incorporate

other's names into their own, witness the plethora of Blondins—the American Blondin, the Australian Blondin, the original African Blondin, the Female Blondin, etc. In the early 1860s in the United States a child by the name of Eddie Rivers ascended to fame as an extraordinarily gifted rope-walker, under the pseudonym "El Niño Eddie." In fact, he was in London in the first months of 1866 and was causing a bit of a stir at the Alhambra Palace, the very place where Farini and his El Niño would soon appear. Rivers could hardly complain about theft; after all, he liked to bill himself as "the Infant Blondin."

If there indeed was a child left "motherless" after Mary Osborne's death in Havana it seems unlikely that it was El Niño (the possibility that he and Master Alphonse were the same person is greater). It is known that El Niño was not Farini's natural son, that he was born in Maine some time in the second half of the 1850s (late in life he gave his birth date as February 1855, but some time between then and 1858 seems more likely), his Christian name was Samuel and his surname was either Wasgatt or Wasgate. He once told a reporter that he did not know his parents, but his daughter's statement that he did not get along with them and ran away with a circus seems closer to the truth. Farini found him, probably in Boston in 1864 or 1865, either in a show of some sort, in an orphanage, or on the streets running around like the Artful Dodger (shortly after Farini's appearances in Quebec City in 1864, when he was experimenting with young protégés, he spent several weeks in both Boston and Maine for undisclosed reasons). Whether this relationship was completely amicable from the beginning or more like a "kidnapping," as Sam's daughter later characterized it, is not known for certain. It was common for nineteenth-century circus people to adopt children and teach them the business; kidnapping them was not beneath the ethics of some performers and many court battles were fought in those days as parents struggled to reclaim their children. Farini was likely capable of something like this and there is no doubt he exercised a strict control over his little protégé,

pushing him to try the most dangerous of feats. But
Farini also gave him a thorough education so that he
matured into a successful and well-rounded young man,
remained his friend and adviser through most of his life
and looked on approvingly when he married into the Hunt
family, all indications that their partnership had more
friendly beginnings or that any initial animosity was
eventually set aside.

El Niño was a very attractive little boy, Farini made
sure of that. His silky blond hair, parted on the left and
full of gorgeous curls, framed a shy little face of fair complexion and flawless shape. Later, when his hair was
somewhat longer, falling in beautiful waves almost to his
shoulders, he was, if anything, even more striking. Farini
promoted him as a beautiful "Circassian," claiming that
he had found him in the Caucasian region of Russia near
Turkey (a fashionable belief of the time was that
Circassians were the purest Caucasians in existence and
hence the most attractive people in the world). El Niño's
deceptively slight build, long skinny arms and well-
formed legs made him seem vulnerable, almost effeminate, and the whole package endeared him to audiences.
But obviously this former street urchin wasn't the sweet
little thing he was presented as, and his performances,
brought to perfection by Farini's superb training, betrayed
his precocious strength, agility and daring.

However, when Andrew Nimmo first took Farini to see
the mighty E.T. Smith, little Sam wasn't entirely finished
with his training and not really part of the presentation.
The great man was an astute judge of talent and aware of
the Niagara daredevil's reputation; as soon as he saw him
perform he knew he had the stuff to make an impression
in the tough London market. Off the wire the strange
Canadian, dark-bearded, elegant and muscular, nearing
his twenty-eighth birthday, somewhat world-weary and
becoming more withdrawn at this stage of his life, projected an air: he seemed pretentious but mysterious, as
though there was always something brewing in his mind.
He was a character all right, and that appealed to Smith.

But it was after the exhibition that the impresario saw something truly wonderful. The Signor brought little Sam Wasgatt, reputed to be just seven or eight years old, up onto the trapeze to practise. As Smith learned later, Farini had been secretly preparing the boy for a sort of "sensational" act for some time. A meteor-child flew through the air, at one point flinging himself nearly forty feet from bar to bar. Moving to the sound of his dark Svengali's clear instructions, he did everything with precision and elegance. Throughout the whole nerve-wracking exhibition Smith couldn't get over the appearance of the child: he looked fragile and beautiful, like a little girl, and yet he smiled the smile he had been taught, projecting a sense of devil-may-care ease. When Smith opened his pleasure gardens in Chelsea the following month there were two Farinis in his show.

The audacious Everlasting Torment Smith was four decades into one of the greatest careers in show-business history. He at one time or another ran so many of London's large venues that one critic estimated he controlled just about every hall in the city. Included in his stable were the famous Drury Lane Theatre, the Lyceum, and the hallowed Panopticon at Leicester Square which he transformed from a kind of "science centre" meant solely for the edification of minds into one of England's hottest show venues. He also owned the Cremorne Gardens, a twenty-two-acre, carnival-like "Pleasure Garden" that sat between King's Road and the Thames River about three miles south-west of Westminster. Despite its beautiful grounds and theatres, dancing platforms and bandstands, it had lapsed badly in the late 1850s and needed a shaking when Smith acquired it. He immediately put up new structures, including an outdoor one with four thousand seats which was used for circus and equestrian shows, and began signing a wide variety of presentations, hoping for a sensation. In quick succession London saw jousting tournaments, balloon ascensions and the Female Blondin in a very shaky walk over the Thames. This helped attendance, attracting not only ladies and gentlemen but also many of the rowdier classes, who made up the bulk of the customers. Prostitutes and pickpockets swarmed to the Cremorne, going through the elegant main gates on King's Road and mixing in immediately. It soon became known among the upper crust as one of the least uplifting places in London. It was in this atmosphere, in Smith's new amphitheatre, that the Farinis flew onto the London scene.

The Cremorne did well in 1866, starting with a block-buster program for the Grand Opening on May 14th. The gates were opened at four o'clock and from that instant until midnight when Farini's old friend Buono Core (now just months from death) walked through huge jets of fire, there was a long list of entertainments. Acrobats, singers, balloons, learned goats came one after the other, and at a quarter to ten the little boy who would prove to be the star of the show made his debut. El Niño Farini performed his "graceful act, entitled 'Le Tambour Aerial.'" *The Daily Telegraph* commented:

> ...a boy scarcely eight years old—who at a height which it would be painful to contemplate but for the precautionary net spread forth below, takes some astounding flights, and plays a remarkable solo on the drum whilst swinging through the air, with his head bent back over the bar of a trapeze, his only means of support. The gracefulness of the child does much to lessen the feeling of peril attached to the performance, but despite the smiling confidence of the youthful gymnast, who takes care to impress the spectators with an assurance of his skill being quite equal to a control of the danger, there is a general sense of relief in witnessing his descent in safety.

There are a number of interesting aspects to this performance. Firstly there is an obvious similarity to Verrecke's act, secondly there is Farini's strange desire to make someone fly (which continued to grow throughout the following decades), and finally the intriguing presence of a safety net.

Farini has several times been given credit for the invention
of the net, a piece of equipment now standard in any
"death-defying" act. There seems to be no evidence for its
existence prior to 1866, though Farini himself may have
been using one the previous year while practising with El
Niño for his London debut. In February the Hanlons
appeared indoors in Boston and papers noted the use of a
net, spread above the heads of spectators to protect them
as well as the performers. The fact that Farini's net was
employed at an outdoor show indicates that he used it as
part of the performer's standard equipment, not just as
something to protect audiences. For centuries acrobats and
funambulists had disdained any safety measures, believing that danger was a part of their art. Deaths or crippling
accidents were common well into the late nineteenth century and it was not unusual for a theatrical journal to
record several fatal or at least blood-curdling accidents in
a single week. Just a few years before the Farinis came to
the Cremorne a wire-walker fell from a sixty-foot cable
there and plunged to the ground, breaking his collar-bone,
fracturing his skull and suffering numerous other injuries
that proved fatal. Even one such accident in the late twentieth century would bring immediate calls for censoring
anything "death-defying," but it seemed to be part of the
show in Farini's day and eyewitness accounts were horrific.
Many spoke of the bone-breaking sound heard throughout
the hall as a performer dropped like a rock onto the surface
beneath the wire or came flying into the wooden stage after
missing the trapeze bar, often screaming in terror.
Spectators usually did two things: some rushed the stage,
often preventing the immediate medical attention needed
to save the acrobat's life, while others ran screaming or
weeping up the aisles and out into the streets. Farini, perhaps moved by the death of his wife, would have none of
that. He wanted to terrify people, and did it better than
almost anyone in theatrical history, but he would not tol-
erate incompetence and a bad fall was really just that.

Mattresses used to be set on stages to help break acrobats' falls but often performers would bounce off or hit

sideways or miss entirely, and then lie unconscious on the
floor, bones at grotesque angles and blood oozing from
their heads. Sometimes accidents were contrived to create
a sensation and bring larger crowds for the next show, but
too often they were real and audiences were left stunned
as they saw the star removed quickly from the stage as a
distressed showman attempted, in the ensuing chaos, to
restore calm by assuring everyone of the good health of
the fallen hero. The most common injuries short of fatali-
ties were hip fractures and dislocations, which seldom
could be righted by Victorian doctors and left stars disabled for life. The early nets weren't much better than the
mattresses. At the Cirque Napoleon in Paris in November
1866 two gymnasts fell into a net which immediately gave
way, causing them grievous injury, and the following year
Risarelli thought he had an excellent net, so he purposely
dropped into it, whereupon it broke and left him with a
fractured shoulder. Farini abhorred such errors. Unlike
other show people, who were really nothing else, his abilities were varied. His consummate mechanical skills, for
example, were practically equivalent to those of a professional engineer. He invented a net based on sound principles: it wouldn't break and it had a good deal of give to it.
Though his protégés had some accidents, none suffered
serious injuries while in his employ, despite performing
some of the most dangerous acts ever seen.

El Niño's solo performances at the Cremorne took about
fifteen minutes. He finished each night at ten o'clock and
was followed by the comic ballet "Mad As A March Hare."
Such madness set the tone for Signor Farini's arrival on
his high wire, exuding presence, the dark goatee now
grown into a short beard, just as elegant in another of his
bright costumes as he had been on the grounds during the
day dressed in an expensive suit, gold chain strung across
his vest and a suave, confident air about him. He was still
billed as the man who had walked Niagara Falls on stilts,
but despite such a starry introduction was beginning the
process of deflecting attention away from himself toward

his protégés and the inventions he was putting into the acts, so he kept his funambulism brief and quickly brought back El Niño for their performance in tandem, "duopangymnastikonaerostation." It was a double flying trapeze act, utilizing the speed of the child, the strength of the father, and the intriguing sight of the difference in their sizes.

Their London debut was an unqualified success. And most importantly for Farini, El Niño was the real star. They continued at the Cremorne for several months, and a number of big names appeared with them, including the one and only Blondin who started in late May and stayed for nearly a month, performing for a while right after the Farinis. There is no word as to how the two old foes got along—no further fist fights were recorded. A young lady named Mlle. Victoria was also a sensation. She was not a particularly gifted wire-walker, but a beautiful woman in peril was too much for London to resist. Later she appeared in Barnum's show and not long after that was killed in a fall from her wire in Berlin.

El Niño and his father, immediate sensations, were snapped up by another extraordinary man and his famous theatre. The place was the Royal Alhambra Palace, the former Panopticon Smith had transformed, and the man was John Hollingshead. Though wealthy Frederick Strange was the actual lessee of the building, Hollingshead was its stage-manager and the dominant creative force behind the shows while the Farinis were there. They would become almost its resident artists, staying there off and on, for more than a year and a half.

The Royal Alhambra Palace was a sight to behold: a century after its heyday no building on earth is even remotely similar. Named after, and built in a style vaguely reminiscent of the great palace of the medieval Moorish kings in Granada, Spain, it was six elegant storeys high. Complete with dome and Moorish decorations, it looked down upon a wild and dirty Leicester Square known, before it was cleaned up in the mid-1870s, for the many scurrilous characters in its swarming crowds of revellers, and the rotting vegetables and dead cats on its grounds. But all but the greatest of snobs adored the Alhambra. Every night more than 3,000 came to eat, drink and be entertained, and some evenings there were as many as 5,000; during 1866 nearly a million people pressed inside its doors.

Acrobats performing at the Royal Alhambra Palace.

Theatre Museum, V & A

And what an indoors! Upon entering, a newcomer was immediately struck by its vastness: a huge lobby opened into the panorama of a beautiful auditorium and a stage with statues on its proscenium, and three tiers of floors rising above you with their huge, curving balconies. Everything was polished and shining, and a brilliant light, created by gas jets, gave the hall a startling sharpness. On the main floor spectators popped champagne corks as they sat at long tables overflowing with food; and every class of person but the poorest mingled and talked and laughed, far from those elegant sorts with reserved upper seats who disdained the pit-like atmosphere below. The entertainment lasted for four hours every night, but there was more to do than just watch. Those who knew the right people could have a drink with the performers in the mysterious "canteen" below the main floor. Here they might meet one of the painted dancers, known for their beauty and loose ways.

The building's sometimes racy, and occasionally government-censored, shows were of a decidedly mixed nature. In between "ballets" and pantomimes (with as many as eight hundred performers and effects such as a cascade of 150 tons of water shooting over the stage), the individual stars appeared: dancers, singers, comedians

and, of course, gymnasts, daring death as they flew
through the vast auditorium above the heads of the
patrons and their meals. The Alhambra was the big
league in the world of the flying trapeze, its reputation
growing from the moment the great Leotard performed
the first such act within its walls and made entertainment
history. Ladies flocked to Leicester Square to see his
svelte, muscular form perspiring above them, and
Leybourne captured the jealousy felt by every man in
London when he immortalized Leotard in song:

> He'd fly through the air with the greatest of ease,
> A daring young man on the flying trapeze.
> His movements were graceful, all girls he could please,
> And my love he purloined away.

"Signor Farini and Son, the Flying Wonders" took up
residence at the Alhambra beginning August 20th, fast on
the heels of El Niño Eddie. Though he had done well, the
Farinis would do even better. During their run here at
London's most spectacular downtown show-place they
were its stars. El Niño Farini performed solo after the first
ballet production, thrilling the crowd with his drum feat.
Later, to the strains of the sixty-piece orchestra, Signor
Farini appeared, his son by his side: this was when they
really wowed the big London crowd. "The wondrous
trapeze performances of Signor Farini and son," wrote
Bell's Life in London, "are...at present the chief attractions
of the hall. The ease, skill and certainty with which these
athletic feats are accomplished rob the exhibition of any
sense of peril which would otherwise accompany it.
Anything so extraordinary has not been seen even in sight-
seeing London." Moving to waltz time, sentimental or fast-
paced music, they performed "The Flight in the Air," "The
Flying Leap," "The Aerial Somersault," "The Terrific
Suspension," the "Forty Foot Drop" and "The Picturesque
Descent." Double somersaults were only accomplished in
those days by the very best gymnasts but The Flying
Farinis seemed to do them effortlessly, sailing above the

heads of the crowds in their blood-red costumes. Farini's effective net allowed them to perform frightful leaps from the heights, while his enormous strength enabled him to hurl Sam around the hall as if the boy were launched from a catapult. This wonderful combination of strength, speed and daring enchanted Hollingshead, and he kept them at the head of his shows for as long as he possibly could.

Within a short while there was even a song about them, entitled "The Farini," composed by R. Coote. The sheet music had drawings of El Niño flying toward Signor Farini, who was hanging upside down from a trapeze bar. Inset portraits presented a dashing Farini, moustache devilishly waxed, and an aggressive-looking El Niño.

Their initial stay lasted two months, and their absence afterwards was only for a month-long stay at the Philharmonic Rooms in Southampton on the southern coast. The Philharmonic, also owned by Frederick Strange, was really just a "little Alhambra south" and featured many members of the mighty moorish Palace's company. The Southampton and Portsmouth area was navy territory and shows here attracted a large proportion of sea-going toughs and good, loud crowds. It was a place Farini would return to many times in the future, being the home of his future wife, the mother of his children. Since this was his first visit to the area and he married her fewer than five years later, it is possible that twenty-one-year-old Alice Carpenter came into his life that autumn in 1866.

After the Southampton run the Flying Farinis returned to the Alhambra and performed for a marathon seven-month string of nightly appearances from November 1866 to June 1867. Farini was constantly changing their act and now he made another adjustment, a little gem which charmed audiences. At the conclusion of the performance, when little El Niño alighted delicately upon the stage, instead of bowing off he approached the footlights and in a soft voice sang:

I'm but a little boy just now,
Not very old you know,

> But as the rolling years go by
> I guess I'm sure to grow:
> I hop, I sing, I swing to please,
> I do the best I can,
> But some day I'll do something more:
> Just wait till I'm a man!

The song pre-dates the poetry Farini would one day write (badly, for the most part) in great profusion and another song he published many years later. It made such an impression on those who heard it that many years later Victorian regulars at the Alhambra could still recall it quite clearly. It likely was given birth due to a slight controversy about El Niño which Farini may have encouraged: because the boy had such a pretty face and slight build there were rumours that he was really a girl. Other performers recalled seeing him go to the ladies' restroom with "his mother" (he certainly had no mother with him at the time though there may have been a Madame Farini). Later circumstances will make this memory more understandable. Farini loved such things: latching onto a little misperception and turning it into a mystery. He may very well have insisted that El Niño act effeminate, secretive, and make a show of going to the wrong restroom. "Wait Till I'm a Man" put the icing on the cake.

El Niño Farini's beauty was such that his father made sure he had legal control over the selling of his image, and photographs of the little star were some of the best sellers in England. Farini later claimed that his take for the photos "often exceeded eighty pounds a week." This continuing interest in the boy's appearance and the questions about his sex struck Farini as things he could exploit even more. But it took him several years to figure out how...then he did so in spades.

In June 1867 the Flying Farinis left the Royal Alhambra for an extended tour of the British Isles, going out as part of a combination whose other half was the renowned magician Professor Sylvester. Money and fame were certainly large considerations in Farini's life, but secondary to his search for adventure: magic and spiritualism intrigued him, and observing it performed up close for several months by one of its best practitioners would be fascinating.

Alfred Sylvester was thirty-five years old when he took up with the Farinis, and climbing toward the height of his popularity, which he would reach in the early 1870s under the wonderful name the "Fakir of Oolu." He has a place in the annals of magic history because of his continuous work and eventual success with the trick of levitation, or suspending someone in mid-air with no visible means of support. Many magicians had tried similar feats and it was common to see a performance in which someone was made to lie flat as a board in the air, with only one narrow piece of support under their upper body. But at the Egyptian Hall in London in early 1873 the Fakir of Oolu dazzled his crowd with his "Last Link Severed" when he removed that final means of support and displayed his subject apparently completely suspended in mid-air. Farini's name has been connected with the invention of the trick; though there is no real evidence for this, it is interesting that he toured with the man who was to become the mighty Fakir just prior to the creation of the feat. In the late 1860s Sylvester would have been working hard at solving the levitation problem and Farini's brainy imagination would have been an invaluable ally. In 1867 Sylvester was best known for the brilliant lectures he delivered as he performed, and in them he displayed his well-earned reputation for intelligence and the requisite disdain for the spiritualist fakery that Farini so despised. All in all, he was truly Bill Hunt's sort of man.

By September the combination had arrived in Dublin, Farini's first trip to the Emerald Isle. They packed them in, El Niño continuing to be a great crowd-pleaser. But by November Farini had had enough of touring and brought the act back to London, to the Alhambra again, equipped with another new twist. Later in life he loved to boast about this new feat: "[it] has never been successfully imitated," he told one reporter, "for it needs a man of herculean strength, and a boy of phenomenal skill and daring." And indeed it did. The ad in *The Times* called it "new and startling..."

This is what audiences at the Alhambra saw: near the end of their performance the Flying Farinis ascended to a peculiar collection of three trapeze bars, one fourteen feet above and midway between the other two, which hung about a man's length apart. Signor Farini extended himself between the two lower bars, facing upward to the ceiling, setting the back of his head on one bar and his feet on the other. As he lay in mid-air on the bars, his son walked out onto him, stopping on his abdomen. When El Niño had settled into position Signor Farini bent slightly downward, summoned his strength, and snapped his torso upward, firing the boy fourteen feet up to the higher bar. For the finale El Niño flew, face down, off his high trapeze toward his father; as they came in contact Farini grabbed the bar near his head and allowed his feet to fall, and the boy slid along his body until, at the last second they hooked their feet together, El Niño hanging down toward the crowd, his little body an extension of his father's. It was another sensational Farini idea and Hollingshead and the crowds who flocked to see the daring pair loved it.

John Hollingshead grew to know Farini well and it is interesting to note his opinion of his star. Years later he remembered him as a clever, well-educated man, "a master of languages" who was brilliant at "mechanical contrivances," a man whose acrobatic talents were exceptional, and yet not nearly as impressive as his intellect. Farini's ingenuity would always intrigue his colleagues, sometimes to the extent that it scared them: he seemed driven to constantly create new and dangerous sensations.

Hollingshead was a good man to impress. He had just the rudiments of education, but was one of the masters of journalistic prose in the Victorian era, writing in what his friend Thackeray called "a very pure style." In his early days he had worked with Dickens, trying so hard to measure up to the great man that he would even accompany him on some of his legendary walks, one being a sixteen-

mile jaunt to visit a haunted house. He knew all of
London, from the streets and the parlours of the rich, to
the halls of Westminster and the floor of the rowdiest theatre. He was looked upon as a kind of progressive, writing
about the misery of unemployment, and taking a liberal
approach as a drama critic. He also brought the can-can
from Paris, successfully fought oppressive theatre laws
and hammered away at other legislation he felt interfered
with the liberty of the individual. His energy and imagination were indefatigable and his post-Alhambra theatrical accomplishments were even more impressive than
when he and Farini were associates.

In late February Farini appeared at the Crystal Palace.
This was God's venue—if you played a star-turn there,
you had hit the top. The day the Flying Farinis performed,
more than 22,000 people came to see them.
    The Palace of the people's pleasure was the most
famous of all Victorian buildings. It was created to exhibit
the empire's progress to the world, but when it was moved
from Hyde Park in 1854, to a beautiful spot on the top of
Sydenham Hill in the suburbs, its purpose was to be
slightly different, leaning a little more toward entertainment. Joseph Paxton's original building, influenced by his
former days as a gardener in the Duke of Devonshire's
estates, looked like a giant greenhouse, but was made
even bigger when it was moved, and the new monster-
building that sat on Sydenham's two-hundred-acre park
was an awesome sight, stretching for nearly half a mile,
well over a million square feet of glass and iron. An average of two million people per year took the nine-mile jaunt
from London, or came from other parts of the world to see
and be seen. Easter Mondays drew 50,000. Monsieur La
Thorne, an American showman, once exclaimed that his
first glimpse of the Palace gracing the hill at Sydenham
made him think "of one of those fabled castles in fairy
land."
    The Flying Farinis played the Palace on March 2 as
part of a grand collection of stars who gave their services

for the benefit of the Oxford Music Hall, the recent victim
of a terrible fire. There was a ballet, an opera, songs by
George Leybourne, a performance by renowned "negro
delineator" E.W. Mackney, the Alhambra's corps and then,
at three o'clock, feats by Blondin on the wire, Ethardo on
his terrifying spiral, and the Farinis. The last three were
the most popular thrill acts of the day, a feast for spectators, not to mention a chance to compare.

The Times picked a few artistes for special praise, intimating that these were the big crowd's favourites: the
Farinis (and not Blondin) were among those singled out.
The correspondent called their feats "almost alarming," a
pleasing description from Farini's perspective. They performed in a section of the Palace called the central
transept. This was the main, arch-like part of the building
at its middle, two hundred feet high, shaped like the nave
of a church (the whole building was somewhat like an
enormous glass cathedral). In front of a crowd that
jammed the whole floor of the transept, the five floors of
galleries and the orchestra stage, Signor Farini started out
from a gallery on a wire strung seventy feet high. This
could have been a rearranging of his duel with Blondin but
Farini didn't see it that way: those days were long gone for
him. Instead he took El Niño out with him and gave a
stunning performance, both on the wire and flying trapeze.
And so they played God's venue, and were a smash.

By the late 1860s Farini had put down a few roots in
London and even joined the Masonic Lodge. But his life
was driven by his great desire, and he was always restless
and seldom stayed put. After his Alhambra runs he and El
Niño toured the country again and spent extended periods
in Manchester where he briefly operated a theatre, and
even helped introduce the roller-skating craze to Great
Britain. Then he suddenly disappeared, vanishing from
the world of show business and taking his meteor-child
with him. Though they may have spent some time in Asia
and certainly lived in France for a while, first they went
home.

Some time around Christmas 1866, while the Flying
Farinis were the toast of London, a fire ripped through
the Hunt home in Hope Township. Though the family was
not left destitute by their terrifying experience, Hannah
Soper Hunt suffered so badly, either from shock, smoke
inhalation or the freezing Canadian winter (into which
she fled to save herself), that by New Year's Day she was
confined to bed. By January 10th Willie Hunt's mother
was dead.

This tragedy, and events which quickly followed, did little for Thomas Hunt's reputation within the family he had
always ruled with an iron fist. There appears to have been
some resentment about the circumstances surrounding
Hannah and the fire, whispers among the children (most
of them now adults) that her safety had not been given
the priority it deserved. Then, just nine months after her
death, Thomas dropped a bomb. And he delivered the
blow in Niagara Falls, of all places.

Emma Neill was about twenty years old when she married Thomas Hunt in St. Peter's Episcopal Church on the
New York side of the Niagara gorge. Thomas was fifty-
three. Only three of his nine children were younger than
his wife. And to make matters even more difficult, two
years later his new wife presented him with a daughter
(named Grace, but called "Birdie"), who was thirty-three
years younger than her half-sister Ann and thirty-one
years Farini's junior. Though the Hunts had always been
an eccentric family, this appears to have been a little too
unusual even for them and put a strain on relationships.
Young Mannie, Hannah's only child still in need of
parental care, was sent off to private school at Rockwood,
near Guelph in south-western Ontario, a move which he
seemed to have resented for some time. Thomas, Sr., who
had been so critical of the so-called immorality of his
eldest son, now felt what it was like to be similarly
doubted, and his young bride was not entirely accepted as
a stepmother by his children. But this marriage makes an
interesting point: it indicates that Farini's flair for the
unusual, his willingness to take chances and his disdain

for others' criticism, may have been inherited more from his father than had previously been suspected.

Just a few months before the marriage Farini had purchased his first tract of land in Hope Township, the ninety acres beside his father's ten acres (and the Hunt home) on the north side of the road. He paid $2,350 for this piece, hardly a pinch from his rapidly expanding bank account, and then laid out $6,000 the following year to get the one hundred acres of rolling land on the south side of the road from his father. Now, just nine years after he left home in disgrace, he owned all the land surrounding his father's property, much of which had belonged to the Marshes. He had also freed Thomas from financial burden. Over the next decade he would continue to purchase land in the area, eventually becoming the biggest landlord in the township. Slowly he was proving himself to his father, though he likely could never have quenched that thirst, had he bought all of Canada.

He had made the initial land purchases while in England, but now he came home, a swaggering and rich showman, to see the young girl who was his stepmother, the father who now had little moral and no financial control over him, and the etched stone, sunk into the earth to mark his mother's grave, across the gravel road from where he used to attend the log schoolhouse in the forest of Canton.

Farini knew he could not go on forever as a daredevil gymnast, the odds were it would eventually kill him. And nowhere was there a better example than in the bizarre fate of Thomas Hanlon, one of the greatest acrobats who ever lived. In early April 1868, after a show in Harrisburg, Pennsylvania, he began behaving strangely, first believing that everyone was laughing at him and then making several attempts to commit suicide. They locked him in a jail cell, and there he presented the most gruesome acrobatic feat ever seen. Running the length of his cell he flipped himself up into a half-somersault and came down on his head, landing with as much force as he could muster (which was considerable) on a three-inch brass nut that protruded from the floor. This he did repeatedly, at one point almost killing guards who came to stop him, until a large group of officers rushed in to subdue the powerful gymnast, whose scalp hung in shreds from his skull. In the corridor, as they tried to pin and chloroform him, he escaped momentarily and smashed his head against the brick floor with terrific force. When he died the following day, the doctor told his heartbroken brothers that a fall he had suffered while performing two years earlier had left splinters in his brain.

Farini was still of healthy mind and body, but well aware that tragedy was always just a slip away. As he headed into his early thirties, suffering just minor problems with his abdominal muscles from the strains of launching El Niño into the air night after night, he began thinking about retiring from performing. As a trained medical man, someone always interested in health, he understood that the career of an athlete should be short and that testing the fates with an ageing body was foolish. "Farini and Son" remained in business into 1869, but some time later that year, either at home or in Europe, he put away his rope and his trapeze for ever. Any future performances would be done in private, for exercise.

But he couldn't live without the thrills his life of adventure had been giving him. He had to feel that charge of excitement course through his veins...or live it through someone else. So he decided he would become a creator, a magician behind the scenes, manipulating others to do his will on the stages and in the circus rings of the world. Now his protégés would provide the thrills. They would live honest lives: full of the danger and passion Farini knew everyone wanted, deep down in their hearts.

His first creation was a marvellous one.

CHAPTER 14

The Weird and Wonderful Lulu

*"The climax of sensations has been attained
by the wonderful leap of Lulu...
It is impossible to conceive of a more daring
gymnastic exploit. It is so intensely emotional
as to impart an electric shock to the beholders."*
Sunday Mercury (New York), May 18, 1873

Farini grew a long black beard that made him look evil, and started working on a secret invention.

Before 1870 dawned, it was perfected. By then he and Sam were residing in France, secluded from the public eye, in training. For a while, supported by the money they had earned in previous years, they lived in the southern port city of Marseilles, a place frequented by sailors and with a rough-and-tumble reputation. In his spare time Farini became fluent in French. In the spring he patented his invention, and then waited for the right moment to unleash it on the public. It came on July 29th.

When Signor Farini debuted this new act in Paris at the Cirque de L'Impératrice, El Niño was gone. In his place was a stunningly beautiful and graceful young girl named Lulu, over whom her master seemed to have strict control.

Paris was the second largest metropolis in the world and becoming more breathtaking with every year of Louis Napoleon's (III) reign. Transferring the elegance of his court and his person (Blondin and Farini copied their imperial moustaches from him) to the architecture of his great

188

city, he built wide boulevards, huge railway stations and scores of monuments, creating beautiful open spaces and vistas. Paris was the only city which truly rivalled London for entertainment, some might even say it was the champion. It was often racier stuff: late hours and much wine, and little fear that shows like the can-can, a French original, would ever suffer censorship. In the circus business, showman Louis Dejean dominated most enterprises: one of his stunning amphitheatres was a 4,000-seat building on the Champs Elysées named for the Empress, Napoleon's beautiful Spanish bride, Eugenie. The Impératrice was built for the circus: circular, with seats rising from the ring to the roof, and apropos of the French respect for this art form, a huge chandelier hung from the ceiling and dozens more glowed in a circle above the spectators' heads.

Despite the impressive superficial changes Napoleon had made to his country, there were many ways in which his dictatorship was waning by 1870. In that year he drew France into a war with Prussia which could have been avoided. Immediately war fever seized Paris.

Arriving in the midst of this excitement Farini's new protégée was a hit; the French press, then devoting almost every line to the war, found room to rave about her. Here in the land of the great Leotard and Blondin, where gymnastic exhibitions were considered displays of some artistic importance and writers carefully examined performers for faults, she instantly bounded into acrobatic history.

Billed as a beautiful sixteen-year-old Circassian, her appearance and grace captivated the crowd from the moment they saw her. She had long blonde hair, blue eyes, and long earrings that sparkled next to her cheeks; she was beautifully proportioned: petite and slim, and yet muscular, her svelteness emphasized by her smooth walk. A satin gymnast's costume, dark blue with frilled edges at the bust, showed off her shoulders, arms and white-leotarded legs. She smiled at them. Then she started a performance that took their breath away. No one had ever seen its like in a circus ring before.

Two trapeze bars hung high above the ground and a
long carpeted plank, about eighteen inches wide was suspended by ropes just beneath them. Lulu walked over to a
small pedestal sitting in the sawdust. She mounted it and
stood still for a moment. The crowd grew silent. Suddenly,
she jumped twenty-five feet straight into the air! As she
rocketed upward her arms moved away from her body as
though she were a bird directing her flight. She whizzed
past the plank and then landed on it with a gentle bend of
the knees, her leather slippers making no sound: she was
a dove settling onto a lookout.

The effect was electric. The crowd had been completely
unprepared for what they had seen. For a split second
there was a sense that they had just witnessed a miracle:
a human being leaping upward like a god! They gasped
audibly; when Lulu turned and smiled they rose and
exploded.

The adults knew that the pedestal had done the trick;
but how it was done was another question entirely. The
children, with their mouths agape, were thinking something else: Lulu was a superwoman.

Now she went through her performance, wowing the
crowd with her grace and daring, causing *L'Avenir
National* to compare her to a "vas de cristal." She threw
somersaults on the narrow platform, landing on her feet
each-time with a delicate sureness. Then she leapt from
the board, caught a trapeze bar, swung until her momentum was enough to allow her to let go and flew through
the air to the other bar. Later she hung by her legs and
then dropped toward the platform, turning a half-somersault and landing on it; and for the finale, leapt from the
platform and turned a triple-somersault while falling into
the net, a feat never before accomplished by a human
being. As she dropped from the ceiling the crowd cried out,
and when she landed in Farini's strong webbing the
applause, held back for a moment to see if she were alive,
was thunderous.

Lulu was one of Farini's greatest inventions and her
debut was a special moment in his career. *Le Figaro* called

her "extraordinary...truly incredible..." and another writer instantly crowned her as Leotard's rival in grace, a compliment of the highest order from the French. Over the ensuing weeks she continued to be the star attraction of the Cirque de L'Impératrice and word began to spread about her throughout the show-business world. She raised as many questions as compliments. Who was she? Where had the ingenious Farini found her?

But that summer in Paris there were greater questions. The French were losing the war and losing it badly. Bismarck and his mighty Prussian army kept pushing them until on September 2nd a catastrophe happened: at the battle of Sedan the main French army surrendered and Louis Napoleon was captured. The Prussians and their German allies then moved into France at a veritable run and were almost immediately on the doorstep of Paris. They surrounded the city and laid siege to it. Though the people went on bravely, hardship hit them like a cannon blast and for four months they were without normal food and services; the papers dwindled to a page or two, every line full of the darkness of the city's plight, and soon the theatres closed.

Though Farini was conscious of the danger that swirled around him from the outset of the war, it would have been prescient for anyone to have predicted that the Prussians would be in the environs of Paris just six weeks after the first shot was fired. Always aware of what should be done in a tight situation, he had presented Lulu's debut as a benefit for the wounded men of the French army. But by September such gestures were almost meaningless and what he did from then until the end of the year is unknown. He either fled as the enemy approached or hung on as long as the Cirque stayed open, and then somehow made his way out through the lines, Lulu in tow, proving to the Prussians that he was a North American and uninvolved in this fight.

By Christmas he had made his way back to London, returning to his adopted home for the first time in a long while. He quickly arranged for an English debut for Lulu at the Concert Hall of the Cremorne Gardens in the second week of January, inviting only London friends, agents, "the elite of the profession," and members of the press. This worked splendidly, mostly because, as was becoming obvious, Lulu was the genuine article, a real star about to be unveiled. Press notices were all raves. *The Era* said, "The term extraordinary was never more properly applied to any entertainment than to that given by Mdlle. Lulu... If [she] is an angel, her wings are hidden; but flying is, without doubt, her peculiar forte.... Is she shot from a Krupp gun, or have the projectile resources of Dr. Gatling been brought into requisition?" Farini found himself able to choose almost any venue he wanted for Lulu's extended London run. His choice was the spectacular Royal Holborn.

The Royal Amphitheatre and Circus on Holborn Street, only three years old when Lulu appeared there, was a big, beautiful venue with both a stage and a circus ring, and three balconies of seats encircling the action. On the floor the audience was packed in around the orchestra, so close to the performances sawdust hit them as it flew from the thundering hooves of the horses. The best circuses, gymnasts and equestrians in the world came to the Holborn, but when Lulu arrived they cleared the boards, gathering sundry comedians, performing dogs and acrobats around her, stitching together a show rather than using a full circus so she could be given centre-stage attention. They anticipated her instant stardom, and were not disappointed.

The advance publicity was extraordinary for a new performer (much was made of the supposed raising of the roof twenty feet, enticing customers with the prospect of a truly high aerial performance); Farini advertised her as "The Eighth Wonder of the World," an appellation that stuck with her throughout her long career. When she opened on February 6th an overflow crowd packed the Amphitheatre. Farini appeared first, explaining the safety precautions and the effectiveness of his net, like a professor describing a respectable exhibition. Then the gymnastics began, now with fourteen feats, involving essentially the same components as earlier but fleshed out, and saving the sensational bound to the ceiling for the end. The effect of the latter was even more magical now because the means by which she was propelled was concealed in the floor.

London fell in love with Lulu. The papers sang her praises, amazed at her beauty, her "perfect training," her grace and her "extraordinary strength and agility." But most of all they were startled by that unearthly leap. One journalist wondered if he'd seen a miracle:

What would be the feeling of an average individual, possessed of no particular theories on scientific subjects, should he see a lady in front of him standing on her own doorstep make a spring and land herself on the roof of her house! He would, we suppose, discredit his own senses. Yet this feat, or one uncommonly like it, is executed nightly by Mlle. Lulu.... A sort of whizz is heard, the girl disappears and is perceived easily reposing on a narrow platform...twenty-four feet above the place she formerly occupied. How this is done we do not pretend to explain, we simply record a fact, leaving the reader to comment or explain. How the ordinary conditions of science are thus violated is a mystery to be solved. In ancient days they would have settled the matter quite easily by putting Mlle. Lulu to death, a ready and pleasant method of meeting difficulties, which of late has gone out of fashion. People will now pay their money to see her and will puzzle their brains to account for her performance. He will be a bold man, however, who in presence of this spectacle will maintain that fairy land has entirely disappeared, or that Mlle. Lulu is not herself a denizen of elf land.

Much was made of her appearance. She was called a "beauteous little blonde, petite in form...altogether an exceedingly pretty figure," and "young, shapely and handsome." Victorians, sexually repressed, were outraged at a lady showing even a bare ankle in public, and had to find some outlet for their yearnings, whether it be through prostitution, naughty underground publications or bare limbs at the circus. Nineteenth-century accounts of gymnastic performances, in which artistes, both male and female, are extremely scantily clad for their day, often betray a sexual intrigue, the writer describing the gymnasts' bodies at length, noting their heaving chests and their perspiration, and the excitement they aroused in their observers. Lulu seemed to be filling the need again, in spades. "A bright-eyed girl of seventeen," *The Daily Telegraph* called her, "...her symmetrical form and muscular limbs free from the restraint of superfluous apparel..." Farini knew what they wanted.

Lulu's ascent to stardom in England was as instantaneous as her bound to the ceiling: suddenly she seemed to be everywhere, especially idolized by children and the men who fell in love with her. Besides the thousands of photographs of the "Queen of the Air" that soon flooded the country, there were "Lulu hats," "Lulu sacques" and "Lulu shoes and gloves." At the Grecian Theatre the comic actor and acrobat George Conquest imitated her in his burlesque "Playing at Loo Loo." Gentlemen brought her flowers and some (of high standing it was rumoured) even offered marriage. Everyone on the streets of London knew about the "Lulu Leap," and *Punch*, the reigning journal of English wit and insight, couldn't resist a poetic comment:

Unless you're sceptic, as Colenso's Zulu,
In revelations fresh she's sure to school you—
That fair Circassian, acting in this new lieu,
The plastic LULU!

From other admirations she may cool you,
She's just the girl whom Nature forms to rule you,
And with her acrobatic feats to fool you;
Bewitching LULU!

You'd like, you say, to see the female who'll you
Enchant, and gently down life's roadway tool you.

Now, please, don't brag, you obstinate old mule, you,
Go and see LULU.

In April Mr. J.L. King lectured about "The Art of
Balancing" at the Royal Polytechnical Institution and used
a life-sized figure of Lulu to explain his theories, causing
it to spring upward to a great height. He spoke of how difficult it would be for anyone to maintain his or her balance
when propelled upward with such force, and called her
leap one of the most remarkable feats of the day. Such
respectable admiration was just what Farini was after.

Even the Chancellor of the Exchequer felt the explosion
of Lulu's fame. Robert Lowe had just introduced a tax on
a recent invention, matches, and the public was upset
both by it and the possibility of income tax increases.
Punch was again to the fore. Their political cartoonist
drew Lowe as "LoLo," dressed in Lulu's costume, "springing at one bound from a box of matches" from a circus ring
to a platform bearing the inscription "increased income
tax." It was displayed in double-page extravagance, the
Chancellor's stern, white features sitting atop Lulu's lithe
form, and on another page was an accompanying poem:

LU-LU vs. LOW-LOWE

LU-LU she can spring,
Like a shaft from the string,
Or a stone from a sling,

Five-and-twenty feet clean;
As, for weeks past, hath been
At the Holborn Cirque seen:

And as posters display
To the people who stay
From the circus away

How she does it, none knows:
If by spring from her toes;

Or by springs in her clothes:

Or some artifice neat,
In the boards 'neath her feet;
Or some counter-weight cheat—

Such as Lambeth essays,
Its shop-profits to raise,
And win pudding, not praise.

Cheating counter-weights do
High a shop-profit screw,
Then why not a LU-LU?

But if up LU-LU go,
Like an arrow from bow,
What's LU-LU to LOW-LOWE?

Who like him, now alive,
Ever jumped, at a drive,—
Four times twenty and five?

Punch, May 13, 1871

And on it went, insisting that Low-Lowe's "leap unmatched" put even the wondrous Lu-Lu to shame. "Could the force have been hid," they asked, "neath so tiny a lid"?

But there was something strange about Lulu. Many noticed it, but few could put their finger on it. She was secretive, and never seemed to speak to anyone except Signor Farini, who always accepted gifts on her behalf and deflected offers of marriage or even requests for introductions. She was rarely seen in public, her complexion was a delicate white, and her manner disarmingly shy. People clambered to know more about her, but she remained an impenetrable mystery.

Then Blondin, the one and only Blondin, who *could* put his finger on just *exactly* what was strange about Lulu, did so in public. It was his chance for revenge.

A report circulated in a New York paper in February
that the marvellous Lulu who was knocking them dead in
London was really...a boy. Blondin had apparently written a public letter in which he said he had seen Lulu,
scrutinized her closely, and quickly realized that this
beautiful little blonde was none other than El Niño Farini.

It was a curious accusation. Lulu walked like a girl,
apparently talked like a girl, seemed to be built like a girl,
and above all, excited gentlemen in a manner most persuasive. Few believed Blondin. The newspapers kept
referring to "her," the admiration kept coming from men
and the beguiling Lulu remained a success. But those who
did doubt her sex maintained their belief with conviction
and slowly a controversy arose, whispered in the press and
stated bluntly in the streets. Lulu's every movement was
watched closely and eventually doctors and scientists were
asked their opinions. A not uncommon feeling was that El
Niño had actually been a girl and now that her figure had
grown to the point where it could no longer be concealed,
Lulu was finally assuming her correct sex before the public. Performers and managers began saying that they
could remember El Niño going to the ladies' restrooms in
theatres and that the child had always been very effeminate, had in fact been teased for it by other children and
had taken to staying indoors. So now there were three
sides to the argument. But most wanted to believe that
she was the beautiful "she" they hoped she was.

This was not the first time a sexually ambiguous performer had confused the public. Years earlier Farini had
often seen the great Ella Zoyara. Ella's real name was
Sam Omar Kingsley. At age seven he was apprenticed to
an equestrian performer who dressed him up as a girl,
instructed him in feminine ways and surrounded him
with female friends. His soft good looks and acting ability
made the transformation convincing and by the early
1860s Zoyara was a major star, so confident in her dis-
guise that she sometimes performed as the male equestrian Omar Kingsley on the same show with her female
persona. It took a few years before the public began to

question her sex but slowly the controversy grew and it helped her popularity immensely.

And there were other well-known transvestite performers. Among them equestrian Alfred Clarke who was Mlle. Isabella in the 1880s, Alfred Jones who appeared as Miss Beatrice in the early twentieth century, and the beautiful Barbette who achieved fame as a trapezist and wirewalker. But Lulu (with the possible exception of Zoyara) was the most extraordinary: she combined remarkable beauty and ability with a wonderful act, and was able to cause a truly heated and prolonged debate.

But who was Lulu? Was she really a boy? A girl? Was she El Niño? Had El Niño been a boy? The answer was that Mlle. Lulu Farini was...Sam Wasgate, and Sam was very much a boy.

When Farini first noticed how audiences responded to El Niño's beauty he didn't consider turning him into a female. But slowly the idea grew. Sam and Farini generally kept to themselves on the road, perhaps a reflection of the foster father's concern about the deleterious influences of circus people. Farini insisted his adopted son learn to read and write, and study languages; he wanted him to be a respectable man, worldly, affected by the cultures he experienced as he travelled; there were even singing and dancing lessons. Thus Sam became a little mannered and elegant, something rather strange in a young boy. Any playmates he had found him eccentric and he acquired the reputation of being slightly effeminate.

By the late 1860s Farini may have begun to encourage some controversy about El Niño's sex. Several factors then contributed to the creation of Lulu. First, and most obviously, he realized how easy it would be to turn this pale, slim child with the show-stopping beauty into a girl; secondly, he remembered the great success of Zoyara; and finally, just as his idea was being born, female acrobats were everywhere, drawing larger crowds than men.

Though women had performed on high wires for many years, their numbers had been few, and most like Madame Saqui, Maria Zanfretta and Marietta Ravel,

were meticulous professionals presented as capable
funambulists, not sexual characters in peril. But in the
1860s this began to change. There is some debate about
who deserves credit as the first female on the flying
trapeze. Both Mademoiselle Azella and Madame Senyah
claim the honour, and both certainly debuted some time
between 1866 and 1868 in England. Crowds flocked to see
them, staring up at their scantily clad figures flying
through the air, the prospect of their fair bodies suffering
terrible injuries paramount in everyone's minds and promoted by impresarios. *The Illustrated London News* contributed to their popularity by doubting that such acts
were in good taste. But ever since the mid '60s when the
voluptuous Menken was strapped to a stallion and Selina
Young fell from her high wire, people had loved to see
females in desperate circumstances; it was so much more
thrilling than watching men. Soon Azella and Senyah had
scores of imitators.

So Farini had a good deal of motivation for the Lulu
transformation. By the time he and Sam reached France
the decision had been made. Farini took his son into seclu-
sion and sought no dates for an extended period, purposely removing the image of El Niño from the public.
Sam's hair was grown down past his shoulders, he dressed
constantly in women's clothes, his ears were pierced, he
was taught how to apply make-up, and given lessons in
how to walk and think and move like a woman. Farini
worked on his voice, changing its tone and inflections. And
when Mlle. Lulu finally appeared in 1870 no one seemed
to have the slightest idea that she was a man, that is,
until Blondin saw her in London the following year.

Farini never made any public comment about why he
gave his protégée the name Lulu, but it was a fitting title:
a not uncommon name in the late nineteenth century, it
can be traced to dark origins. In Hebrew legend Adam's
first wife was called Lilith and her name, evolved as it was
from the Sumerian word *lilito*, or debauched, is the source
of Lulu. Lilith was a sort of demon in the Talmudic tradition, whose haunting presence was felt in stormy weather

and in people's dreams. She was expelled from Eden for
refusing to be inferior to Adam. In Arabic mythology she
married the Devil and mothered evil spirits. Farini would
have read about her in Goethe's *Faust* and perhaps in
Dante Gabriel Rosetti's *Eden Bower* (which appeared the
year Mlle. Lulu was created). In the late nineteenth century and into the twentieth "Lulu" settled into the role of
the almost amoral, sexually overheated temptress,
because of the controversial character of the same name
who dominated two plays of Frank Wedekind, a German
writer who, intriguingly, used a circus motif, and worked
for a circus during the time Farini's Lulu was a major star.

It may also not be a coincidence that Napoleon III's only
child, the boy who wore the Legion of Honour in his crib,
was godson of the pope and went off to fight Bismarck
with his father at age fourteen, was commonly known as
"Loulou." The "child of France" was a much-discussed figure, especially since he was expected to one day be
Napoleon IV. During the build-up to the Franco-Prussian
War, Farini was training Lulu in France and her debut
occurred on the very day Napoleon and Loulou left for the
front. The war sent the Prince Imperial into exile with his
parents in England, but Farini and Loulou's paths were
destined to cross again.

And as Sam was becoming this enticing woman he was
also learning how to use Farini's latest invention. They
practised until Lulu could do it perfectly. The acrobatic
part of the performance, though extremely well done, was
really no marvel, just the result of Farini's expert training.
But what of "Lulu's Leap"? How in the world was it done?

Hidden from the audience, directly under the stage
where Lulu stood prior to her leap, was an awesome-look-
ing machine. It had the projecting power of a cannon and
indeed at first glance might easily have been mistaken for
some sort of instrument of war. It was an eight-foot-high
wrought-iron frame with four two-inch square legs. Three
sets of iron crossbars ran between the legs, one at the top,
another in the middle and a third at the bottom; a series of
hooks were attached to each crossbar. Up the centre of the

frame were two cylinders and through them ran a seven-foot-long, two-inch diameter piston. The top of the piston was covered with rubber and attached to the trap door in the stage on which Lulu stood. Powerful rubber straps, like huge elastic bands, were attached to the hooks on the crossbars. Before Lulu leapt, powerful leverage forces pulled the piston down and the straps were distended to their utmost and then pulled over the hooks at the bottom of the frame. Simultaneously less powerful bands were stretched the opposite direction, pulling the piston upward. At the instant Lulu leapt, an electric battery was activated which tripped the lower hooks, releasing their powerful straps and firing the piston (and Lulu) upward with great force, and a fraction of a second later the less powerful bands pulled the piston downward, snapping the trap door back into place faster than the human eye could see. A small aperture in the floor near the machine allowed Lulu to signal the workers below, and she wore "a steel mechanism of novel description" under her dress which kept her body stiff on impact, preventing the fracture of her legs. She threw the mechanism into gear with a movement of her arms and released it, in mid-air, by a similar action. With this amazing machine beneath her, Lulu actually flew, and her spectators gasped in amazement.

On February 20, 1871 the Prince and Princess of Wales came to see Lulu at the Holborn and Farini, dressed to the nines amongst the glittering audience, may have reminded Edward that this was the second royal performance he had the honour to present. In June he patented "improvements in projectors," the mechanism's second patent in as many years, so anxious was he to protect his ingenious invention. And all the while Lulu continued to be a smashing success, headlining throughout an incredible six and a half months at the Holborn, giving nearly 250 performances until her last show on August 19th.

Two days after Lulu's final leap at the Amphitheatre, she and her father were back in the Southampton area on the

English Channel. There was a small matter to attend to:
Guillermo Antonio Farini was getting married...again.
And Lulu was the best...man.

It must have been a curious sight at the Portsea
Church of England on Portsea Island near Portsmouth
that August 21st in 1871. Twenty-six-year-old Alice
Carpenter came up the aisle escorted by her father to wed
her thirty-three-year-old husband: the mysterious-looking
Farini's long black beard was combed perfectly, his deep
blue eyes were watching, and by his side stood the bizarre
Lulu, dressed momentarily as a man, his blond hair flowing down almost to his lower back. William Carpenter, a
grocer in the area, and his wife, Charlotte, must have
wondered just exactly what their daughter was doing.

Little is known of Alice Carpenter Farini, other than her
age, the fact that she came from just north of the
Portsmouth area, from a working-class or merchant-class
family, and likely met Farini while he was performing in
her part of England (one rumour claims they met in
Brighton). If Farini indeed married his Halifax heiress in
1864, then she had left the scene in just a half-dozen years.

Their honeymoon was very brief because in little more
than a week the Farinis were back in their rooms at 2
Vernon Place (near Bloomsbury Square, adjacent to the
theatre district) in London getting ready for Lulu's second
English engagement. She was booked for a shorter run
this time, at the Royal Britannia Saloon in the suburb of
Islington, north-east of the city.

The manager of the Britannia was Frederick Wilton
and he told his diary some intriguing things about Farini
and his mysterious Lulu. She was scheduled to start at
his theatre the first week of September, and he recalled
seeing her on stage after the other acts had finished on
the 2nd, examining her ropes and net, and executing a
dive or two. But her father was apparently distressed
about problems she was having with her knees and said
aloud that he "didn't know what the hell to do" about it.
For the following week Lulu was incapacitated and Wilton
wrung his hands every evening as crowds came to see the

famous Lulu only to be disappointed. Farini took to the
boards several nights to explain the situation, even bringing Lulu the first night to introduce her. Finally, aided by
a mustard plaster, she began to get better and appeared
on the 11th, drew big crowds for nearly two months, and
had her benefit on November 9th. Throughout Wilton's
association with the pair, Farini exercised complete control over Lulu—she barely uttered a word and he contracted all their business. Wilton never had the slightest
sense that Lulu was male, even though he actually visited
the Farinis at their lodgings! It is apparent from this that
"her" life was *very* carefully controlled: "she" was never
seen in men's clothes, on occasion had to take on her dis-
guise at home and was from time to time seen in public
dressed as a woman. Sam, understandably, soon grew
frustrated with these conditions.

Farini didn't keep her at the Britannia for the same sort
of extended run as at the Holborn because he was negotiating a contract to take his illusion on an extended tour in
1872. He envisioned something marvellous, travelling in
luxury around the capitals of Europe, dazzling his new
bride and thrilling big crowds. It was the sort of thing he
had dreamed of as a boy in Bowmanville. And the tour did
prove to be like a dream come true. Lulu became a
European star. They swept through Vienna, Berlin, St.
Petersburg, Paris, Pesth (in the Hungarian part of the
Austro-Hungarian Empire) and every other place they
wanted to visit, spending eight months on the road. Much
or all of the tour was made with one of the world's most
prestigious shows.

   Lulu was the star attraction of the mighty Renz Circus,
on a six-month contract which began in March at the huge
salary of 750 pounds per month. The deal also stipulated
that steps be taken to prevent anyone else from performing on machinery similar to hers. Farini's concern about
others stealing his inventions continued over the next few
decades.
   Ernst Jacob Renz, the son of a rope-walker, who had

worked his way up from apprentice to an equestrian, owned an empire of beautiful circus buildings in Hamburg, Breslau, Berlin and Vienna, and was advertised as the world's greatest circus director. His hold on the industry was almost absolute in Germany and considerable elsewhere on the continent. He was sixty years old when he won the rights to Lulu, and at the peak of his powers, with a reputation for presenting star-studded circuses that ran like clockwork. According to another performer, Herr Renz in person was rather formidable: "[he was of] above average height, with harsh features, small eyes, overhung by heavy brows, a decided and broken aquiline nose, heavy black moustache, a husky, unpleasant voice, pitched for a basso profundo, of uneven temperament, irritable and imperious, but easily subdued by a master spirit." Of such spirit was Farini. Though there is some evidence that they once had a slight disagreement, generally these two formidable personalities appear to have worked well together, toward mutual prosperity.

Europe had changed a great deal in the last few decades and by 1872 had evolved from a ragtag collection of states into fewer, more powerful countries: Germany, which the Renz Circus toured in March and April (and where Herr Renz was called "the Emperor"), was a huge autonomous bloc comprised of all German-speaking people except Austrians; the Italian peninsula was a united country; as was Spain and republican France. There was a sense of prosperity and political calm throughout the continent, a kind of settling-in after the revolutions of 1848 and the Franco-Prussian War. Show business was more profitable than before. Vienna, the capital of the dual monarchy of Austria and Hungary, reflected this prosperity. One of the world's most elegant cities, its streets boasted beautiful opera houses and its air was filled with the strains of the Viennese waltzes of Johann Strauss. Farini seemed to enjoy his visit there and loved to tell two stories about Lulu's appearance in the Prater.

Farini liked to advertise Lulu by simply stamping her name on available public spaces, leaving people to discover for themselves what "Lulu" meant. In Vienna the authorities did not take too kindly to this, wary as were many European governments that "Loulou" the French Prince Imperial might return at any moment from exile in England to upset the status quo just as his great-uncle Napoleon had done over half a century before. When the secret police began seeing the word "Lulu" everywhere in Vienna they were concerned some plot was brewing. Farini was brought before mysterious men several times to answer questions but seemed to relish it: he responded to demands that Lulu be examined by police officials by telling them "it is an advertisement for which I would give five hundred pounds." Not wishing to contribute to the income of a mountebank the police declined and the undressing of Lulu was narrowly avoided.

A journalist reconstructed another story from Lulu's visit to Vienna:

> One evening an Austrian Count swaggered behind the scenes, and, after complimenting Farini on his "daughter's" performance, coolly intimated that he would "call tomorrow evening and take her and Mrs. Farini out to dinner." Farini quietly inquired if Madame la Comtesse was in Vienna. The Count, in some surprise, demanded the reason of his question, when Farini remarked that, as the Count had done him so much honour, he would like to return the compliment, and take his (the Count's) wife out to dinner. The Count was considerably surprised.

Later in life Lulu remembered the time in Germany when a nobleman appeared backstage and requested an interview with Farini. After introductions he presented the Signor with a "formal proposition...for his lovely daughter's hand in marriage." It was respectfully declined.

But it wasn't all bouquets and proposals: the spectre of a medical examination of Lulu loomed again in another continental city, pushed by someone behind the scenes. Renz may have been the culprit. Farini claimed that "a

circus proprietor," trying to avoid paying the balance of
Lulu's salary (not surprising since she was one of the
highest paid performers in the world), asked authorities
to proceed with an examination, perhaps using the ever-
present "Loulou" controversy as an excuse. Farini's *modus
operandi* was so secretive that it is likely the proprietor
was not entirely certain that Lulu was a man; however, he
was more than a little shocked when Farini agreed to the
examination and Lulu passed with flying colours, a real
live woman after all!...Farini had fortuitously found
another young woman who looked a good deal like Lulu.
A few cosmetic adjustments later and (after getting the
real Lulu out of sight) the examination was completed...and the proprietor was confused.

Throughout Lulu's early career she often found herself
sent off to sleep in women's quarters. It was only through
Sam's expert handling of these situations and Lulu's legendary modesty that he was able to avoid detection. But
few Victorian men saw so much female nakedness.

Their trip took them into Russia to Moscow and St.
Petersburg. Here they entered a world very different from
the dour days that country experienced in the twentieth
century. In 1872 Czar Alexander II and a wealthy aristoc-
racy reigned and the appearance of the circus in one of the
city's glittering theatres often brought out blue blood.
Lulu, a hit there as elsewhere, performed for some of the
highest of Russian society, something which Farini no
doubt cherished. When they returned to England late in
November they were considerably wealthier (Renz had
twice extended their contract) and more famous than
when they started out. They were also a family of four: on
August 2nd Alice had given birth (possibly in Germany) to
William Leonard Farini. And Sam, in his teens, was growing out of his Lulu suit.

That Christmas Lulu played the Agricultural Hall,
another of the London's big venues. These holiday shows
had a wonderful mixture of performers, the kind of large-
scale line-up unique to that time, not seen before or since.
In addition to "Lulu, the Flying Beauty" and the ubiquitous

Blondin (billed below Lulu), there was a gigantic 5,500-foot painting of the Siege of Paris complete with scenery and live armies which attacked each other in the foreground, a high diver named Johnson "the Hero of London Bridge" (who had recently leapt into the Thames to save someone from drowning—a man planted there by the hero), Mlle. Gertrude's miniature circus, pony races with monkey jockeys, a Siamese troupe of gymnasts, several of the world's greatest boxers, wrestling matches in which celebrated grapplers took on all comers, and a jousting tournament wherein everything from foils to bayonets or any other self-defence was allowed.

On January 10th a benefit was held for Lulu at the Cambridge Theatre in London and her performance here was one of her great triumphs, eliciting screams from uninitiated spectators when she purposely fell from the roof to the net, and bringing her bouquet upon bouquet of flowers at the show's end as she was recalled to the stage four times. In February she played the Canterbury and the Metropolitan in London, sharing the bill at the latter with a group who did a popular burlesque called "The Fakir to Do You," a spoof of Farini's old magician friend Sylvester; and by March she had gone north to Liverpool where she created her usual sensation in a building appropriately called The Star.

But Farini was anxious to get Lulu to America.

CONCLUDING AN ENGAGEMENT AT

FOX'S AMERICAN THEATRE, PHILADELPHIA.

FIRST WEEK'S RECEIPTS, —

$6,725.50.

SECOND, OVER

$7,000.

THE GREAT

LuLu

MANAGERS WISHING THIS

GREAT SENSATIONAL NOVELTY

apply to

G. A. FARINI,

Agent,

care of CLIPPER Office.

SHARE OR CERTAINTY.

TEN WEEKS AT NIBLO'S GARDEN, NEW YORK. 38-1t*

New York Clipper, December 20, 1873

CHAPTER 15

Lulu
Undressed

*"If she is not a she, then I don't know
what a woman is at all."*
Bath Express, February 6, 1875

ulu was actually becoming known in the United
States without making a single appearance there: in
fact, there would soon be rumours in the American press
that Barnum was vigorously pursuing her; someone
named Geraldine was creating a sensation doing the Lulu
Leap in the States in 1872; a showman was advertising
that he had the sole rights for "the Lulu Sensation Act" in
North America; and Geraldine's partner M. Leopold was
presenting a young protégé with the appropriate name of
Leo in "a spring from the stage to the dome of any theatre" (this boy was terribly injured doing the feat, suffering a permanently deformed hip-joint). All these
performers may have been absconding with Farini's
invention, but it is more likely that most were paying him
a stiff fee.

About the 1st of April Farini left Liverpool on the ocean
steamer *Adriatic* of the White Star Line. Behind him he
put Harry Wieland in charge of his London affairs.
Wieland would later be the creator of the wonderful female
gymnast Zaeo and have further connections with Farini.
For the time being, much of his job was to publish caveats
in the press, warning other impresarios to keep their
hands off the patented Lulu feat. This fear of plagiarism

was becoming an obsession, fuelled by the fact that so many American acts wanted to use his inventions.

The Farini party on board the *Adriatic* reflected their growing wealth and position: as well as Signor and Madame Farini, there was a veritable entourage of servants, a nurse for infant Willie, another protégé, and of course Lulu, who signed herself "Miss Farini." The few times she was seen on deck she was elegantly dressed as the beautiful lady her fans adored.

Their arrival in New York on the evening of the 12th was noted in several newspapers. In just over two weeks "The Eighth Wonder of the World" was to open for an extended engagement at the elegant Niblo's Garden on Broadway, the most famous of all the famous New York theatres. On the day the Farinis arrived "The Scouts of the Prairie" featuring William F. Cody as Buffalo Bill ("a good looking fellow, tall and straight as an arrow, but ridiculous as an actor") was playing at Niblo's to horrible reviews; Charles Fechter starred in the "Monte Cristo" romance at the Grand Opera House; Anton Rubenstein was playing the piano at Steinway Hall; and over at Tony Pastor's Opera House in the Bowery, Billy Pastor was delighting crowds with a new batch of comic songs. Two circuses—Barnum's Traveling World's Fair, Museum, Menagerie and Hippodrome, and Lent's New York Circus—were playing to good houses. And both outside and inside the metropolis a plethora of actresses named Lulu were making appearances.

Again that "cabalistic" name appeared on nearly every available space. "Who or what is Lulu?" asked the *Sunday Mercury* in a big front-page article entitled "Lulu's Leap": "This has for some time been the prevailing question in the street, the store, the car, and the workshop." They sent their reporter to a rehearsal at Niblo's Garden to find out. He discovered a veil of secrecy around the performer but was able to watch her practise. Initially taken aback by the complex arrangement of apparatus at the roof of the theatre's dome he was even more surprised when he saw Lulu go through her act, executing everything with grace, so concentrated that she even bowed to an imaginary audience, before darting upward from the floor a distance described as thirty-five feet. "So amazing is the feat," said the startled journalist, "and so instantaneous its accomplishment, that the beholder can scarcely realize the conditions of its achievement." Captivated by her appearance, especially her "lovely blue eyes," he swallowed the story of her Circassian birth whole. "Lulu," he reported, "adds to her many accomplishments those of a linguist and pictorial artist. Her knowledge of the continental languages enabled her fully to enjoy the polished circles in which she everywhere mingled" (in London, Berlin, Paris and St. Petersburg).

All the New York papers gave her wide coverage and anticipation grew. The *New York Herald*, while informing readers that she had been born at Orkotsk on the Danube in 1854 and spoke five European languages, explored the intriguing question of her sex: "nobody is certain whether Lulu is a boy or a girl...[she could be] a beautiful girl, with the strength and agility of a boy, or an exceptional boy, with the rosy freshness of a girl."

On the strong wind of this build-up (one paper was now saying her jump was forty-two feet!) "Lulu the Sensationist" opened as the star attraction of Niblo's on April 28th, appearing alongside a lavishly produced pantomime. An overflow crowd, packed into the Garden's 3,000 plush seats, saw Farini bring her to the footlights in the second act and help her into a stirrup attached to a rope. She was then raised to her plank and began her performance before this particularly attentive audience. When she descended to the stage and stood ready for the leap, a sudden silence fell over the house; and when she shot upward and landed safely they gave her the kind of boisterous applause for which New Yorkers were known. Later, they were silenced again when she climbed almost to the dome of the theatre and dove toward the stage, turning her triple somersault and landing in the net. The applause was then more like relief, a "temporary repose to the extremely excited spectators."

As good as the pantomime was, in the critics' eyes Lulu was even better. The *New York Times* called her the "sensation of the night"; and another journalist exclaimed, "It is impossible to conceive a more daring gymnastic exploit. It is so intensely emotional as to impart an electric shock to the beholders..." The *Clipper* maintained that there could be no doubt as to her sex, "[she is] a young girl with blonde hair." Everyone who wrote about the leap felt compelled to say it was mechanically powered, but none could explain it, and all admitted that to the naked eye she simply jumped more than thirty feet into the air.

Soon Lulu was headlining the Garden's advertisements, rather than sharing the billing with the pantomime, and every night the "Lulu Waltz" was played during her performance. The show was called the best entertainment in New York, and in mid-May, Lulu was re-engaged for an indefinite period. Meanwhile, a little further along Broadway at the Olympic Theatre where legendary comic actor G.L. Fox was re-creating his famous "Humpty Dumpty" for big crowds, another gymnast, also billed as a Circassian and doing a routine similar to Lulu's, made his American debut on May 12th. This was "Ala," the second protégé Farini brought from London. In the future he would occasionally be advertised as Lulu's brother and there was even a speck of intrigue about his gender, but for the most part, despite his reputation as a particularly daring and speedy acrobat, he would play a secondary role to Farini's star attraction and initially did only double somersaults and not the Leap. He was successful in New York and would continue to prosper throughout his career, much of it guided by Farini. Ala was just one in a long line of gymnasts to whom Farini would teach his art: the Signor's reputation as a superb trainer of athletes, perhaps the world's best, began to grow during the 1870s.

Lulu continued at Niblo's into June and such was her popularity that on the 10th, when she was unable to appear due to a stiff neck, a riot nearly ensued in the theatre, erupting after one of the staff stood before the curtain and made the announcement in a tremulous voice. By

July 1st the theatrical season was almost over but Lulu
was prevailed upon to stay for a few more days, fronting a
new pantomime through Independence Day and finishing
her long and glorious Broadway engagement on the 5th.
Farini boasted that his star's appearances had netted
them a profit of thirteen thousand dollars.

Lulu was now a major star in the U.S. Farini engaged
New York show-business agent E.W. Woolcott to put
together a combination of theatrical stars, with Lulu's
name at the helm, and take them on an American tour.
Then he took Alice, now well into her second pregnancy,
and little Willie home to Port Hope. On July 10th they left
Rochester, New York on the southern shore of Lake
Ontario, steamed across the water on *The Norseman* and
by the evening were back in Canada, at their beautiful
new brick home on the property he had purchased in the
countryside near Canton. But by the first week of August
he was in Niagara Falls, visiting old haunts, taking pleasure that his very appearance, now as a powerful and
wealthy impresario, was noted by the area newspaper
(which he told he owned a gymnasium in Port Hope).
Some time between August and the end of the year Alice
gave birth, perhaps in Hope Township, to the couple's second child, a boy named Harry Ernest.

Woolcott had found a host of performers willing to go on
tour with Lulu. Billy Pastor, the veteran comic singer who
was a member of America's most famous variety-show
family was the most prominent, but there was also Miss
Fanny Beane, a twenty-year-old beauty known for her
strong singing voice, several "comedians" for pantomimes
and plays, and to make the show truly a variety, a cornet
player, and the LeClair Brothers, two veteran acrobats
who could do everything from tightrope walking to hat
spinning; and of course Ala would perform as the male
counterpart to Lulu. Woolcott left his agency on Broadway
and went on the road with the troupe as their business
agent, doing the legwork for Farini, who was officially
manager of "The Lulu Combination." Their plan was to
tour the old Southern Confederacy for three months, a

trip that promised adventure.

They intended to start in New Orleans, and move along the Gulf of Mexico to Houston, Texas, but the old demon yellow fever began to plague them early on and they found themselves chased by it throughout the deep south. The changed itinerary included Jackson, Mississippi; Montgomery, Alabama (where the local paper spoke disdainfully of the idea that "the negro is capable of civilization"); appearances in Tennessee and Atlanta; then up the Atlantic coast from Savannah, Georgia to Richmond, Virginia. Lulu, who was the hit of her Combination, added a backward somersault from the high trapeze onto her eighteen-inch platform to startle the South (she was also advertised to do a quadruple somersault during a Charleston show in late October—if she did it, it was the first ever accomplished); and Farini built a canvas floor suspended by huge elastics for Ala so that he could drop onto it and leap up again to his horizontal bar. Ala's gender came under scrutiny, much to his creator's pleasure.

By late November the Combination had broken up and Lulu started a two-week run at Fox's American Theatre in Philadelphia, where a journalist compared her to "a projectile shot from a cannon." It is interesting to note that her performances here were sandwiched between appearances by LoLo "the Eighth Wonder of the World," an artiste whose most sensational turn was flying from balconies to stages through flaming hoops covered with tissue paper; she also did various feats similar to those taught by the master trainer Farini and may have been connected to him. At that time other gymnasts began appearing using names like LaLa, Lola and Little Lulu.

After spending the Christmas holidays in New York, Farini took "LuLu, the Flying Wonder" on a tour through the eastern states and then westward across the country, with notable stops in Chicago in June and a stay in San Francisco at the Palace Amphitheatre on a bill with Herr Holtum, a gentleman whose speciality was catching cannonballs fired at him from a real cannon.

Where they went for the next four months is not certain. Always afflicted with wanderlust, Farini travelled a great deal during his life: few of his contemporaries saw such diverse geography, language and culture. Whenever he disappeared for an extended period it was usually because he was travelling abroad. He and Lulu may have boarded a steamer in San Francisco that year and made their way, via Hawaii, to Australia and New Zealand. He travelled in both those countries more than once, his busy mind investigating everything he saw and enjoying, in particular, an eccentric interest in their indigenous ferns. It was even said after his death that he authored a book entitled *Ferns Which Grow in New Zealand* (published in 1875, it was found in his possession at the time of his death), an erroneous claim, though he indeed became a botanical expert, fellow of the Royal Horticultural Society, possessor of an extraordinary fern collection full of samples from Australasia, and even an author of a book about begonias.

In early November people began spotting them on the streets of New York. What they saw was startling. There was Farini, colourfully dressed with walking stick in hand, big luxurious black beard dominating his dark face, strolling along Broadway with a decidedly strange looking young man at his side: slim and graceful, he too was dressed elegantly, and had freakishly long hair, flowing down in blond tresses to his shoulders. It took people more than one look and some reflection before they realized that this young man was none other than Mademoiselle Lulu.

Farini and Lu decided to go out in public this way because they were finished with North America for now: both knew they would soon have to give up the deception anyway. Not only was Lulu getting bigger and more muscular but he was also tiring of living a secretive life and had been pressing Farini for a change. This stroll down Broadway was the first step.

On November 11th, just as Ala, "the greatest living gymnast" (in the "Great Lu-Lu Sensation"), made a second appearance at the Metropolitan Theatre, the Farinis sailed

for Liverpool. By the time Lulu reached land he was a
young lady again. Now she went out on tour in England,
Wales and Scotland, going to several places she hadn't been
before. There were appearances with Lord Sanger's and
Hengler's circuses during this stretch, two of Britain's legendary shows. By the end of June Lulu was back in
London, opening for a long engagement at the Cremorne
Gardens, where El Niño had once caused such a sensation,
and by the 1st of August she was booked at the Alexandra
Palace for four weeks, despite the fact that she was still in
the midst of her shows at the Cremorne. This indicates the
immense drawing power of Farini's star, playing simultaneously in two of the greatest amusement parks in the
world. The Alexandra, named for the Princess of Wales,
was basically a copy of the Crystal Palace and the only
place to truly rival it; it was built on a hill that commanded
a wonderful view of London from the north the way the
other Palace looked back on the city from the south.

Despite their hectic pace during the summer of 1875
Farini and Lulu didn't slow down when they finished at
the Alexandra. They kept careering forward, on an endless tour it seemed, commanding top salaries (in Belfast
with Powell and Clarke's Circus they received more than
five times the fee of the previous highest earner). And
other Lulus turned up on other continents, some apparently real women and perhaps part of the ingenious
Farini's growing stable. He was in his element, constantly
on the move, seeking the excitement around the next corner. But at this speed his life was nearly out of control.

First, there were cracks on the domestic front. His
inability to remain at home for more than the shortest of
stretches was difficult for Alice, who was responsible for
making some sort of a home for her two little boys; and on
the road there were temptations he had never been very
good at resisting. A look at his addresses during the 1870s
and 1880s shows how the restlessness of his soul related
to his life. Not only did he move to and from continents
and countries, living in New York, Hope Township, on the
road in the old Confederacy and in the south Pacific, but

even at home in England he seemed to be always moving about. The rooms at 2 Vernon Place in Bloomsbury were maintained throughout these two decades, but he also periodically took residences or offices at 123 Chancery Lane near Fleet Street, two or three locations in Westminster, in the beautiful Lincoln's Inn Field area, another in Islington, and for a while at 5 Spencer Villa on Lewisham Road in the upscale southern suburb of Forest Hill. He and Alice, who had gleefully toured so far and wide together in the early days of their marriage, found themselves apart more and more as the seventies wore on.

But there was another, more spectacular problem just ahead. When Farini and Lulu raced into Dublin in early August 1876, Lu now at least in his late teens and finding it harder to hide his bulging muscles beneath his tight blue dress, little did they know what awaited them.

Dublin was an intriguing place, the nerve centre of Ireland, bursting with art and literature and the craft of storytelling, the city where the minds of young men like Bernard Shaw, Oscar Wilde and Charles Parnell had recently been formed. In the summer of 1876 its pubs and newspapers were full of talk of Home Rule and they gloried in the eloquence of young Parnell giving it to the English in the House of Commons. The Farinis came to Dublin looking for a different kind of glory.

He had agreed to another contract with Charles Hengler's wonderful circus, for a short run in the city, and Lulu's first appearance was on August 7th, a bank holiday that brought a huge crowd to the spacious Rotunda. Most came to see the famous Lulu. As her moment approached a sense of anticipation reigned and when the band struck up her music and the people caught sight of her strolling into the arena, so blonde and beautiful in her well-known blue suit, attended by Signor Farini and a phalanx of circus staff, everyone rose and gave her a thunderous welcome. After gracefully acknowledging the warm reception she ascended to the roof of the Cirque and performed her gymnastic routine, drawing more applause. When she

descended and stood on an elevated platform, the crowd
grew quieter, and when she bent forward, her eyes cast
upward to her landing place near the roof, silence fell over
them. After a pause a loud click was heard and Lulu was
still standing on the platform. She looked around at
Signor Farini, who motioned her to dismount. He turned
to the crowd and announced that a slight malfunction had
occurred, so slight that in moments they would be able to
proceed. Lulu filled up the wait by ascending to the roof
again and entertaining the spectators with more of her
graceful manoeuvres, thrilling them with her triple somersault to the net. But they all knew that the biggest thrill
was yet to come.

Farini motioned for her to remount the platform. Some
who were there that day thought she did so with apparent
nervousness. She clenched her fists as she stood in the
ready position.

Farini had changed a few things in the Lulu act to
make it even better. Now the leap was higher (Dublin
reporters thought it was fifty feet), part of the net was
ingeniously rigged to shoot out beneath her the instant
she was in the air, and high above the landing place were
other ropes she could grasp if she missed the plank. So,
now she had a clever combination of more apparent danger yet more safety.

She stood on the platform looking up, wondering if the
spring was still faulty. Farini gave the signal, Lulu
responded, and like an arrow she was launched upward at
breathtaking speed.

Instantly everyone knew something was wrong.

The crowd groaned in horror: instead of firing on a forward angle toward her plank and out over the net, she
went straight up into space, her head almost reaching the
ceiling. Then she started descending, going limp like a
wounded bird, while women screamed and men cried out.
Down she came toward the floor at tremendous speed. On
the ground Farini responded instantly, racing toward the
spot where he was calculating she would land. By the
time she neared the edge of the net that hung between the

orchestra pit and the ring's fence she looked as though she had been fired downward, so frightening was her speed. Everyone except Farini, who was now nearing her, braced themselves for the ugly sound of her bones cracking against the floor. But she was lucky, at least momentarily: she came down onto the edge of the net and it gave with her weight but didn't break. She bounced off it at an angle and was about to hit the fence when Farini arrived, his big arms extended toward her. He caught her for an instant, but she glanced off, crashed into the fence and rolled into the orchestra pit.

Pandemonium ruled the Cirque. There were screams and wails of horror and people started pouring out of their seats into the circus ring, charging across it toward the fallen star as Farini fought to find her. The Hengler's physician, Dr. White, rushed toward her also, and together they lifted her up and took her, apparently unconscious, backstage. In moments they had revived her and carried her into a cab which took her to nearby Hardwicke Hospital.

Many years later, a gentleman who had gone to see Lulu at the Rotunda, clearly recalled the excitement that prevailed inside and outside the building. Since he was a medical student at the Hardwicke, he hotfooted it over there, and got one of the great surprises of his life. As the doctor cut Lulu loose from her costume, a naked human being decidedly unlike a woman was revealed underneath the padding. Stretched out on the examining table, still in shock from the fall and badly bruised between the shoulders, the man who played the part of the famous beauty was still alive, but the female Lulu was beginning to die.

The accident caused a sensation. From the Irish press it quickly spread to England, Europe and North America, but the greatest reaction was in the London papers. Not only were the entertainment publications and the sensational dailies running stories but so was the normally staid *The Times*, who assured one and all "she" was not badly hurt, wanted her fans to know the accident was but a trifle and would soon be performing again. A public letter from Lulu was published in several papers, including *The Penny Illustrated Paper* where it appeared alongside a huge drawing of Lulu leaping to the roof of a theatre and an article headlined, "Lulu on Lulu's Fall." The writer began with a few opening paragraphs about how she had begun her career "in the guise of a curly-haired lad," and followed with demands that her performances be stopped immediately; they were far too dangerous to be allowed, even Queen Victoria had spoken out against similar death-defying feats (perhaps she had forgotten to tell her son to stay away from the Holborn Amphitheatre in 1871). More than a few citizens now agreed, and Farini, whose reputation was growing as the genius behind many of the bizarre thrill acts that were currently terrifying the public, was the target of a great deal of criticism. Both his shadowy notoriety and attempts to ban his inventions, some from official circles, would increase drastically over the next five years.

The Penny Illustrated Paper, March 13, 1880

Dangerous performances including Lulu and Zazel's

In his letter Lulu described the circumstances of the accident, and claimed the problem originated with the bolts on the mechanism, which were drawn a little, thus causing the projecting board, normally tipped forward, to be flat, and sending her straight up instead of toward her plank. He insisted that she was not seriously hurt and even walked to a waiting cab afterwards. He vented some anger at *The Daily Telegraph* for calling the safety net a farce, claiming that it had, in fact, saved her from serious injury and was so well adapted to gymnastic performances that it would have saved her even if she had landed on her head. He claimed her "father" had also been instrumental in preventing further injury: "...I set myself to receive the shock, felt something soft [my father who caught me]...." The letter sounded like Farini and the flourish that always came from his pen; it was at times preachy, and claimed others had false perceptions. For example, there was this defence of the intelligence of their act and their verve for life:

> The pitcher going to the well is true enough, but I should not like to go thirsty nevertheless. The front wheel might run off an omnibus, but that will not cause me to become a pedestrian. The recent railway accident and terrible loss of life will not prevent people travelling by rail....That the public do appreciate high-class gymnastics is proved by having crowded houses wherever we appear. As for the public thinking that I, or any other artist, am foolhardy...they are mistaken, as we love and enjoy life more than other people, as our calling gives us vigour and health to do so. I never take a chance, even in learning. Our appliances are such that we can try anything without danger.

Lulu was ready to work again before the end of the Hengler engagement and not so much as a beat was missed in her schedule. Her popularity seemed to be unaffected, so much so that a well-known gymnast named Avolo tried to get away with doing the Lulu act at the Crystal Palace that very summer—Farini stopped it and published advertisements warning others. But something had irrevocably changed with Lulu that night in Dublin and Farini, sensing that rumours about his star's true identity would now grow into factual accounts, whisked him off to Paris in

September for a few shows at the notorious Folies-Bergère: perhaps they could steal another run for Lu as a woman in a foreign country.

"It is ugly and it is superb," said author J.K. Huysmans of the Folies in the 1870s, "it is of an outrageous yet exquisite taste." Maurice Chevalier, Josephine Baker, Barbette and some of the world's first nude shows would eventually be seen on the stage of this "the most famous music hall in the world." When Lulu got there in 1876 it still had a huge indoor garden at the entrance, and spiral staircases leading up to second-floor galleries, and large statues and fountains on the floor. Walking through the garden past huge pillars customers came into the "promenoir," from which a gentleman could see the stage, even as Parisian ladies of the night propositioned him. Here, as Huysmans put it, the air "reek[ed] of the make-up of paid love and the bark of the wearied corruptions." It was racy and it was classy, it had sex and it had style. It was a long way from Hope Township, and yet not really foreign to Farini's heart.

Lulu played here in the days when many theatres were closed for the summers to allow rich customers to adjourn to various vacation spas, therefore their September 15 opening date was actually that season's debut performance. This was at least Lulu's third set of appearances in Paris and she did well, despite being on the edge of a major change. After they returned from Paris "he-she" went out on another series of performances around Great Britain, but rumours about Lulu's true sex were now much more than that and Lu himself was exasperated with his carefully controlled private life and even his long hair. Beyond that, he wanted to get married.

Edith May Hunt, Farini's younger sister, despite being several years Lulu's senior, had struck up a more than friendly relationship with him during his visits to Hope Township. His elegant, sensitive ways, slim muscular form and his fame, to say nothing of his prepossessing appearance, must have charmed her. Another relative once

described him as being quite striking to encounter during
his visits with Signor Farini to the Hunt and Marsh farmhouses, sweeping into rustic kitchens and living rooms
with his flowing blond hair and a black cape tied theatrically to his suit coat. Edith, or Eda as Lu called her, was a
handsome woman, extremely neat and tidy, with a reputation for being the best and most elegant dresser in the
family; she had the squarish face of the Hunts and the
somewhat snobby air that sometimes was a part of their
personalities. She had little use for the circus. But Lulu,
who had been forced to live such a strange, remote life,
loved her serious ways and may have felt comforted in the
arms of this tall, stylish twenty-four-year-old (he was, at
most, twenty-one) who represented security with her age,
her attitude and her connection to his adopted family.

In a private letter, mailed from the Farinis' rooms in
Lincoln's Inn Fields, sealed with a large, green and red
"LULU" sticker and dated December 3, 1876, Lu revealed
to his new niece Lucia Marsh (daughter of William Marsh
and Ann Hunt) a sudden change in his life: "I no longer
wear *long hair*," he wrote with pride, "which was ever a
source of annoyance to me when I had it."

His short hair and his marriage to Edith signalled his
return to his true sex, but it was not the end of his career.
In fact he would perform for several more years and
remain quite popular, dressed in the familiar Lulu costume
but not pretending to be female. He wore short hair for the
rest of his life (it began thinning almost as soon as he cut
it), grew a moustache (and later a beard), eventually took
to wearing circular, wire-rimmed glasses and actually had
them on during performances the last few years of his
career. The whole tone of his performance was entirely different by the end of 1876. Not only was there no mystery
about his sex, there was little deception about the leap
because earlier in the year, about the time his accident was
signalling the beginning of the end, W.H. Cremer published a book in London de-mystifying the magical tricks of
the great conjurers of the day. And there, in several pages
of minute description was "Lulu's Leap Explained."

Then, to top everything off, Edith became pregnant and in August 1877, Mademoiselle Lulu was the father of a daughter named May.

There was a certain amount of public indignation expressed as it slowly and finally became evident that Lulu was a man, particularly from those gentlemen who had fallen in love with "her" and especially from those who had offered marriage. But Farini wasn't concerned about people who bought the deception and then felt betrayed. Despite his prodigous imagination, he was a practical man and expected others to have at least enough practicality to understand that show business was about deception—if they couldn't see that, then they were just deceiving themselves. The public had bought the Lulu illusion for simple reasons: they wanted to see her fly, and they wanted all the erotic sensations she could give them. Now they were angry that they had actually felt such things, under Farini's spell.

The death of Mademoiselle Lulu wasn't even a blip in the rush forward that was Farini's life. In fact, things were speeding up. Early in 1877 he was approached by influential London entrepreneurs who wanted him to mastermind a huge but failing entertainment enterprise. He accepted their offers and told them exactly what they needed to solve their problems. They needed something spectacular, something that would startle London and the whole show-business industry, something absolutely frightening, previously thought impossible...and he had an idea.

CHAPTER 16

The Wizard of Westminster

"Farini, who was unfathomably dark and silent, was the original of Svengali in Du Maurier's 'Trilby'"
Mrs. Lucy Buck, daughter of the Royal Aquarium's
medical adviser, in *The Radio Times* (London) 1933

*"The following Titles, with Lithos, Registered:
...the Human Cannonball...the Living Projectile..."*
Farini's ads in *The Era*, 1877

The Royal Aquarium and Summer and Winter Garden, Westminster, was the rather pretentious name given to an ominous brick and glass building that began rising across Broad Sanctuary from Westminster Abbey in the spring and summer of 1875. Its purpose was equally pretentious. And when it opened on January 22, 1876 in the presence of Queen Victoria's son (the Duke of Edinburgh), the Lord Mayor of London, the American, Austrian and Turkish ambassadors and thousands of distinguished and not-so-distinguished guests, all entertained by Arthur Sullivan's four-hundred-piece orchestra, there was reason to believe it would live up to its mandate. The Royal Aquarium (soon affectionately known as "the Aq," and not-so-affectionately as "the Tank") was supposed to be a respectable institution, providing classical music, art, drama, high-brow entertainment and marine biology to Londoners right in their own backyard, a place where a British subject could see history and culture in three-dimension.

Sitting along the north side of Tothill Street opposite the Westminster Palace Hotel, it could be seen not only from the Abbey but from the windows of Parliament some

three or four hundred yards away, and reached on foot
from St. James Park or Buckingham Palace in ten or fifteen minutes. It was six hundred feet long and two storeys
high, thick and dark and dominated by heavy red brick;
there were cathedral-like towers at its entrance, and over
it arched another glass roof. Columns of polished granite
tried to relieve its looming presence, but nearby carved
sea creatures reinforced the darker effect, intimating that
strange, underwater beings lived within its doors. The
Alexandra and Crystal palaces, still sparkling on their
hills, now had an evil downtown sister. *The Times* correspondent said, "Beautiful the exterior cannot be called,
nor altogether in harmony with the venerable buildings in
the immediate neighbourhood."

Coming into the Aquarium from the eastern end visitors found themselves in a large vestibule with small fish
tanks on tables. From here they entered the main part of
the building, the central hall, nearly 350 feet long, with a
strange chocolate-and-blue colour scheme, dominated by
the huge, curving glass ceiling and filled with fountains,
statues, stalls for exhibits and huge salt-water and freshwater tanks. Here there was room for thousands of chairs
for exhibitions and opposite the Tothill entrance at the
hall's centre was a large main stage. The orchestra sat at
the western end, arrayed before a massive pipe organ,
which looked gothic and haunting as it rose in front of a
big, church-like window. Leading off from both stories
were libraries, restaurants, smoking rooms and an art
gallery presided over by John Everett Millais. The company also intended to open a roller-skating rink (almost a
necessity at the time) as well as a two-thousand-seat theatre under the direction of John Hollingshead.

The thirteen huge tanks of the central hall were supplied by reservoirs built into the basement containing
700,000 gallons of water, but on opening day visitors saw
few fish. Though this was considered to be merely a result
of a hasty opening it was actually a harbinger of problems
for a dismal first year.

Aquariums had been springing up the past few years

throughout England, the United States and Europe, the
one in Brighton, England being particularly successful,
and it was thought a London model would be a cinch to
succeed. It was the brainchild of impressive, capable men:
the distinguished Wybrow Robertson and his brilliant
though unpredictable colleague Henry Labouchere, and
involved the likes of Sullivan and Millais. On their
Council of Fellows sat a glittering array of theatrical
giants, such as Hollingshead, W.S. Gilbert, Henry Irving
and E.A. Sothern, and an enviable collection of princes,
dukes and earls (including a Rothschild). But despite such
stellar leadership the Royal Aquarium somehow got it all
wrong right from the outset. The Duke of Edinburgh
proudly stated its purpose in his opening remarks: "to
stimulate the love of natural history and the acquirement
of scientific knowledge." But such lofty ideals were part of
the problem. In order to survive, this huge building
needed to consistently draw big crowds from all classes of
the populace, not just a few thousand well-heeled citizens.
The Aq limped through its first few months, open from
eleven in the morning until eleven at night. Still without
even its tanks full, it provided beautiful paintings, an elegant library, good food and first-class music to a partially
filled, poorly ventilated and over-heated central hall. By
the end of the year it was in real financial trouble and
something had to be done to keep it from going under.

The Board decided there was one man who could save
it, turn its fortunes around immediately and bring huge
crowds to the doors. He was controversial and a little
secretive, and there were questions about his methods: he
was the creator of the marvellous Lulu and the mastermind behind many dangerous "thrill acts" that made
money hand over fist.

As soon as Farini arrived at the Aquarium things began
to change. His title was "technical advisor," but in fact he
was in charge of most of the entertainment. He lined up
his old friend Dr. Lynn to bring his bizarre and bloody
magic act and his "Hindoo Snake Charmers" from India to

the Aq, and signed acrobats and dog trainers and sword
swallowers to get things moving. Many citizens were
aghast. But they didn't worry him any more than the old
ladies in Bowmanville had. He set out to shock them. He
wanted to create something spectacular for the Aq, to fix
it in the public's imagination. He decided on a big bang,
literally. He invented the human cannonball act.

It didn't happen overnight, inventions seldom do. In fact,
the first documented public performance of the feat of
shooting a human being out of a cannon occurred two
years earlier, on March 15, 1875, at Wood's Museum in
New York, presented by old American circus proprietor
Yankee Robinson. Even though it is unknown whether
Farini had any connection with this first presentation, it
is still correct to consider him the originator of the act.
    First of all there is some question about whether or not
the human bullet was ever really fired from the cannon in
the Robinson presentation. *The New York Clipper*, for one,
thought it a "ghost illusion." The feat also didn't generate
much publicity, again calling into question its veracity and
indicating that it wasn't very spectacular. Albeit once it
went out on the road with Robinson's circus that year it
was often at the head of the bill, advertised as "The Great
Sepoy Gun Feat," and the show specified it was not an illusion, but this is over-shadowed by the fact that this minor
circus drew badly and collapsed in financial ruin part way
through the season. There was a similar act attempted in
Paris in late November 1875, in which someone named
Mayol was to be shot forty-five feet out of a "mortar" to a
trapeze bar; but it failed badly and the gymnast narrowly
escaped death after landing on his head on the balustrade.
    Farini patented his projecting springs for use in a
"Theatrical Cannon" in December 1875 (the only major
change was that an explosion of gunpowder was used to
release the catch which moved the springs—he had been
using springs in the Lulu Leap for several years by then),
while Robinson never patented his act, leading one to
believe that it either wasn't competent, or was based on

Farini's Lulu-leap mechanism, first registered in 1870. Even gymnast George Loyal's unsubstantiated claim that he was doing the feat as early as 1872 in Australia is undermined by Farini's 1870 patent. Acrobats who purchased his Lulu-leap machines often advertised in trade papers that it could also be used for the cannon act. Toward the end of 1877 he placed his own ad in *The Era Almanack,* staking his claim to the invention so aggressively that even the phrases "Shot from a Cannon," "The Living Projectile," and "The Human Cannonball" were proclaimed his property.

He was certainly the first person to project acrobats through the air and the hundreds of types of similar bounding acts which have followed for more than a century have their birth in his ideas. He is the father of show business's "thrill acts" or "the big thrill."

When it came time to make the Royal Aquarium a paying proposition Farini decided to unleash the real cannonball feat. Unlike Robinson's tentative beginning there would be no question about whether or not a human being actually came out of Farini's cannon and the act wouldn't die a quick and ignominious death. It was an absolute and terrifying smash from its opening night (and remains so to this day).

Farini, of course, didn't do it the way anyone would have expected (not that anyone in England "expected" to see a human being exploded out of a cannon). His first instinct was to use a girl as his bullet, a tactic calculated to make the feat even more terrifying. Later in life he was asked about the use of young girls in these sorts of acts, the implication in the question was that this practice was not only in itself cruel but that cruelty was likely used in her training. He insisted that he was "entirely opposed to cruelty...[and that]...when you are instructing a girl you should secure that she never hurts herself ever so slightly. That keeps their nerves intact. Give me, for my part a good girl, that is a credit to my home as well as to my entertainment. A girl of loose morals is rarely a conscientious artist."

Farini may have been training the girl whom he chose
to be his human cannonball for five years prior to her
debut. But regardless of how long he was working with
the feat and the gymnast, he didn't put the two together
until some time in 1876. The girl was then fourteen years
old. She may or may not have been the noble creature he
claimed his protégés always were, and her training may
not have been entirely free from what some would consider cruelty, but one thing is certain and not surprising:
her early years with Farini were controversial.

Her name was Rosa Matilda Richter and she was born
April 14, 1862 on Agnes Street, Waterloo Road, London,
the daughter of German circus and dramatic agent Ernst
Richter and his (English) wife Susanna. She first went on
the stage as a small child, a singer and dancer, and performed for a number of years at some of London's premier
theatres under the tutelage of some of the best pantomime
directors and ballet masters. At about ten or eleven years
old she began taking gymnastic lessons from respected
teacher Herr Stergenbach and soon, borrowing from the
greatest "female" gymnast of the day, made her trapeze
debut as "La Petite Lulu" (a name which makes an early
Farini connection plausible). Subsequently she toured
Europe as part of a Japanese troupe of acrobats, but then
her story becomes a bit muddy.

Her father and mother did not get along and a separation was worked out. Not long after this she was appearing in Germany and was approached with a business
proposition by a gentleman named Lorenz Stolberg, who
had seen her perform and was very impressed. Soon she
was signed as his apprentice. It was understood that she
would be a singer and dancer with her new employer. This
shadowy German gentleman's real name was G.A. Farini.

Or so said Rosa's father, but his version of the events
leading up to the creation of the world's first important
human cannonball performer is a little suspect. First, it
was published in a three-page scandal-piece in Henry
Labouchere's London journal *Truth*, a title which was considered by its many critics to be chock-full of irony.

Labouchere was a part-time show-business impresario, involved with the Royal Aquarium's launch, and eventually a colourful and controversial member of parliament— Queen Victoria was said to have told Gladstone to keep him out of the cabinet due to his questionable journalism. He pretended to not know Farini during this interview with Ernst Richter, but he obviously knew him well and violently disagreed with the style of entertainment then dominating his beloved Royal Aq. In addition to Labouchere's bias, there was also the fact that Richter and his wife, who were on the worst of terms, had very different views about their daughter's apprenticeship. The father claimed that he didn't know "Lorenz" was the famous, mysterious Farini, and said that "Farini should never have a dog of mine, much less a daughter, for his dangerous performances"; while his wife knew all along with whom they were dealing, and approved of it.

If the father's version is accurate, it speaks volumes about the dark side of Farini's personality and his genius for foreign languages. But since the mother seemed to have little problem with the arrangement and in fact Rosa was taken into Farini's home and clothed and fed by him, the Richter-Labouchere story is not entirely believable.

Farini promoted his dark image—it helped to sell tickets. But it wasn't always just an image and it is important to not summarily excuse accusations about sinister conduct on his part. Obviously Richter and Labouchere were not the first people to have concerns about him, and it seems likely there was some truth in the article. Then there is the fact that he seems to have made great sums of money from the human cannonball performances, at least 120 pounds per week even in the early days, and paid his protégée and her mother a very small percentage of the take—his critics claimed just five pounds. Farini was always indignant at such criticism, taking laymen to task for accusing him of sitting back and profiting from artists who risked their lives, "but look what I have done," he said, "I have invented, patented, and constructed apparatus at a cost of two thousand pounds. I have taught the artist his or her business. I used to supervise every detail of a performance, and I never had an accident. My pupils have not always been so fortunate after leaving me." He should have said his students never had a "serious accident" (and was not including Mary Osborne as a "pupil") and he certainly could have paid his protégés more. However, his statement is essentially true and, unlike many impresarios, he also risked his own life during his career and demonstrated his inventions to his students while training them. His dark image persisted for many years: it fit this unusual Victorian so anxious to explore his passions, the more dangerous the better.

Given Rosa's earlier career her training likely went fairly quickly. Farini taught her three main feats: a spectacular dive from near the roof of the Aquarium into the net, an elegant wire-walking performance and, of course, the cannon act. Obviously he had great confidence in his safety net: not only did it have to catch Rosa in her high-dive but it was also her landing spot after she flew out of the cannon. Farini taught her how to keep herself absolutely rigid while inside the mortar, especially at the moment of the release of the spring (the cannon's insides were soon known to an intrigued public as "the vampire trap"), and then how to make herself go limp in the air just before landing. The reverse: limpness at the point of explosion or rigidity while falling, could be fatal.

Once the training was done, he needed a name for her. This time he didn't dig deeply into mythology. Instead he created a name designed solely for its sound. It wasn't uncommon in those days to invent stage names that had a number of Zs, giving them as much pizzaz as possible. Farini called Rosa...Zazel. It had the requisite flare and rhymed with and sounded like gazelle, an animal whose grace and speed Zazel would appear to possess.

The first advertisement was in the newspapers in late March, buried in a long list of attractions for the Easter holidays. It merely said: "First Appearance of the marvellous Zazel, specially engaged for the Royal Aquarium." No mention was made of a cannon. The following week, on April 2nd, just ten days before the artiste's fifteenth birthday, the debut took place.

The Aq, likely due to Farini's prodding, was beginning to get itself in order by the time she was ready to appear. On April 2nd visitors actually saw fish in the tanks and both baby and "monster" alligators. Once inside the great hall they were entertained by various comedic and musical troupes, a group of performing dogs and a "man flute." And then, just about the time the skies began to darken, Zazel gave a graceful performance on a high wire and a trapeze fastened almost at the roof. In the evening after everything else was done, the grand finale was readied for a large crowd, drawn by rumours that Farini was going to do something never done before.

Zazel's appearance was perfect. As the band played, the crowd spotted her coming toward the fearsome-looking cannon, accompanied by Signor Farini and his assistant (both decked out in evening dress). She seemed small and slight, and looked pale. She had dark, almost black, curly hair and a round face described by one onlooker as possessing "a certain fascinating beauty." Two earrings in the shape of stars sparkled in the lights, setting off the shy visage; a thick, dark necklace with a large stone hung around her neck; and her beautiful ruby red outfit, frilled with pink and cut low on the chest and in the back to scandalize everyone in just the right way, was charmingly complemented by her pink tights and slippers. Farini had an eye for how to dress his protégés, being particularly good with matching colours, especially vivid ones.

The crowd was suitably upset by the juxtaposition of this lovely little girl approaching the ominous-looking cannon, hanging as it was from the roof and wall of the Aquarium, black and massive, supported by numerous cables and one huge rope, tilted upward at a 45-degree angle. Across the hall in the direction it pointed stretched perhaps the largest safety net ever seen. Ignoring the mortar for the moment Zazel ascended to her wire and trapeze bars and gave another performance, much

applauded by the crowd. For her finish she leapt into the
net, turning a somersault as she went, putting the hearts
into the mouths of many spectators. But the calm they felt
when she landed safely was about to be exploded.

The band began playing again and Zazel dismounted
the net and climbed the ladder behind the cannon. As she
entered its huge mouth, looking scared and unsure, every
spectator stared, now certain that Farini was really going
to do what everyone was saying: he was going to fire this
little girl out of the cannon, like a human cannonball!

Zazel's head disappeared. The band stopped playing.
Farini stepped forward, dark eyes intense above a big
black beard, his muscular frame, now a little weightier,
bulging in his suit. There was almost an aura of evil about
him. In his hand he held a lighted torch. He spoke clearly,
his voice projecting well in the large hall, as he assured
the doubtful spectators that there wasn't the slightest
danger in this feat. Over the buzz of the crowd that had
increased at his first words, he then said loudly: "During
this part of the performance I must request strict
silence...in order that I may hear when the fair artiste is
ready for the applying of the torch." He turned toward the
cannon. "Are you in?" he asked. There was absolute
silence. Then a small, sweet voice said, "Yes," and Farini
moved abruptly to the base of the cannon. He lit the powder.

Suddenly an explosion rocked the hall, its concussion
seemingly capable of smashing every inch of the huge
glass ceiling, frightening the transfixed spectators and
making them shudder where they stood. Instantly, almost
too fast for the eyes of people who had never dreamt they
would see such a thing, a human being was flying out of
the cannon, a red flash as quick as a bullet firing through
the smoke from the mortar and out across the hall, landing in a perfect hit in the centre of the net. Zazel appeared
limp as she struck Farini's web and it gave four feet as it
took her weight. All eyes watched her, the echo of the
explosion still ringing in the hall. Would she rise?... She
came up slowly, onto apparently shaky legs, her face

pale...but then the band started up, she smiled, and applause burst from the crowd like a second explosion and reverberated up and down the great hall.

In that instant Zazel became a star.

In the following days the Royal Aquarium attracted the largest crowds it had ever drawn, its interior a dense mass of people waiting for Zazel. More than 20,000 came one day during the Easter holidays; and they kept on coming week after week, and soon month after month. For the holiday performance in May the Aq's gate receipts showed that 17,000 more people came that day than on the same occasion the previous year.

Arthur J. Munby, a curious Victorian gentleman who was fascinated by working-class women (so much so that he secretly married one) and female trapezists, went to see Zazel at the Aquarium a few weeks after her debut and recorded his thoughts in a diary:

> To the Aquarium at 5, and again saw "Zazel" and again astonished (as everyone was) at the courage and coolness and skill of this girl of 18 (sic): who, drest as an acrobat, walked the tightrope without a pole, lay down on it and rose again on one leg, and the like: then swung herself about on the trapeze like a monkey, and sat on it like a strong man, with big arms folded, and sitting thus, flung her body round and round it, holding it by the hollow of her knees: then leaped 60 feet down, head fore most: then let herself down, feet first, into a cannon, and was literally fired thence into the air, falling flat on a net: and 15 minutes afterwards, was seen in neat woman's clothing, walking quietly home with her sister, as modest and demure as any school girl.

Now it was Zazel's turn to be the principal sensational performer in London, for her photograph to be one of the most sought after in the city, for her portrait to appear on the cover of magazines, for her to receive professions of love from gentlemen, and of course, for *Punch* to put her charms into verse:

ZAZEL
(With Mr. Punch's Compliments)
POLICEMEN, I have lost my heart
Here in the Westminster Aquarium,
Since first I saw her rapid dart
Across the diaper'd Velarium.
A form, that PHIDIAS might confess
As graceful as a young gazelle,
With raven hair, and ruby dress,
And winsome eyes, make up ZAZEL!

Like swallow swiftly starting South,
She safely skimmed the air, and yet
'Twas then my heart into my mouth
Would jump, as she did in the net.
But see, she rises like a partridge—
And now becomes a true live shell,
Or shall we say, a living cartridge?—
I wish you were 'my' charge, ZAZEL!

Discharge you! Blow you up! Not I—
I could not do it if I tried.
But let me off: you'll see me fly,
To fall in 'your' net—at your side!
A poet's loftiest flights come short
Of praising your High Art, 'ma belle',
Your aim's as good as your report:
You've hit the gold—and me, ZAZEL!

There were a few who did not join in the applause,
though the nature of their grievances was not new to
Farini: just more criticism from morally righteous people
disturbed by his ideas in action. The Home Secretary, Mr.
Cross, gave notice on April 21st that he was considering
consulting Licensing Justices if Zazel's act was continued
and that those in charge at the Aquarium were to be held
responsible should an accident occur. Farini had taken
pains to ensure Zazel's safety, using a state-of-the-art
forty-foot-wide net, and informed reporters commented on

the precautions in the act; this didn't matter to his opponents. But far from letting his critics destroy him, Farini found a way to use them. First he published statements from prominent medical men about the high likelihood of Zazel's continued good health and then issued a statement saying that he would be pleased to demonstrate the safety of the act to the Home Secretary in person by giving him "the novel and pleasureable sensation of being fired into air." He also used Cross's comments on placards to help draw crowds. Needless to say, Zazel's act was not withdrawn; in fact, its popularity grew.

In May *The Illustrated Sporting and Dramatic News* produced a full-page illustration entitled "Zazel at the Royal Aquarium." It had a dozen or more drawings of her, in a revealing costume complete with ample cleavage, in the various stages of her act: sitting daintily on the high wire with an umbrella, hanging from the bar, diving downward, etc. Also depicted was a gentleman stuffing his mother-in-law into the cannon, a lady leaning on her husband's breast pleading, "You're a fellow of the Aquarium so darling blow me up for once!!" and a whole row of men reaching out to catch Zazel as she dives, under the caption "Prepare to receive the enemy!" Dominating the whole drawing was Zazel flying out of a cannon inscribed with the words "A Palpable Hit"; and standing on the cannon, looking rather dark and evil, long black beard billowing on his chest, stood Farini in an athletic pose, lighting the mortar: "Farini finds his match," read the caption.

An accompanying article dealt with Farini's renowned training skills and advised women that Zazel's figure, pronounced almost perfect, was gained from the "athletic education" her trainer had given her; a message distinctly like Farini's own views about the importance of exercise.

New bits were added to her act. Like El Niño, she sang a song: hers was called "It Is So Easy." And before long she took to falling from her apparatus, frightening the crowd as she suddenly dropped like a rock to the net. Farini also came up with a new phrase to advertise her, from Shakespeare of all sources: "Seeking the bubble reputation, at the cannon's mouth."

Though she was far and away the main attraction and the Aq's most lucrative presentation ever, other acts of a distinctly Fariniesque nature helped to draw crowds. Dr. Lynn and his snake-charmers were there, as were the Gilfort Brothers' strange strong-man act, the Mountaineers of the Apennines, the Performing Fleas, and a "General Volunteer Assault of Arms" wherein people were invited to test themselves against one another in a gigantic brawl using bayonets, sabres, tug-of-war, single sticks or whatever struck their fancy. In mid-July P.T. Barnum was booked to lecture at the theatre and Farini billed him as "proprietor of The Greatest Show on Earth (always excepting the Royal Aquarium)." The legendary American impresario was one of the most famous people in the world and Farini admired many things about him. The feeling appeared to be mutual: the great man was enchanted by Farini's wonderful ideas, right from the moment Lulu leapt into space. Just before he left London that year he offered Farini two hundred pounds a week for eight months of Zazel's services with his great circus. Farini was tied to an extended Aquarium contract and turned him down, but saw an irresistible advertising opportunity in this private bid. A few days later the Royal Westminster Aquarium issued the following statement:

ONE THOUSAND POUNDS REWARD, or $5,000—It having come to the knowledge of the undersigned that a conspiracy exists on the part of the Hon. P.T. Barnum for the abduction of Zazel, the above reward will be paid to any one giving such information as will lead to the conviction of the said Hon. P.T. Barnum. (Signed),
W.W. Robertson, G.A. Farini—Royal Aquarium.

The publicity gained was tremendous, perhaps one reason why Barnum later called Farini "the most talented showman" he knew. One paper even produced a drawing of Barnum flying toward the United States clutching Zazel, powered by a blast from the cannon.

That same week, as sharks were put into the tanks, Farini continued his pursuit of the unusual by bringing "The Only Gorilla" to the Aq. Mr. Pongo, the first of his kind to be transported to Europe without dying, was three years old, three-feet-nine-inches tall, hugely muscled around his chest and abdomen, had a black face, grey hair and big hands, which he clapped together when excited, and other human-like habits (like constantly wrapping himself in a cloak), intriguing Victorians to no end. He had been at the Berlin Aquarium for more than a year, where a quarter of a million people had been to see him. In London the Prince and Princess of Wales dropped by, and well-known animal expert Frank Buckland decided to teach him to write: this curious idea, obviously inspired by the current fascination with Darwin, ended when Pongo devoured a good chunk of "the best Cumberland lead."

Francis Trevelyan Buckland, who thought he could converse with animals, fit right in with all the weirdness in Farini's realm. The son of a distinguished scholar, he had been fascinated by natural history and four-legged beasts from childhood, when he often startled classmates by walking about with his pet monkey and bear. After attending Oxford he took up medicine but soon became known as a writer and journalist. His subjects ranged from pisciculture (he was later appointed Inspector of Fisheries) to sideshow freaks and unusually gifted acrobats. An eternally happy and eccentric man with a scruffy black beard, his home near Regent's Park was legendary, packed as it was with bizarre pets and guests, from famous giants to Chinese dignitaries and Zulu chieftains; one giant even wrote his signature on the ceiling. Buckland and Farini hit it off right away at the Aquarium, and with two of Frank's best friends, renowned scientist Henry Lee and A.D. Bartlett of the Zoological Gardens, they made an interesting quartet. Farini was then experimenting with a fish hatchery on one of his farms in Hope Township, and the scientists, impressed with his piscicultural abilities, encouraged him. Besides Buckland's interest in the gorilla, he was involved with Farini's later exploits with whales

and Zulu warriors. The two friends were a perfect fit:
clever, inquiring and eccentric. Buckland held many
Victorian niceties in contempt and did not seem to care
how he was regarded, a trait which allowed him to hobnob
with acrobats and sideshow freaks on the same day he
might sit down with the Prince or Prime Minister Disraeli
(whom he took to see Pongo). In this he was aided by his
father's reputation and his own significant accomplishments in the field of natural history (he was the most popular writer on the subject during the Victorian era).
Farini's own background and the nature of his accomplishments did not always give him the same social confidence.

Farini's influence at the Aquarium grew during 1877.
By late September Zazel was billed as "Farini's Last
Invention"; and after adjustments to raise the roof, he had
her doing the "Eagle-Swoop," a hair-raising high-dive into
the net from a much loftier spot than her earlier leaps. It
started about one hundred feet above the floor. In October
her still controversial act received a peculiar endorse-
ment—from the Reverend S.D. Headlam, Curate of St.
Matthews, Bethnal Green, who commented in a lecture
that, "...the pluck, the nerve, the agility which we see in
Zazel at the Aquarium are as admirable in my mind as
her exquisite grace and beauty of form." But despite this
and other successes, Farini already had another strange
attraction well past the planning stages. He was going to
bring a live whale to England and put it in a huge tank in
the great hall; no one had ever been able to show one of
these sea monsters to Europe before.

The whale was acquired through connections Farini had
recently established with an exceptional American showman about his own age named William Cameron Coup. It
was W.C. Coup who convinced Barnum to get into the circus business in a big way, who ran his shows for a number
of years and was responsible for many important innova-
tions in sawdust-ring history. He took the seminal step of
transporting the big show by rail, was instrumental in
raising the first Madison Square Garden in New York and

after leaving Barnum in 1875 erected the New York Aquarium on Broadway with famed animal importer Charles Reiche. The following year he built another aquarium at Coney Island and it was while he was acquiring the first whales ever put into captivity for this enterprise that Farini came calling.

The whales Coup captured (off the coast of Labrador in the Gulf of St. Lawrence) were belugas: the small white whale that looked like a dolphin and whose full length at adulthood ranged between fifteen and eighteen feet. Hunting them involved cornering them in bays at high tide, lifting them out of the water with huge nets and heaving them into travelling cases. These watertight cases were filled up to the whales' eyes but not above their blow-holes, in order to allow them to breath. Periodically salt water was poured over them, but despite this, Coup had trouble keeping them alive and of the eleven he captured in the early summer of 1877 only one survived. The first to make it to New York died the day it entered its tank and the second three days later. It was the third "white whale," a young female nearly ten feet long which had lived an apparently healthy existence for several months swimming in a continuous circle in her round aquarium home, that was dispatched across the Atlantic to Farini on September 15th. It took ten days for the steamer to cross and the whale, sitting in its water-case on a bed of seaweed, fed by bushels of eels, salt water thrown over it every three minutes, appeared to have problems before they were even halfway over. Its handlers were emboldened by its ability to survive a longer trip after its initial capture, but stupidly did not account for the diminishment of its health during its stay in New York. By the time it arrived in Southampton it had a severe cold and its blow-hole was filling with mucus.

Farini was at the docks with the Aquarium's naturalist to receive the whale. Concerned with its condition, they raised it onto a railway car and whisked it up to London. Meanwhile a huge hole had been dug in the Aq's floor, big enough to encase a 50-by-25-foot, 50,000-gallon tank,

larger than the whale's New York home. Just before noon
they arrived at Waterloo station and in front of a gathering crowd put the whale into a "van" and rushed it to the
Aq where the big tank was still being filled. At five minutes to four on the 26th they eased it into its new home.
Incredibly, the tank did not contain salt water, a fact that
Farini and his colleagues desperately regretted, but which
was forced on them when they realized that pumping
water between the whale's tank and all the others, as was
normal procedure, would poison the other fish.

Everyone watched and waited. Initially the beluga
dropped to the bottom like lead but slowly seemed to find
itself and started swimming in the little circles it had
known in New York. Eventually it discovered it could
swim straight ahead for some distance and began doing
this, coming up for air at intervals. The *Times* correspondent was worried about the whale from the moment he
saw it, noting it was considerably below its proper half-ton
weight, that it seemed frightened by noises caused by
nearby workmen and, above all, that it needed to be in
salt water in order to survive. At seven o'clock the public
was let in and they came in droves to see the small white-
skinned whale, as they did on Thursday and Friday. At
midnight on the latter day the naturalist John T.

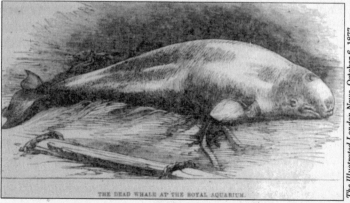

THE DEAD WHALE AT THE ROYAL AQUARIUM.

The Illustrated London News, October 6, 1877

Carrington sat up with it, deeply concerned about its health. No doubt the freshwater was causing it problems but its greatest difficulty was the cold it had caught on its voyage, which had developed into pneumonia before it even got to the Aq. Carrington saw that its breathing was becoming more laboured by the hour and that mucus was rising from its blow-hole when it blew hard at the surface. Around one o'clock it became strangely excited, swimming up and down the tank at high speed, sometimes hitting its head against the end. A few hours later it stayed down for fifteen minutes, rose for a gasp of air, swam across the tank and struck its head again. Then it turned over on its side and died. Immediately the eels, meant for food, glued themselves to the whale's skin.

Farini was undaunted. Within a day he announced he had concluded a contract to acquire another whale. Rather than considering the possibility that it too would come to a pitiable end, he vowed to succeed, stating that the problems encountered the first time were solvable and would not be repeated. He would have to wait nearly eight months.

Zazel's popularity continued unabated through attractions like Pongo and the ill-fated whale. She appeared twice daily, her performances often free, to draw people to the Aquarium. There were cartoons about her in popular magazines and even an accomplished thoroughbred race horse named after her. The inimitable Leybourne, England's "Lion Comique," advanced her popularity even further by prancing about London's stages, cane in hand, hat set at a jaunty angle, singing a song about her. Entitled simply "Zazel," it told the comic tale of a country bumpkin coming to London and being dazzled by its cornucopia of sights. A Londoner tells him that Zazel is a particularly "grand" attraction, and at the Aq he is so captivated by her beauty and her frightening act that he still dreams of her many days later, and sings:

Zazel, Zazel, have you seen Zazel?
Zazel, Zazel, my beautiful belle.

It's wonderful fun when she's shot from a gun,
I could live and die for Zazel.

Leybourne was also performing "Lounging in the Aq,"
the story of a swell's love for the mighty "Tank" and its
racy attractions. Farini's haunt (which attracted more
than its share of prostitutes) was definitely the place for
something illicit:

I've tried all kinds of gaiety, I've seen all sorts of sport.
And concert, theatre, and ball, have each been my resort.
Yet pleasing as they all may be, they somehow seem
to lack,
The charm of the Aquarium, or as we say the "Aq".
Lounging in the "Aq", Lounging in the "Aq",
That against all other modes of killing time I'll back!
Fun that's never slack, eyes brown, blue, and black.
Make one feel in Paradise while lounging in the "Aq".

On October 13th as Zazel neared her 350th performance
at the Aquarium, the Gaiety Theatre in the West End,
managed by John Hollingshead and famous for its bur-
lesques, took advantage of her fame and the mysterious
man behind her, in their production of H.J. Byron's parody
of Goethe's *Faust*. Nellie Farren, then England's greatest
burlesque performer, starred as "Little Doctor Faust." In
this interpretation the evil Mephistopheles was presented
as a showman, tempting "her" to view his exhibition. "Will
you walk into our show sir?" sang Edward Terry in the
devil's role, "There are many things you know sir...there
never yet was seen sir, Such a scorching exhibition as this
here particular show." Terry, a remarkable comedic actor,
dressed dark and bearded, was immediately recognizable
as the mysterious Farini, and the comparison was brought
to a climax when Mephistopheles stuffed young Faust into
a cannon and appeared to fire her across the stage onto
Marguerite's balcony. "Are you in?" asked Terry in his best
"American" accent before lighting the torch, "Are you far
in?" he asked again..."Are you Nel-lie Far-in?" Known to

many playgoers as the Zazel Burlesque, this show enjoyed great success, running for 151 consecutive performances until it finally stopped seven months later, in April 1878. Then in August it started another run.

The show increased Zazel's fame, and its characterization of Farini contributed to a legend about him. More than half a century later Lucy Bond (daughter of Dr. Bond, physician to the Royal Aquarium) publicly stated that Farini, whom she recalled as "unfathomably dark and silent"…"was the original of Svengali in Du Maurier's 'Trilby.'" If this is true it casts his personality forever in history, since the concept of a Svengali is a part of languages worldwide. The *Webster's International Dictionary* defines "Svengali" as "one who attempts usu. with evil intentions to persuade or force another to do his bidding." This was certainly the image that the Gaiety players were toying with in "Little Dr. Faust" when they made Farini into the devil. His ability to train young performers to perfection and convince them to mount his terrifying projecting machines, and the ingenuity of those machines, never explained by him and so mystifying to most, was a wonder to the public. He seemed to be able to make people fly, explode them out of guns and off bare stage boards. And by the turn of that year rumours abounded that he was building a catapult onto which he would actually put human beings and shoot them two hundred feet through the air. Even the British government was worried about him, as will soon be seen. There was speculation in London that Farini had control over a whole group of young girls and called them all Zazel. If one balked at entering the cannon's mouth, he merely substituted another. It was a strange accusation…and absolutely true.

Zazel's fame soon reached the U.S. without her ever leaving England. On October 6th her portrait was on the front page of *The New York Clipper* and the following week the paper announced that she ("of exquisite shape") would soon be coming to America, possibly under Barnum's management. This didn't happen, but a few months later a cannon feat was announced for the Great

London Show at Gilmore's (Madison Square) Garden. Other human cannonballs began appearing, the most prominent Mlle. Geraldine, who (with Farini's permission) fired herself out at Coney Island. Later she did it with the help of famed magician Professor Herrmann, who had his own cannon show. Then there was George Loyal, in the midst of a lucrative career as a missile that would make him a star with the great Forepaugh Circus. Like many of Farini's imitators Loyal had a few accidents, including a celebrated one in New York in 1879, but his act, wherein he flew into the waiting arms of Ella Zuila who hung upside down from a trapeze bar, was a winner.

Farini held Zazel back from a trip overseas, waiting for an opportune moment. Besides, he still had a great deal to do in London. For Christmas the Aq's great hall provided a diversion to the theatre's pantomime of "A Frog He Would A-Wooing Go" with Ethardo, the famous spiral ascensionist who climbed to the absolute peak of his apparatus in their building, the Dare Brothers, Benedetti the sword swallower (a good exponent of an art which Farini admired), a female Abyssinian snake-charmer named Lualla and a whole village of Laplanders complete with sleds, reindeer, dogs, songs and even white foxes, whom Farini had signed after learning about them while one of his importers was searching for a walrus.

He also set plans in motion for 1878. First he had a new act for Lulu, who had continued touring and was still immensely popular, despite performing in his frilled woman's suit and sporting a moustache and glasses. In May 1877 Lulu had even returned to stardom in London, playing the Alexandra Palace and the prestigious Canterbury simultaneously. He was becoming more and more independent from Farini, whose involvement with Zazel, the Aquarium attractions and a veritable stable of gymnasts kept him busy, though the two men certainly did not sever their business partnership. For a long time (several years in fact) Lulu's advertisements had been announcing that he would soon go to the colonies and India to perform, and then retire. This may well have been his plan, and retirement was definitely on his mind almost from the moment he married, but by the end of 1877 he was still going strong. However, both he and Farini were tired of the Lulu Leap. In January Farini announced that his awesome catapult would soon be completed and Lulu would take the first flight. Though this act's debut was farther in the future than he anticipated, he wasn't going to have to wait as long for two other big attractions. The first was his second whale.

In May he went to the Labrador coast, supervised the capture of four belugas and transported them directly to Liverpool. Leaving three in northern English aquariums as reserves, he brought a big (more than thirteen feet long) two-year-old female to London. It was healthier from the start and its popular stay at the Aq lasted a couple of months, but late in the summer, just as it was sent off to the World's Fair in Paris, it died. (It was also announced at this time that he had gained exclusive whale-fishing rights off a stretch of the Labrador coast and had even purchased an "enclosed bay, serving as a kind of 'whale preserve.'" Farini told a reporter later in life that in total he imported twenty whales.)

To top the whale he wanted a mermaid.

The legend of the these half-women, half-fish, who like sirens of mythology seduced lonely sailors into watery graves, was so popular in Victorian days that many actually believed it. Barnum once presented a fake mermaid but Farini, always trying to be scientific as well as spectacular, decided to show the public what a mermaid really was. Though popular entertainment now dominated the Royal Aquarium, they still struggled to maintain a higher tone than the music halls. The way they dealt with the "mermaid" was in line with these goals.

Farini knew that a large, herbivorous marine mammal called a manatee gave rise to the mermaid legend. They could reach a length of ten feet, had a flat tail, paddle-shaped flippers, a head vaguely the shape of a human being's, small ear holes, a nose of sorts, eyes that blinked, a mouth which appeared to have lips and breasts in the chest area. Its habit of standing up on its tail to look for food and feeding its young by pulling them to a breast made the resemblance to a human being not entirely ridiculous at a distance. In legend the mermaid is often pictured combing her hair, a mirror in one hand and comb in the other. This pose was not unlike a position commonly struck by the manatee while peering above the surface of the water. Early in the summer Farini or one of his agents captured a particularly large manatee near the Demerara River, off the coast of Guyana. On June 22nd it debuted at the Aq in a large glass tank, its nine-foot length perpendicular as its round face stared out above the water's surface. Only one manatee had been brought to Britain before and it had been much smaller and died in two or three days. This one, called "Manatee, the Mermaid" fared much better, living for nearly a year.

The presentation was a decided success. Human beings had rendered the manatee extinct in many parts of the world, so just getting one was a coup. Debunking a lie rather than creating one gave the Aquarium some credibility and yet still drew large crowds. In fact the first weekend "Farini's Zazel," "Farini's Live Whale" and the mermaid were combined, they drew the largest crowd in the Tank's history, and both *The Times* and *The Daily Telegraph* wrote lengthy articles about the mermaid myth and how the Aq was solving it.

One would think that with all of Farini's success the summer of 1878 would have been an exciting time. But the fact that he and his wife continued to drift apart dampened things. Due to the frenzied pace of their schedule, their two boys were sent to live with a Mr. and Mrs. Tier in Emsworth, a small place just a few miles northeast of Portsmouth. Despite frequent visits, this distancing became another source of problems within the marriage. At the height of Farini's triumphs in July, a month after his fortieth birthday, they agreed to separate. Alice went down to Emsworth to be with the children and Farini lived in his rooms near the Aquarium, his periodic sojourns to the coast being solely for visits with his boys.

He seldom spoke with his wife; in fact, she often left during his time there and gave her bedroom over to him. But the greatest storm in their personal lives was yet to come.

Fresh on the heels of the mermaid, Farini signed one of the most famous "freaks" of the late nineteenth century. This was Millie-Christine, given two names because she was two people: black Siamese twins born into slavery in the U.S. They were often called the "Two-Headed Nightingale" because the greatest part of their act was singing. In a few years Farini would become much more involved in the "freak" world, but the association with Millie and Christine was one of his first. That same month he also presented dwarfs Baron Littlefinger, Count Rosebud and the Countess of Lilliput.

But not everything at the Aq was freakish. Farini needed respectability too, so he booked many highly regarded magicians, as well as inventors and explorers, some displaying different versions of the telephone, others lecturing about journeys to far-off parts of the world and even a group who crossed the Atlantic in a nineteen-foot flat-bottomed boat.

About halfway through the year Farini and Lulu finally got the catapult act operating. When one contemplates the danger of the feat it is difficult to understand why Lulu consented to do it. He and Edith had taken a few months off toward the end of 1877 and vacationed in Hope Township for the Christmas holidays, but in England Farini was making announcements about Lulu returning in a new act, and Lu himself issued a statement that it was imminent: by early in the year he was in training at Plymouth. A few months later his show debuted: he entered the amphitheatre wearing his Lulu costume and lay down on his back on a huge iron arm, held in place against powerful resistance by a lever. Suddenly the lever was released, causing the arm to snap upward at tremendous speed, shooting Lulu through the air in an eighty-foot arc. As he flew he turned several somersaults, heading for a net at the far side of the building.

On August 19th Lulu and Ala opened in Blackpool at

the Winter Gardens. Lulu was the headliner and much
was made of the fact that "she" was now a "he," and that
his performances were completely new. They drew large
crowds and presented the image Farini wanted: of daring,
but scientific athletes. Though Lu was unable to use the
catapult the first two weeks in Blackpool, his remarkable
skill as a gymnast compensated so much that the Lulu-
Ala show was an early hit and held over. One of his tricks
was to walk a high wire made of piano wire, another was
to bounce almost up to the ceiling after landing in the net.
He was also displaying his musical skills, playing several
songs on the violin, the concertina and the harmonicon as
he walked the wire. And once the ominous catapult was
put into play, the show was even better.

On February 8th Zazel had played the 1,200th and final
show of her first Royal Westminster Aquarium run, a
stand that lasted nearly two years (and included at least
two performances before the future King Edward VII) and
would prove the longest consecutive set of appearances in
the history of the building; so far as the Aq ever had a
Queen, Zazel was it. Now Farini booked her with
Hengler's Circus
and she went out
on tour. She was
still very much an
item in the enter-
tainment papers:
Punch, responding
to some strange

Half-past Five.
PERFORMANCE BY THE MARVELLOUS
FIRED FROM THE CANNON.

rumour that she was about to marry an Archdeacon, had
recently quipped that she was about to be delivered "out
of the mouth of a Canon into the arms of an Archdeacon."

During late 1878 and into the new year P.T. Barnum
wrote to Farini discussing the possibility of signing Zazel
as a headliner for The Greatest Show on Earth. He had let
it be known to friends that this act, of all the acts in the
world, was the one he really wanted. In February G.F.
Bailey came to England on Barnum's behalf to open negotiations for her services. He offered twenty pounds per

week and Farini responded by taking the offer as merely an opening gambit. "(Bailey) MAY be a VERY clever man." Farini wrote cryptically to Barnum. Then he went on to explain that he had put 650 pounds into mounting the cannon on a carriage for Hengler's street parade and that when it had been seen by the citizens of Manchester, drawn by four horses with six men in artillery uniform, they followed it in the thousands and people were turned away at the circus's doors. He knew Barnum's love of advertising and the importance of an effective street parade. Such were his negotiating tactics, fearless in the face of dealing with America's greatest salesman. It would take the legendary showman another year to get Zazel.

This February 20th letter to Barnum also discussed the continuing difficulties he was having preventing others from doing the human cannonball feat. Part of his problem arose from the fact that he took out patents under two different names: Hunt and Farini; so he acquired new patents that cleared up the problems. Then he took steps to protect the name Zazel as his "trade mark," even issuing long advertisements proclaiming that "Zazel" was his private property and that he had the name registered throughout Europe, in England, the U.S., Australia, India and South Africa. He also warned that he had now patented the human cannonball act in five different ways: compressed air, steam, rubber springs, metallic springs and gunpowder. He offered a reward for information about showmen using his inventions and warned that he had solicitors on several continents who would prosecute. These salvos give more credence to his claim as the inventor of the act, and show that the pride and independence he had as a small child were still with him. He would take on anyone who crossed him.

During the next year he would need that attitude, as his growing list of sensational acts became even less politically acceptable and those who opposed him increased in number.

The house where the Hunts lived in Bowmanville in the early 1850s.

The young Signor Farini

The Hunts' barn in Hope Township. It was to this building's roof that Bill Hunt built his first high wire.

Jack Gordon

Blondin "the Magnificent" over the Niagara gorge.

Farini hanging from his high wire above the Niagara River, 1860.

Signor Farini carrying a washing machine over the Niagara gorge, September 5, 1860.

Farini shortly after he came to London.

Naudin's photograph of El Nino Farini on the flying trapeze, taken about 1866, is one of the earliest images of a subject in motion.

The Flying Farinis during the height of their fame in London.

El Nino and Signor Farini,
mid-1860s.

Sheet music cover for
"The Farini Waltzes,"
by R. Coote.

Mademoiselle Lulu (left), Farini (seated) and an unidentified performer about 1873.

The Royal Westminster Aquarium, London, where Farini reigned from 1877 to the mid-1880s.

Lulu, the Eighth Wonder of the World, about 1871.

Lulu (below), in a rare photograph showing him out of female attire.

Poster for P.T. Barnum's Greatest Show on Earth in 1882, featuring Lulu as a man.

Zazel at the cannon's mouth,
the Royal Westminster Aquarium,
1877. Farini is below her at right.

Rosa
Richter,
"Zazel,
the Human
Cannonball," as she
appeared in her prime.

Farini in the late 1870s,
as the dark Svengali
of the London
entertainment world.

Farini with "Krao, the Missing Link," about 1883.

Krao Farini in later years.

Krao, seated middle row second from left, on the Barnum and Bailey Circus sideshow, 1903.

The elegant Fräulein Müller, well-heeled lady and concert pianist.

G.A. Farini and Anna Müller, about the time of their marriage in Berlin in 1886.

Guillermo Antonio Farini in his mid forties.

*Cartoon of (left to right) Gert Louw,
Farini and Lulu arriving at Cape Town
for their 1885 African expedition.*

*Mr. Lulu Farini, photographer and
proprietor of Farini Photographs of
Bridgeport, Connecticut.*

*Expedition deep in the Kalahari
Desert, photographed by Lulu. Farini
is seated, wearing sombrero-like hat.*

Farini, top, with one of
his theatrical troupes in
the early 1890s.

Left to right: May Farini,
G.A. Farini, Lulu, and
Edith Hunt Farini, about 1890.

Knapp's roller boat in the Toronto harbour, 1897 (F.A. Knapp in inset).

Madame Anna Farini
and Signor G.A. Farini
in old age.

Farini the artist,
on his calling card.

Farini Hunt
in Port Hope in
the late 1920s,
as he neared
age ninety.

CHAPTER 17

Dangerous Performances

"Flying at Last Accomplished!"
Farini's ad for the human catapult, 1879

"These dangerous tricks of the ingenious Farini
have been performed for the last time…"
The Penny Illustrated Paper, February 1879

Farini's kind of poetic justice was briefly achieved that
March when Blondin was signed for a series of performances at the Royal Aquarium. The god who had disdained
him, fifty-five years old and still a rope-walker, was now
essentially in his employ. But there were things of much
greater importance in Britain in early 1879 than Blondin
or even Toby, the Tank's wonderful performing seal.

Problems that had been brewing for a long time
between the English, the Boers and the Zulus in the cluster of homelands in southern Africa were about to boil
over. The Zulus were viewed by Victorians as warlike people with a taste for savagery, and their King, Cetewayo, as
a man who was searching for opportunities to "wash his
spear" in battle. Authorities in British Africa, anxious to
remove Cetewayo from power, sent him an ultimatum in
late 1878, demanding that he disband his army, using a
few minor border incidents in the area as justification.
The proud king could not capitulate, and in January the
British Governor declared war. The white men expected to
win quickly: the might of the awesome army of the
Empire would descend upon these uncivilized black men,
led by an "ignorant and bloodthirsty despot," and
instantly bring them to their knees. But eleven days after

the war's declaration the unthinkable happened. At
Isandhlwana inside Zulu territory the "impis" of King
Cetewayo attacked a British force, and in a bloody massacre, wiped it out. When the Zulus finally drew back,
eight hundred British soldiers and five hundred of their
black auxiliaries lay dead, their bodies punctured by mis-
sile-like javelins called assegais, which had been thrown
with deadly accuracy.

Shocked and embarrassed by this defeat, the British
sent more troops to southern Africa. Stories began growing in England about Cetewayo's savagery and cunning,
and how his huge, fearsome warriors mutilated the bodies
of fallen enemies. Zulus were awe-inspiring. Among the
troops sent to Africa during the rush of patriotism in
February 1879 was the exiled French Prince Imperial,
Loulou, the son of the now-deceased Napoleon III. Farini
and Loulou's paths had already crossed, and now they
were about to do so again.

The prince had been educated at a British military
school, and demanded that he be allowed to fight. On
June 1st, while on an insignificant mission in supposedly
friendly territory, he and a small group of men were
ambushed by Zulus. As others deserted, he fought bravely,
before falling under a murderous hail of eighteen
assegais. In England people were horrified: the only heir
to the Napoleonic throne had been cut down by savages
while under the protection of the British Army, and the
Queen's soldiers had fled from the attack like cowards.

Despite the fact that the war went much better for the
British from this point onward, Zulus continued to be big
news. Cetewayo, who was captured and imprisoned in
Cape Town, became an almost mythic figure in the British
Isles.

Here was danger and horror that Farini didn't need to
make up. If people really wanted to understand what was
going on in Africa, he would bring it to their doorstep.
After the Isandhlwana massacre he began searching for a
way to present a Zulu-related show, and as soon as the

prince was killed, he dispatched Nat Behrens (a former Barnum associate) off to Durban, Natal, with orders to bring real Zulus to London for exhibition at the Aq. (A little book entitled *The Zulu Spy* was published a few years later claiming that Farini had been in Africa in 1879, witnessed several battles, and through cunning and bravery, arranged to bring the very natives who killed the prince back to the western world for exhibition. The fact that this booklet was used to promote Barnum's circus puts its veracity in serious doubt.) He had actually presented his first African show some time earlier.

Initially there was the Zulu Kaffir Boy and then two women, presented as Pawchee and Flycheia Letiaway, who were the "dusky daughters" of a Maravi chief and had been kidnapped out of central Africa by Zulus at a young age. These "Wild Women" from the "Dark Continent" gave spectacular demonstrations of their customs, but as expected, the centre-piece was their war methods. The Aquarium's publicity characterized it this way:

> The manner in which they illustrate the method of killing their war victims is in itself enough to strike terror into the stoutest heart. The fiendish reality of their war dances and songs is marvellous in its true and horrible intensity.

The effect this sort of thing had on Victorians is difficult for people of the twentieth century to understand. Across the ocean their own soldiers were being killed and mutilated by people they had never seen or in the least understood, people whom they feared as though they were devils on earth. And here the whole bloody scene was being vividly enacted for them right before their eyes by women who had supposedly been there and seen it happen. Farini loved it, and took pains to tell the public that this was a "genuine show" (whatever that meant). Whether these two women were really from Africa or just two black actresses is not known—it was common to discover, years after an "African" show, that its "Zulus" were from places like Harlem or Hoboken. In fact, acting was often the primary skill needed in a so-called "freak show."

Toward the end of May in southern Africa, Behrens completed negotiations to bring six young Zulu men to London. The utmost care was taken in proving that they were whom Farini said they were, and that they had come willingly. A letter was published in the London papers from George James Forrester, Sergeant of Police over the Licensed Native Labourers in Durban, signed at the police station, testifying that these men were genuine Zulus, that no other Zulus had ever gone to England, and cautioning Behrens to "Take good care of the boys and bring them back safe." Forrester also indicated that he had helped Behrens convince the men to go and that if harm came to them there could be bad consequences. At mid-ocean on June 10th (Farini's 41st birthday), Behrens had every crew member and passenger (some of elegant address) of the *Balmoral Castle* sign a statement confirming that the Zulus were real Zulus on their way from Africa to England.

When the ship arrived late in the month it was met by a big crowd at the Southampton docks (fellow showman Coup liked to say 100,000 were there that day). More information was released about its exotic passengers: apparently one was the eldest son of Chief Somkali and they were "friendly Zulus," loyal to the British Crown, a fact that Sir Theophilus Shepstone of Natal, who was also on board the *Balmoral Castle*, consented to put in writing. Their loyalty was particularly stressed, almost as if there was fear for their safety.

But that wasn't good enough for the British government. The Secretary of State for the Home Department (Mr. Cross), who had tried to censor Zazel, now let it be known that the government did not approve of Farini's Zulus, friendly or not: the Zulu War, though in its final days, was still raging. Captain A.P. Hobson, the new manager of the Royal Aquarium, who had been anxious to get the Africans to his venue just the week before, suddenly got cold feet. The Aq was often the target of moralists, both in Parliament and elsewhere, Farini's frightening acts being the most criticized, and Hobson desperately wanted to be rid of this reputation. How could they justify presenting the horror of a Zulu war dance when British boys were dying such ghastly deaths at the hands of Zulu warriors? So with the Zulus on English soil, Hobson cancelled the show. One can imagine Farini's anger. It wasn't his way to knuckle under when pressured by anyone.

On July 8th "Farini's Friendly Zulus" opened at St. James's Hall, Piccadilly and Regent Street, which ironically was famous for its black-face minstrel shows. The Zulus stayed there for nearly a

FARINI'S FRIENDLY ZULUS

Bernth Lindfors Collection

month, putting on "illustrations" of their daily life and customs, including the obligatory war dance. Despite Cross's dictum, London was enthralled and crowds showed particular excitement when the Africans threw their deadly assegais with such terrifying speed and accuracy. They would take up these five-foot-long spears with their five-inch iron blades that cut both ways, make them quiver in their hands and launch them like arrows, usually burying them six inches into their targets. The newspapers came out in full force to review the Zulus and their accounts provided Farini with excellent advertisements.

Everything was presented as an exchange of cultures: the peoples of two nations at war exploring their differences. But the exhibition wasn't really so noble: for the English it was just a spectacular show of savagery (and, by implication, of their own supposed racial superiority) that made good theatre and generated cold hard cash. Time would reveal that behind the scenes cultures were clashing more than melding.

The show finally transferred to the Aq in August.

Hobson changed his mind for several reasons: primarily because of the exhibition's success, but also because the Zulu War was now won and Cross's comments couldn't carry the same sting. Other venues began reacting to the Zulu fad. The Agricultural Hall, for example, spoofed them in their minstrel show, advertising that "Farouti's Unfriendly Zulus" would be incorporated into the act. It was also said that they "appeared by the unkind permission of Mr. Cross." "The Only Genuine Zulus" continued at the Aquarium right through Christmas 1879, on display almost all day and giving special performances upstairs in the Reception Room twice daily. Soon Farini contracted with another group of Zulus to add to the show.

But they (five in number) complained about their situation from the outset, apparently because other promoters had offered them more money once they arrived in England. Farini refused to substantially increase their salaries and informed them that he would not release them from their contracts. They decided to leave the Aquarium, but Farini confiscated their clothing. Within days their disagreement was in the courts and reported prominently in the press. Theophilus Shepstone and Bishop (of Natal) Colenso's son attended the proceeding, speaking with the Zulu men, attempting to help them. But cultures clashed without apparent solutions. The Africans, understandably, could not comprehend why they were not free to make their living with other showmen. Farini told the judge he would pay for part of their trip home and would not stand in the way of their finding other work in England, but he would *not* consent to let other English promoters exhibit them, and that this was his legal right. "[A] bargain was a bargain," he claimed, and the Zulus had known the details of their agreement. The judge seemed inclined to agree with him but there appears to have been much sympathy for the Zulus' situation, especially from Shepstone and Colenso.

It is evident that Farini was not paying the Zulus very substantial wages, though it seems they were reasonably looked after. He was not technically guilty of anything, nor could he be accused of cruelty, but he took a narrow stance in a difficult situation. The British press was often harsher, the *Telegraph* racist, saying that the Zulus were really just lazy and didn't want to work at all. After another appearance before the judge the disagreement was solved amicably and things got back to "normal" at the Aquarium. Farini even used the court publicity for advertisement, often referring to his new, "discontented Zulus, who are now becoming contented." One and all continued as a major attraction into early 1880.

But controversy wouldn't leave him alone, and during these days his Svengali reputation loomed like a huge shadow over the Aquarium and his many frightening acts. In May Zazel suffered her first accident, falling through the net during a show in Portsmouth. Though she wasn't badly hurt and quickly resumed her tour, several members of the press and government lashed out at the nature of her performance. From now on, her every move would be scrutinized. And the act Farini proposed to offer at the Aquarium that September didn't help matters.

The *Times* ad read "Flying at Last Accomplished." And that was it for several days: no further explanation. Then on September 26th the Aquarium made a "special announcement" which explained things: "The manager begs respectfully to announce the FIRST APPEARANCE of Mr. Farini's world-renowned LU LU, at the Royal Aquarium, on Monday next, when will be presented an entirely new and extraordinary performance...." Lu was going to do a terrifying version of the catapult act for London, and show them how to fly.

Despite the use of the phrase "Farini's Lu Lu," and the fact that Farini had invented Lu's new act and still managed him, Lu and Edith were making further attempts to be more independent and show the public that he was no Svengali-puppet. It was publicized that he now "gave his entertainments alone and unaided," that he was going to soon take a seaside vacation at his own behest, and it was made abundantly clear to the great London audience that

Lulu was a fully grown adult male. Now in his twenties, a husband and father, he was taking an active part in running shows at the Aquarium, functioning as Farini's second-in-command, and often conducting business in his foster-father's absence. Soon he would branch out into his own show-business ventures and was beginning to lay the groundwork for his early retirement from gymnastics.

But on September 29th he was supposed to place his body on a new, more powerful human catapult and fly two hundred feet across the Aquarium, turning somersaults as he went. This was a decidedly juiced-up version of the act that had been presented in northern British cities: Farini really wanted to let fly with Lulu's body in London. Despite his great courage, Lu may have finally been frightened by a Farini invention: his appearance set for the 29th didn't come off, apparently due to problems with the apparatus, and it was rescheduled for October 6th. But the 6th came and went without Lulu becoming the first human being in London to fly. Then he gave a performance: he climbed the ladder to the top of the gallery, where he lay down on a "sloping surface." Suddenly the surface catapulted him across the great hall, shooting him at a tremendous height until he landed in the net at the other end of the building. A few days later it was announced that Lulu was ill, suffering from "severe mental and physical strain." Though a medical certificate, signed by Dr. Bond, was reprinted in the papers, one wonders how much of Lulu's illness came from an enormous dread of the consequences should he continue to trust his life to that terrifying machine. It was announced that the show would return after Lulu had rested for a week, but it never again saw the light of day at the Aquarium.

There were other explosions that year in the Farini family. In February the senior Farini, who had been going down to Emsworth regularly to visit his two boys, came upon a private collection of Alice's letters. They made his blood boil. In them he found evidence of a love affair (of a "criminal nature" as it was later put) between his wife and a butcher named Charles Miller from the neighbouring town of Havant. He took possession of the letters and sued her for divorce. With all the cards in his hands he appeared in Probate and Divorce Court on January 23, 1880. This divorce, noted by the papers, came just weeks after his two court battles with the Zulus. Alice did not appear and Farini won his divorce and custody of the two boys without active opposition. The case was so decisive that Mrs. Farini was only given access to the children whenever (if ever) her former husband chose, and it was merely recorded that the court "hoped" the petitioner would provide some maintenance for the respondent.

The harshness of Victorian morality had come crashing down on Alice Carpenter Farini. Her dynamic, globe-trotting husband was probably less than attentive to her during their marriage; he was often away and had never been blind to the charms of other women, and it is not unfair to speculate that their initial separation was not entirely her fault. But in Victorian society an adulterous woman, regardless of the possible surreptitious conduct of her husband or of the state of the marriage at the time, was always guilty. Alice soon married Charles Miller, but died just five years later of chronic peritonitis brought on by cancer of the stomach: she was thirty-nine years old. It is not known whether she was ever given access to her children.

Farini was beginning to reap what he had sown. He had wanted this life of adventure and danger, he had wanted to boldly explore his passions, but with that came instability and constant exclusion from the very respectability he wanted. As the 1880s approached he seemed to be blamed for everything negative that happened in the British world of entertainment. Late in October 1879 while rehearsing her "Balista Flight" for an appearance at the Alexandra, the gymnast Zaeo shot out of the spring-release box that projected her into the air and struck her face on a wire on the way up, badly cutting herself. She fell heavily into the net, her face covered in blood (this disfigurement never entirely disappeared). The press was outraged. *The Illustrated Police News*, which made its money from sensationalism, raged that women were "physically unfit" for such acts and compared these shows to bull-fighting and Roman gladiatorial combat. But Farini was the real villain of the piece:

> Only recently Mr. Cross informed the proprietors of a place of public entertainment, in which a young girl was allowed night after night to go through an undoubtedly dangerous exhibition, that if a fatal accident occurred to her they would be held liable for the result. The rule thus laid down in the case of Zazel will, it is to be hoped, be followed in that of Zaeo. Such exhibitions are a public disgrace.

But this time it wasn't just the Home Secretary who was after him. Another M.P., Edward Jenkins, was putting his indignation into legislation. All of this governmental righteousness is somewhat ironic when one considers that the Aq was a favourite haunt for members of Parliament, especially on days when a "count-out" found there to be fewer than the requisite forty in attendance in the House and a move to adjourn was made. Distinguished members were then seen scurrying between the Commons and the Tank, usually hatless since placing one's hat on one's seat in Parliament ensured that others would assume it was occupied. They spent many a thrilling afternoon watching Zazel or Zaeo while their hats sat for them in the House.

Despite the pressure that was building on Farini and the Aquarium proprietors that year, they signed Zaeo for late December. When she started the Balista Flight at the Aq on the 29th, all eyes watched for even a hint of trouble. And the worst possible thing happened. Just over a month into her engagement she was knocked unconscious doing the act and had to be helped from the hall. It looked like the last straw: reaction in the press and in Parliament reached a crescendo. Farini immediately substituted LaLa (an extraordinary black gymnast who, upside down, held a cannon suspended from her teeth as it was ignited and fired) for Zaeo and the Royal Aquarium Society met to decide what to do. At first they stood their ground, but under mounting pressure and concern for their licence, they buckled. On February 29th they announced that "all performances with mechanical projecting power" had been stopped at the Royal Westminster Aquarium. "These dangerous tricks of the ingenious Farini," said *The Penny Illustrated Paper* "have been performed for the last time there."

The opposition had won, at least for now.

The history of public concern over dangerous performances obviously goes back many centuries but intense discussion about it really began in Great Britain not long after Lulu made her first leap. Initial concern was over the use of children in such acts: in 1872 Lord Buckhurst put together a bill "to prevent children under 16 taking part in acrobatic performances that were dangerous to their lives or injurious to their health." This bill was withdrawn for redrafting that year, offered again the following year and withdrawn again for redrafting. In 1879, aided by growing concern about Farini's activities, a bill with a similar purpose finally made it through Parliament and became law. It was intended "to regulate the employment of children in places of public amusement" and specified that "no child under 14 should take part in any public exhibition or performance which in the opinion of the Court would be dangerous to life or limb."

But Edward Jenkins wasn't satisfied. There were several performances in England he thought were not only dangerous, but immoral. He took aim at the evil Farini and his kind and by March 1880, aided by the apparent flurry of accidents and the Royal Aquarium's surrender, had his bill ready. "The Dangerous Performances Bill" was designed "to prevent the exhibition in places of amusement of acrobatic performances dangerous to life and limb"; it sought to control the height at which gymnastic performances were done, forced artistes to use nets and greatly restricted the activities of women and children in dangerous feats. And it specifically outlawed "Any performance in which the performer is forcibly projected into the air by machinery, springs, or any explosive force, to any

greater distance than six feet." Several meetings of prominent gymnasts were convened in London to discuss the
proposed bill and offer criticism. Old Farini colleague
John LeClair and his former protégée Ala were among
those in attendance. They were concerned about their
livelihood and told Jenkins's representative that there
were five thousand gymnasts and acrobats worldwide who
could be detrimentally affected by this legislation. But as
the evening wore on and they examined the bill's details
it became obvious that Jenkins was after particular people and was willing to make compromises in the wording
to exclude the majority of performers. As this became
clear, the feelings between the two sides grew more amicable. A short while later Jenkins met with several of the
gymnasts in his office. Before long the two sides were pat-
ting each other on the back and bad-mouthing mechanical
projecting acts: in fact, by the end of the meeting some
artistes were actually intimating that there was little skill
in such things. Afterwards, one explained to the press:
"The act was really to prevent Lulu from being hurled
from one end of a building to the other; Zazel from being
forced from a make-believe cannon..."

Though all concerned departed on good terms and
seemed to reach a consensus on what could be done, the
fact that the acceptability of a number of mainstream performances (including the feats of rope-walker Wainretta
and spiral ascensionist Ethardo) was discussed did not
augur well for the future of the bill. If the legality of such
acts could be questioned then it seemed Jenkins's net was
going to be cast very wide indeed. Therefore it was not
surprising that when the proposed bill was laid out in *The
Era* many acrobats and gymnasts, representing a large
portion of the profession which disagreed with those at
the London meetings, wrote expressing their opposition.

But the letters attacking "dangerous performances" kept
coming into the Home Secretary's Office, and most journalists sided with them. In mid-March *The Penny Illustrated
Paper* printed a two-page illustration of the kinds of feats
Mr. Jenkins's bill would "suppress," depicting Zazel col-

lapsing into a torn net, Lulu springing toward her platform, and even Blondin with a man on his back. (See illustration on page 219.) Captain Hobson of the Aquarium
was quoted as saying that he and his directors regretted
having such acts and presented them solely to make a
profit for their shareholders.

Despite all this noise in favour of the bill, and pronouncements like one by an M.P. who called these types of
shows "this growing and scandalous evil," Jenkins was
unable to get it into the House before the spring dissolution, and thereafter (fraught with sweeping generalities
and ineffectiveness) it died. Efforts to resurrect it later in
the decade also failed.

But by then Farini was gone: as the furor swirled
around him, he fled to the United States.

Early that month the Aquarium announced that "Lu
Lu" was to make a glorious return. Much was made of his
legendary status: "With iron will and nerves of steel,"
puffed the ads, "He wildly dashed through space, And
thousands stood amazed"; "The most graceful and accomplished artiste in his profession in the habitable globe."
"Lu Lu's Great and Truly Magnificent Idealisms are the
Wonders of a Wondering Wonderful World", said another.
But Lu wanted to try the catapult again: so Hobson waved
the white flag and the show was cancelled.

British Parliament and the finest of British society had
blanched in the face of Farini's dangerous ideas, just as
"old croaking grumblers" had in the backwoods of Canada.
So he ran away again, in search of uninhibited adventure.
On March 20th the steamship *Greece* sailed past the
Statue of Liberty with Zazel, Farini and a few of his Zulus
on board: in America there was a law preventing children
from being used in hazardous performances but not even
the thought of a bill against adults doing the same.

Farini was free. And Zazel was about to put a jolt into
"The Greatest Show on Earth."

CHAPTER 18

The Greatest Shows
on Earth

"An Immeasureable and Paralyzed Flood of Grandeur!"
Courier for The New United Monster Shows, 1881

*"...the moral worth, original excellence and stupendous
proportions of our Mammoth Consolidation."*
Advertisement for The Greatest Show on Earth, 1882

Farini hadn't been to New York for four and a half years. As usual the city was bustling, but now it seemed even busier. The United States was in the midst of what was called the Gilded Age (after an 1873 book by Mark Twain) though it might have been called the Age of Invention or the Urban Age. American cities were exploding in size as immigrants poured in; mass production was becoming reality and inventions to aid growth seemed to happen daily. Just over the New Jersey border in Menlo Park, Thomas Edison was entering his creative prime, having just invented the phonograph, and was turning his attention to electricity. Andrew Carnegie created the first large steel furnace, the Brooklyn Bridge approached completion and public telephones were a new phenomenon. But corruption accompanied growth, in politics as well as industry, and many felt the soul of the country was dying, caught in the feverish rush of "progress."

Entertainment was becoming big business too and Broadway was alight with stars. At the head of the American ship of diversions was an entrepreneur as capitalistic as Carnegie and as clever as Edison: the inimitable P.T. Barnum. He fit this age perfectly. When the

264

masses needed to be entertained, he provided in a BIG
way. His "Greatest Show on Earth" was, without a doubt,
exactly that, and as he prepared to descend on New York
from his quarters in Bridgeport, Connecticut that year,
seriously challenged for the first time by several burgeoning sawdust extravaganzas, he made sure he had the
world's most spectacular act.

Getting Zazel into his show was the culmination of several years of effort. And there were other Americans who
wanted to see her in their country on the world's most
high-profile stage; even former Vice-President (under
Grant) Schuyler Colfax. He wrote to Barnum in 1878 suggesting that she be enticed across the ocean. The old showman replied, "I have seen the woman shot from the cannon
and I have been trying to get her. Hope to succeed."

Now he had. The ingenious Farini, the Svengali of
thrill, had delivered her, and his terrifying Zulus, and a
few other blood-chillers. By the beginning of April things
were ready to roll. The big show opened a scheduled two-
and-a-half-week run in the big city on the 8th as a starter
to their seven-month tour through fifteen states. Their
venue that year, the American Institute Building, was
located on the upper east side at the corner of 63rd
Street and 3rd Avenue. Barnum had used it in five of the
last seven seasons, despite having his new Roman
Hippodrome available downtown on Madison Avenue. The
older building was thought to be nearly fireproof (Barnum
had a bad history with fires, losing two museums and the
Hippotheatron) and had a substantial seating capacity,
but was considerably smaller than the new one and did
not have good sightlines for aerial acts. This would be the
last year he showed here, moving back to the Hippodrome
the following year after it was freshly renovated and given
a new name: Madison Square Garden.

Street parades were an essential part of the circus in
the nineteenth century and The Greatest Show on Earth's
was second to none. Two days before the New York opening great coloured wagons, bands, calliopes, acrobats, elephants and Zazel's ominous cannon came down Broadway

watched by crowds that thronged the sidewalks, stood in doorways and perched in open windows.

Opening night drew 4,000 people to the Institute, the foyer which encircled its interior so full soon after the doors opened that ticket-holders could barely move. The menagerie was on display right beside them: Namibian lions, Bengal tigers, black leopards and hyenas. People pushed and shoved to see these wonders. The following night the crowd was somehow even larger, filling up every seat, every standing-room position, and all the extra chairs and even the tops of cages, on which people stood to see the action. By the eight o'clock starting time the show's officials had to refuse admission to hundreds and close the doors on a crowded sidewalk.

Inside the throng was entertained by the circus's orchestra, until a signal to start the show was given just past the hour. Out marched the beautiful procession, sparkling in tinsel and dominated by purple. First came some of the performers, dressed in bright, scanty costumes, then the animals, some still in their cages, the crowd alerted to their arrival by the sound of shrieks and growls. The "living curiosities" were next, bizarre human beings, striding into the arena with all eyes riveted on them. Captain Costentenus, the headlining freak, came first. He was one of the greatest sideshow attractions of the 1870s and '80s: an Albanian Greek with long dark hair tied in braids, a big, fleshy body covered by perhaps the most tattoos a human being has ever possessed and a wonderfully contrived life story that made children's eyes wide with wonder. He claimed to have led a wildly adventurous life, at one point being tortured by an Oriental Khan who tied him to stakes and ordered a woman to tattoo every inch of his body, including the skin between his fingers, his eyelids and his genitals. Farini's involvement with this strange man was substantial, in fact he may have been managing him at that very moment.

Farini acts opened and closed the show. First came his four Zulus, Dingando, Possomon, Maguibi and Ousan, running into the ring. Described as well-built, copper-coloured men standing taller than six feet and wearing just a single "girder" with a few ostrich feathers (the scantiness of their costumes intrigued American spectators—journalists characterized them as nearly naked), they began hurling their assegais, frightening much of the audience, particularly those who sat behind the target. It was some time before they were convinced of the Zulus' accuracy and settled back into their seats. A war dance followed.

Then came a myriad of equestrian feats, many performed by famous stars. Dressed in gaudy costumes, they would leap about on their horses, turning somersaults as they went, standing on their heads, or clinging to their animals' bellies, faces just inches from thundering hooves. Acrobats and gymnasts were just as numerous. Barnum even had a troupe who performed acrobatic feats while playing violins. And there were other strange acts, like Charles White's crowd-pleasing performing oxen, said to be the only trained ones in the world; and Mme. Nelson, who had magical control over a flock of doves. Everything came fast and furious, in and out of the ring, often followed by armies of clowns. The show was a kind of colourful, dizzying succession of emotions that thrilled a crowd whose expectations had been high to begin with. Barnum published signed letters stating that this was the best and most expensive show he had ever produced, but that was to be expected from the Prince of Humbug. Still, as the *New York Herald* said, the word Barnum was synonymous with "the longing of human nature for the unusual" and in 1880 he gave the big city all it desired.

But the best was saved for last.

Zazel was the show's headliner. She was paid like a star and was responsible for filling the seats. Her name dominated the Barnum ads in the New York papers that spring and every newspaper in every town they visited that summer and fall. Zazel, the greatest star in the greatest show on earth, was expected to perform like the world's number-one draw. Signor Farini, announced as the inventor of the human cannonball act, led her into the ring. She was dressed in her scarlet costume and pink tights, and as she stepped into the lights the band struck up "The Zazel Galop." Quickly she ascended almost to the roof of the Institute and began walking a nearly invisible high wire, delicately holding an umbrella on her first crossing, but discarding it on the way back. Then she did her trapeze act, flying with admirable grace high above her wire. She alighted on a platform and suddenly leapt out into thin air, falling face forward, her body seeming to drop for minutes as the crowd, forced to the edge of their seats, felt their stomachs go down with her. But she landed safely in Farini's net, and the applause, coming from many who had never seen a high-dive before, was thunderous. All eyes then went to the huge black cannon that hung from the trusses of the roof. Zazel climbed up to a platform just above it and lowered herself, feet first, into the big mortar. Most people in the crowd had never experienced anything like this either and a mixture of pity and fear grew in them. Signor Farini mounted the net beneath the cannon, holding a long wax light in his hand. He stood still for a moment and then in a loud, clear voice asked the young girl if she was ready. In the ensuing silence a small voice responded. Farini lighted the fuse, a huge explosion shook the Institute, and Zazel rocketed out of the cannon and landed in the net on the other side of the ring. The *Herald*, which wasn't kind to every part of the show that year, said the cannon feat "arrested the beating of many hearts." The real human cannonball act had finally come to America.

Zazel must have been a major hit because The Greatest Show on Earth was a winner in New York in 1880. Hundreds of chairs were added near the ring and still there wasn't enough seating; night after night the doors were closed early on crowds pressing to be admitted.

One of the show's biggest attractions was P.T. Barnum himself. Now in his seventieth season, his presence at his circuses (he appeared briefly in the ring on opening day in 1880) could outdraw even his living curiosities. He is often remembered as standing at least six feet two inches tall and possessing a high-pitched voice. But these observations seem to have come from people wanting to see something strange in him. In reality he was just a bit under six feet, heavy set at about 215 pounds, with a bulbous nose, grey hair encircling his bald dome and a clear, well-modulated voice. His personal history was familiar to most Americans, pressed upon them by the aggressive marketing of his autobiography, and yet many thought of him as a circus man, an occupation he had really only embraced in a big way for the past decade. First and foremost he was a businessman and a matchless promoter. Though Farini was also a "prince of humbug," it was there that the similarity between the two men ended. Barnum had never been a performer, and lacked the Canadian's versatility, his daring and his darkness.

On April 26th the show's tenting season began on the Capitoline Grounds in Brooklyn, where they raised their huge green tent (250,000 metres of it), advertised as being able to hold from 10,000 to 11,000 spectators, and two smaller tents for the sideshow and the menagerie.

The American circus was entering its golden era. It had prospered to some degree before, but in the old days even some of the best circuses were really just small "mud shows" that plodded from village to village by wagon, plagued by bad reputations. Ever since Barnum entered the fray with Coup in the early 1870s, expanded his show, put it on rails and brought out the best in his competitors, things had improved. Performers' reputations were on the rise as was their fame and their salaries. Circuses were now big businesses, worth millions of dollars. They employed regimented phalanxes of advance men who blanketed cities with extraordinary new mass-produced colour advertisements, drew modern-arena-sized crowds into their big tents, and ran their shows like little cities on the move. No longer did their people hole up in questionable hotels in small places: now they had their own huge sleeping quarters, kitchens, barber shops, blacksmith shops, all on the move in brightly coloured trains, run by managers with the precision of a military operation. They sped from town to town, covering whole regions

of the country, usually leaving at midnight or the small
hours of morning, packing up after two shows in one place
and rushing on to meet their next date the very next day.
There they would raise a huge entertainment complex in
a matter of hours, ready to show before thousands. The
circus was becoming the most popular form of show business in the world.

After a week in Brooklyn, The Greatest Show on Earth
headed north into Connecticut. They continued to do well,
selling out every show in Hartford, despite Zazel's absence
from one program due to the cannon's malfunction. On
May 10th they rolled into Boston for a one-week stay on
the Coliseum grounds. That day they drew 20,000 people
to the first shows. Acrobat John Batchelor's double somersault over seven elephants seemed to be a particular
favourite but even that couldn't beat Zazel, whose
thrilling performance filled the huge crowd (or so said ads
in the *Boston Daily Globe*) "with love and admiration for
the daring little foreigner." "[The] inventor, Professor
Farini" was in command of her portion of the performance
and assured the crowd that precautions, like his well-
made net, guaranteed her safety.

The circus then headed west across upper New York
State, making stands on its way to Buffalo, and reaching
Detroit on the far side of Lake Erie in late May. Posters
for these dates depicted five images of Zazel: being blasted
from her cannon, flying toward a trapeze bar, hanging by
her toes, doing the high-dive and sitting daintily on a wire
with her parasol. But it was the Zulus who gained the
most press in Detroit, for reasons not pleasing to Farini.
After a smashing day inside the canvas where 22,000 people witnessed two shows, one of Farini's Zulus disappeared into the Detroit night. Unable to speak English
but not otherwise looking unusual when in his street
clothes, the "Chief" was seen drinking in a saloon in the
Potomac section of Detroit the following afternoon by a
policeman. The officer didn't know the man was wanted,
so no effort was made to communicate with him—by that
evening he was nowhere to be found, despite a thorough

police search. A few days later he was discovered, report-
edly intoxicated, "at a negro settlement" about eight miles
from Windsor in Canada. At first he refused to return, but
after a conversation with someone described as Zazel's sister (who, as a Farini employee, had learned to speak some
Zulu), he consented to go with her to meet the show in
Chicago for its opening there on June 1st, returning to
work apparently without being forced.

It was said that 100,000 people came to their thirteen
shows in Chicago in the first week of June, and thereafter
their success continued, through Illinois, Wisconsin and
Minnesota. "Zazel," wrote a Minneapolis reporter, "...who
laughs at danger and who dives into the hearts of the
audience and the center of the huge net simultaneously, is
certainly the most novel feature of the entertainment." In
July and August they toured the smaller towns on the
edge of the American frontier in Iowa, Kansas, Nebraska
and Missouri, where the fabled American Wild West was
in its final decade. At one stop, a young Buffalo Bill even
visited them and brought their equestrians a wild horse
he had captured on the plains. By the second week of
August they were working their way back east, where
urban centres were larger and the possibility of filling
their huge tent greater. A few weeks later they blew into
St. Louis, a city that was growing in leaps and bounds,
and played there for an entire week. The crowds were
large and the press coverage was long and unusually
detailed. After opening night the *St. Louis Daily Globe-
Democrat*'s reporter was even taken behind the scenes so
that he might tell his readers about being introduced to
Zazel. Describing her as "small...young and pretty," he
was amazed that just seconds after being fired out of the
cannon she seemed composed and none the worse for
wear: he could detect only a small bit of black dust on her
face and some grime from the powder on her tights.
Signor Farini appeared almost immediately with a "white,
fur-tipped mantelet" which he threw over her shoulders,
and he stood nearby, watching and listening. Zazel was
apparently having a wonderful time as the star of

Barnum's show and laughed often as she was questioned
and "danced away to her dressing room supremely happy."

Farini decided he would put a little charge into Zazel's
performance on the second last day of their sold-out St.
Louis run. He made a secret agreement with a journalist
prior to the show, that he could shake her wire, and her
talent and his precautions were such that no harm would
come of it. It was said Zazel knew nothing of this and
when she was twenty feet out on the wire the nefarious
deed was done: she threw up her arms and "uttered a
small cry; ladies in the audience shrieked, men put out
their arms as if to catch her..." But, relying on her training, she fell gracefully and safely to the net. This of course
brought an enormous reaction: "the attention and
applause bestowed upon the artiste made good her title as
the great sensation of the day." For Farini this Svengali-
like trick was a little triumph: it proved his thrill act was
almost foolproof.

Zazel continued a big hit as they swept through several
more states that summer and autumn. In Indianapolis a
newspaper featured a long article about her, stating she
was Farini's daughter and he the son of an Episcopalian
minister; in tiny Little Rock, Arkansas they drew 8,000
people to two dates; and in the wild state of Texas in
October they played frontier towns full of saloons with
cowboys' horses hitched outside. By then the show's season was in its final days, and just a few performances
were given as they moved back into the eastern states,
making a beeline for Barnum's winter quarters in
Bridgeport, which was reached on November 12th.

Farini went home to Port Hope when the season finished.
The local press reported he was in town with Zazel and
had made six hundred dollars a week with Barnum (more
than eighteen thousand dollars for the season). During his
stay he began negotiating another land purchase, adding
to his baron-like holdings in Hope Township.

Lu was running his affairs at the Royal Aquarium, so
Farini spent some time in New York during these days.

There Sarah Bernhardt was all the rage, making her American debut in early November, not long before Zazel appeared at Niblo's Garden for a short Christmas run. Farini cleared up a small bit of business in January by getting a patent for his huge iron catapult, then plunged into negotiations for a much bigger venture: a partnership with W.C. Coup in his New United Monster Shows.

Farini's desire to try something new and Coup's interest in enlarging his show so it could seriously challenge his old partner Barnum, came together in 1881; both men were talented self-promoters (and adept at spinning a tall tale or two) and both craved respectability, kindred souls of a sort. Coup had recently left the Aquarium business and had been running a travelling show dominated by equestrian acts, expanding it each year, making it a fully rounded circus and reaching the point in 1880 where he felt he was on the verge of something big. G.A. Farini's considerable power in show-business circles overseas, his extraordinary sensational performances and his ability to deliver a big star or two were just what he needed. "Farini's Paris Hippodrome" was often listed as the principal show which joined Coup to make up The New United Monster Shows, and Farini and Coup were the major partners, but this giant combination was really an amalgamation of the talents and reserves of several successful impresarios, among them George Middleton, an old circus man and sideshow expert who owned a renowned dime museum in New York's famous Bowery section and W.L. Jukes, a manufacturer of "musical steam chariots." It was not unusual for circuses to combine their powers to present the biggest possible show, and "Combined" or "United" were common adjectives in shows' titles. Bigger was always better in those days: each show was scarier, more sensational, better run, blessed with more seats, etc. than the next. Competition, evident in huge advertisements (some of them gorgeous, one-hundred-sheet colour lithographs that could cover the walls of an entire town block), was nearing its peak. Ads warned the public about the lies in the opposition's publicity, advising them to wait for the real thing, the really BIG show. This approach gave birth to the three-ring circus, which gave the impression of great size. Afflicted by "giantism" himself, Farini was an invaluable ally in this sort of fight.

Coup called for seventy-five people to post bills that season. Then he unleashed the show's gigantic name: "W.C. Coup's New Colossal Amphitheatre, Roman Hippodrome, Imperial Trois Rond Circus, Museum, Aquarium, L'Ecole Physicotechnique and Anthropologique and Conservatory of Living Wild Beasts," a fitting title for a show partly owned by the pangymnastikonaerostationist himself.

A huge track, said to be forty feet wide and nearly half a mile long and stretching around the show's three circus rings inside the big top, was the defining feature of "Farini's Paris Hippodrome." It was used for horse races of all types, but most notably a thundering and often dangerous Roman chariot competition of a distinctly sensational nature. Farini also contributed the Zulus, Mlle. Geraldine now doing an awesome high dive from the roof of the tent into the net, Mlle. Zaco in a new act where she slid along a wire from the roof to the ground attached solely by her hair, and several other acts. But his most spectacular contribution was Lulu's iron catapult feat; it was a show-stopper. "Lulu, The Man Bird," dressed in his female costume and watched at ringside by his wife and child, actually did the terrifying feat they had tried at the Aq. Each night the show was stopped while he was wheeled into the spotlight in a gorgeous wagon drawn by four white horses. At a signal he mounted the catapult and was shot the full length of the huge tent, ninety feet above the three rings, a human being in flight. He was the show's star and drew the largest salary.

Coup and Farini's circus was often compared favourably to Barnum's. It attempted to project a highly moral tone and was well connected. The two owners, though impeccably dressed and coiffed and looking respectable from their heads to their toes as they travelled in the sumptuously appointed cars of their brightly coloured train, often

exaggerated the show's qualities to the press. This knack
for white lies was something all showmen had to be adept
at, but Farini and Coup were particularly adroit. There
were times in 1881 when one might have thought that
their show, advertised as having over 1,000 special attractions, 1,200 musicians, 600 workers and covering eight
acres of ground, involved fifty shows and that Barnum's
was but a flea next to theirs. Later in life Farini liked to
say that he ran the first three-ring circus the world had
ever seen, a distinction history bestows upon Barnum.
Though he may be referring to something he created prior
to the 1880s, it seems probable that he meant Coup's
show. Barnum's first three-ringer opened on March 28th,
1881 at Madison Square Garden. However, more than
eleven weeks before, the United Monster Show's January
8th advertisement in the *The New York Clipper* referred
to his "Imperial Trois Rond Circus," and makes the question of who was first an interesting one.

In February Farini placed an advertisement in a New
York entertainment paper warning one and all that he
was the sole inventor of the human cannonball act. The
names of his Philadelphia-based lawyers were included.
He stated that he had been "reliably informed" that several showmen were planning to use the act without paying him. He concluded, "I shall and will protect all parties
using my inventions by my authority." This indicates he
had sold the act to several shows; the Batcheller and
Doris circus was one of them. The Zazel who headlined
their show was none other than Rosa Richter herself. The
other prominent Zazel, the star of the Shelby, Pullman
and Hamilton show, was a Mrs. Elizabeth Ann Roche, one
of the early substitute Zazels Farini employed at the
Royal Westminster Aquarium. Farini's influence on the
American circus world that year was remarkable: in addition to the two Zazels, Forepaugh's great show had a cannon feat as its feature act and Barnum had a catapult feat
and was only without Farini because he was running his
own show. The *Clipper* claimed that 1881 was the most
competitive circus year they had ever seen, but didn't

mention the invisible force behind all the thrill acts.

That season began for Coup and Farini at the corner of Broad and Dickinson in Philadelphia on April 6th. This city was not their original choice for the opener but they jumped at the wonderful chance of starting in the country's second largest urban centre when it became apparent that Forepaugh was not going to open in his home town that season. With Barnum in New York and Forepaugh in Washington, Coup and Farini put last-minute ads in the Philadelphia papers and began with a bang. Farini's Zulus, stricken by the recent death of their "Chief" in London, and seven train-car loads of armour, costumes and Roman chariots, appeared just days before they were needed. The opening week drew huge numbers, tens of thousands, crowds thrilled by the spills (and there were a few) and chills on the hippodrome track. And Philadelphia was given a bonus when the one and only Zazel made a few appearances, available because Batcheler and Doris were just across the Delaware River in Camden, New Jersey.

Before the show left for northern Pennsylvania, Farini was paid for a "commercial" for St. Jacob's oil, the rubbing liniment which was publicized through ostensibly unbiased interviews with famous people. It was made known, for example, during a conversation with Buffalo Bill that that noble hero relied on the oil to keep himself supple in case of sudden Indian attack. "Both Mr. Farini," stated the interviewer, "and his ward 'the original Zazel'...have received great benefit from St. Jacob's Oil. In cases of bruises from accidents, sprains, etc. they have invariably found speedy relief by rubbing with the Oil." Such was the life of a star.

From Pennsylvania they moved up into New York State, and then east to Massachusetts. They spent a week in Boston, drawing great crowds. But as they played dates in New York on their way to Syracuse and Rochester in early May, word reached them of the terrible death of a young performer in the Barnum and Bailey show at Wilkesbarre, Pennsylvania. A Farini-style act had been the death instrument.

Lizzie Davene (Elizabeth Power) was just twenty-one
years old when she was killed doing the iron catapult feat.
Apparently the great speed at which she was propelled
caused her to lose control in the air and she landed on her
head in the net. She was instantly paralyzed from the
neck down and ten days later died in hospital in New
York. She had been doing sensational gymnastic feats
with her sister and brother-in-law in the Davene Troupe
for a number of years and was a competent performer, but
the iron catapult was a challenge for which she was
apparently not ready. Though this machine was patented
by William Davene, it was not part of the Davenes' performance and she had agreed to do it for a separate fee.
There was a lesson in this: a Farini act was dangerous
enough, but a Farini act without Farini was especially
hazardous. Harry Carey replaced her on the catapult and
Barnum's show went on, now with a feat that audiences
knew was a real killer.

Lulu seemed unfazed by Lizzie's death and as the New
United Monster Shows moved through New York State,
Michigan and Ohio the act continued to draw crowds. In
Columbus a reporter wrote of Lulu: "[His act] is worth the
price of admission, and more than Mr. Coup is able to say
of it on his bills." In Cincinnati they had to turn people
away and when they appeared in St. Louis for a week in
early June, on the same lot where Farini's acts had performed the previous year inside Barnum's great green
tent, they claimed 18,000 people came one evening to see
new ideas materialize under Coup's gleaming white canvases. Strange happenings on the track were particular
favourites here: a steeple chase, four black horses driven
by a woman against a man, and Indian braves chasing
down an Indian maiden on horseback.

They kept rolling through the big cities of the west and
in July ventured into Kansas. If it wasn't evident in the
streets of small Kansas towns that you were close to the
frontier, then all you had to do was open a newspaper. "It
is usual on circus days," said Atchison's paper the day
Coup, Farini and Lulu hit town, "for Missourians to come

to Atchison with pistols, and shoot somebody." Two officers checked citizens for guns that day and the first seven men searched had six pistols. Atchison was obviously not all gun-play, but the atmosphere was charged with an attitude that was surprisingly like a Western dime novel. Even their humorous approach to their expectations of Coup's show revealed a rough-and-tumble spirit: "We hereby give Coup's clowns fair warning that if they attempt any of the bald-headed puns of their profession, a tall policeman will walk across the hippodrome track into the particular ring wherein the infamy is perpetrated, and beat them to death." Actually, the show did well in Atchison, so well that the newspaper declared it the best the town had ever seen, high praise when it is considered that Barnum had been there the previous year.

The United Monster Shows followed an unusual route that year by appearing in New York City in mid-campaign. On the 6th of September, they opened at Madison Square Garden for a three-week run, and pulled out all the stops. The Garden was even refitted for them, with 3,000 extra chairs placed very close to the action, on a beautiful carpet laid between the track and the rings. Lulu was now given his third opportunity to headline in the big city and he did not disappoint; in fact many Farini creations, Geraldine, the Zulus and the hippodrome in particular, came in for specific attention from New York critics. As in every other city, reporters here loved to write about accidents on the track: riders flying off their mounts or being flung out of chariots as they careened around a corner or crashed into each other. Despite the fact that many went headfirst over the fronts of their horses or were run over by other vehicles, and a number were (apparently) carried off insensible, no fatal or crippling injuries occurred on the track that season. Their crowds fell off a little after the first two weeks, affected by the death of President Garfield, who succumbed on September 19th to wounds an assassin had inflicted earlier that summer.

About the time the circus reached New York, Farini was getting restless again, looking toward the future. He

worked out a deal with Coup, allowing himself to be bought
out, and began preparing for his return to London. It was
reported at the time that Lulu was involved in the trans-
action, temporarily taking on Farini's portion of the show.
Lu was now in his mid-twenties with a four-year-old
daughter and was spending more time with his family in
the Port Hope area; in fact Edith and little May were in
Hope during the Coup show's New York run, visiting all the
Hunts but spending most of their time at William and Ann
(Hunt) Marsh's farm, called Locust Lawn. Perhaps they
even saw the humorous piece in the *Port Hope Times* about
a gentleman accidentally performing what was termed a
"Zazel leap" when he was thrown out of his buggy after it
hit a bump on the road between Port Hope and Cobourg.

When the Coup show left New York at the end of
September 1881 it headed south, going to the Washington
D.C. area, and then into the old Confederate states. Farini
was with them for a while but left for good in October and
headed back to New York. The big 1881 show, with its
curious configuration of three rings encircled by a race
track, had been a resounding success. But now Coup and
Farini went their separate ways.

On November 2nd Farini left New York for London on the
ocean steamer *Queen* of the National Line, taking with
him Captain Costentenus, Zazel and a freak called the
Leopard Boy. "Freak shows" were becoming popular, and
Farini, influenced by the censoring of his thrill acts and
the money to be made in this sort of venture, became more
involved with "freaks" as the decade wore on.

His return to London was announced prominently by
the Aquarium, which had had a rather dreary season without him. "Farini's New Sensation" as Costentenus was
called, opened November 21st, presented four times a day
to make up for the dearth of other excitement. He drew
well and was given a great deal of play in the press. Farini
showed him as a kind of "aggrandized" freak, one with
refined characteristics rather than merely an oddity: a
Greek nobleman of unusual courage. "7,000,000 Punctures

of the Quivering Flesh," read Farini's advertisement. He offered 10,000 pounds "for the production of half so extensive and perfect a piece of tattooing, or for the correct deciphering of the hieroglyphics upon his body." The Leopard Boy was his other "ethnological phenomenon": supposedly twelve years old, he was presented as coming from a white tribe in Africa. Though he was Negroid, he had large white patches all over his body. An army major, curiously named Pinto, corroborated the story of the boy's origins. Though the boy may have been an albino Negro, it is most likely that he was "piebald," his skin having "localized depigmentation," a characteristic he inherited because he possessed an autosomal (non-sex linked) dominant gene.

Farini lectured about his exhibits ("most interesting variet(ies) of mankind") at what he called "receptions," often quoting legendary American physician, writer and raconteur Oliver Wendell Holmes on Costentenus; cartes de visite were produced of the famous tattooed man, entitled "Farini's Latest Wonder." By December, no longer fearful of politicians, Farini brought Zazel back for a month's run; and in January he debuted his third prominent freak, The Elastic-Skin Man. This "novelty," also called "Farini's India-Rubber Man," was really Heinrich Haag, a gentleman with incredibly pliable skin which he could pull away from his body and wrap around things as if it were part of a deflated balloon. Though one journalist claimed that such looseness of skin could be attained by liberally rubbing vinegar on one's body (shades of Pentland's worms), Haag's condition was a medical one: he had Ehlers-Danlos Syndrome, described as "a defect of the connective tissues of the dermis characterized by thin, delicate hyperextensible skin."

In January Farini presented "Farini's Mystery, the Suspended Head" in the Picture Gallery at the Aq. This was a magic trick, more than a little spooky, and one of the few examples of an actual bit of conjuring done by him. It was featured for a number of months and may be another reason why he was credited with the invention of the illusion of levitation. Before mid-February he closed

Zazel's and Haag's performances and accompanied the two
artistes and several of his Zulus on another steamer back
to America, leaving Costentenus, Professor Stokes lecturing on memory, alligators, and an insectorium to entertain
at the Aq.

Several months earlier Barnum, Bailey and Hutchinson
had asked Farini to return to The Greatest Show on
Earth for the 1882 season. Though he wasn't a partner,
his contribution to the world's greatest circus in one of its
greatest years comprised a major portion of its program.
Not only would Zazel be returning but so would the Zulus,
and Lulu on the catapult, and several other Farini acts. In
addition Farini himself would make an appearance as a
"ring lecturer," introducing his many protégés and informing audiences about the intricacies of their acts. He
arrived in New York on February 20th and before the
week was out presented Princess Ama, Chief Newcomo
and the other Zulus at the London Theater. But before he
even left the docks on the day of his arrival he made news,
in the form of an announcement for the press. He told
them that the big elephant Barnum had recently purchased from the Zoological Gardens in London would be
shipped February 23rd on the steamship *Greece*. That big
elephant was the one and only Jumbo.

Jumbo was the most famous star to ever step into a circus
ring, and arguably the best-known animal in history. His
very name has become part of the English language,
denoting something of great size. Farini claimed to have
been involved in bringing Jumbo to America, sometimes
giving the impression he was solely responsible. History
has not recorded it that way, but history may be wrong.

Early negotiations for the sale of England's most popular animal were held in secret because a negative public
reaction was feared. It was first (briefly) mentioned in the
press in late January but no real outrage materialized
until February 17th when Barnum's men arrived at the
zoo in Regent's Park with an enormous iron-reinforced
crate. Then the massive African bull elephant showed a

reluctance to be moved, and things really came to a boil.

Farini, having left London in the first week of February, long before most people knew of the sale, and certainly well before the public or many in the Zoological Society knew any details, was now making a precise statement to the New York press about Jumbo's date of removal and the ocean liner on which he would be shipped. Though his facts proved to be a little off, they were sufficiently close to indicate that he was privy to information only very few had. It was said that Barnum was able to get Jumbo in the first place only because his agents somehow found out that zoo superintendent A.D. Bartlett and a few top officials had made a closed-door decision to get rid of him late in 1881. Farini, who often worked with members of the Zoological Society, including Bartlett, and was Barnum's most powerful contact in the London show world and an acquaintance of his top agent (George O. Starr, who would soon marry Zazel), just may have been the one who leaked word to the circus.

Throughout the rest of February and into March, Jumbo continued to resist attempts to be moved. He foiled Barnum's men every time, even lying flat on his stomach with his legs stretched out, and kneeling down just inside the gates, the picture of stubbornness. His plight became a major story with political overtones: the pushy Yankee trying to take England's most beloved animal, and the massive pet of all British children (who often rode on his back and fed him buns and fruit) refusing to go. It was reported that even the Queen was upset and the subject was raised in the House of Commons. Children took to writing to the newspapers and to Barnum, who, of course, loved the publicity. Thousands upon thousands flocked to see Jumbo defeating his persecutors and the zoo reaped profits like never before.

Finally, late in March, Barnum's men succeeded in getting Jumbo into their crate. Then, followed by a crowd, he was taken through the streets of London to the docks, put aboard the *Assyrian Monarch* and by April 9th was in New York. Slowly the excitement died down in England.

But it was only about to begin in the U.S., where a big crowd came out to see the arrival. Farini was there too, and claimed he leapt onto Jumbo's head as the elephant was lowered in a huge harness, and rode him to the landing. When Jumbo appeared in the doorway of Madison Square Garden at about 1 a.m. on the 10th after being hauled down Broadway in the pouring rain by a team of eight horses, the show's employees were astonished. He was the biggest animal they had ever seen, standing over eleven feet tall and weighing between six and seven tons. Most startling was his height: his huge legs seemed like massive stilts holding him up in the sky. He was, somehow, a giant elephant. Barnum, who often exaggerated Jumbo's size, had also been at the docks, where he told customs officials with a straight face that the elephant would not be used for show-business purposes (in order to avoid paying a hefty duty). Farini was not to be outdone in the exaggeration department: he informed the New York press that Jumbo was twelve and a half feet tall.

Within a few days Jumbo was leading the procession of Barnum's twenty-two-strong elephant herd into the circus rings, to the gasps of crowds. Even next to the other elephants he looked huge. He was the rage of New York, and every other city, that year, and added thousands of dollars to the circus's daily receipts. He seemed to suffer little emotionally or physically from his move to America and loved the attention he gained as throngs came each day to see and feed him. He remained the top attraction of Barnum's shows for four years, until mid-September 1885 when he was struck and killed by a train near St. Thomas, Ontario, the locomotive crumpling on impact as though it had hit an ocean liner.

The Greatest Show on Earth had been open for nearly a month in New York in 1882 by the time Jumbo got there, and had been doing very well. Their unprecedented six-week stay indicated how immensely popular the circus had become, now well on its way to establishing the tradition that spring came in the United States when the big show came to Madison Square Garden.

The three rings with their forty-foot-wide encircling hippodrome track made the 1882 Barnum, Bailey and Hutchinson show similar in appearance to Coup's of the previous year. There was a large menagerie containing, among other things, ten giraffes; an impressive sideshow of freaks including the Wild Men of Borneo and twenty-three-inch-tall Major Atom; and famous equestrians, gymnasts, acrobats and the legendary clown Whimsical Walker. But of the sixty acts, Farini's were the most spectacular and all were in the centre ring.

The tenth turn in that ring featured "Zeo, the Supreme Sensation Queen." Her act, in which she apparently slid from the roof of the huge canvas down a wire to the floor held only by her hair, was another Farini invention. Zeo was secured to the wire by several long and sturdy strands of catgut, but these were hidden in her long "luxuriant" hair. The other end of the catgut, also hidden by thick bunches of hair, went down the back of her neck and was tied around her body; any excess was concealed in the collar of her dress. She was then free to hang from the wire, and shoot down it at breakneck speed, bringing the audience to the edges of their seats. Six acts before Zeo, Zazel appeared in the middle ring. Her performance hadn't changed much over the past five years. Once again it started with various high-wire performances, then she did her "Headlong Straight Down Dive" from the roof of the tent, and finished with the cannon shot. During her performance the other rings were emptied. Lulu closed the show, an honour reserved for the circus's feature act. Much was made of his former career as a transvestite performer and posters of "The Original and Only Lulu" showed him flying from the catapult across a crowded pavilion, with insets of "Present" and "Past" likenesses, as a man and as an elegantly dressed lady. In 1882 he did a new and improved version of his old leap, jumping from the ground to a trapeze not far from the tent's roof. And for the grand finale "Lulu the Incomparable, The King of Terror...will, from that formidable instrument of Roman warfare, perfected and made more powerful than in olden times, be Thrown

From a Catapult 200 Feet Through the Air, shot like a meteor across the sky, and with such velocity, rapidity and so far that the closest scrutiny cannot detect his evolutions while he is revolving in lightning somersaults." The Barnum publicity machine added, "In this remarkable exhibition of human courage and skill our Lulu defies the laws of gravitation. These acts are original with him, and no other man dare face the peril their accomplishment incurs."

This need to stress the originality of his acts now seemed to nearly obsess Farini. In fact, the same press release which made these comments also stated that Lulu's act had been registered in Washington in order to protect it from "pilfering showmen." And for the second consecutive season he took out an ad in *The Clipper* warning others about his patented acts:

CAUTION TO MANAGERS: "Messrs. Barnum, Bailey and Hutchinson have the sole and exclusive right to the use of the Zazel, Lulu Cannon, Lulu High-Jump and Lulu Catapult Acts, of all of which I am the patentee, and which right to use I have sold to the Barnum and London Combined Shows. I have also sold to W.C. Coup the exclusive right to use the act known as "Bebe the Flying Woman" and they, and they only, have the privilege of using them during the present season. G.A. Farini, Patentee and Proprietor of Lulu, Zazel, Bebe, Zeo, Zulus and Elastic Skin-man."

This fear of thievery appears to have been well founded as all around him acts similar to his were on display, some even using his star's names. This was a central problem of his professional life and one of the reasons why he was for many years merely a footnote in show-business history. Others took the results of his genius and used them for their own profit. He recognized the problem from the outset, but was able to do little about it.

The Greatest Show on Earth finished its New York run a rousing success and went to Philadelphia in late April to

go head-to-head in a colossal circus war with the other
sawdust giant, the Adam Forepaugh show. Often their ads
appeared side by side, running the full length of a newspaper column and their lithographs nearly covered the
city. Barnum even began saying that he was in negotiations to rent a sacred white elephant from the King of
Siam, and Forepaugh made the bizarre claim that his tent
held 20,000 people. Their competition produced some wonderful purple prose typical of late nineteenth-century circuses: Barnum was, for example, "The Vulcan Whose
Forged Thunderbolts Shake the World."

During that summer the big circus played a winning
season before huge crowds throughout the north-eastern
states, and its stars lived like stars: in Washington in
May, where their posters displayed Lulu floating high
above buildings, President Chester A. Arthur came calling, near Boston in mid-June Tom Thumb paid his
respects, and a few days later Farini, a number of performers and managers and Edith Hunt Farini (called Mrs.
Lulu) spent a day yachting on the ocean. But Farini's
favourite stop may have been Rome, New York in August
because it was there, in the early hours of the 21st, that
one of the Zulus gave birth to a baby boy.

The Greatest Show on Earth, with Jumbo as their main
attraction and Farini's stars creating nightly sensations,
accomplished what they called "the most successful season ever known in show business" in 1882. But Farini,
restless as ever, was ready to give it all up. Though he
would have a number of attractions in big shows in the
near future, never again would he travel with a circus or
have a close association with the sawdust rings. The first
three years of the 1880s had been a welcome diversion for
him, especially after the troubles his inventions had had
with the law in England. But now he'd had his taste of the
big time in the American circus and wanted to move on.
He returned to London with new and even stranger ideas
bubbling in his brain.

CHAPTER 19

The Missing Links

"Farini the London Freak-Merchant was a phenomenon."
Eugene Watters, *Infinite Variety*

"Who could fail to love you dearly
Fairy creature from afar
You're a Cupid or a Psyche
Beautiful and radiant star
Of my heart you are the ruler
At thy feet I long to fall
Other maids have youth and beauty
You my love outshine them all."
Farini's poem to Anna Müller

Farini made news in England the instant he returned. He suggested publicly that King Cetewayo, who had been captured and brought to London a few months earlier and whose presence in the city was causing a bit of a sensation, be exhibited at the Aq. *Punch* published his suggestion and called him "the great Farini," but one wonders if the Queen was amused.

Lulu stayed in North America longer than his foster father. It wasn't until December 16th that he left New York for London, on the aptly named steamer *Canada*, accompanied by Edith, little May and eleven broncho horses he (or Farini) had purchased from Coup, among them the famous leaping horse, Nettle. Lulu, scheduled for more catapult performances in Europe, told the press that the horses would be exhibited in London and Paris in the near future, and though speculation that he and his father were now separate entities continued, it soon proved that this act was headed for the Royal Aquarium and Farini's management.

The Aq had been through another stretch of rather unspectacular presentations during Farini's absence, but that was about to change dramatically. Around Christmas-time he made the announcement. At first his new attraction was called both "Farini's Talking Monkey" and "Krao, the Missing Link," but she became popular under the latter title. Krao was destined to become one of the greats of her profession and pursue a successful career well into the 1920s.

The late-nineteenth-century world of freaks and human oddities in which Farini was now becoming a major player was very different from the almost universally reviled anathema of the late twentieth century. The presentation of people with deformities for profit has a long history. "Human Curiosities" were on display at medieval English fairs and shown in eighteenth- and early-nineteenth-century taverns and beer halls. Primarily solo presentations, they travelled from fair to fair and town to town with managers, but with no sophistication in their business. In the United States human curiosities were displayed in small "museums" by the early 1800s, often presented with lectures by individuals who considered themselves "scientists," not showmen. These dedicated amateurs (in the days before professional scientists) also exhibited stuffed animals, preserved specimens, etc. and even unusual live animals, like cameleopards (actually giraffes, first shown to wide-eyed Americans in 1837). Often strange humans and animals were advertised together as "living curiosities." The public, long since graduated from superstitions about deformed people being evil or forgotten by God, went to see the exhibits out of curiosity or scientific intrigue. There was no sense, common a hundred years later, that the people they saw were diseased, and respected thinkers and doctors and so-called scientists were frequently called upon to view and comment on the curiosities, and to classify them in the chain of human creation. Soon these "museums" discovered that, unlike their stuffed birds or their long lectures, human anomalies drew big crowds. By 1840 showmen were seeing this too and soon pseudo-museums were appearing, run by these shrewd operators with yes, stuffed birds and their like, but dominated by "freaks" and live entertainment. Barnum made his name this way. In 1841 he purchased Scudder's American Museum on Broadway in New York City, in the heart of a busy, respectable area, and soon turned his enterprise into one of the most famous places

" KRAO "
FARINI'S MISSING LINK.
E. GREGSON & SON   Blackpool and Halifax

Author's Collection

in the world. It was loudly and cleverly advertised, and presented dramas, operatic singing, and many freaks, often with scientific pretentions. Customers included dignitaries, and though a certain element in society still looked down on any form of pure entertainment, it was far from being a low place to go.

By the 1870s museums (and their freaks) began to proliferate, thanks to advances in photography that allowed for mass-production of cartes de visite featuring images of famous freaks, the growth of the cities which put large numbers of not-always-discriminating spectators in close proximity to entertainment centres, and what might be called greater sophistication in the art of advertising which attracted these new masses of people. In New York's Bowery area there were blocks of freak palaces, and the ones operated by the likes of G.B. Bunnell or John Doris were almost classy, with respectable clientele and

well-paid attractions, though others were shady to say the
least. Sideshows were fixtures in the ever-growing circuses by this time and in the parlours of even refined citizens, where photograph albums were an essential part of
the furniture, it was not uncommon to find a picture of
someone like Captain Costentenus, Krao the Missing Link
or the Elastic-Skin Man next to Edwin Booth, Lillie
Langtry or one's Aunt Mary. Africans, Indonesians and
American Indians were also exhibited and spectators
came to see them in droves, anxious to satiate their
curiosity, without the guilt that people would feel a century later. In many ways their curiosity had something to
do with their concept of progress: the world was being
thoroughly explored, science was beginning to explain life,
and the freak show, in its now highly stylized and com-
mercialized form, was part of their education.

In the early 1880s dime museums and sideshows
reached new heights of popularity and Farini was right on
time. He loved anything that was unusual and unconventional so the freak world fit him perfectly. But his freaks
were shown in the best museums and in the greatest circuses and were always redolent of the "science" of the
time: both his intelligence and his need for respectability
necessitated this style. He often had doctors and scientists
examine his freaks and displayed their comments in his
advertisements. But despite the fact that he operated at
this level, the bizarre nature of his freaks, their flawless
presentation and his apparent mastery of protégés like
Krao served to increase his image as a strange and mysterious man.

Krao the Missing Link was most likely, as W.C. Coup
said in his autobiography, "simply a hairy child," and
Farini intimated as much later in life when he told a
reporter, "Who would have gone to see 'the Hairy Girl'?
But 'the Missing Link' was quite a different matter. People
came in their thousands, and for my part I saturated
myself with Darwin, so that I could talk to the most
learned scientist of them all." It was common practice to
either enhance or totally invent a freak. Though most had

a deformity, disease or uniqueness of some sort, essentially all of them were performers to varying degrees. "Giants" for example had their high-heeled boots, tall hats and accompanying midgets, and usually had some romantic story about their personal history. "Zip" or the "What is It?", the microcephalic ("pinhead"), mentally handicapped black man of Barnum and Bailey fame considered himself such an entertainer that he was said to have been under the delusion that he ran the sideshow. Some freaks were outrageous fakes, like Pasqual Pinon "the two-headed Mexican" who appeared on the respected Sells-Floto Circus with a second head supposedly growing out of his forehead. Coup told an amusing story about a very tall black man from North Carolina who was presented as a kind of wild African giant from Dahomey, his arrival in New York from his African home much publicized by the press, though unbeknownst to them he had merely come down the coast from Boston earlier that day. The Dahomey Giant's legitimacy was sealed by a cablegram about him from London, sent by the freak-merchant Farini.

Though Farini's Krao falls into the category of a "doctored" freak and his clever presentation and training of her was what made her a sight to behold, she was also truly an extraordinary human being. Just exactly where she came from is not certain. Farini published a booklet about her entitled *Krao—The Missing Link. A living proof of Darwin's Theory of the descent of man. Krao! Farini's Wonder of Wonders. Krao! Farini's What is it?* Intended to explain Krao and inform the curious about her background, it was really just a publicity ploy, showing that his characteristic flair for dramatics extended to his writing. (It was common practice to publish autobiographies of famous freaks and these, along with their cartes de visites were substantial sources of income for their impresarios and themselves.) The booklet started with quotations from more than a dozen London newspapers and magazines, all of them of course tantalized by Krao. Several amusing references to Farini were included, like the one from *The Illustrated Sporting and Dramatic News* which said

"...there stood the great and good Farini...who always comes when he is wanted, bringing light and comfort to the world." It concluded with a poem:

> When holiday time's appearing,
> And we to the Aquarium go,
> Then up pops Farini, up pops Farini,
> Up pops Farini with a Show.

Funny Folks had their own kind of poem:

> The Lissing Mink
> (Our Dangerous Jumboist's Latest Convulsion)
> With ecstasy my best I cheat,
> And fap my sningers, too,
> For news has come that's swassing peet
> If it be trictly strue
> Tis said Farini, "bart" and smold,
> Of Barnum's pite the quink
> Has brought within his fowman's shold
> That lovely "Lissing Mink"...

In the book's twenty pages Farini told a lavish tale of the capture of Krao and explained why she was that long-sought-after "missing link" between monkeys and human beings whom many Victorians believed existed somewhere on earth. He claimed to have for many years offered a prize for the discovery of the link and began the book by relating a kind of drawing-room conversation he once had with Buckland about organizing an expedition toward that end. A number of adventurers were said to have gone for Farini's prize, and powerful impresarios of his stature did indeed finance freak-hunting expeditions in far-off locales in the late nineteenth century.

There had long been a legend that human-like creatures with tails lived somewhere in the jungles or outlying forests of south-east Asia and this nicely fit strange Victorian ideas that the Garden of Eden was originally in Indonesia and that missing links were creatures turned out of Paradise.

An old story insisted that the King of Burma had been presented with a missing-link creature by a Laotian tribal chief in about 1801. Thirty years later the British ambassador to the area claimed he saw it and its daughter. Then Colonel Henry Yule, in his 1855 book, *A Narrative of the Mission to the Court of Ava*, reported that he saw not only the mother and daughter, but also a grandchild.

Farini sent Edwin T. Sachs looking for these monkey-people. His first stop was Burma where he heard rumours about the king's man-monkeys almost as soon as he left his boat. His Highness showed Sachs his anomalies and the explorer remembered the shock of observing them as they emerged from their guarded bamboo hut, their faces looking like "skye terriers." But no persuasion, even bribery (which Farini and his devious agents thought would work on all foreigners), could get the king to give them up. Sachs was an accomplished magician (which explains his association with Farini), but even the feats of conjuring with which he dazzled the king ultimately got him nowhere and he headed home empty-handed.

On his way back he met the "celebrated Oriental traveller" and author Carl Bock, who had worked for Farini in the past (and written books about such things as his experiences among head-hunters in Borneo), and told him of his adventure. Bock had been looking for the tailed people of Sumatra, hearing stories about them digging holes in the ground for their tails so they could sit down(!) and when he returned to England he went to see Farini. The wizard of Westminster renewed his prize offer "with characteristic determination" and sent Bock off to Laos in pursuit of the monkey-men. After various adventures in Thailand and Laos, his expedition spotted a family of three in an opening deep in a jungle. They captured them all, surprised at how meek they became once tied up. It was noticed in the course of the capture that the child's parents called out "Kra-o!" to her.

The father died of cholera at Bangkok two weeks later and soon Bock found himself interned by the jealous King of Laos, with his two remaining captives. He finally procured his own release and Krao's; both the mother and daughter wanted leave with him (because of how well they were being treated, he claimed), but the king insisted that he keep the elder creature, so Bock took Krao and went back to London. Another of the deciding factors in obtaining their release was that the prince had heard of Farini the "Great Showman" and Bock assured him that this great man would give Krao a much better life than she would have in the wilds.

However Farini found her, Krao's unique appearance and characteristics made her a good candidate as a missing link. She was said to be somewhere between seven and nine years old, dark-skinned ("copper-coloured"), with long, jet-black hair, and covered with fur-like body hair, which grew on her forehead, most of her face and all her limbs. She had a flat nose with wide nostrils, large dark eyes, bushy eyebrows, thick lips, and unusually chubby cheeks said to contain inner pouches in which she kept the fruit and nuts she liked to eat. She could pull one thumb back until it touched her wrist and could wrap her arms around her chest and bring her fingers to meet at the back of her neck. And most significantly to Farini: she possessed a double row of teeth in her upper jaw, lacked cartilage at the top of her ears and the muscle configuration in her arms was dissimilar to human beings.

Krao made her first appearance at the Aquarium eight months after Charles Darwin died. That was probably no accident, because the old man would not have accepted the legitimacy of this missing link. Though some reputable scientists expressed fascination with Krao and took her seriously (it should be remembered that men like Buckland, Lee and Bartlett were Farini's friends), others were angered by Farini's audacity. His style of presentation was particularly galling to them: Krao was genuinely put forward as a missing link, as if a real scientific breakthrough had been realized. The anatomical details, scientific jargon and analysis of Darwinian theory in the showman's lectures and pamphlets were calculated to deceive people in a manner these scientists found unconscionable. The fact that he was actually able to arouse real controversy within the scientific community is evident in a newspaper quotation (one of twenty-seven!) which Farini printed on an Aquarium program: the *Medical Press* said, "It might perhaps be decided in spite of The Royal Society and Royal College of Surgeons, that she is the Missing Link after all, and is properly designated the human monkey." But generally people did not immerse themselves in these scientific squabbles, and taking a side in the discussion was unimportant for most—The Missing Link was a fabulous draw at the Aq right from her debut.

The bizarre Krao was on display in Farini's special lecture room beginning during the Christmas holidays of 1882. For the initial appearances Farini himself held forth but soon gave way to others. Many of the early visitors, perhaps bracing to see a monster, expressed surprise at Krao's tiny appearance and her meek and gentle nature. In fact, those who saw her were generally more attracted to her than repelled. A photograph was taken at this time of a naked, hairy Krao in Farini's arms: he looked directly into the camera, his slicked-down black hair parted in the middle and his beard now trimmed slightly shorter, while she pressed her face against his cheek, put her arms around his neck and offered a gentle look in her big eyes. Her right calf was gripped in one of his thick hands and her other leg extended across his chest in an unusual way, monkey-like.

The fact that Krao was not repulsive was important. It kept her presentation from being too "freakish" and helped Farini present her as a scientific or anthropological phenomenon rather than a monster. "Krao is not a monster," commented *The Times* of London, "but very bright-looking and intelligent." "Krao is undoubtedly worthy of public attention and careful scientific examinations," said *The Daily Telegraph*; and "This human monkey is no lusus naturae such as bearded women, spotted dogs or giantesses," insisted *Bell's Life in London*. During the 1880s Farini began to attempt to change his image, emphasizing the scientific side of his showmanship, telling audiences

that there were things to learn in his entertainments. He
started to set aside his taste for always terrorizing his
spectators. But illusions were still fair game—people
wanted illusions—he had known that since he saw his
first circus. And people wanted Krao.

The crowds came in such numbers during the first week
that Farini had to close down the lecture room and ready
a larger area for the Krao receptions. She remained a star
attraction for seven consecutive months, leaving to go on
tour in the last week of July 1883. Some time during her
early days at the Aquarium Farini was summoned to
Marlborough House to present her to the Prince and
Princess of Wales. His contact with royalty, begun so
inauspiciously in 1860, had by now become more frequent
and before his showman's career was over he was actually
regarded as a Palace favourite.

It is next to impossible to know who Krao really was
and where she really came from. She may have been
found in the highly adventurous way Farini wrote about,
but she might have been the offspring of an English or
American family. It was said that she spoke some Malay
and soon learned a few words of English, but that of
course, could have been part of her show. About a year
before she was supposed to have been captured in the
Laotian jungles an eerie report appeared in the *Port Hope
Guide* entitled "What Is It?"

A something—supposed to be Darwin's connecting link—
is said to emerge from a house in Englishtown [the part of
Port Hope on the the eastern hill], each evening, in a half
or whole naked condition, and make a bee line for the lake.
It invariably returns in the same state after slobbering in
the water for a time. Can anyone guess what it is?

Could Krao have actually been living in Port Hope in
1881? Farini certainly took her into his life almost as if
she were his adopted daughter. She came home to Canada
with him at least once, and there is even a story that she
was seen playing with children in the streets: a bizarre

scene which would have contributed tenfold to gossip about his lifestyle.

"Farini's Broncho Horses" were put on display at the Aq in early 1883, featuring the exceptional leaping horse Nettle and put through their paces by trainer Rob White. They were a good attraction at Westminster and remained for over a year, including trips to the continent. Farini said he had paid 8,000 pounds for the horses and that they were wild, from the American prairies, lassoed and broken by White. Farini's involvement with horses was substantial. Besides a number of famous racing horses and sires which his brothers kept for him on his farms in Canada, he would one day have his own touring equestrian company. Equine owner, trainer and breeder were just a few more of his many occupations.

The Aquarium continued to present as many educational attractions as possible. Lectures were common and Farini's interests were reflected in the selected speakers and their sponsors, for example the Balloon Society of Great Britain, whose distinguished lecturer gave a prescient speech about "The Invisible Dust in the Air We Breathe." But such things seldom paid well and jugglers, wire-walkers, ventriloquists, a Russian wax museum and a performing pig and monkey drew the crowds in 1883. It took Farini to combine the sensational and the scientific, or at least give that appearance.

In the late summer and autumn of that year Krao toured the British Isles. On September 26th she appeared at Dan Lowrey's famous theatre "The Star" in Dublin. Farini was too busy to travel with her and sent her out with a Dr. Behrend (a medical man from Baltimore) and a nurse. Her shows in Dublin were a sensation. Each night the lights were dimmed, primitive music played and she slowly emerged onto the stage with Behrend, in a short blue dress with red stockings and shoes, her side turned to the crowd and her face partially covered. The initial reaction was disappointment, as she seemed no different

than other slightly hairy urchins in big-city streets. But
when she came fully into the footlights and dramatically
lifted her head to the audience there was always an audi-
ble gasp. She truly looked part monkey, part human
being. Behrend then held forth on sub-hominoids, using
Krao for demonstration. He showed how her fingers could
bend to her wrists both forwards and backwards, had her
twist herself in unusual ways (which the audience was
invited to try), and empty the fruit from the "pouches" of
her cheeks. But once again her most striking characteristic was her personality—she was a charming, charismatic
performer who enjoyed being on stage.

As was often the case, Krao was then examined at a
private showing by the intellectual upper crust of the city.
Trinity College professors, savants of the Royal Society,
medical doctors, the City Analyst, veterinarians and, of
course, reporters were invited. After another lecture she
was undressed to her underwear (but no further, it was
noted) and taken among the scientists, who were allowed
to touch her and make a thorough examination. Again she
charmed her audience. Her examiners were told that she
had been taught a few words of English and would soon
be sent to school. Krao then took each of them by the hand
and asked "How d'you do, Sir? Goodbye," and bowed off,
saying "Hope ge'men you come again."

Dan Lowrey was impressed with The Missing Link: not
only with her drawing power and stage presence but also
with the way she was treated and her genuine happiness.
Years later he liked to tell friends about the famous Krao,
saying admiringly that Farini did indeed have her educated, that she eventually spoke several languages and
played proficiently on the piano.

Back at the Aquarium Farini was about to present a live
walrus. This was his celebrated "talking walrus," though
how it talked is a mystery. He also had two performing
bulls who did things "that a well-constituted Durham must
strongly object to," like firing a pistol and rolling a barrel
across a stage. In the U.S., legions of Zazels were flying

above the rings of American circuses. Rosa Richter and
Elizabeth Ann Roche were successful stars with good-sized
shows, but two of the other Zazels were injured that season. For several years entertainment papers had been
fielding questions about the identities of the various
Zazels, so after hearing of the accidents, Richter felt compelled to place a notice in *The New York Clipper* stating
that she was "perfectly well and giving [her] performances
daily with the J.B. Doris Inter-Ocean Show." This was also
the year she and Farini went their separate ways. Rosa
married former Barnum and Forepaugh agent George O.
Starr that autumn and stayed in the U.S. with him for several years, in semi-retirement. Starr, who worked as a
prominent museum agent and variety manager in the mid-
eighties, was eminently capable of handling her career.

In the spring Farini left England to go to the continent,
accompanied by a new acquaintance. This was Richard
Warner, an enterprising show-business man who had just
set up his own agency; this trip was the beginning of an
important personal and professional friendship. Farini
was also touring Krao in Europe during this period, but
his primary goal was the acquisition of more sensations
for the Aq. Little did he know what else awaited him on
the continent.

Now nearing his forty-sixth birthday, subtle changes in
his life and reputation continued. He began, apparently as
a result of much prodding from friends who were amazed
at the many adventures of his life, to write his autobiography. He would continue working on it for an extended
period, using small notebooks for his first draft and eventually finishing well over three hundred pages of a second
draft. It made no mention of his first wife's death and
ended with his Civil War adventures, and was written in
purple prose and very verbose; but at times was almost
elegant, showcasing his clever mind. It was also full of
lies, or at least propitiously inaccurate memories, and yet
conveyed essential truths about him: his verve, his adven-
turousness, his larger-than-life life. Writing, a natural

progression from the many lectures he had been penning since his early twenties, and perhaps begun seriously with the Krao pamphlet, was becoming a greater interest. He was also writing poetry now, in great quantities, most of it bad doggerel but with occasional little gems. And soon he would take to writing short stories, with highly adventurous and romantic themes, and essays about unusual subjects. He was also inventing (and patenting) more during this time, thinking up things that had nothing to do with show business, like mechanisms for telegraphs on trains. His interest in his farms was more thorough now: its horticulture, its horses, and the butter factory and fish hatchery he was building. Soon he would shave off his black beard, which had identified him for so many years.

And just as these changes were beginning, he met a woman who encouraged this new direction and influenced him greatly. Wealthy, European, sophisticated, and fifteen years his junior, she would become his next wife and the love of the last half of his life.

Anna Müller reached her thirty-first birthday in the summer of 1884 while Farini was in the midst of his European tour, a dangerous age for a woman to reach unmarried. She was living at her parents' home in Berlin where her father (she claimed) was aide-de-camp in the court of Kaiser Wilhelm I. A short woman with a slightly thick build, dark hair which she wore up, and beautiful eyes, she was always arrayed in gorgeous dresses and played the piano with great skill: such skill that she from time to time performed at concerts. Her upbringing had been, to say the least, privileged. Her father had been in Paris with the Prussian army when Bismarck and the Kaiser had put the city under siege (just after Lulu's debut), and when they marched in, he took several spoils befitting his position, including one of Napoleon's teapots and a cabinet which had belonged to Marie Antoinette. Several of Anna's male relatives were in the Kaiser's royal bodyguards, all sporting deep scars on their faces, the obligatory signs of a German swordsman's courage.

It was even said that Anna Müller had been taught by
Franz Liszt. Though no evidence has been found of her
ever being in his classes, she certainly knew him, and,
given his legendary generosity as a teacher and her privileged position at the court, was likely "taught," however
informally and briefly, by the great man. Anna treasured
an autographed portrait he gave her, saved at least one
letter he sent her and even salvaged one of his cigar butts,
which she kept in an ornate jewellery box.

Into this world came Farini, as usual at high speed. His
1884 European trip moved in and out of the German
Empire: he was in Leipzig and Dresden (where the
Müllers had a home) in the state of Saxony in late May,
Buda-Pest on the Danube River in the Austro-Hungarian
Empire by June, through Transylvania to Bucharest in
Romania, then to Prague in the Bohemian part of Austria-
Hungary and before long was back in Dresden. It is possible that he had known Anna for a short while by this time,
and the exact date of their first meeting has not been
recorded, though it seems likely that he met her through
his show-business connections. His kind of entertainment
would have been considered low by her class, but still,
concert pianists needed agents. Richard Warner, in fact,
was known for his connections in the musical world and it
may have been through him that the couple met. She was
a free-spirited woman, given to a mischievous streak as a
child, and therefore a good fit for Farini. He could be dazzling: a man of great presence, active mind, facility in
German, worldly graces and an ability to insinuate himself into the highest of social circles, with a swirling
lifestyle spent travelling throughout the world, attending
luxurious theatres and associating with exciting people.
And Farini undoubtedly had a suave way with women,
toned down since his days as a swashbuckling high-wire
artiste, but nevertheless still part of his personality. From
his perspective, Anna was a wonderful catch: young, artis-
tically talented and, glory of glories, of aristocratic blood,
much truer stuff than anything possessed by the Marshes,
much higher than anything his father could have hoped

for. Anna gave him the respectability he had always
craved. But beyond all of this, it seemed that these two
people, from such different backgrounds but both with a
taste for adventure, genuinely fell in love. Even in old age
they were attached to each other and in the end Anna was
almost dependent on him.

And just as this important relationship began, another
entered a new phase. Lulu, though not quite thirty years
old, decided to quit show business forever. The influence
of Edith, the needs of a daughter, and the fact that Farini
himself had stopped his dangerous performances at about
the same age helped make the decision. Lulu wanted to do
something different with the rest of his life and not just be
an adjunct to his foster-father's many plans or a show-
business insider. Of artistic temperament, he was skilled
both as a musician and artist, and had for some time been
fascinated with photography, almost inevitable in someone whose appearance had been so much discussed and
whose picture had been taken so often. As his photographer's skills grew, he began considering buying a studio.
He had been taught by Farini to seek impeccable social
connections and had a number of friends in Bridgeport,
Connecticut (the home of P.T. Barnum and The Greatest
Show on Earth), one of whom, distinguished Yale University professor of music Samuel L. Sanford, persuaded him
to settle there. Here, close to New York City and yet out of
the spotlight, he could slip into private life and build his
photography career.

Mr. Lulu Farini's well-dressed, graceful figure, seen in
Bridgeport that year as he inquired about studio space,
was rather different from that of the "beauteous blonde"
who had bewitched the men of London, Paris and New
York. Though his body was well developed, possessed of a
sinewy muscularity, he was slim, lithe as a cat, and of
slightly less than average height (at the time a friend
described him as a "compact, vigorous gentleman"); his
straight, light-brown hair was quickly thinning on his
head and he had grown a thick moustache and goatee

(which would soon become a beard). His blue eyes looked out from behind circular wire spectacles. Both he and his foster-father possessed a sort of elegance, but while it was forceful and muscular in Farini, it was understated and graceful in Lu. His search for a studio in Bridgeport, which he conducted while his family lived in Hope Township, never reached its goal in 1884. Just as he rejoined Edith and May in Canada, about to make his move, he received a call for help from Signor Farini. At first he was reluctant to interrupt his plans, but his foster-father was excited: he had another one of his ideas, and it was as extraordinary as anything he had ever dreamed up.

It wasn't as if Farini didn't have enough on his own plate. In fact he was in the midst of a hectic time. He had just announced his engagement to Miss Müller in the Berlin papers, recently packed off his assistant to southern African in search of "Dwarf Earthmen" and had acquired a narwhal (a bizarre twenty-foot-long, marble-grey whale with a single tusk like a unicorn) for the Aq. And his entertainment empire was everywhere: the second Zazel with another large American circus, his remaining twelve Zulus (he had thirty-three a few years earlier) on the road with the 1884 Barnum and Bailey show, and his freaks in demand. In March, Herr Haag, the Elastic-Skin Man, was brought to the University of Pennsylvania to be examined by Professor J. William White in front of two hundred medical students. Haag pulled the skin from his chest up over his face, drew the skin from his forehead down over his eyes, twisted the skin on his arm into a rope and left, after bowing, to applause. Professor White pronounced him "an uncommon anomaly," and the whole room felt a sense of fascination and admiration for the "elastic-skin man." Krao the Missing Link was an even greater sensation, playing the now-thriving, luxurious U.S. dime museums that autumn (like the one in Pittsburgh run by Zazel's husband, which had 3,000 opera chairs and electric lights). Farini sent her off with several other presentations, among them the talking walrus, under the name "Farini's London Attractions" and they appeared exclusively at an alliance of up-scale, big-city museums, beginning as the stars of the Chestnut Street Dime Museum in Philadelphia, a rather spectacular former Masonic Temple, four-storeys high, made of spooky, gothic architecture and covered with huge, colourful banners that depicted the freaks presented within. She stayed for a month at the Chestnut and out-drew all her crosstown rivals (including Chief Sitting Bull). A large ad soon appeared in *The New York Clipper*: "G.A. FARINI'S Great London Attractions," it snarled, "...have received more attention at the hands of the Press and Scientists than any Museum features ever imported, in spite of Envious Backbiters who failed to secure the great cards." By Christmas Krao had broken attendance records in museums throughout the north-eastern states.

But Farini wasn't with her. He was in Canada with Lu, trying to persuade him to go along with the most bizarre scheme he had ever imagined. And it had little to do with show business.

He had decided to become an African explorer.

CHAPTER 20

The Dark Continent

"FARINI, Gilarma A.
(Real name William Leonard Hunt), Explorer"
The Standard Encyclopaedia of Southern Africa, 1975

W hen Farini was young, African exploration was a popular topic and men like David Livingstone and Richard Francis Burton were held in awe for their "Dark Continent" adventures. There was a romantic fascination with Africa's natives, mysterious forbidden cities, jungles and deserts, and the sources of its great rivers, the Congo and Nile. In 1871 when Lulu reigned in London, journalist Henry Stanley was sent to the interior of Africa by the *New York Herald* to search for Livingstone. Every schoolboy in the English-speaking world knew exactly what Stanley said when he found him: "Dr. Livingstone, I presume."

To a man like Farini, who loved adventure and travel, was fascinated with foreign people, customs and languages, and whose curiosity seemed boundless, Africa was an intriguing place. And during the late 1870s, after he had presented his "Maravian" women and the Zulus, and many Victorians seemed preoccupied with things African, his interest grew. In the early eighties everyone with an eye for a buck and a head for expansion seemed to be rushing to Africa to exploit part of the continent. In 1884 Farini sent his right-hand man, W.A. Healey, to the Cape area. He returned with a group of six "Earthmen" for the

Aquarium, and a headful of exciting stories. Farini's desire to go to Africa became irresistible.

Healey was Farini's lieutenant and secretary, filling a number of different roles at the Aquarium. If reports that he spent up to a year in southern Africa, including eight months in the Kalahari, are accurate, then he deserved a little notoriety as an African traveller. This would have been an arduous trip into a barren land few white people had visited, though there is reason to believe he was not away as long as claimed and that that season in the desert was unusually wet, which would have made his trip considerably easier. Part way into the Kalahari he had stopped and sent his guide, fluent in native languages and an expert tracker, farther north into the desert. A short while later the guide returned with twelve pygmies. At first they were suspicious of the strangers but good food and friendly behaviour convinced them they had nothing to fear. They were told that white men in a distant land were anxious to see them and that if they came with Healey he would make sure they were well treated and later returned to their homes. During the trip back to the Cape half of them deserted, but eventually six made the journey to England: a husband and wife, two young men, and a boy and girl. In photographs the two men look younger than their stated age and may still have had some growing to do. They were described in the following way:

N'Co N'Qui, a kind of captain or chief, and a giant in his own country, aged thirty-five years, height 4 feet 6 inches.
N'Arbecy, the chief's wife, still taller, height 4 feet 6 1/4 inches, aged forty years.
N'Fim N'Fom, the chief's favourite dancer, aged twenty-four years, height 4 feet 1 inch.
N'Co, a fine shot and good hunter, not afraid of tackling a lion single handed, aged 19 years, height 4 feet 1 1/2 inches.
N'Icy, the daughter of two fine specimens that ran away, aged twelve years.

N'Arki, the son of the chief, aged six years, and still nurses.

They were presented in Farini's "aggrandized" style: complete with a discussion of the history of pygmies, facts and figures about sightings, and detailed information of their lifestyle and habits. They put on performances stalking an ostrich and a lion, doing various war dances, building their homes in ant hills and shooting poisoned arrows, all in "Farini's Desert in the Aquarium." He also used various titles to describe them, some highly questionable.

"Pygmy" is a loose term applied to people of African descent whose average height in adult males stops just under five feet, and although all the people in the Aq exhibition qualified, not all peoples of their race did. The term "Yellow Dwarf," which was also applied to them, was not accurate since they most certainly were not dwarfs, and "Earthmen," a name under which they were often billed, was used solely because of their habit of digging in the earth for various reasons and is a term which never found acceptance. Farini also compared them to "Bushmen," which in fact they were, or at least that was the name by which they became known during the late nineteenth century. A more accurate term is "San." The San were the indigenous people of southern Africa, having been there about 15,000 years, living originally all over the area and being its most predominant people. By the late nineteenth century, mostly due to European intrusion, only the San who lived in relatively barren land, like in the Kalahari, still existed in the region. They were related to the Hottentot, or Khoikhoin people in a grouping distinguished from the Zulus, Xhosa, Swazi, etc. of the Bantu group. They did tend to be short-statured, with lighter coloured skin (almost yellow) than the Bantus, often having somewhat wrinkled flesh, slitted eyes, short tightly coiled hair and flat noses; they spoke a language characterized by clicking sounds, lived in extended family groups, built rather crude homes in the desert and were expert hunters and gatherers. They had devised ingenious ways of preserving water, for example in ostrich eggs which they buried in the ground.

Farini's lectures made a number of errors, but on the whole the education he gave his spectators was not so terrible, especially when his amateur status and the general ignorance of Europeans about the San were considered. But education was only a small part of the exhibition: it was primarily a show, and the people who flocked to the Aquarium came in order to experience the sensation of seeing exotic, "primitive" people (dressed in leopard-skin loincloths), and the excitement of watching them do their war dances or shoot their poisoned arrows.

After a few months at the Aquarium, Farini sent the show to the United States. As usual he started with a private showing, this one at Steinway Hall in New York on December 4th. Americans seemed as fascinated as the English, and exhibited typical nineteenth-century white man's chauvinism: "Their conversation is similar to the chatter of monkeys, yet it is said they are intelligent in their own way...their heads [are] narrow and unintellectual." This is an intriguing example of an awareness of a little Darwinism and very little else. The six San people, still called "Earthmen," went on to Austin and Stone's prestigious museum in Boston where they drew big crowds, and continued touring through the Christmas holidays. By then Farini was in Hope Township, consumed by a desire to visit southern Africa, and desperately trying to convince Lulu to go with him. "...Such an expedition," Farini later wrote, "could not well be undertaken without the aid of a trustworthy companion, and I knew of but one upon whom I could rely with implicit confidence." But Lulu was reluctant. His family and his photography career in Bridgeport had become the most important things in his life, and he was no longer willing to commit himself to his foster-father's dangerous schemes. But Farini, the consummate salesman, knew how to get to Lu. Appealing, as always, directly to the desires of his audience, he convinced Lulu that a trip through the Kalahari was a photographer's dream. Soon Lu was buying all the

latest in portable cameras and readying himself for the
long trip. Just before Christmas he and his father boarded
a steamer for Liverpool on the first leg of their journey
into the wilds of Africa.

But what had happened to Farini since the San people
arrived in England to convince him, absolutely, to attempt
this perilous trip? The lure of adventure was at the heart
of it, but there were more specific motivations. One came
from an interesting man of true Kalahari stock.

Gert Louw (always called "Kert" by Farini) was at least
in his fifties and perhaps well into his sixties when he
first met G.A. Farini. He had been recommended to
Healey in the course of the first African trip and was
found to have extraordinary abilities in the desert, as an
interpreter, tracker, etc. It was Louw who found the San
and brought them from their homes. He was a Baster
(originally termed Bastaards, not "bastard" as Farini
called them), known in the twentieth century to South
Africans as "coloured." The Basters were the offspring of
Boer fathers and Hottentot mothers, who lived in the
desert or close to it, often in somewhat tribal settings with
chiefs, etc. They were conscious of their white heritage,
and yet had the abilities and often the language of their
native side. They therefore could be proud and somewhat
superior in their ways and at the same time as cunning
with nature as any San or Zulu. It was claimed that Gert
was a Baster Chief and well known for his skill as a
trader and hunter, and if his ability to tell a tale was any
indication of his powers then this can hardly be doubted.

Gert told Farini two particularly intriguing things: first
that, contrary to popular belief, parts of the Kalahari were
fertile, there were thousands of acres of grass perfect for
ranching, and he claimed there were diamonds in the
desert, in fact he had found a 188-carat stone in a secret
location. A short time after their conversation, as Farini
just happened to be rifling through the Sans' possessions
(he claimed to be looking for poison), he found a few small
diamonds. This convinced him that a search for Gert's

mine field was worth the effort. The stories about fertile
plains interested him because of his farming background
and also because he had a partnership in a cattle ranch
(or so he said) in Arkansas. He began considering purchasing a large tract of land in the Kalahari. And the
thought that he might also try his luck as a big-game
hunter tantalized his Victorian-male soul. Obviously there
were also professional reasons for making this trip: who
knows what wonders worthy of exhibition he might find
in these regions where few white men had ever been?

Then there was his health. In the early 1880s, for the
first time in his life, he had put on extra weight, and was
having recurring problems with indigestion. Always a
robust-looking, tanned man with what he called an "iron
frame," he now looked a bit flabby, there were dark circles
under his eyes and his face was pasty and puffy, with even
the hint of a double chin. He felt, as many doctors did at
the time, that a change of climate would help. So he travelled a great deal during the years leading up to his
Kalahari trip, and never once, whether it be in Russia,
South America, the American plains, or back home in
Hope, felt the climate helped his problems. The Kalahari,
so arid, and so different from any place he had ever been,
struck him as worth a try. And curiously, after his African
journey he was never unfit again.

But what most interested him about the trip, even more
than the fortune it might bring, was the wonderful adventure of it all. Money-making attracted him throughout his
life and his schemes were many and varied, but the
romantic idea of exploring, and searching for diamonds in
a strange land, performing daring deeds in the effort,
excited him enormously. Notoriety on the scale of the
noble Livingstone was thrilling to envision. There had
been nothing like this in Hope Township: and if there had
been, it never would have been allowed.

The desert into which Farini proposed to wander was
really, as he soon discovered, misnamed. A huge and
widely varied place (covering all of modern-day Botswana

and beyond), in terms of climate and vegetation it was more accurately a "thirstland." True, it had miles upon miles of sand, more than any other place in the world in fact, and very high temperatures in summer months (October to March), reaching an average daytime high of 117 degrees Fahrenheit in the shade, and very little rain; but as Gert had intimated, it also had regions, especially in the north, that received good rainfall, where much of the area was covered with grass, trees abounded in places, wild game ran in huge herds and temperatures could be cool in the winter. But in the mid-1880s this was not generally known to people outside its borders. Much of it had not been seen by Europeans: there wasn't even a proper map. Striking off into its wilds was a courageous thing to do, and death, especially from thirst, but also from hostile animals or people, was never more than a mistake away.

Livingstone and Oswell had been the first white men to cross the grassy and sandy plains of the Kalahari in 1849, but not many had done so since. Disasters were frequent. Just six years before Farini and Lulu, a Boer group with 300 wagons had tried a desert trek: 250 people and 9,000 cattle died. So what Farini was proposing, despite his ideas about diamonds and his health, was no Sunday stroll in the park. He and his son were about to encounter a mysterious and contradictory place, and if they did not keep their heads about them, they might never return. But danger had always pushed Willie Hunt forward, so off he went.

Lulu and Farini arrived in Liverpool on New Year's Day 1885 and on January 7th were on board the *Roslin Castle* as it left England, via Madeira and St. Helena, for Cape Town at the southern tip of Africa. Writers who researched this celebrated expedition would make much of the fact that Farini disguised his identity on the passenger list. He and Lulu took their real names, Hunt and Wosgatt, and Gert was recorded as K. Love. Farini commented, "finding that somehow or other Kert's story about the diamonds had leaked out, we took our passage under assumed names." This seems like a hilarious example of Farini's concept of his life as an adventure story. Apparently he and Lu continued the deception on board and Farini, ever the devilish boy, took great fun in discussing "Farini" with others and hearing their "very frank opinions" of him. He commented, "One gentleman in particular told me a story of how he had made 'that stingy fellow, Farini, stand drinks; a thing he had never been known to do before'—a story which naturally gave me a much worse opinion of Farini than I had previously entertained." Despite occasional disagreements, Farini and Lu were perfect allies, the deepest of friends, carrying with them decades of unique experiences together, and holding similar, sometimes intolerant views on the frailties of others. They had deceived the public in a celebrated way and now enjoyed deceiving the ship's passengers in this minor way. They often thought of themselves as "two-against-the-world," a world they felt didn't have their flair, inventiveness or courage.

The *Roslin Castle* docked at Cape Town at 6:30 a.m. on January 29th, though Farini, for whatever reason (deception?), recorded it as June 2nd. It was still summer here and the view of the settlement from Table Bay as the sun rose on the west side of the Cape Peninsula, about thirty miles north of the Cape of Good Hope, was breathtaking. Towering in the distance were two dark mountains, the peaked Devil's Peak and the huge wall of Table Mountain, and at their feet lay the town, nestled on a tract of green land.

They stayed in Cape Town for more than a week and had a wonderful little holiday. Farini made the most of his time, visiting the well-placed people to whom he had introductions, dining with hosts nearly every night. He delighted in the near-perfect Mediterranean climate, and enjoyed the sights and sounds of the town, explained to him in detail by those who knew it best. Here he saw a wealthy, mostly English place, with "old Dutch" amongst them; and lower classes: Malay servants and workers, from the far east, "coloured" Basters like Gert, and occasionally

Hottentots and blacks, mostly servants and menial workers, from the interior. Narrow Dutch streets ran parallel
to the Bay lined by old Dutch homes, and the wider
streets of the English areas boasted solid Victorian
houses. Trees shaded the streets and everywhere things
seemed green. Lulu, who was always less concerned about
status, didn't spend so much time making the social
rounds. Instead, struck by the beauty of the place, he was
frantically trying to capture it with his photographic
skills. Not only did he shoot the town and mountains from
the water, but he climbed 3,000 feet nearly to the top of
Table Mountain and made an exposure from there.

But they had more serious tasks inland, so on February
6th Lulu, Farini and Gert gathered with their possessions
on the platform of the Cape Town railroad station to catch
the train for Hope Town, about five hundred miles to the
north-east. The luxury of the preceding week was about to
come to a grinding halt. But at first Farini did not realize
this. Told that a Pullman sleeping car was available, he
eagerly anticipated settling into comfort. But the beds
turned out to be little better than canvas hammocks
strung above the seats with a thin mattress on top and no
blankets. Somehow he fell asleep quickly and only rose
when the train slowed in the Hexe Mountains. Here, high
above sea level, he expected a beautiful view but was disappointed, and to add to his misery, found himself shiver-
ing, blanketless in the cold as the temperature dropped
dramatically in the mountain night. Within hours he
would have given nearly anything for a moment of cool
air, as they descended into the Great Karoo, an arid
region which had been suffering through a drought for
two consecutive years. Here the heat was unbearable, so
much so that Farini could not even gain relief by standing
on the platform at the end of the train: the wind hit like a
furnace blast. They saw no living animals except vultures,
which gathered high above the corpses and skeletons of
dead animals. The farmers were beggars and their land
parched clay. Farini was astonished, "Hell could not be a
great way off this place," he wrote in his notes. Lulu

agreed: to him the Karoo was "the most God-forsaken country under the sun."

Now for the first time Farini came in contact with Boers, the tough, often racist farmers and adventurers of Dutch descent who lived in the interior. Their ancestors had been in southern Africa for more than two centuries. Farini took an immediate dislike to them. He disdained their attitude toward other races, even though some of that disdain arose from his sense that Englishmen were superior to them. "It is a common opinion that the colony will never do much good as long as the Boer element predominates," he said and added, referring to their remaining as beggars in the arid Karoo, "...no Englishman could live on hope, while his hands were idle at his side."

Passing out of the Karoo at Beaufort West they began climbing again and the climate, though still hot, became a little more bearable. Now they saw a few shrubs and even passed an ostrich farm. Farini's judgemental attitude reached a new low as he condemned even the poor ostriches for their stupidity because they could not escape over low fences that penned them in. Before long they came to lower land and soon reached the Orange River Terminus of the railway nine miles outside of Hope Town. Everyone climbed out of the train and proceeded to the coaches which would take them the remaining seventy-five miles to Kimberley. Farini, Lulu and Gert, not being able to get on regular coaches that were packed full, were forced to hire a mule wagon. This primitive object soon raised the ire of its occupants: it was meant to carry six passengers but that day fifteen were crammed into and on top of it, along with 1,500 pounds of baggage. The treatment of the mules, which were harshly whipped, also did not sit well with Farini and Lu. At the Orange River, whose width and banks of white sand made the cranky Farini finally look upon something with admiration, they took a scow across the water, the male occupants getting out at a sand bank and being carried across on the shoulders of a "stalwart" Zulu (Lu and Farini balanced on his shoulders must have been an interesting sight).

North of the Orange the heat came on again and they
entered another land of drought and parched earth, and
rotting animal corpses. Farini claimed the heat reached
140 degrees. After several more stops and starts, encoun-
ters with Boers (to whom Farini spoke Dutch) and a bit of
flirting on Farini's part with a young woman whose legs
were nearly intertwined with his in the cramped confines
of the mule wagon, they reached Kimberley.

Lulu seemed particularly disgusted by the trip. At one
point he had felt so claustrophobic in the oven-like wagon
that he decided to try walking. When this activity, "performed" (as Farini was wont to say) in nearly suffocating
heat, nearly did him in, he lashed himself to the tail board
of the wagon for the rest of the trip. Farini who always got
a kick out of Lulu's adventures, described his adopted son's
appearance on arrival at Kimberley: "...he was the picture
of what Adam must have looked like in one of the earlier
stages of his manufacture out of the dust of the earth."

Kimberley sat just a couple of miles west of the Orange
Free State in Griqualand territory controlled by the Cape
Colony. Diamonds had been discovered here in 1869, but
it took a few years for the settlement to thrive and feel the
effects of a real diamond rush. Still a rough place full of
rough people, it was nevertheless a step back toward civilization for the tired and dirty pair. In the burning heat of
the mid-afternoon sun they arrived at the Transvaal Hotel
and booked one of its peculiar accommodations. The sitting rooms, which faced the street, were made of mud and
"deliciously cool," while the attached bedrooms, made of
galvanized iron, faced the other way and "felt like ovens."
Farini used his considerable powers of persuasion to convince the owner to allow Gert to stay with them in the
hotel. "Black men," it seemed, were prohibited from sleeping anywhere but in the stables. Gert therefore ended up
in the sitting room, the best room of all, much superior to
the heated confines of Farini and Lu's chambers.

Farini's kind intervention on Gert's behalf is an
instance of his contradictory nature concerning questions
of race. He was class-conscious, and this informed his

view that there was a certain hierarchy amongst races. In
Africa he referred to blacks as "niggers," and "kaffirs," and
made observations about Jews, Malaysians, Boers, etc.
that were unkind and unthinking. Other times during his
life he had also been guilty of racism. He seemed to
believe racial stereotypes. For example, on a number of
occasions both in the U.S. and Africa, he dwelt on what he
thought was a genetic laziness in black people (in this typ-
ically chauvinist Anglo attitude, he was no different than
most of his contemporaries). He also had his own personal
demon of feeling insecure about who he was: his desire to
be "somebody" not only drove him forward with unsinkable determination but made him anxious to find a great
many "nobodies" in the world.

  And yet at times he offered stinging criticisms of the
way that whites treated blacks (in America as well as in
Africa), and vigorously argued for Gert's equality. His real
fault was that he strictly judged *everyone*. And, in the end,
he did it regardless of skin colour. It was difficult for anyone's courage, cleverness or energy to measure up to his
own. He could even set aside class distinctions when he
judged: Gert Louw was almost as bereft of social standing
as one could get, but he impressed Farini on a one-to-one
basis, and that was why he fought for him against all
comers. Farini was a rugged individualist to the core, one
could say he believed in it: he had made himself rich and
famous through hard work, brainpower and bravery, and
had little use for those incapable of similar self-reliance.

After a bath and a home-cooked meal, Farini, Lulu and
Gert collapsed into their beds and slept. The next morning
preparations began for the trek into the Kalahari. First
they purchased a wagon and team of six mules from a Mr.
Caldecott who, in keeping with Farini's impeccable connections, was the Principal of the School of Mines at
Kimberley (Farini had met members of the Caldecott and
Sauer families on board the *Roslin Castle* and had brought
with him letters of introduction to and from some of the
most prominent men in southern Africa). Other provisions,

like powder and shot for his rifles, coffee pots, kettles, blankets, etc. were bought and an advertisement was put out for a good shooting-horse. He was quite taken by a Cape area invention—a "water-bag" made of linen which could keep water cold in the hot sun. Soon he had acquired so many things that Lulu complained their room had little space for themselves.

The wagon would not be fully fitted up for a while so the dynamic duo decided to spend a week in Kimberley, mostly exploring its mines. Farini, ever confident, felt that if he could observe diamond mining up close he would be able to master the craft should he come upon jewels in the desert. Dr. J.W. Sauer introduced them to various owners and even arranged for a descent into the open pits. Sauer was a cabinet minister in the Cape Government and well placed as an associate of the legendary Cecil Rhodes, who would one day dominate the diamond and gold industry in the region, become prime minister of the colony, and have both Rhodesia and Rhodes Scholarships named after him.

Farini and Lulu got into an iron bucket and allowed themselves to be lowered into the pit. Farini remembered everything he saw with his steel-trap mind and later was able to recall it in the minutest detail. The thievery and graft in the business at Kimberley was described to him— much of it, he was told, perpetrated by various non-English people. He of course had solutions at hand, and came away with a feeling that blacks were often being wrongly accused of stealing. He also felt that Kimberley, while undeniably rough and crime-ridden, was not as bad as its reputation, and he favourably compared it to other "rush" towns he had visited.

One day Lulu, apparently as impervious to fear as his father, climbed down into the mine and tried to photograph the explosions. Everyone was supposed to vacate the area during the blasts, and a frantic Farini scrambled into the pit to retrieve Lu (who didn't budge until he had taken his plates). He recalled this confrontation in his notes, his concern for his son's safety showing in an uncharacteristic tenderness. "Never mind the camera," he said when Lu complained about a rock the size of a table that had just missed his tripod, "If it had hit you, what a fix I should have been in. I couldn't get another Lulu in this country, or any other."

On February 17th their wagon was finally ready and a crowd of "idlers," as Farini called them, gathered as Lulu put the finishing touches on his packing job. He tried to pile most things on top but in the end had to hang many pots, pails, shovels, etc. from rings underneath the wagon. Food for the mules was stored in a trunk attached to the axle; utensils, clothes, blankets and Farini's saddle were on top; and the valuable items, like Lulu's cameras, their "drug-chest," provisions, guns and a box of cartridges containing 9,000 rounds of ammunition (so heavy it took four men to lift it) all went inside. Their driver was a short, forty-five-year-old man named Jan, of mixed blood, born in St. Helena, and the fact that he was called a "boy" by others and "bought" like a slave for this trip, struck Farini as bizarre. They wheeled out of town at a brisk pace to the cheers of the bystanders and began following a primitive road, Farini riding behind them on his horse. A few miles out, rapidly becoming sore because he hadn't been in the saddle for a few years, he fastened his mare to the back of the wagon and climbed inside. That night they stopped within the light of a farm, Farini and Lulu sleeping comfortably on mattresses stretched on boards on the seats while Gert and Jan (who had taken to calling Farini "boss") were equally content under the wagon.

This first part of their adventure would last a week or more and bring them out to the edge of the shimmering desert. They stayed on the crude roadway, heading straight west over Griqualand toward their target. Hardships hadn't really begun yet and Farini enjoyed himself. Rising with the sun most mornings he hunted Namaqua partridge, turtle doves and other fowl, knocking them from the skies in startling numbers, impressing Gert with his marksmanship. Mowing down wildlife would be a very big part of this trip. He toyed with the Boers he met, telling them he was an American, reminding these

English-haters that Americans had rebelled against the
Brits; then he smugly ignored their "political vapourings."
They crossed the Vaal River on a scow, and travelled into
Campbell where they were stunned to see green fields and
a modern reaper in a farmer's yard and met a "half-breed"
son of an old missionary named Bartlett who lived in a
thatched house near the place where Livingstone had met
and wed Mary Moffat. Out in the country they saw a
40,000-acre farm with 12,000 sheep, cattle and horses,
run by an Englishman. At Griquatown, surprised to find
themselves on real streets with a court-house, a church,
hotels and shops, they encountered James Christie, the
Commissioner and magistrate. He lived in a real house,
much better than that belonging to the ex-King of
Griqualand, a surly alcoholic old man who reluctantly
agreed to let Lulu take his picture. Everywhere around
these settlements Farini saw natives in desperate conditions and poured his disgust into his diary.

> The black man is not improved by a veneer of civilization.
> The real "savage", who has never been in contact with the
> whites, has a certain amount of honour and chivalry about
> him, and one cannot help admiring him; but the half-
> Christianized black is a lying, lazy scoundrel, without a
> spark of self-respect...

In places the heat was so intense it brought out blisters
on Farini's hands and yet twice they were caught in freakish thunderstorms. They ate their canned goods sparingly,
trying to depend on what they killed (like two steinbok
Farini claimed he did in with a single bullet) and occasionally bought food, a luxury they knew would soon be
gone. Water was a trickier problem and they were always
relieved to find some. One day Jan vanished after chasing
off after an animal, disturbing Farini but not the unflap-
pable Gert who insisted that the "boy" would be all right,
alone in this wilderness. The first week their wagon
moved smoothly along the road and Farini purchased two
new horses to help, naming one Lady Anna. And a friend

of Gert's joined in too, bringing along another wagon. But
as the Kalahari loomed they encountered more sand and
soon it deepened. Before long they were in a wasteland of
dunes and their wagons bogged down. Gert was sent to a
nearby town to buy oxen and the others moved slowly
onward using the mules in the miles of sand, interrupted
periodically by kopjes, strange natural rock formations
that presented even greater challenges to the wagons.
When they finally reached the far side of the first stretch
of sand, they came to something almost worse: the Devil's
Kloof, a mountainous region filled with sharp stones and
huge squarish boulders. They made several bumpy trips
over it, amazed that their wagons survived, and found
themselves just six miles from the Orange River.

Gert returned with the oxen just as the expedition
approached the boundary between British territory and
the Kalahari. When they made camp that night they were
on the edge of the desert. They saw what looked like a sea
of red sand ahead.

The next morning their great experiment truly began. Not
only were they finally entering the mystical desert but
they were a scant day or two from the the spot where Gert
insisted he had found his diamonds. Farini, sweat-stained
and dirty, was thrilled. But first they saw people: naked
and semi-naked San who seemed to come from nowhere
and then followed them with interest. Basters were also
nearby and Gert was happily met with handshaking and
the clicking sounds of the San's greeting. He was in his
glory. As usual his trusty felt hat with its colourful ostrich
feathers was perched on the scarf wrapped around his
head, but he had also put on a British admiral's jacket
and was proud of his appearance. He said to Farini, "See,
I am a great man here. These are my people. We shall
soon have food and water." But the Basters were suspicious of the white men, and disinclined to give them anything until they produced money. And like nearly
everyone else in southern African, they immediately
asked Farini about an anticipated war between the

British and the Boers—they sided firmly with the British.

One of the problems which plagued their trip was the constant need to chase off into the desert after their animals, who frequently escaped when not attended to. During this visit with the Basters it happened again, and Farini exploded:

> After all my recent experience and the warnings the men had had, this was too much for me. My temper was up. I let fly at the Bushman with my most refined Afrikander-Dutch, and introduced my bootmaker to the boy's—well, he never had a tailor; while I christened Kert with several new pet names he had never owned before, and threatened him with kind treatment. They flew away after the animals...

This uncharacteristic outburst was followed by almost equally uncharacteristic tenderness when Jan unexpectedly returned to their camp, nearly starving, with a horrific tale of being temporarily lost in the desert. Farini was genuinely moved by his reappearance...and then was nearly moved again just before they left, by the sight of San women eating the raw entrails of sheep.

At their next stop, a spot with an unusual amount of vegetation, Farini examined plants, some of which the Basters and San frequently ate. Most interesting was the tsamma, a melon similar in both taste and appearance to the watermelon. It contained a great deal of water and seemed able to grow in the sand. Farini tasted it, aware that in the immediate future it might be their sole source of refreshment. He also captured some unusual ants for his friend, prominent entomologist Jenner Weir, and some bees for his brother Myndert (who was in the bee business near Detroit). They got going again that day around 6 p.m., as was their habit, to make the most of travelling in the cooler part of the day (they moved during the mornings, camped during the hottest part of the day, and headed out again in the late afternoon or early evening), and started into a difficult stretch of sandy terrain. They didn't reach Wilgenhoutsdrif until midnight. Farini was

worn out and slept well that night, but perhaps he should-
n't have, for he was lying on the very ground where Gert
had insisted he found his big diamond.

In the morning Lu, Gert and Farini started searching,
scanning every inch of the area, scratching off the surface
as they went, paying particular attention to a spot under a
tree. This first long search proved fruitless and they grew
sceptical about their guide's tale, but when an old man
appeared, intent on questioning Gert about the diamond
he found long ago, they became convinced that he wasn't
lying. The following morning they were up early, this time
digging, but after hours of hot, back-breaking work, there
was still no sight of diamonds. Lulu had soon had enough.
To Farini, the adventure of searching for a treasure was
nearly as interesting as finding it, but Lu begged to differ.
He scolded his father, as he often did during the trip:

> I'm quite satisfied that Kert has told the truth about that
> diamond, and that he did actually find it here. Perhaps
> you are sitting at the mouth of the richest diamond-mine
> in the world. But I would not stay here to work it for the
> biggest gem in creation.

He followed this with a long account of the hardships
they had endured on the trip so far and his need for something at least approaching the comforts of home. Farini
always took Lu's rants good-humouredly. "Never mind, my
boy," he said with a twinkle in his eye. Ever the optimist,
he tried to convince poor Lulu that the hardships he was
enduring were physically good for him, a concept he had
been trying to sell to everyone, everywhere, for a good
many years. Lulu agreed to put on a brave face. "And so,"
said Farini, "we agreed to think we were having lots of
fun..." But Farini's greatest motivation for coming to
Africa had never really been diamonds, and before long he
called off the search, rationalizing that they could not
make much progress by digging and should get their
claim to this land from the Commissioner at Upington
near the end of the trip. And so, with less than a single

day's search for the precious stones that had supposedly
been so much a part of what drove them to take this dangerous trip, they left. It seemed that an attack by a lion in
the midst of their search would have been much more
interesting to them. As Farini later said, "...we came to
the unanimous opinion that we were not constitutionally
fitted to be diamond-diggers."

Their trip, from this prospective diamond field onward,
did not necessarily happen the way Farini later said it
did. They certainly went deep into the Kalahari, but
exactly how far they went is not certain. Though they
were still looking for prospective ranch lands and possible
Aquarium exhibits, their main objective now was simply
adventure and education, and they wandered around in
this deadly land looking for it. What follows is essentially
Farini's account.

They headed north-east, roadless, further into the desert.
Progress was difficult and their mules were not up to the
task, so Farini traded all six for sixteen oxen, hired a tall,
thin black man as driver and inched forward into an
"ocean of sand" (dotted by the odd rocky protuberance).
They rode from salt pan to salt pan, the large crater-like
holes in the desert which were used both as watering
holes and as guideposts through the wilderness. There
had been an unusual amount of rain so many of the pans
were full. Presently they met a group of Bushmen, who
took them to their homes in the mountains where Lulu
was intrigued by the drawings on the walls of their caves
and copied some. But when he pointed his camera at them
they became afraid and some even ran away. Farini gave
them some docha, a sort of wild hemp with hallucinogenic
qualities, and was intrigued by the spectacular dances
they performed immediately after smoking it.

Then they came to a fascinating stretch of land covered
with knee-high grass that reminded Farini of the
Canadian prairies; it had water just beneath the surface
even though there had been little rain. The land changed
each day over the next few days, from grass to sand, to

hard limestone with small bushes, to a fifty-mile area that
had abundant grass but absolutely no water, forcing the
group to go more than two days without watering their
cattle. Finally they arrived at a stream. Here they hunted
again, as they had done most every day, killing flamingos
and cranes. They continued on through miles of grass-covered sand. They saw tsamma and wild cucumber and from
time to time little clumps of beautiful wild flowers. Soon
they turned directly north and headed toward Bakaris
and Khuis in Bechuanaland. But before they arrived
Farini had an adventure he would never forget.

It all began with another hunting expedition. As usual,
Farini struck out boldly after his prey; before long he was
alone in the Kalahari. But he hardly noticed, intent as he
was on the spoor of wild ostriches. He wounded a couple,
followed them for a distance, and finished them off by cutting their necks; and then was drawn further off on his
own when he found the corpse of a dead "Bushman,"
untouched by predators because he had died of thirst.
Farini made the bizarre decision to cut off the dead man's
head, in order to keep the skull. With his grisly trophy
and his birds he tried to make his way back to the camp,
but had underestimated the distance he had gone and
soon found himself tiring in the mid-afternoon sun. He
took a drink and fell asleep. Upon waking the next morning he discovered, to his horror, that he had dropped his
flask and the water had drained. Instantly he remembered being told how quickly a man would die in the
Kalahari without water. For many desperate hours he
struggled to get back, his throat parched, resorting at one
time to putting a button on his tongue to excite his sali-
vary glands. Then he thought he had found a temporary
answer to his problem by cooking and eating a root, only
to realize soon afterward that it was poisonous. Moments
later, still trying to shoot gemsbok to keep himself alive,
he vomited several times and collapsed, convinced he was
dying. When Gert found him later that day, it was
assumed he was dead.

Lulu, though frantic at the thought of losing his father, remained cool enough to hold a mirror to his mouth and detected very slight breathing. They soon revived him. Gert and the black men were convinced that severing the "Bushman's" head placed a curse on their boss that almost killed him, but Farini would have nothing of that illusion. How much of this story is true will of course never be known: it is a florid tale, with Farini as the hero, musing a great deal on death, thinking he had always wanted to die with his boots on, and imagining himself being torn apart by jackals or lions.

He claimed to have been ready to travel again within a day. They continued straight north through hard stoney land, drinking mud water when clean water could not be found. Tsamma was more plentiful, though much of it was not mature enough to provide them with useful water, and as they made their way to Bakaris they became desperate. Bakaris was a pan which supposedly contained water, but when they arrived they found it dry. Luckily, the tsamma was soon abundant in larger sizes. Within two days they were at a gathering of huts on the Kuruman River where they met a native chief named Makgoe, who tried to make Farini give him his rifle as a kind of toll fee. They added to their expedition here: more people, animals and another wagon, and when they left had a veritable "cavalcade" as Farini called it, consisting of himself, Lulu, Gert, Jan, Dirk and Klas (Basters who dressed in European clothes), the black driver, six Bushmen and one of their wives, as well as twenty-four pulling oxen, six spares, two cows with calves and four dogs; and a huge collection of food, water, tools, kitchenware, skins, etc., and thirty-seven rifles, one hundred pipes, two bottles of Worcester sauce, and due to Farini's tireless collecting, 115 packets of seeds.

They crossed the Molopo River and headed into the heart of the Kalahari, into present-day Botswana. Gert was again in his glory when they fell in with a group of Baster hunters and he regaled them with stories of England: of visiting the Queen (Gert and the "Dwarf Earthmen" had been given a royal audience); of horses

that had their own houses and were brought food from far
away; and of an exhibition in which lions were held in
cages and feared men. His countrymen doubted his stories
and only believed them when Farini corroborated them,
though the circus lion story was too much to accept even
with the boss's approval.

Lion tracks began appearing in this area, disturbing
the Basters who feared lions more than any other animal.
Farini ignored their fears and hunted the beasts, even
stalking and killing one. But each night the wagons were
put in a circle, oxen tied on the inside and fires kept blaz-
ing. It was a peculiar encampment, with naked Bushmen
dancing and singing, Basters telling stories in the firelight
and two "Americans" planning their next move.

Soon Farini went ahead with Dirk and Klas in order to
scout out the next day's terrain—they were coming to an
area with no water and few tsamma plants. As they rode
through many miles of grassland Farini reflected on what
would be his most important African discovery: that the
Kalahari should never have been called a desert. He
returned to his old theory about ranching here and
decided that with industry and proper management of
water, a great success could be made. He wrote, with an
unfortunate racist qualification, "In the hands of an energetic white race this country could surely be made one of
the most productive grazing-lands in the world."

While camping that day a curious little man, evidently
a pygmy San, suddenly approached them out of the
wilderness. Farini described him as "the funniest-looking
little fellow I had ever seen." "Korap" had skinny legs, a
pot-belly and a small wrinkled face; he spoke only two
words of Afrikaans, yet through his desperate pantomim-
ing and clicking was able to tell them that his master, a
white German trader, was in trouble. After a trek into the
desert Fritz Landwer was found, nearly dead, shoved
under the thorns of a noi bush so animals wouldn't eat
him. Fritz told a colourful tale of being ambushed by
Hottentots and left bleeding to fend for himself with only
his San slave. Farini revived him, mostly with quinine

and laudanum, and gladly enlisted him as a member of their strange party. A muscular, 6-foot-1-inch man with a thorough knowledge of the desert and of industrious habits, he was soon put in charge of the wagon, in place of Gert who was not as useful at this stage of the trip. Farini was to give him the nickname "I'll-vatch-it," a phrase the ever-vigilant German often used.

Lulu came forward with the other wagon presently and, taking Fritz's advice, they steered away from the water-less area they were in and kept to a stretch of tsamma-filled land leading toward Lehututu, where Chief Mapaar of the Bakalahari lived. They were then within a few days of the Kang Pan area, several hundred miles into the Kalahari Desert. They plunged on in the heat, carrying their city on wheels, travelling for several days through grasslands as ocean-like as the sand. Here was Willie Hunt, deep in Africa with Lulu his creation by his side, still desperate for adventure. Nearing Lehututu they met two black men and a bizarre, "copper-coloured" individual with a necklace of lions' claws, hyenas' toenails, wolves' vertebrae, etc. His presence shook Gert and the Basters: he was a witch-doctor.

Ever since childhood Farini had bristled at the idea of any human being possessing actual magical powers. Being an illusionist himself he loved conjuring, but real magic was something he scoffed at. The next morning, accompanied by Lulu and the three awed Basters, he went to see the witch-doctor (sarcastically calling the meeting a "seance"). First there was a long recital of pre-dictions from the "soenya," which Farini inwardly laughed at (feeling they had been extrapolated from things the man had picked up during conversations with Gert). He felt right at home with this "wily old fortune-teller" who seemed to him to employ the same techniques as the shams he had been observing in show business for decades. When the witch-doctor was finished, Farini sud-denly scooped up his magical bones and began palming them, swallowing them and placing them on Gert's unsus-pecting person; he also pretended to swallow a knife, which he and Lulu contrived to secretly drop into the soenya's possessions. Then he reproduced the bones and the knife out of thin air and proceeded to divine details about the others' possessions, aweing even the soenya himself. Undoubtedly Farini was ridiculing these people and their beliefs, but he was acting no differently than at seances in Port Hope, or even New York and London.

As they headed toward Kang Pan they entered the K'gung Forest, a well-treed area in the midst of the desert. Underfoot there was still sand and grass and no water, not even tsamma. They marvelled at the enormous nests grosbeaks built in the trees, like umbrellas in the distance, made of thatches of grass, some six feet deep and weighing a ton. When they arrived in the Kang Pan they were shocked to discover there was no water there either. Lulu was especially distressed because he suffered the most in waterless conditions. For some reason the tsamma juice, which he did not like, fuelled his thirst rather than quenching it. He also smoked heavily, on a pipe, which Farini, ever health conscious, abhorred, and which he speculated caused his son even greater thirst. In the midst of one of their numerous discussions about these matters, in which Lulu loudly complained of his predicament, Farini made a revealing comment. "No; I don't *like* the sama, but I make the best of it. This kind of life is a pleasure to me, and I would put up with anything for the novelty of the thing."

They dug in the pan and got some muddy water. Even this was essential because they were approaching the Tropic of Capricorn and the heat was intensifying (though the nights were cool). That evening, while Farini was lying in a hammock enjoying the coolness, disaster struck. Without warning, a lion leapt into the camp, snatched one of Klas's legs into his mouth and pinned him to the sand. When he screamed, Farini came to the rescue. Remembering lions' fear of flames, he grabbed a charred stick from the fire and rammed it into the back of the growling beast and kicked hot coals at him. The lion roared, dropped Klas and jumped on one of the oxen, tearing at its shoulder and knocking it to the ground. Instantly Fritz was after him, firing as often as he could, but it was only when Lu, roused from sleep, took aim and shot, that the lion fell. Luckily both the ox and Klas would survive their wounds.

At Lehututu they found a collection of huts, gifts from the king, a wonderful spring in which to bathe (which they did almost in ecstasy, since they had been unable to wash themselves, except in the gooey tsamma juice, for extended periods) and a number of nude women whom Farini eagerly described as "well-built." The next day they had an audience with King Mapaar, a large, heavy-set man about forty years old. Gert, a match for Farini as a storyteller, introduced his boss as "the great London captain" who brought greetings from the Queen of England, immensely pleasing the king. When Farini returned to his hut, a beautiful (though apparently smelly) young woman was waiting for him, an interim wife, provided for him as part of Kgalagadi hospitality. Though Fritz and the Basters took advantage of similar hospitality, Farini could not bring himself to sleep with the woman and ended up back in the wagon. This caused a fuss in the village and a confrontation with the king. But Farini was ready with a tall tale and extemporized about being an English witch-doctor, therefore unable to take a wife because intimacy with a woman, according to English custom, would sap his powers. Fortunately this was accepted.

But the king now wanted London's great witch-doctor to predict the weather. Farini scrambled back to his wagon, studied a Cape Town almanac and decided to tell his royal acquaintance that rain would come very soon. And so it did, in such quantity that it nearly drowned the king's garden and all his huts, and made him angry with the English witch-doctor. But Farini extricated himself from this too and soon was allowed to leave. Just before departure, Lulu was able to snap a clandestine photograph (the king and all of his people were frightened of the camera) of Mapaar and his wife.

Not long after leaving Lehututu they entered forests again, though the trees here were closer together and the ground was harder. They crossed the Tropic of Capricorn and covered the 175-mile distance between Lehututu and Ghanzi (south of Lake N'Gami) in a little more than a week. In this very area an earlier explorer had gone nineteen days without water, so they felt fortunate when it rained toward the end of the first week.

Once they had passed Ghanzi and neared Lake N'Gami water became more plentiful, even lying in pools close to the crude road, and watermelons were everywhere. Five days of easier travelling through the sandy plains of this region brought them almost to the lake. Here they came across the "M'Kabba (possibly Koba) dwarfs" whom Farini had heard of, and was anxious to exhibit at the Aquarium. Pygmies averaging just slightly more than four feet in height, they were described as shy, completely naked people with wrinkled faces who had the peculiar habit of tattooing themselves with a blue dye and amputating the first joint of the little finger of each hand. Farini also thought their "great projecting stomachs" made them look like "so many dwarf aldermen of the desert." He immediately set to work to convince them to accompany him to England; his trump card seemed to be the promise of rifles when they were returned. While waiting for the M'Kabbas to decide, they went off closer to the lake for an elephant hunt. Farini recalled a dangerous, thrilling adventure in which they were almost trampled but, through bravery (mostly his own, at one point he even disdains their own ambuscade, claiming "open attack is more in my line") and pinpoint shooting, succeeded in bagging two. That evening the natives cut the feet off one elephant and all, including Farini, ate them. The following morning they ate its heart.

Several M'Kabba decided to go back with them, and together they reached the northernmost point of the journey (less than one hundred miles south of present-day Angola) and turned westward. This would take them through new land on the way back and steer them clear of

Mapaar's territory. After touring through miles of undu-
lating, lush "golden" grassland that reminded Farini of an
English corn district, they turned south and began the
long trip home. Nothing extraordinary occurred during
the first part of the return trek, except at Rietfontein (present day Namibia), which was situated on an elevated
area near Damaraland, where Farini was fascinated by
an encounter with the Damara people, an exotic "jet-
black...powerfully built, stalwart race..." who had been at
war with the Namaqua Hottentots for some time.

Nearly two weeks of travelling south brought them past
Anerougas and Kerses (through what is today the
Kalahari Gemsbok National Park), down to Mier
(Rietfontein, South Africa). Here, in the middle of a group
of huts stood a large kraal and a stone house, where Gert
excitedly introduced Farini to Dirk Philander (Farini
called him Verlander) "the self-appointed chief" of the
Basters. An interesting confrontation ensued, though one
wonders how Farini managed to concentrate, so taken
was he by the "firm and round...well-shaped breasts" of
the "Bushwomen" in the building.

As soon as he began conversing with the Baster chief he
discovered that Gert had told him a bit of a yarn: that
Farini bore a letter from the Cape government to the chief
and inside information about the administration's plans
for land north of the Orange River. Thinking quickly,
Farini produced one of his letters of introduction and read
an excerpt which asked all "Commissioners" to assist him
and to sell him any land he wanted. Philander, dressed in
shirt-sleeves and corduroy pants, seemed pleased with
everything he heard, though he insisted that present
negotiations for the sale of his land would probably pre-
clude any sales to Farini. For his part, Farini did not
think much of the Basters; he considered them lazy and
immoral, and despised their inability to think beyond
their next meal nearly as much as he abhorred their
propensity for begging. But a few days later they would
take him on an expedition that would forever make him
part of southern African folklore.

CHAPTER 21

A Vision in the Desert

*"...as one who has long been a slave to the
enchantment of the Kalahari, and to this particular
mystery...I believe in Farini's account..."*
Fay Goldie, *The Lost City of the Kalahari*

It started as merely a short excursion off the main
route. At first there were a few adventures, dangerous
as always, though lacking in substance. But this aimless
little jaunt was destined to have every inch of its distance
closely scrutinized for more than a century, because at its
end, Farini and Lulu stumbled onto a legend....Or did
they?

Coming to the Nossob River, they followed its dry bed
north as if it were a road until they reached the Ky Ky
Mountains; from there they headed north-east and around
in several circles. Near Khatia in the K'gung forest they
went out in search of giraffes. First a twenty-footer was
killed and parts of it eaten, including its intestines. But
Farini was actually tiring of all the killing and pitied the
animal as he was shooting it: "There was despair in his
drooping eye," he recalled. And he felt badly about a baby
giraffe they orphaned too, saying it seemed to be pleading
for its mother; he even refused to capture it, because he
felt its rightful place was in Africa. Meanwhile the dead
adult giraffe was buried under bushes and gunpowder
was strewn around, to keep scavengers away until it could

be butchered the following day. Farini then announced
that he was going to spend the night strapped high in the
branches of a nearby tree, in order to observe nature.

During his dark vigil he saw vultures, jackals and hyenas coming to devour the carcass, but scared them all off.
In the early morning three lions appeared. Just as he was
about to shoot them he spotted the expedition's wagons
coming to a halt about sixty yards away, Lulu rushing forward with his camera and tripod in hand, and Fritz in
tow. Lu was so excited at the prospect of photographing
the lions that he seemed to disregard his own safety. His
frightened father later recalled, "...he never did know
what fear was." Lulu rushed straight at the largest lion
who came directly toward him, tail snapping. On Lu
came, pointing the camera into the lion's face, until,
finally, it turned and ran off, apparently intimidated by
the bizarre sight of a man's trunk with a black box on top.
Afterwards father and son engaged in a comical, mutual
scolding about each other's foolhardiness, ended by Lulu's
salvo about Farini's decision to spend the night in the
tree, "Just like you; always doing some foolish thing. You
are old enough to know better."

The group split up for about ten days, Lulu and Farini
staying in camp with a few others in order to collect but-
terflies and insects, or at least father did so; son was not
inclined to rush about in the heat chasing nearly invisible
game. It must have been quite a scene: Farini, in his large
sombrero, built like a Clydesdale, running back and forth
in the sand "like a big schoolboy" while Lu looked up from
time to time to criticize him and tell him to act his age.

Farini and Lulu loved each other dearly. Despite their
bickering, they were irreplaceable in each other's lives.
Now, just a short while after they played together in the
heat of the African sun, so wonderfully removed from the
rest of the world, they were about to experience perhaps
their greatest adventure. It would produce a mystery that
only they held the key to. And neither of them ever gave
away the secret.

All the travellers were back together again and moving
onward in the sand. In the distance they saw something
that looked unusual. They drew closer.

His account of his strange discovery would puzzle many
well-respected anthropologists, historians, writers and
adventurers for many years after both he and Lulu were
dead and gone. Because of him, a ghost would rise that
still haunts the Kalahari. Here, deep in the desert, he
found, or said he found, the ruins of an ancient civilization
that no one had ever heard of; he might as well have said
he had discovered Atlantis, peeking up through the sand.
Thus the legend of the Lost City of the Kalahari began.

He later described it this way:

> We camped near the foot of [a mountain], beside a long
> line of stone which looked like the Chinese Wall after an
> earthquake, and which, on examination, proved to be the
> ruins of quite an extensive structure, in some places
> buried beneath the sand, but in others fully exposed to
> view. We traced the remains for nearly a mile, mostly a
> heap of huge stones, but all flat-sided, and here and there
> with the cement perfect and plainly visible between the
> layers. The top row of stones were worn away by the
> weather and the drifting sands, some of the uppermost
> ones curiously rubbed on the underside and standing out
> like a centre-table on one short leg. The general outline of
> this wall was in the form of an arc, inside which lay at
> intervals of about forty feet apart a series of heaps of
> masonry in the shape of an oval or an obtuse ellipse, about
> a foot and a half deep, and with a flat bottom, but hollowed
> out at the sides for about a foot from the edge. Some of
> these heaps were cut out of solid rock, others were formed
> of more than one piece of stone, fitted together very accu-
> rately.... I told [Jan] that here must have been either a city
> or a place of worship, or the burial ground of a great
> nation, perhaps thousands of years ago.

Farini and Lulu began digging, without the Basters,
who thought this waste of energy on old rocks insane. By

Lulu's depiction of the ruins of the Lost City.

the next day they uncovered something that fascinated them.

> On digging down nearly in the middle of the arc, we came upon a pavement about twenty feet wide, made of large stones. The outer stones were long ones, and lay at right angles to the inner ones. This pavement was intersected by another similar one at right angles, forming a Maltese cross, in the centre of which at one time must have stood an altar, column, or some sort of monument, for the base was quite distinct, composed of loose pieces of fluted masonry.

They continued digging, Lulu took some photographs (or at least Farini said he did) and within three days, rather unceremoniously, they were gone, leaving behind them a place, either real or mythical, that may never be found again.

It has somehow disappeared.

CHAPTER 22

The Illusive Legend

*"Most authors, either in preface or introduction,
apologize for what is to follow:... I hardly think
an apology is required."*
G.A. Farini, *Through the Kalahari Desert*

"Is There a Lost City Under the Kalahari Sand?
Sunday Times (Johannesburg), November 10, 1963

Now they were ready to go home. But first they had to trek back to Mier, a long and arduous journey. Initially it seemed it would be easy going since at the Ky Ky Mountains they found a large pool and treated themselves to drinks and a swim. Thinking they wouldn't need much water they added little to their reserves. But the following week was the most harrowing, waterless time of the entire trip. Their oxen began to starve as did Farini's horse and at times they feared the end was near. Several oxen were mercifully shot, as was Lady Anna, which almost broke Farini's heart. But finally, within a few days of Mier, they found tsamma and were saved.

They spent several days amongst Philander's people before moving on. The chief's secretary, an Englishman named Halliburton, told Farini someone had made a deal with his boss to acquire all the Basters' land but the deal could be broken if Farini could get the English government to annex the area. Farini agreed to the idea, but really didn't take it seriously; he was more interested in being bitten by a poisonous snake so he could try the native antidote of injecting himself with powder extracted from a highly poisonous reptile.

Shortly they moved out of Philander's realm and headed south, leaving the Kalahari Desert. They crossed an enormous dry salt pan, one mile long and a mile and a half wide with six feet of salt in it. As they went further south, past Abeam Pool, the land turned to clay. Here the group split up, most returning to their homes, and Gert going off to Upington, while Lu, Farini, Fritz, Morap and two Basters continued on to the Orange River to explore the Great Falls.

Passing through Zwartmodder the next day, a place of not much more than two stone houses and a few huts, they approached the banks of the Orange. People here warned them that anything more than a view of the falls from above was unthinkable, and that was only possible because the water was low at this time of the year. Farini, ever confident in his ability to do what others thought impossible, was undaunted.

The falls they were about to visit were among the most spectacular and inaccessible in the world. A whole series of cataracts, so numerous Farini named them The One Hundred Falls, they joined together into a single, giant sheet during the rainy season. Today called the Augrabies Falls, after a Korana word meaning "big waters" or "water that thunders," they have a drop of 480 feet and during extraordinary flood periods their flow can be greater than Victoria Falls. The first non-African saw them in the late 1770s, but it is doubtful many others were so fortunate between then and 1885; and everyone viewed them from distant vantage points. But water, height and daring were right up Farini's alley, and he and Lulu proceeded to climb in, around, and almost behind the various falls, probably the first human beings to get that close and certainly the first to photograph them while in their midst. Only people blessed with their skills could have accomplished these things. As they themselves pointed out: few explorers were also world-class gymnasts.

They stayed at the falls about two weeks and early on established the pattern of leaving Morap and the two Basters at the wagon while the three white men went off exploring. Fritz, though admirably brave, was often unable to keep up with his two acrobatic friends and would stake out a spot part way through each daily expedition to cook meals. Off on their own, Lu and Farini tried things that would have meant certain death to others. Farini's devil-may-care attitude was summed up in a self-righteous comment he made to Fritz when the poor German, shocked at the chances his companions were taking, exclaimed that it was his policy not to play with death. Farini replied: "That's where the fun is. But you need not be afraid on our account. It's easy enough to us. You're like the rest of the world, what you cannot do yourself, and don't understand, you think wonderful."

They soon discovered that a great deal of swimming, and wading stripped naked with one's clothes held aloft, would be necessary. They also were forced to build rafts and use them to ferry things across the streams. Farini, by far the best swimmer (or so he said), almost lost Fritz a few times in the water, but seemed to think it all good fun. With Lu toting his camera, they went far into the various rocky gorges, doing whatever it took to get there, not only to explore but also to find good vantage points for photographs. Lu was intense about his art and often more interested in finding the right aesthetic blend for a shot than in his own safety. They used ropes to get to precarious ledges, lowering each other down long distances, dangling in the air high above rapids, and climbing back up, hand over hand. The beauty of their surroundings captivated them and like children they seemed nearly obsessed with throwing themselves into its deep chasms and rugged ravines.

Farini began naming various falls, assuming he had the right to do so; mostly he named them after himself and his friends and relatives: there was Farini Falls, Lulu, May, Anna, Müller, I'll Vatch It, and Louw Falls, but also ones called Mariposa (a place in Ontario), Kaffir, Bushman and Springbok; and others named for southern African dignitaries whose friendship he courted.

The adventures of Lulu and Farini were sometimes a

little like those of two knockabout comedians. Such a bickering, wisecracking, intrepid duo the rocks and sheer cliffs
of the Augrabies Falls had never seen (nor will they ever
again). One day, while attempting to climb up a steep wall
via a rope, Lulu, first up, found himself in trouble as he
neared the top because the rope lay flat on the side of the
cliff, making it impossible for him to get his fingers under
it. Quickly he wrapped his legs around the rope, let himself hang upside down, and then used his leg power to
throw himself up and over the top. It was an old gymnastic trick. Then it was time for dad:

> ...it was a hard struggle for me to get up. As I reached over
> the edge Lulu grabbed me by the collar, at the same time
> pulling his shoe out from under the rope, and down went
> my knuckles against the stone, grinding the bark off them,
> and squeezing some hard words out of me... "What did you
> pull the shoe out for, Lulu?" I asked, when at last I gained
> the top. "Because I could not get my foot out from under
> the rope unless I did," he replied.

They even injected comedy into the most dire circumstances. One day as they all found themselves stranded on
a rock for the night, Farini wisecracked to Lulu about eating baboons to stave off starvation:

> I wish some of them would come to us, instead of howling
> and barking in that tree over there; roasted baboon isn't
> bad, when there's nothing else; besides, it would save you
> and Fritz, for I shall have to eat you both if we have to
> stay here very long.

Fritz commented that he was going to "vatch it" that
Farini didn't eat him. Later, after a baboon was indeed
sacrificed to their hunger, Lulu would have no part of it.
"I draw the line at eating my cousins," he said, perhaps
thinking of Krao.

The day and night on the rock was the result of being in

the midst of an excursion when the water suddenly began
to rise (the rainy season was just beginning). They had to
race to higher ground, fearful they would be engulfed, and
the following day barely escaped with their lives while
swimming their way to safety. Farini, ever aggressive and
muscular, took the lead in these situations, despite being
forty-seven years old. The water rose on them almost every
day and many times they would go out on a certain route
and find it full of new waterfalls when they tried to return.
But this phenomenon also created the most moving scene
of the whole adventure. One day at Hercules Falls a sudden rise in the water joined other falls to it, and the result,
though frightening, was breathtaking. "On every side fresh
cascades sprang out, as if by magic, from the rocks,"
remembered Farini in awe. For as far as they could see
everything was suddenly a single majestic waterfall.

Though he actually found diamonds in sand between
rocks one day, such a discovery paled next to the sheer
adventure of those two weeks. He said nothing of the diamonds later, but the impression the Augrabies made on
him stayed forever.

When they left the Falls their expedition was essentially
over. They stopped briefly at Upington, where they
enjoyed the sight of a white Christian church in a real
town and stayed in a brick house where they were treated
to an English-style meal, "presided over by a lady...." A few
days later they recrossed the Orange River, and in a week
reached Hope Town. Farini arranged to have the oxen,
wagons, etc. sold at an auction. Though Lulu was concerned that his father would suddenly decide to trek to
Cape Town over the deadly Karoo, they were on a train a
few days later speeding straight south.

They took a room at the Masonic Hotel when they
arrived in Cape Town on July 21st. Their steamer *The
Drummond Castle* was leaving at 4 p.m the next day, so
they quickly readied themselves for the long trip home.
The next morning a journalist from the *Cape Argus* cor-
nered Farini for an interview. In the article he was

described as "bronzed from the sun, but tough and in excellent form," and sounded very much like a typical, opinionated Yankee (indeed he told the reporter he was American). He spoke forcefully about how the Kalahari was not as desert-like as most people thought and how it could be used by Americans, mostly for ranching, but also for other purposes, and had a full-blown scheme for moving and marketing cattle. He also spoke at some length about his ranching operations in America. Perhaps surprisingly, he told Gert's diamond story and gave the location they had searched. For the first time he mentioned that he was planning a book about his adventures and left the journalist with an impression of a man of considerable intelligence, boldness and energy.

The newspaper reported that he had just one "pygmy" with him (the rest were reputed to have run off or been induced to leave) though the passenger list of *The Drummond Castle* indicated that G.A. Farini and L. Farini had "2 servants" with them. Ever of a scientific bent, he also hauled on board a substantial collection of Kalahari flora, mostly for the Royal Gardens at Kew, Sir Joseph Hooker, and the Berlin Botanical Gardens; insects for J. Jenner Weir; and various skins which he intended to send to the British Museum. During the voyage he met George Baden-Powell (brother of the famous Boy Scout founder) and their discussions appear to have been many and lengthy. Among the contacts Baden-Powell gave him for future references was Reverend John Mackenzie, a prominent missionary and politician of the day.

They arrived off Plymouth on August 13th and docked the following day. How strange it must have been to be back in England after nearly six months in the desert! But despite the culture shock he sprang into motion immediately. Within days he sent his specimens to appropriate institutions and soon received letters of thanks, one from Sir Joseph Hooker himself.

He also began putting his notes from the journey into book form, and by the last week of September signed a

contract with Sampson, Low, Marston, Searle and
Rivington, a large London company which also published
Thomas Hardy, Louisa May Alcott, Jules Verne, and
Henry M. Stanley (*How I Found Livingstone* and *Through
the Dark Continent*). And he was quickly by Anna's side in
Germany. On November 7th he read a paper about his
Kalahari trip, in German, before the Berlin Geographical
Society. He continued to practise his fluent German,
spending time in Berlin over the succeeding months, and
marrying Anna there on January 21, 1886. When not in
Europe he worked on his manuscript at his latest residence at 7 Canonbury Lane in the north-east London suburb of Islington and drove himself so hard at it that a long
sample was ready for the February 20th issue of *The
Graphic* (an impressive, four-page fold-out with nineteen
illustrations).

On the evening of March 8th Farini's paper, entitled "A
Recent Journey in the Kalahari," was read in his absence
before the Royal Geographical Society in London. This
was a prestigious organization with a great deal of government support, both political and financial, which specialized in African exploration and had subsidized Burton
and John Hanning Speke when they discovered Lake
Tanganyika, Livingstone's Zambezi trip and numerous
other expeditions. On the day Farini's paper was read the
Marquis of Lorne was in the chair, a former Governor-
General of Canada and son-in-law of Queen Victoria.
Farini would have dearly loved to have read his own
paper, but his whirlwind, itinerant lifestyle betrayed him
this time. Off in Berlin on one of his many business trips,
he was apparently unaware or misinformed as to the day
he was to appear. Anna wrote in her diary, "Most unfortunate misunderstanding at the Geographical Society.
Willy's paper read without him." The prestige afforded by
the Society was of the sort he desperately wanted, and he
was deeply hurt by this lost opportunity.

The paper told essentially the same tale as the book,
though there were a few changes in detail. It was a well
composed, serious presentation with more attention to

geological, economic and political concerns than the adventures in his manuscript. He went to some length to criticize the Boers, but his central theme was the revelation that the Kalahari was not a completely unpopulated, barren wasteland but in places grass-covered and full of game, some areas having many trees and pockets of population, that could, with industry, be turned into excellent cattle ranching land, a place where immigrants could thrive. And, despite the racism he had shown in the past and his desire to get English people onto these lands, he ended with this thought:

> I have also endeavoured to point out that the Bushmen and other local tribes are too little known, and if properly studied in this, their free homes, before they become first contaminated and then exterminated by civilisation, much important ethnological information will be obtained. But I will conclude with the hope that now this great district has become part of the British Empire, these interesting native races will be preserved, and that the English public, in opening up this district for civilisation and trade, will also give lasting protection to the natives.

The discussion which followed the reading of the paper brought comments from several distinguished members and while some expressed surprise at the "abnormal garb of plenty" which Farini saw in the Kalahari no one offered much criticism. The question of water in this "desert" dominated participants' thoughts and the president felt it wise to not be too optimistic about the area when recommending it to immigrants.

Baden-Powell had spoken to Reverend Mackenzie, so just before the book's publication Farini sent proof sheets to him, asking if he would "be kind enough to wade through them." Few men were better suited to give him an informed opinion. Mackenzie was an old associate of Moffat and had lived in southern Africa as a missionary, mostly north of the Orange River, for nearly thirty years. He had published a great deal about his experiences and become involved in the area's politics. He had just completed a controversial (and brief) term as Deputy Commissioner of the Bechuanaland Protectorate (or Botswana, made up almost entirely of the Kalahari) and was in the news for his advocacy of direct British Imperial rule over the area. Having such a man read the manuscript gave it a certain legitimacy.

Through the Kalahari Desert: A Narrative of a Journey with Gun, Camera, and Note-Book to Lake N'Gami and Back by G.A. Farini appeared in Great Britain in April. It had a greenish blue cover with an engraving of a Kalahari scene, and featured drawings from photos by Lulu. It did well, as evidenced not only by reviews, like those in the *New York Times* and *New York Daily Tribune* and a report, full of pride, in the *Port Hope Times*, but also because an American edition was published almost simultaneously, by Scribner and Welford of New York, and a German edition was brought out entitled *Durch die Kalahari-Wüste*, published in Leipzig by F.A. Brockhaus. The following year a French edition appeared, published in Paris by Librairie Hachette, with the rather exaggerated title *Huit Mois Au Kalahari: Recit D'Un Voyage au Lac N'Gami*. A South African limited edition was published in 1973.

The book opened with two large photographs. The first was of Farini, and a lavish shot of a lavish man it was: he stood nobly in front of a building with a high staircase, his hair cut short and parted in the middle, a bushy moustache with no beard, and an obviously thick build; he held a top hat in his hand, a cape was tossed over his right shoulder, and pencils were evident in his breast pocket; he wore a high-collar with stick-pin, and a dark suit jacket that split near the top to reveal his fancy vest; his vision was cast into the distance. Lulu's portrait (which wasn't in every edition) was much more humble, showing a young man in a neat, but quiet suit and tie, photographed from the chest up, with well-groomed, receding hair, a moustache and goatee and smiling eyes behind circular, wire-rimmed glasses.

Farini was not without abilities as a writer, though his style betrayed the verbosity and purple prose typical of his time. He exhibited a good vocabulary, moved the story quickly (albeit with a bit of wandering here and there, and a number of examples of his bad poetry) and wrote, for the most part, believable dialogue (and there was a great deal of it), often difficult for inexperienced writers. His ego was evident throughout. In fact, he

G.A. Farini, age 47, on the frontispiece to his book Through the Kalahari Desert.

set the tone in his wordy introduction. "Most authors, either in preface or introduction, apologize for what is to follow," but he made it clear he didn't deign to apologize. What followed was an entertaining story by a man obviously well acquainted with several foreign languages, Latin, Shakespeare, numerous countries, geology, geography, anthropology and other fields of science. The narrator was a daring fellow, so highly opinionated and ostensibly unconcerned about others' opinions of himself as to be rather boorish at times, and always the hero of almost every adventure, with Lulu a close second. It seemed there was nothing he encountered that he did not know something about, and if he found himself ignorant, he soon learned. For example, his description of diamond mining in Kimberley was so full of details that one wonders if he was a mining engineer in his spare time. And he was capable of intriguing insights. In the 1960s Kalahari expert A.J. Clement made the following comment: "Farini was an enlightened man and, in many ways, far ahead of his times. Eighty years ago he foresaw the tremendous ranching potential of the Kalahari and, foreseeing the ultimate benefits which would accrue to mankind, advocated the adoption of business-like measures for its full utilization. It is a sad indictment of modern times that little progress has been made in this direction during the intervening years."

His hard-headed, egotistical attitude had occasional touches of sensitivity. For example, in the endless tales of hunting down and killing wildlife, done with bloodthirsty glee and a sense of heroism, come moments of tenderness for the victims. He wrote again of his basic respect for native Africans, though he also made it clear that he thought them beneath Englishmen, and sometimes harshly criticized them. His criticism of the Basters and certainly the Boers ran much deeper. His rage at the way natives were treated by the Boers echoed Livingstone's thoughts and was similar to much of the world's feelings following the institution of apartheid in the mid-twentieth century. He wrote:

> ...the poor Bushman is hardly dealt with. The big game is driven from the country by the Boers and their flocks; the small game he cannot hunt, as his poisoned arrow and bows are always taken from him; so he is obliged to steal some of the flocks to exist, for which he is punished by depriving him of his liberty which he loves so well. Is it a wonder he resists capture so desperately? But the march of civilization has no ears for the cries of those poor wretches whom it crushes if they stand in its way.

Despite these and other serious conclusions (there is a lengthy appendix full of minute details about flora, animals, distances between places, etc.) it should be emphasized that the book is, more than anything else, a tale of adventure. It even begins with a scene like an opening from a novel, on the platform of the Cape Town railway station, and proceeds in almost episodic style, to relate the ups and downs of life on the road with Lulu and Farini (interspersed with long and subjective analyses of their surroundings). It would not take an enormous leap of the imagination to term his book a picaresque novel, with Farini as the roguish "picaro" hero; the book's frequent humour, tall tales and occasional satire fit this style.

There has always been a great deal of criticism of the accuracy of Farini's Kalahari book. Not only is his discovery of the ancient ruins considered suspect but so is a large portion of the journey itself. A number of critics, especially in the twentieth century, have come to believe that the northern part of his trip was fictional. But analyses which dwell solely on the book's factual details miss the point. Farini was a merchant of entertainment, a man of invention, whose greatest search in life was for adventure and who from childhood turned his very existence into a story. Primarily, readers are meant to enjoy the book. One wonders if even the know-it-all narrator of these *Adventures in Africa* (the original subtitle) is not always taking himself perfectly seriously.

There are certainly things to be learned from the book, but one must tread carefully. And nowhere is that more advisable than in the mysterious, still-living-and-breathing legend of The Lost City of the Kalahari.

When the book first appeared there was, surprisingly, not a great deal of discussion or public reaction to his "discovery" of the ruins of an apparently highly developed ancient civilization in southern Africa far south of where the Egyptian dynasties lived. In addition to the description in the book, he discussed it in the geographical society papers. Generally the papers were more cautious, saying for example that the city's wall was an eighth of a mile long while the book said the ruins themselves could be traced for a full mile; not a contradiction, but a kind of scaled-down analysis. There were other minor discrepancies, like the omission of "cement" from the description in the lectures and the reduction of several table-like structures to one. For the most part people believed his story, primarily because they did not have the means to verify it. The place where the ruins were supposed to be was in a remote part of the desert seldom seen by human eyes. The Kalahari is deadly primarily because it lacks water, but also because it has few landmarks, and the ones that do exist can disappear virtually in hours. The shifting sands, the sudden hard rains, can effect transformations and change particular landscapes forever. Saying that you discovered something deep in the unmapped Kalahari of 1885 was almost like saying you had found a needle in a haystack. And Farini knew it.

In 1886 and 1887 distinguished German scientist and traveller Dr. Hans Schinz, who had been to the Kalahari, published reviews in the popular *Petermann's Geographische Mitteilungen* denouncing the book. Some of this criticism seemed to stem from the fact that many eminent German anthropologists, including Virchow, had been highly critical of the Krao exhibit and had not forgiven Farini for it. Schinz speculated that the Kalahari book and its wild claims were nothing but a publicity ploy for similar exhibitions. But despite this kind of attack the book received positive comments from informed sources, like noted ethnologist Dr. A.H. Keane and gold-mining expert J.M. Stuart, and was even called "a standard work on the subject [of the Kalahari]" by one journal. However, after the turn of the century it faded into obscurity and by the 1920s was a collector's item.

But in 1923 Professor E.H.L. Schwarz of Rhodes University in South Africa began taking Farini's Lost City seriously, and soon widespread interest was brewing. In 1930 F.R. Paver, editor of the *The Star* (Johannesburg), and Dr. W. Meent Borcherds, a medical doctor at Upington, started investigating and soon the former was writing articles about it in his newspaper. In 1931 the South African magazine *The Automobile* organized an expedition to search for the ruins, and from that year onward Farini's Lost City developed into a mystery that has intrigued a great many people, a legend in South African history. The press began talking about it and San and Khoikhoin legends about a lost city were taken more seriously. Even the

Minister of Lands, Piet Grobler, became interested. In
1932 the first expedition went into the desert, led by
adventurer R. "Tinky" Craill. They went up the Nossob
River and found a number of interesting things but no
Lost City. The following year Paver and Borcherds visited
the same area. Dr. F.D. du Toit van Zyl's trip in 1949 was
the first of a string of at least twenty-four separate expeditions by a wide variety of people over the next sixteen
years: several times three expeditions went out in a single
year and never did two full years pass without an
attempt. Among the participants were novelist Alan Paton
(*Cry the Beloved Country*), French explorer and writer
François Balsan, eminent university professor P.V. Tobias,
author A.J. Clement, a senator, several doctors, military
men, distinguished ladies, and the Northern Rhodesian
Boy Scouts. The most relentless searcher was Dr. J.N.
Haldeman, a chiropractor from Pretoria who led eight
expeditions between 1957 and 1965 and several afterwards. Searches have been conducted on foot, in wagons,
trucks, jeeps, Dakota aircraft loaned by the South African
Department of Defence and various other airplanes.
Thousands of square miles have been examined on land
and in the air, sites have been photographed and exca-
vated, and analyzed by academics. Answers have been
found only to be shot down.

The Boy Scouts with their leader J.F. Leech thought they
had solved the mystery in January 1964 when they found
a freak geological formation in the northern Kalahari that
looked to them a great deal like the Lost City. Their discovery was carried by the press not only in South Africa
but by such leading papers as *The Times* of London and
the *The Globe and Mail* of Toronto. However, the fact that
the rocks were found in north-western Botswana several
hundred miles from Farini's locations and near the Ky Ky
Hills, mistakenly taken for the Ky Ky Mountains, rendered their solution highly questionable. The walled-city
ruin Klaus Dierks discovered not far from Rietfontein in
1986 seems a better candidate, though its location, to the
south-west in Namibia, also clouds its tenability.

Over the years natives have reported intriguing sightings of similar "ruins," and cranks and adventurers have
made numerous assertions. Some have even claimed to
have photographs of the ruins, but all of these turn out to
be unsatisfactory in one way or another. One gentleman, a
police officer from Kimberley named Jack Hauser, claimed
he and a friend were caught in the Kalahari during a
severe sandstorm in 1950: wrapping themselves in their
clothes and putting their faces down they rode out the
storm, but when they looked up afterwards they saw
before them the ruins of Farini's ancient city, uncovered in
the desert. Hauser's attempts to relocate the site later
failed. L.S. Du Plessis of Pretoria claimed in the mid-1960s
that he had visited three ancient ruins, one of which was
Farini's fabled city (with underground vaults filled with
treasure). Du Plessis was guided to these spots by San and
Khoikhoin and speculated that they were connected to the
ancient city of Atlantis. Another claimant, D.J. Herholdt,
insisted for years that he had several times found an
ancient city in the desert submerged under the sand. And
a legend still persists of a line of ancient ruins running
from Zimbabwe through Farini's area out to the western
coast, all containing fabulous treasures.

A number of books discuss the legend at varying
lengths, and Fay Goldie's *Lost City of the Kalahari: The
Farini Story and Reports on Other Expeditions* and A.J.
Clement's *The Kalahari and Its Lost City* are entirely
about it. Some writers are highly sceptical, others
unabashedly supportive, but most are captivated by the
romance of it all. "My favourite 'lost city' will always be
the ancient ruin Farini reported in the Kalahari," wrote
Lawrence G. Green in *Thunder on the Blaauwberg*; Goldie
said Farini's discovery was "a spectacular and tantalizing
contribution to the records of the famous explorers" and
theorized, "The Lost City of the Kalahari, if never found,
will always remain one of those fascinating enchantments
for which Africa is famed, and over which our great-grand-
children will nod a speculative head and be as intrigued
as we are." K.E. Lloyd Hooper, who got into the right

351   Shane Peacock

spirit of things in *Travellers and Adventurers* by recounting Farini's expedition like an adventure story, accompanied his tale with a cartoon of Gert, Lu and Farini on the dock at Cape Town. Michael Main, on the other hand, presented Farini as a complete crank, and incorrectly speculated that he borrowed much of his story from a land surveyor (who actually copied things from Farini's book, rather than the other way around).

The most peculiar book about Farini and the Kalahari is Nicholas Luard's *Kala*. An adventure novel by a best-selling author, it was published in 1990, and tells a lurid tale, in the tradition of best-sellers, with all sorts of plots, obvious good guys and bad guys, sex thrown in to help sales, and a grand resolution of all the plots at the end. Farini plays the *really* bad guy. He runs the Royal Westminster Aquarium, and his walk over Niagara Falls is dramatized, but the details of his life are twisted to suit the tale. He is presented as a foul-mouthed, not particularly intelligent, driven voluptuary exploiting a group of San people as well as a young African girl named Kala (a descendant of Cleopatra, raised by jackals!) by exhibiting them. He even attempts to rape her when the feeling takes him. Soon he discovers that diamonds can be had in the Kalahari and chases an escaping Kala (freed by an incredibly decent young woman and a disabled young man) to South Africa, veritably drooling for her blood and the diamonds. Kala leads one and all to her home, a "lost city" in the desert, and the evil, cursing Farini therein meets his death. The good guys believe in Darwinism, environmentalism and always side with indigenous people, while the bad guys, like Farini, are associated with the church and show business. Willie Hunt would have been more than a little shocked to see himself thus portrayed.

Of all the books about this legend the most thorough and best researched is undoubtedly Clement's. *The Kalahari and Its Lost City* is virtually, as Clement rightly claimed, a handbook of Farini's trip and his mysterious find. It meticulously analyzes everything: from extensive information gathered by Paver over several decades, to native rumours, to railway schedules, weather reports, accounts of interviews with Gert Louw and another Farini expedition member in old age, expert opinions about Kalahari travel and investigations into the details of Farini's schedule, his maps and his daily movements. Clement also travelled into the Kalahari in search of the ruins and contacted numerous other Lost City explorers.

He begins by examining Farini's life, quite rightly establishes that he was capable of a tall tale or two, and then goes through the trip and concludes that it was highly unlikely that he travelled as far as he claimed. Clement is most sceptical about the extreme northern portion of the expedition, once it left Lehututu and did a loop up to Ghanzi, Lake N'Gami and down the western side of the desert back to Rietfontein and the Philanders. This is mostly based on three things: evidence that Farini only had about 175 days available to him in Africa and yet his book discusses 230; evidence that he travelled about twenty miles per day and yet would have needed to go about twice that speed to accomplish what he said he did; and evidence that Europeans in Ghanzi and the Lake N'Gami region interviewed soon after Farini's trip had not seen him nor heard anyone else in the area mention him.

Clement believes his theory that Farini's Lost City was a fiction gains credence from the fact that no indigenous peoples lived in the ruins area "at a time appropriate" to their construction. He also feels that Lulu's extensively touched-up "photograph" of the ruins, only one of which exists today despite Farini's claim that several were taken, may simply be a drawing, and this apparent lack of any actual photo of the Lost City when photographs of other parts of the trip are numerous, is highly suspicious. Clement makes much of the discrepancies between the book's account of the ruins and the one in the geographical society papers, feeling that Farini purposely toned down his description when speaking to a well-informed audience. He also points to a much different drawing of the ruins in the French edition of the book. The first-hand accounts of an aged Gert and others also cast some doubt on the existence of a Lost City.

Clement deals with the many serious expeditions that have searched for the ruins and while he has respect for them, and even for Haldeman and others' continuing belief in the Lost City, theorizes that they all searched the wrong areas (in this he was not unique: just about every expedition was certain that the others were off-course).

Finally, Clement makes a bold statement at the end of his book: he claims to have found what everyone was searching for. It is not the remnants of a lost city, however, but a natural rock formation eerily like Farini's ruins. He made his discovery just fifteen miles east and a little south of Rietfontein, where Farini began his little diversion from the main route with Philander's men. This was about one hundred miles south-east of the area that had been the focus of most searches. Clement's discovery fit his theory that Farini often exaggerated the distances he travelled.

What Clement found was the Eierdop Koppies (or Eggshell Hills), an amphitheatre-shaped collection of rocks and boulders (dolerite) about a mile long and a third of a mile wide, with (what appeared to be) double walls, perfectly square rocks like building blocks and even a table-like slab strikingly like one in Farini's picture. Many of the boulders were smooth, as if cut, and looked piled on top of each other, often ten or more feet high. "One or two of the rocks showed a kind of fluting...and a few were shaped like a basin." There were even white streaks on the boulders, looking much like cement mortar, actually produced by natural, chemical weathering.

However persuasive, Clement's book did not solve the mystery. Haldeman, for one, did not accept its conclusions and remained convinced of the existence of the Lost City. He based much of his belief on first-hand knowledge: many expeditions into the Kalahari (many more than Clement) convinced him that Farini had actually been in the places he wrote about. He found Farini's descriptions accurate and his comments about his surroundings convincing, and continued to find natives who recognized the photograph of the ruins. Three years after Clement's book was published he stated unequivocally in a letter to one of Farini's descendants, "We do not feel he made the 'Lost City' up as we have confirmed everything else in the book."

Though it is difficult to find major holes in Clement's argument, it does seem rather strange that on his one and only attempt to find the ruins he went up to Rietfontein, drove fifteen miles outside of the village and there it was, right in front of his eyes. It is also not convincing to argue that because Farini may have exaggerated parts of his journey he necessarily did the same with the Lost City story. And knowing that Farini had a propensity for stretching the truth, it is curious that Clement analyzed everything in the book as if it were the truth when it suited his purpose. In other words, if Farini claimed he stopped somewhere for eight days for some outrageous adventure, Clement seemed to want to believe him, so he could mark him down for eight days and add up the time he spent in the desert until it was well beyond a believable limit.

A newspaper report filed by Lulu on February 17, 1885 confirmed that they left Kimberley on that date, so deducting the three weeks it took them to get on the road at the beginning of their journey and get back to Cape Town from Hope Town at the end, they were travelling by wagon for about 150 days. During this time they covered anywhere from 2,500 to 3,000 miles (or less if Clement's theory is correct), giving them an average of somewhere between 13 miles and 20 miles per day, a more than reasonable rate of speed. This of course, does *not* account for rest days, and their inclusion would put their miles per day up somewhat but not necessarily past a believable figure. Clement's assertion that there were approximately eighty-eight rest days seems wildly off and is only believable if you accept everything that Farini wrote. It is more accurate to theorize that, rather than indiscriminately making things up, he merely exaggerated here and there. A judicious shaving of several days off a few adventures and a hundred miles here or there in the northern

Kalahari would have given Clement a more accurate perspective.

This is not to say that Farini definitely went north as far as Lake N'Gami. Clement is not entirely unfair with him, but he rarely gives him the benefit of the doubt, or much credit. Farini and Lulu were bright, industrious and physically capable people and to argue, as Clement did, that Mary Moffat and Livingstone were able to trek between thirty to forty miles a day (on albeit relatively easy terrain) and yet this rate of speed would have been nearly impossible for Farini underestimates him. Clement argued that "she and her husband were both young at the time," but one wonders how she would have done on a tightrope over Niagara Falls or dead-lifting 1,000 pounds. One must always take Farini with a grain of salt, but his ability to do extraordinary things is well documented. He unquestionably went to the Kalahari, explored places few if any had been in before, followed the general if not exact route he mapped out, and may have found a lost city. To present him as a semi-capable, unfit blowhard doesn't paint an accurate picture.

Another gap in Clement's argument concerns maps. He cannot figure out which map Farini had with him, but it is now known that he used a German map called "Das Capland" by Von A. Petermann. And, most importantly, that map is still in existence, with Farini's own handwriting on the margins, his main route distinctly marked out, going well up to Lake N'Gami, and a sort of lighter side-route and arrow pointing to the very area where he claimed he found the ruins!

All of Farini's critics (including Clement) make a crucial error when they assume that he stated categorically that he had found the ruins of a lost city and tried to publicize it. The truth is that while he wondered if his find might be some sort of old-city ruins, his unremarkable account takes up only a couple of pages in his long book, and is only briefly mentioned in the geographical papers. Neither the *New York Times* nor the *New York Daily Tribune* reviews note it at all. In fact, the story of the Lost

City has been blown out of proportion by those who became fascinated with it in the twentieth century. It is these people who present Farini's short, sometimes vague report as a specific claim of historical importance, and then proceed to call him a fake when they think such a claim unjustified. Sometimes they seem almost angry that their own balloon has been burst. Even the renowned Laurens van der Post fell into this trap: "Farini...claimed at length...to have discovered the ruins of a lost city in the desert... In my youth the newspapers from time to time carried special pieces about yet another expedition... It is only now that Farini has been thoroughly discredited..."

Most of the analyses of his Kalahari mystery contain a great many errors about his life and his character is usually misjudged. The general inaccuracy even extends to his conclusions, which were serious ones about the true nature of the Kalahari, its suitability for agriculture and that it was actually not a desert (which was correct). But one would think from reading his critics that he came home boasting, solely about an elaborate ancient ruin.

A final and intriguing fact relating to the legend is that some climatologists have recently come to believe that thousands of years ago the Kalahari actually had many lakes and its land was perfect for agriculture. It was therefore, quite conceivably, well populated.

Farini likely did see something unusual in the desert that day, but whether or not he ever believed it was an ancient ruin probably went with him to his grave. He had known about stories of lost cities in the Kalahari long before he went to Africa so when he came upon whatever he saw in those sand dunes at the foot of those unfindable Ky Ky Mountains he knew he had a story, either real or just in need of a little dressing up, and so he gave it to posterity.

One of the great ironies of the whole mystery is that during the 1930s, when intense discussions were taking place concerning it, Lulu Farini was living at his country home in upstate New York, the answer to the secret of the Lost City of the Kalahari still there in his active mind.

It is interesting to speculate about Farini's psychological make-up when it came to deception and exaggeration. It is tempting to think that he loved to make fools of people, whether by convincing them that there was a lost city in the middle of a desert that was just a collection of stones, a beautiful female gymnast who really wasn't, a missing link who was taught to be so, or a human cannonball who was never once really blown up. As a child he felt the adults of his town pushing him to repress his passions, to be something he wasn't, to opt for illusion. He came to believe that most people never really sought the truth, that what they *said* they wanted was not what they *really* wanted. Human beings were hypocrites. In the circus he found ways to give them those illusions, and then packed them with jolts of very real terror. Watching his sensational deceptions, people found themselves suddenly connected to their passions in great adrenalin rushes.

But deep down he was embittered by the stupidity of the gaping crowds who believed everything they saw. Always disturbed by his father's judgement of him as a mountebank, he ultimately hated others for believing the mountebank in him, for being so low and stupid as to be taken in. But this snobbery was also a great source of inspiration: it drove him to be more than a mountebank, to make his illusions ingenious things, to be mysterious, a Svengali. The Lost City of the Kalahari may be the greatest of all his deceptions: something sensational and yet open to serious intellectual debate, and so mysterious it may be unsolvable.

CHAPTER 23

Coming Down to Earth

*"Baldwin was followed by the Italian G.A. Farini,
who also invented a flexible parachute."*
Gerald Bowman, *Jump For It*

*"Very slowly then and very gracefully the Professor
came down and alighted...the crowd rushed at him
and cheered him mightily."*
The Era, August 4, 1988

Despite the fact that Farini expressed so much interest in the Kalahari and was apparently given some
sort of option to buy land there, he never again returned
nor did he dwell much on it. He was rolling on in life.

While he was away his acts had been working on two
continents. Early in the year Behrens had the Zulus in
Berlin, various exhibitions continued at the Aquarium,
and the Elastic-Skin Man, the Earthmen and Krao were
all in the U.S. While Krao was touring, John Doris was
trying to offer enough money to get her onto his
Consolidated Monster Show. Finally, she opened with
them at Indianapolis in mid-April. They crossed into
Canada, played Toronto, and on July 22nd, the same day
Farini left Africa for home, the Doris show with Krao as
their feature act, played Port Hope. But the town was not
exactly in a circus mood.

Farini once said that while he was in the desert he
thought of how isolated he was from the outside world,
and worried particularly about deaths back home. In April
and May, while he was in the midst of the great hunting
trip which unveiled the Lost City, rebellion broke out in
Canada's western territories, and deaths were numerous.

The little town of Port Hope was especially affected.

Their most respected citizen, A.T.H. Williams, who had been their member of parliament (as his father had been before him), Conservative Party "whip" and aide-de-camp to the Governor-General, a favourite son who was everything that was upright and proper to them, was one of those who lost his life. He had been a Lieutenant-Colonel in the fight, and by leading the charge which overran native-Métis leader Louis Riel had become a national hero. But on his way home to a massive welcome, he had fallen ill and died. On July 21st a funeral was held the like of which has never before or since been seen in Port Hope, attended by a crowd of 15,000 (the largest since Farini's walk) and numerous national dignitaries. The town was draped in black and an arch was erected over Walton Street with the words "Our Country Laments the Hero of Batoche." That evening Farini's Krao arrived in town with the John B. Doris Consolidated Monster Show.

But Farini, the rebel son of Port Hope who would never receive their praise, knew nothing of this. Neither did he know that Alice Carpenter Farini Miller was stricken with stomach cancer while he was heading home on the Atlantic and died two months later, on September 25th at the Infirmary in Ryde, on the Isle of Wight, leaving behind husband Charles Miller, journeyman butcher of the island. Whether the children spent much time with her after the divorce is unknown, but after her death Willie and Harry (aged thirteen and twelve respectively) lived permanently with Farini and Madame Anna when not away at school.

One of his stars also died while he was in Africa. On March 12th Elizabeth Ann Roche, the twenty-two-year-old native of England who had been famous as the second Zazel, expired during childbirth at Norfolk, Virginia. Her death caused much confusion among show-business fans, who were anxious to know if the mighty Zazel really was no more. The *New York Clipper*, looked upon as final arbiter, was besieged with letters. "...there have been at least two Fs and at least two Zs," said the harried editor.

Lulu went back to North America after returning from Africa, resolved to leave the Farini-created world of sensation forever. By spring he was well on his way to setting up his studio, in the Warner building at 61 Fairfield Avenue in the centre of Bridgeport. Here in Barnum's city he made a commitment to maintain his home. There was even a little biography of him published, called *Chapters in a Human Life*. Someone named E.K. Stimson was the author and though he claimed he was moved to write the booklet because he was impressed with Lulu's life story, it also promoted Lu's photographic skills, had an ad on the back for "Farini Photographs" and appeared just as the studio was opening. (Information from this booklet was used in a biographical sketch that later appeared in the *Boston Globe* which noted how intriguing it was to have your picture taken by the great Lulu, such an extraordinary man with such a cache of marvellous stories—it was also made clear that, even though he may have once affected a falsetto voice, it now had "the strong manly cadence.")

The details in the biography are interesting. Lu told about having no idea whom his parents were, of his life as El Niño and Mlle. Lulu with Farini, and claimed for some reason that his final performance was at Niblo's Garden in 1873. He also changed a few things about the Kalahari adventure. His emphasis was on his photography: like the view he snapped of the peak of Tenerife with clouds floating below its summit as they passed by the Canary Islands and the shots he took of the Augrabies Falls. He, like his father, understood what a good story was: he mentioned, for example, the night the "tawny lion sprang into their camp." And he switched roles with his father at the Augrabies, describing himself as the man to the fore, boldly forging across treacherous waterways before helping others to get over. The booklet also said that when sixty of his African photographs were shown at the British Photographers' Exhibition, "[it was] the highest compliment ever paid by that critical institution to the work of any one individual, and Mr. Farini was (in consequence of this display) elected a member of the Society."

Whether everything he said was perfectly true or not, and one can certainly forgive a bit of exaggeration in anyone raised by G.A. Farini, there was little doubt he was a gifted photographer. He was meticulous in his approach, always attempting to give his pictures an artistic quality (and it is evident that he considered photography an art), trying to out-do what he had done before. His friend Stimson described him as ambitious. Not long after he came to Bridgeport he attempted to photograph a train moving at high speed through the city, and unlike others who had tried this before, did not use a series of cameras. How he did it is unclear and what the final result was, which he showed as a sort of moving picture in a public hall, is not certain. He was obviously inventive like his father: this experiment was coeval with Edison's early attempts at movies.

Lulu Farini, post-show business, was an elegant, kindly man who kept an elegant studio. He would continue working in Bridgeport for more than twenty years, first solely as a photographer and later in the more experimental field of cinema. From 1886 onward he had no more direct business connections with his foster-father, nor did he ever perform again.

Lu was the most important person in Farini's life. Mostly because Farini had sculpted him into an understated, slightly more serious version of himself. A father who had felt people's imperfections intensely, made his son perfect: a being who would embrace his brand of excitement and exploration and do nearly anything to get it, including becoming Mlle. Lulu. They were dear friends and mortal enemies, and Lulu was (almost literally) the best replacement Farini ever found for Mary Osborne. He always felt alone in life, opposed from the start, and Mary had been his first real ally, but Lulu was his greatest. In later years their meetings were said to be electric. May Farini commented about a prospective get-together in 1896: "If the roof of [the house] remained upon its accustomed support during the time when Papa and Uncle Will...[are] assembled beneath it, it would be a triumph for the architect."

As Lulu was settling down in Bridgeport, Anna was getting a taste of what marriage to a whirlwind named Farini was going to be like. He ensconced her in his (new) rooms at Vernon Place in Bloomsbury Square, London, and proceeded to leave her for long periods, tearing off to the continent on business for weeks at a time, attending to things at the Aquarium and other venues. Her diary records her constant longing for his return from his many absences. Reappearing, he would sweep her out to one theatre after another, tickets on reserve, and then be gone again. Occasionally he took her with him, like on a memorable trip to Liverpool where she had the strange sensation of being privately introduced to Krao. Loneliness was the constant companion of Farini's wives, though Anna somehow reconciled herself to it. She dealt with the monotony by playing the piano for hours, entertaining friends and delighting in letters, one which arrived from Franz Liszt late that June, speaking of an illness that would soon prove fatal.

In September he finally took her on a proper honeymoon. They spent the better part of two months in North America, where they visited Port Hope (staying for two weeks, attending church with the Hunts and causing no major family quarrels), Bridgeport, Niagara Falls (where the newspaper noted his presence), Chicago, Washington and New York. In Manhattan they and an audience of more than two hundred boats saw the unveiling of the Statue of Liberty, and everywhere they went to the theatre; and when there was no theatre Anna played the piano in her new relatives' homes. They were two elegant, colourful personalities, dressed to the nines, travelling first class, together continuing the adventure that was Farini's life.

Though they often travelled during the next dozen years, frequently visiting the European continent, their home base was London, where Farini again began lending his name and influence to Richard Warner's burgeoning theatrical agency. Now associated with his wife's social position and wealth, and the proud possessor of a reputation as an author and explorer, he started investigating

other talents. He wrote short stories, always full of melo-
drama, and began writing more poetry, including an
eleven-page ninety-four-stanza tribute to Henry Irving,
full of references to great actors and theatres, and praising Irving for popularizing Shakespeare. He also took
more time to work on his inventions and in 1887 patented
nine in Great Britain alone. Among them were improvements in ammunition and cartridges for guns and "the
permanent way of railways" (an idea to make the wood
"sleepers" and steel "chairs" sections of rails into one continuous piece of steel), but perhaps the most important
was a new design for theatre seats, one which made it
easier to fold them up in their place to allow space for people to walk in front of them, and he also created a place on
the chair to hang a hat and coat. Other inventions that
year included one for pistols and another for a fireproof
theatre curtain. And he was still applying his mechanical
genius to the fish hatchery and butter factory on one of his
Hope Township farms. The latter experiment (which was
to be run by water power) was later destroyed by fire and
it was always rumoured that an arsonist, perhaps one
unsympathetic to the evil life of a showman, was responsible. He had also begun to invest in railways, and his
interest in racehorses was in full swing, as evidenced by
an ad in a Port Hope paper for the services of his trotting
stallion Rifleman, Jr. And he continued to study languages: he spoke, wrote and read German and French
perfectly, Spanish, Dutch, Italian and Russian well, and
could even understand some Zulu and San.

In 1888 he made another move in his real-estate holdings. Seventeen years earlier he had taken over financial
control and assumed the mortgage for his sister Ann and
her husband, William Marsh's farm in Hope Township,
five minutes east of the old Hunt place. It seems this was
done to help them financially. Now he purchased the land
outright and allowed them to continue to farm it. Locust
Lawn, as it was called, was often the centre for Hunt-
Marsh family gatherings. Lu, Edith and May were frequent guests, as were the many family members who now

lived in Detroit: Mary Hunt who had wed American businessman Joseph Hartford, Myndert and his wife from
his bee farm outside the city, and Tom from downtown;
other visitors included Mannie from his dentist office in
Hamilton, or Jack and Jim (and his numerous wives) from
close by. But heads turned when Farini and Madame
Anna dropped by, dressed in their sometimes eccentric
and always extraordinary fashions.

In the spring and early summer of 1888 Willie and
Harry Farini visited Locust Lawn, apparently on their
own. In May they went home by ocean liner. Fifteen-year-
old Willie wrote to cousin Lucia Marsh on his return,
excitedly telling her about seeing whales and porpoises off
Newfoundland. At Liverpool they took a train to London
and were met at the station by their father, who evidently
was anxious for them to fend for themselves at a young
age. Willie noted "Papa's" sarcastic comments about the
ship's clergyman not being able to change the roughness
of the sea despite his constant sermons. The boys were
going to a private tutor in those days, though soon they
would take examinations to enter Dulwich College.

That year was also marked by the reappearance of two
stars who had played important roles in Farini's life. In
March Rosa Richter Starr, now in her later twenties,
brought herself back to life as Zazel and took a leading role
in her husband's galaxy of stars in the Barnum and Bailey
show at Madison Square Garden. Unable to do the cannon
act because of Farini's tight grip on the patent, she concentrated on the high dive into the net, even giving demonstrations of its use for fire departments by diving into it
out of fourth-storey windows dressed in a skirt and dainty
hat. In June, Blondin, age sixty-four and apparently a little pressed for cash, performed on the high wire at Staten
Island and Coney Island, carrying his son on his back.

But Farini wasn't thinking of such things; tightropes
were now twenty years behind him. He added nine more
inventions to the holdings of the British Patent office in
1888 (in addition to patents he took out in France), among
them a further improvement to the folding theatre seats,

several concerning gun cartridges, and one for turning a rifle into a machine gun. His applications, full of meticulous explanations, displayed his considerable knowledge of things technical. He continued to write creatively in his spare time, and his poetry was sometimes revealing, as in a three-page piece about a celebrity who had been wrongfully jailed, a metaphor for his sense of how he had been judged and convicted of moral crimes throughout his life.

He was about to commit another transgression: his last great sensation would involve a man and a parachute, and one of the most extraordinary performances London had ever seen.

The parachute was essentially a nineteenth-century invention, even though Leonardo da Vinci had sketched one as early as 1495, and a Frenchman named Lenormand had leapt from the window of a house in 1783 relying solely on a thirty-inch-diameter umbrella for his safety. André Jacques Garnerin invented the first true parachute, which he tested in 1802 by dropping 4,500 feet clutching a stiff twenty-three-foot-diameter model. But in the first half of the century any parachute jump was extremely dangerous, exemplified by Englishman Robert Cocking's 1837 leap in which he fell 5,000 feet to a horrific and celebrated death in Kent county. Still rigid and employing hoops and ribs and often made of cloth or canvas, parachutes were not much improved over the following four decades: in 1874 a Belgian named Vincent De Groof died during a well-publicized performance at Cremorne Gardens. Some called De Groof's invention a "flying machine," but the closest thing to that in those days was the hot-air balloon. They had been around much longer than parachutes and by the early and mid-nineteenth century their flights were almost fixtures at fairs and even some circuses. They were thrilling and dangerous spectacles. Tightrope walkers performed on wires attached to balloons, women with iron jaws clamped on and were lifted up, gymnastic performances were exhibited and...parachutes were tested in daring leaps. The science and entertainment worlds converged when it came to balloons and parachutes, and thus G.A. Farini was destined to be involved.

His connection to the parachute is inextricably bound up with an American named Thomas Scott Baldwin. He was born in 1860 in Quincy, Illinois and at age ten was apprenticed into a circus, performing first as a gymnast and later as a rope-walker. His proficiency was such that he soon set out on his own. By the early 1880s he had incorporated a hydrogen gas balloon into his act and before long started experimenting with parachutes. His first performance was on January 20th, 1887 when he made a 1,000-foot descent in San Francisco, but the first shows which brought him to public attention in a big way occurred that August at Rockaway Beach, Long Island and he continued to make news throughout the rest of the year, having his portrait and biography published by *The New York Clipper* and jumping from extraordinary heights.

In 1886 and 1887 many parachutists gave their lives to their spectacular profession: one descended into the Baltic Sea and drowned, another fell from 1,500 feet, breaking both his legs, an arm and his neck, and another dropped into the ocean two miles off the coast of California and was eaten by sharks. Professor T.S. Baldwin, head and shoulders above the others, never had a serious accident; his efficient, collapsible parachutes allowed him the utmost control over his descents and he always landed lightly, without so much as a bruise. In early 1888 he began manufacturing and selling his parachutes at a factory in Quincy, advertising himself as the inventor. And some time that spring he contracted with G.A. Farini for a series of jumps at the Alexandra Palace in London.

Farini and Baldwin's long associations with circuses and mutual interests in tightrope-walking, gymnastics, flying, inventions and dangerous performances make it possible that their acquaintance began before 1888. So too does the fact that soon after Baldwin arrived in London in early July, they together completed specifications for an invention for major improvements in the design of the parachute. British Patent #10,937 listed Guillermo Antonio Farini first and T.S. Baldwin second, as co-inventors. After examining the patent it is hard not to conclude that Farini and Baldwin were the inventors of the modern parachute. Their creation had all the elements: a flexible and collapsible, mushroom-shaped parachute, ribless with cords sewn into it that reached down to the aeronaut, and a hole in the top to balance it. Though some

PROFESSOR   BALDWIN.

Entr'acte, September 8, 1888

of these elements were in earlier prototypes, this seems to be the first combination of them all. And their drawings looked very much like a twentieth-century parachute.

Curiously, the patent was registered on July 28th, the day of Baldwin's debut at the Alexandra Palace. Farini's publicity had used the wonderful headline "Cloudland," and to Victorians it did indeed seem as if Baldwin was going to fall from the clouds. The ads were vintage Farini, combining science with danger: "The greatest scientific sensation of the age...Professor Baldwin has succeeded in making an umbrella with sufficient surface resistance to land passengers from an aerial ship at any height...[he] will prove the possibility of his invention by jumping out of a balloon 1,000 feet from the ground...and will drop 100 feet through clouds before opening the umbrella...descend in the park in such a manner that every visitor can see him the whole time of this marvellous, stirring and perilous experiment." Soon the ads commenced with, "Farini's Latest Introduction."

But not everybody was thrilled with the possibility that a man could jump out of the sky and fall 1,000 feet. A no-less-august body than the House of Lords was willing to take Farini on this time. On the 27th the Earl of Milltown rose in the House and asked Her Majesty's Government if the Home Office was aware that this performance had been announced, "whether it was believed that the announcement was genuine; and, if so, whether measures would be taken to prevent so dangerous and demoralising an exhibition." The Earl of Brownlow replied that indeed the Home Secretary had been notified, but that at that moment, not being in possession of enough information, the best they could do was send the police to the show and issue warnings. This was the first salvo in a sustained attack on the parachute jump. Journalists were soon asking whose responsibility it would be if the aeronaut were killed.

Despite the presence of the police, Baldwin was at Alexandra Palace and ready for action by mid-afternoon, as were Farini, Richard Warner and a throng of people estimated at anywhere from 30,000 to 40,000. The twenty-eight-year-old aeronaut, of svelte yet solid build, short dark hair combed back and a thick handlebar moustache, stayed in his tent while his balloon was inflated near the racecourse that surrounded the main building. But at the appointed time he made a grand sortie, advanced to the balloon, threw off his hat and overcoat, and in gymnast's costume, turned to the huge crowd and, à la Farini, made a few comments about what would soon be seen. Then he asked for silence. The crowd hardly needed the admonition, mute as they were, their eyes riveted on the scene. One journal commented that while none of them wished Baldwin ill, they certainly would not want to miss an accident should it occur, or have others see it in their absence.

Farini, fifty years old, his hair streaked a little, and his moustache almost completely grey, stood near the balloon, his presence prominent in silk hat and beautiful suit and tie. No longer the silent, mysterious one in the long black beard, but an elegant author-inventor-explorer-theatrical agent, who smiled much more, and whom many knew on sight.

Baldwin seized the ring which hung from the ropes attached to the balloon (it had no basket) and gave the signal for release. Instantly the balloon shot up, bringing a gasp from the crowd. Baldwin darted toward the clouds with it, like an arrow launched skyward, his body becoming smaller as he rose. In less than thirty seconds he had passed the 1,000 foot mark. Farini turned to a reporter and announced with a straight face that Baldwin was now 1,500 feet in the air. People could see the aeronaut struggling, pulling at something hanging from the side of the balloon. Suddenly he snatched it away. Then he began to fall. Downward he plunged toward the spectators, women screaming beneath him. But just as quickly his momentum was checked, the parachute spread out above him, looking, said various observers, like a miniature balloon, a huge mushroom, or an inverted saucer. For an instant he almost seemed to rise again, but soon they saw him floating toward them, holding the strings of his parachute, dropping as gently as a feather, and forty-eight seconds after he left the air ship, he touched ground, without even falling. The crowd thundered its approval and rushed toward him as he stood calmly in the Priory Ground a short distance below the racecourse. In his speech from a cart minutes later he laughed at the fears which so many had earlier expressed. The balloon, which he would soon learn to slit open after his jump so it would fall near him, was found later a few miles away.

The reaction to his leap was varied. Those who were critical liked to say it was merely sensationalism and that parachutes would never serve any practical purpose. The report for *The Stage* headlined "A Deadly Exploit," was in that vein:

...as anyone with the least knowledge of aerostatics is well aware, death is the penalty which the parachute finally exacts from all who, in a spirit of dare-devilry, commit their bodies to it. And it was with this morbid belief that

the vast numbers of spectators assembled on Saturday. We
trust they will not have cause to assemble again, for it is
clearly the duty of the Home Office...to prohibit a performance which the promoters, with the showman's insight
into human nature, freely advertise as perilous. True they
also claim a scientific value for Mr. Baldwin's invention;
but all such pretension is a piece of effrontery... Aerial navigation, far from "being a certainty in the near future...is
not likely to come to us through such a crude contrivance
as his parachute...We look to the authorities to act deci-
sively in the matter...not until all kinds of amusements
are under the control of a separate Government department, shall we be able to expect any intelligent superin-
tendance in general, and immediate restriction in cases of
this kind.

But not all reactions were negative. Many were thrilled
by what they saw, even *The Times* wrote a glowing review,
saying the performance "was certainly one of the most
extraordinary and successful sensational feats of modern
times." But perhaps the most insightful report was in *The
Era*—its author seemed to have spent some time next to
Farini while watching the show:

Mr. G.A. Farini has introduced to public notice a good
many wonders, but certainly none so wonderful as the leap
from a balloon...since its accomplishment it has been
described in all sorts of opprobrious terms, the mildest of
which has called it a disgrace to a civilized country. Well,
some terrible things have been said about most inventions
and discoveries. The talk about railways before railways
came into use gave rise to all sorts of alarmist fears...
Professor Baldwin seems to have discovered the secret of
success [of the parachute], and as Mr. Farini was gracious
enough to say on Saturday, the secret is an open one. That
is, it is an open silk handkerchief with a hole in it. Cocking
and DeGroof failed because of the rigidity of their parachutes. There is nothing rigid about Professor Baldwin's.
Its simplicity is its safety ...

Baldwin gave more than twenty-five performances that season, stretching his stay out fourteen weeks into early November. Farini sent him up every Thursday and Saturday at 6 p.m. and once on holidays, and never did he receive so much as a bruise. And yet this wasn't enough for the authorities. The day after his third descent a long letter to the editor of *The Times* appeared, claiming that Baldwin had been lucky to survive that performance and would sooner or later perish. Several journalists kept up their criticism, the police continued making official warnings, letters were sent to the Home Secretary and memos went back and forth at Whitehall. The police were particularly called to task. Commissioner Huntley, who attended the first show with Inspector Davey, reported to the Secretary of State that, "I did not consider the performance fraught with danger to bystanders, but it appears certain that any mischance with the working of the balloon, parachute or fittings, or failure of muscular or nerve power on the part of Baldwin must be attended with fatal consequences to himself." But an official letter from Baldwin maintaining that "nothing could be safer" and a calming note from the Alexandra's proprietor, kept the parachute in action.

The crowds began coming in huge numbers and Baldwin became one of the greatest sensations London had ever seen. On September 13th the largest crowd ever to attend a Farini-inspired performance gathered—65,000 people. And the press, knowing a good story when they saw one, gave the parachutist thorough coverage. The *Entr'Acte* took particular interest. It published a political cartoon caricaturing the Right Honourable Arthur James Balfour, Chief Secretary for Ireland (and future Prime Minister), as "The Irish Aeronaut" drifting downward in Baldwin's unsteady parachute as he tried to rectify another tight political squeeze, and later Baldwin himself was depicted, standing by his apparatus, with the caption "May He Never Have a Drop Too Much." But he and his notorious promoter still couldn't shake their accusers. Remembering that Farini had slipped through its clutches years ago, the government tried to resuscitate another Dangerous Performances Act (they failed). In mid-October the Middlesex Magistrates considered prohibiting the exhibition: Farini acted promptly, looking danger straight in the face by bringing his aeronaut right to his accusers. Baldwin's testimony at the Sessions House convinced the judges of the effectiveness of the invention and the show continued.

When that storm was weathered it was clear sailing for the rest of the season. On October 31st, Baldwin topped every other leap by dropping 3,000 feet in front of another big crowd that included the Prince and Princess of Wales. The Prince had been away and had rushed back to see the performance. It was said that he spent a good deal of time afterward speaking with the parachutist; no doubt Farini also had a word with his old friend Edward. That was the climax of the exhibitions, though Baldwin returned the following year, created another sensation at the Alexandra and had the authorities on his trail again, to the extent that he was the subject of a question in the House of Commons.

Despite all the forecasts of doom Thomas Scott Baldwin didn't die until 1923, well into his sixties. For many years he and his brother continued to perform and to manufacture and sell parachutes in Quincy, and he was never known to have been injured while jumping. He became a major in the U.S. army and was in charge of balloon equipment (and parachutes one assumes) with the War Balloon and Signal Corps, and after the turn of the century designed several early airplanes. He is a member of the American National Aviation Hall of Fame. In 1888, though surrounded by criticism in England, he received an order from the War Office for a shipment of the Baldwin-Farini parachutes.

CHAPTER 24

Turning Points

*"Nowadays Mr. Farini does not take so prominent a
part in providing for the public entertainment."*
"A Chat With G.A. Farini," *The Era*, June 30, 1894

*"Black Raspberry (Rubrus Occudentalis)
Farini's Prolific...apply to Welsh, Gardener,
Dartmouth Lodge, Perry Vale, Forest Hill."*
G.A. Farini, *How To Grow Begonias*

By mid-1888 Farini had almost completely severed his
relationship with the Royal Aquarium and that
seemed to work immediately to their disadvantage. All
through that year, and especially when Baldwin was the
rage of the city, the Aq struggled. At one point in the late
summer it seemed certain they would go under, but somehow they survived and went on for another decade. One of
their attractions was a little monkey who descended from
high in the Aq to the floor, by means of a miniature parachute. His stage name? "The Baldwin Monkey."

Farini's diminishing role at the Aq was due to his ever-
increasing association with the Warner agency. Richard
Warner was literally a Bohemian, evidently of Jewish
blood, and grew up in the Austro-Hungarian Empire's cultural mix. Fluent in several languages, he came to
Birmingham in his youth fully prepared for English society. For a time he was a businessman but his passion for
theatre and music hall entertainment drew him into making contractual arrangements for various artistes at Day's
Crystal Palace, and before long he moved to London to
work as a theatrical agent. Arriving in the early 1880s, by
the end of 1883 he was well established with Kopf and

Co., whose owner was an old friend, and whose major client was a giantess. Warner was ambitious: by the following year the company was known as Kopf and Warner, and in another year he was on his own. Agents were becoming important and Dick Warner, despite his company's high-flown title (The International Theatrical and Musical Agency) was dissatisfied with its small, stagnant size. And so he sought out G.A. Farini.

That was the year before Farini went to Africa, when he was still the force behind all the strange doings at the Royal Aquarium. Warner knew him by reputation: the ingenious, aggressive showman with the secretive ways, who hid the sources of all his wonderful ideas and always worked independently. It took Warner a while, but he was a forceful man himself and he eventually convinced Farini to accompany him on a talent search to Europe. During the trip Warner was impressed by his new friend's fearlessness: Farini scorned, for example, the accepted notion that unusual novelties or acrobatic troupes could not succeed on the English music hall stage because audiences would only embrace comic singers—he snapped up all the unusual acts he could find and soon made them hits in London, transforming the scene overnight. And this man, who was reputed to have come from a small Canadian town, moved about Europe as though he had been born there, speaking the language of most everyone he met, expertly employing whatever social graces he needed and even causing an aristocratic young German woman to fall in love with him.

But Warner also found the energetic Farini hard to pin down. Not long after their trip he went off to Africa and when he came back spent much of his time writing, inventing and travelling, only entering into agreements with Warner when it suited him. But the Baldwin sensation and other successes Farini brought his way convinced Warner that he absolutely had to make the association formal. In mid-1889 (the recently renamed) Richard Warner and Company announced G.A. Farini as the manager of their Continental Department and two months later he was formally given the position of Co-Director of the entire agency.

Warner's always stressed the fact that their business
was international in scope and they led the way in import-
ing acts from abroad, especially from Europe. The fact that
Farini ran the European end of things is therefore significant, especially in an agency owned by a European! He
spent a great deal of time on the continent in the late
eighties and early nineties and every major act there,
whether French, German or Italian knew his name and
his power. But he seldom appeared at Warner's offices near
Westminster Bridge in Lambeth: employee's memories of
the agency strangely lack intimate comments about him,
even though he ran it as much as Warner did. They could
tell you about his acts, but almost nothing about him.

By the summer of 1890 Farini was the "Co-Proprietor,"
and the company began to grow and grow. An associate
later recalled, "...Warner's Agency in those days was *the*
agency, handling practically *all* the stars and doing enormous business." They were, in fact, the biggest and most
powerful agency in Great Britain and possibly even in the
world. Besides offices in London and Liverpool, they had
places in New York, Paris and Berlin and connections in
Australia. Their contacts included Tony Pastor, the giant
of variety entertainment in New York, and the legendary
Sir Augustus Harris in London; they were connected to
Niblo's Garden and the Folies-Bergère; and in their prime
represented 500 "principal artistes." Some of them were
timeless stars, like the world's greatest male impersonator
Vesta Tilley and the most influential strong-man and fitness guru in history, Eugen Sandow, as well as Lillie
Langtry, comedian Little Tich, famed Russian wrestler
Hackenschmidt, and Cinquevalli, one of the greatest jugglers of all time. And then there was Zaeo herself and a
whole host of gymnastic troupes, like the Flying Eugenes
and the Selbinis, and song-and-dance men, actors, musicians, performing animals, and Fred Karno's Troupe of
knockabout comedians who would soon count among their
members Charlie Chaplin and Stan Laurel. In addition
they negotiated associations for dramas with such luminaries as Sir Charles Hawtrey, Forbes Robertson and Dion

Boucicault. They influenced the style of entertainment in London and their willingness to bring whole troupes into the country ensured that "variety" was the name of the game on the English stage. Their offices were jammed with people trying to make an impression, searching for the one Warner agent who might peek at their juggling, their tap-dancing or their wonderful performing poodle. A few years later (after Farini had left the agency) Willie Farini sought to impress his new bride in London, and found that the mere mention of his father's name ensured him free tickets at any theatre he chose to attend.

Farini's wealth was increasing during these years and late in 1889 he moved his family into a mansion with extensive grounds in the suburb of Forest Hill south of London. There is some evidence to suggest that since his marriage he had rented a home in St. John's Wood, the trendy, nouveau-riche neighbourhood north-west of Regent's Park, but now he took another step upward. He and Anna purchased a huge collection of household goods, from oriental carpets to fancy beddings, so huge that the list of items made out by the distributor was fourteen pages long. Their new home was on Perry Vale, a road which ran from Forest Hill into Sydenham. When the Crystal Palace was brought to Sydenham Hill in the 1850s the area became a popular suburb and wealthy Londoners came to reside in large numbers. By the mid-1870s there was also a large German community in Forest Hill, one of the reasons why Liszt visited, and played the piano in a home nearby in 1886. A beautiful wooded area, just a twenty-minute walk from the palace and six miles south of the centre of London, it was perfect for the Farinis. Over the years the various Earls of Dartmouth had owned a great deal of property here and it was from a descendant, Lord Dartmouth, that Farini rented the house. At Dartmouth Lodge they employed two servants (one a cook and domestic, the other a housemaid) and a gardener. Here Farini had space to work on his inventions and explore his growing interest in horticulture, and Anna could play the piano, teach young friends and make the connections needed to play publicly. Beside their two Dulwich College educated sons, sixteen and seventeen when they moved, they often had visitors from foreign parts, though mostly from Germany, and occasionally from Canada.

In the summer of 1890 Farini's seventy-six-year-old father T.W. Hunt paid an extended visit and even brought his daughter with him. Bella Hunt, or Birdie as she was known, was then about twenty-one years old and must have been thrilled to visit the elegant home of her famous stepbrother and his aristocratic wife, and be treated to nights on the town at famous places with famous people whom she had only previously read of in newspapers and magazines. The fact that Farini's father stayed for three months and on his return excitedly reported details of his wonderful visit to the *Port Hope Guide* indicated that disagreements were long passed, if not entirely forgotten.

Though he was very much the entertainment businessman now, not nearly as "hands-on" as before, his clients still provided him with exciting moments. One came on October 29th, 1889 when Eugen Sandow strode out of a big crowd at the Aquarium and into show-business history by challenging and eventually defeating the renowned Samson in a demonstration of strength. It was a sensational moment, thrilling London and its newspapers, and Sandow, the five-foot-nine-inch two-hundred-pound Prussian, built like a statue by Michelangelo (remembered by Vesta Tilley as a great attraction for women) became a huge star and a Warner client, and eventually the father of modern bodybuilding. He undoubtedly came under Farini's supervision, and one wonders how much "Svengali" had to do with orchestrating his "coming-out" that night at the Aq.

He was associated with another show-biz adventure in 1890, though this was more like a "scandal," in fact one of the most celebrated on the London stage in the late nineteenth century. Warner client and long-time Farini associate Zaeo, who was managed by and married to his old agent Harry Wieland, appeared at the Royal Aquarium that year and into 1891. To advertise her performance a poster was produced of her in costume, smiling out at spectators in what might have been considered a slightly enticing manner; a woman of ample, Rubensesque build (weighing a well-muscled 170 pounds), most of her legs and much of her back were on display. This enraged many moralists in London and no sooner than Warner's and the Aq could say "avalanche of publicity," the Central Vigilance Society for the Repression of Immorality had joined the fray, pushing the London County Council and the courts to do something. Of the posters which were thereafter plastered everywhere in London (not for the Aq to miss such a bonanza) the C.V.S. commented "It is meant to represent a woman in the nude." Newspapers jumped to either side of the argument, one even taunting the other by producing a two-page spread of Zaeo in costume. The Aq published a biography of her, subtitled *With No Apologies Whatever to the Vigilance Society*. Then the whole discussion reached a hilarious climax when certain members of the London County Council solemnly dispatched themselves to the Aquarium to examine Zaeo's back for themselves, close up and personal, on the excuse that the net she was using was injuring her. After these gentlemen were whipped and laughed at for several weeks in the press things finally began to die down and the Aq, running out of posters and their coffers full of money, allowed the "Zaeo Advertisement" scandal to fade into history. This was to be Farini's last connection to a controversy of public outrage.

He was devoting more time to other things. Between 1890 and 1893 he registered twenty-two new patents at the Chancery Lane offices, many of them concerning improvements to steam engines, steam generators and boilers: ways to make them more efficient, to perfect their feeding apparatus, give them fluid-tight joints, inject air into them, construct better tubes for conducting heat and make water gauges for them. So consumed was he by this that he told the census-taker who came to Dartmouth Lodge in 1891 that he was an engine-maker and author, and didn't so much as mention that he happened to be co-proprietor of perhaps the world's most powerful theatrical agency; he was fascinated with machines and power, had the brain of an engineer and identified with that profession. But his inventions weren't all machines: he discovered a new stopper for bottles, created a fastener for window sashes and even invented a clothes peg. And he didn't just patent his inventions in England: he registered them in several countries, including for some reason, Belgium.

One of his first inventions, Zazel, nearly met her death in 1891. This terrifying incident was likely the source of the story that her career was ended by a terrible fall. Farini is often connected to the accident, but Zazel had long since left him. She was with the Forepaugh show that year and fifty feet above the ground on her wire at Las Vegas, Nevada when it snapped and she fell and landed on her back. Though not disabled, she may have been more seriously injured than initial reports claimed. Since her husband had one of the best jobs in show business, the all-powerful advance talent agent for Barnum and Bailey's Greatest Show on Earth, she had no need to continue her career, which she had resumed solely for enjoyment. As she headed into her early thirties she settled into life as Mrs. G.O. Starr.

By the early 1890s Farini was ascending into the role of legend and wise old man of the variety entertainment world; never was this more evident than in February 1892 when British novelist and lecturer Amye Reade waged a campaign against the alleged cruelty of gymnastic and acrobatic trainers in a long letter to the editor of *The Daily Graphic*. The letter, accompanied by a large illustration of a young girl fainting after an arduous practice while an aggressive trainer stood over her, was soon met with a veritable deluge of opposing letters from show-business people, unleashing a roaring controversy.

Reade had actually quoted Farini (as well as Zazel, Starr and Hengler) as an ally, but Farini felt she had impugned the integrity of more than just a few bad apples

and came to the fore of the discussion with the first and
longest letter of response. He considered himself a writer
now and his page-long, illustrated lecture showed it.
Entitled "A Word For the Trainers," it was a reasoned,
articulate piece, full of technical observations about the
industry and the training of gymnasts. He didn't angrily
confront Reade as many others did, but tried to clarify the
subtleties for the public and point out where she had
given them the wrong impression. Sounding almost like a
professor of gymnastic science, he explained the differences between an acrobat, a gymnast and an equestrian
gymnast, even further breaking down the categories of
regular gymnasts into "ariel" (in the air) and "parterre"
(on the ground or horizontal bar). He also described old
and new training techniques, explaining how new ones
which employed safe nets, and pulleys and machines to
hold athletes suspended in the air as they practised, prevented them from falling. "Such scenes as described by
Miss Amye Reade as actually having transpired between
a trainer and pupil, if true, must have been in a very
small circus, as the artists out of their time would never
have permitted such cowardly brutality," he insisted. "As
a rule, there can be nothing said against [circus performers'] temperated habits and morality; the nature of their
work exacts both, and they are much more provident than
either singers or actors. They usually have robust health,
and live to a good old age." He struck the most rational
notes on either side of the argument, so much so that it
could be said he somehow agreed with both.

Whenever his name appeared in other letters, many
from major players in the industry, he was treated with
obvious respect. One performer wrote that he was
"...probably the best known and most experienced—as the
most astute—of acrobatic trainers in the world"; and circus proprietor George Ginnett proudly said, "Farini himself (once) asked me to take an apprentice..." as if this
were an honour. It was apparent that several of the positive changes within the profession, like safety nets and
the concern for the education of apprentices, had been

spearheaded by him. His continuing desire to give his profession respectability was evident during this controversy, as was his need to stay above the rough-and-tumble of a profession with a mountebank reputation. But perhaps his greatest triumph here was a still more subtle one: it became obvious, from the testimonies of Zazel, Zaeo and others, that Signor Farini, contrary to rumours of an earlier day, had never mistreated his athletes and in fact, spawned not only some of the century's greatest stars but also its most independent, best-educated, healthiest, and most financially secure. Apparently the evil Svengali had been just another of Farini's illusions.

He stayed close to home in 1892, a hugely successful music-hall year during which Warner's continued to do well. Always intrigued by horses, late in the year he and Anna decided to invest in the most popular touring horse show in the world: Professor Norton B. Smith's Horse Training Exhibition. Smith was from Canada and managed by former Farini employee Nat Behrens. He made a name for himself in the U.S. in 1891, among his feats the public subduing of a vicious, much-storied horse named John L. Sullivan. By June of the next year he was in London, opening a long run at the Crystal Palace. Though his training technique lacked subtlety, including forcing horses to kneel by almost pulling their fore legs out from under them (a method that did not inspire universal admiration), he was a great success in London and continued so for many years; he later worked for Barnum, and published booklets about his "education" methods. Horses were such an essential part of life in the nineteenth century that people were always fascinated by various ways of training them and anyone particularly successful at it was immediately accorded attention. Anna may have been the Farini with the greatest interest in horses, or perhaps the one with the most money, because it was she who purchased the one-third partnership in Norton's exhibition. The company which ran it was thereafter known as "Farini, Behrens and Smith," with the "original and only Farini" as director.

A string of happy years was about to be interrupted by
one filled with sorrow, perhaps the bitterest of Farini's
life. It started out well: in the spring he became manager
of one of London's great theatres.

The history and prominence of the Olympic Theatre can
be measured by the fact that it had been built in 1806 for
the creator of the circus, Philip Astley. Since then it had
presented some of the greats of the theatrical world and
had gone through several reconstructions. When it was
rebuilt for the third time in 1890 its capacity was enlarged
to well in excess of 2,000 and its interior given a rich
refurbishing. This was done to return it to its earlier glory
and draw people to its seedy location on Wych Street just
off the Strand and Drury Lane (a dangerous little alley-
like road lined with slums, in an area that was no longer
the centre of the theatre district). For a while it prospered,
but by early 1893 it was temporarily closed, refurbished
again, and reopened as the Olympic Music Hall. The
members of the company then called on G.A. Farini to
perform one of his miracles.

By June he was rounding up stars, aiming to open on
the Bank Holiday in early August. The music-hall licence
was secured and the theatre's interior was beautifully
enhanced. It was given a colour scheme of gold and ruby,
the dome was redone sky blue, and electricity lit the
stage. The August 7th opening was a smashing success,
drawing literally an overflow crowd that filled every seat
and spilled onto the floor where people were allowed to
lounge. Farini made himself visible, rushing to and fro
arranging things and greeting people, one of his sons by
his side. He had put together an entertainment that
started just after 6 p.m. and didn't end until nearly midnight, a seemingly unending string of short turns and
sketches in the best tradition of the music hall. His old
Alhambra associate Charles Dubois provided the music,
and among the stars were the Karnos, popular comic team
Tennyson and O'Gorman, and Miss Jenny Burgoyne "the
beautiful," who, dressed to reveal her figure, was strapped
to the wild horse of the Tartary for another desperate ride

in the "Mazeppa." The loud and boisterous crowd, given to
rude shouts from the young "gods" in the gallery, seemed
supremely satisfied.

But despite early success and Farini's experienced hand,
the Olympic continued to struggle, done in night after night
by its location, and four months later a move was made to
liquidate the company. Farini's position and wealth was
such that this sort of setback was really of little importance
to him, though he was frustrated because he was convinced
that the Olympic could have succeeded had the company
been willing to put more capital into it. But other difficulties that year far overshadowed this little problem.

Dick Warner suffered a serious illness, which lingered for
several months and threatened at times to be fatal. The
agency was not quite itself, Farini straddling his duties
there and at the Olympic. By the end of November, Warner
had recovered and the agency was at full throttle again, but
during that very week tragedy struck the Farini household.

On November 13th Harry, who was studying to be a doctor, started feeling unwell and within a short while was
confined to bed. Then he was unable to move his extremi-
ties and before a week was out the family doctor had
given a frightening diagnosis: ascending spinal paralysis.
By November 23rd, with Farini the so-often-absent father
watching at his bedside, twenty-year-old Harry died. Two
weeks earlier he had been perfectly healthy, robust as a
Farini should be, and now his bright future and the family's dreams about the respectability he would bring to
their name, had been obliterated in a fortnight. It was a
devastating blow.

Whether Willie was there when his brother died is not
known. He had had his troubles within the family of late.
While he attended Dulwich College his stepmother had
been stingy with his allowance, giving him considerably
less than the other boys, and in a move he would come to
regret, he had adjusted one of her cheques. When Farini
found out, he was enraged, a rift erupted between father
and son, much like the one that happened thirty-four

years earlier. William told his descendants many years later that he immediately enlisted in the army.

But records show that William Leonard Farini joined the Durham Light Infantry in 1896, at the age of twenty-three, well past Dulwich College age, so there must have been a period after he angered his father during which he struggled to support himself, unemployed and disgraced. It is known that he was living at Dartmouth Lodge with Anna and Farini in 1891, age nineteen, and while his brother was listed as a "scholar," he had no occupation. It seems likely he was brought home from school but did not actually break with his parents for a few years. Whatever happened, he did not get on well with the pampered, aristocratic lady who had replaced his real mother. Years later father and son (and stepmother) would be happily reconciled, but for now he was the black sheep. History had repeated itself—though Farini was too blind to see it.

So within a short time he lost both his sons. In fact, by the middle of the decade Alice, Harry and Willie were all gone, and Lu was on another continent. Except for Anna, he was alone again, and this was somehow fitting. In Port Hope, T.W. Hunt, now nearly eighty, solemnly announced the death of his grandson in the paper: the grandson who would have fulfilled his dream of a doctor in the family.

The way Farini dealt with Willie revealed how uncompromising he could be, a trait he had inherited from his father. Achievement was important to him and he believed that only a tough-minded attitude in all walks of life got you anywhere, so he turned his back on his son. If he ever considered the fact that being the child of Signor Farini was an extremely difficult role to play, his actions concerning Willie did not show it.

The effect that Harry's death had on the family can be seen in the way his memory has survived. William's grandchildren recall that he seldom, if ever, mentioned he had a brother (though he named his eldest son Henry). Either the pain of his loss was too much to bear or Harry's vaulted position in the family remained hurtful to the eldest son. Perhaps Harry's early demise coupled with

Willie's temporary disgrace, gave the youngest a sort of sainthood, like that of a scion killed in a war. Other Hunt family descendants recall rumours of a promising young man cut down in his prime, and one wonders how things might have been different had Harry lived and become a respected London physician.

The Olympic Music Hall's failure and Harry's death took place almost simultaneously, so Farini was not laden with responsibilities as he tried to regroup. During this period he became interested in horticulture in a serious way and began growing a great many flowers at his estate. This preoccupation, much gentler and more introspective than his previous interests, may have been a response to his son's death (soon he would also become interested in painting). Slowly, another stage in his life was being reached, wherein the boisterous, boasting Farini of younger days, somewhat tempered of late, would transform into an elegant gentleman of more refined tastes. But this did not happen overnight, and it didn't blunt his tireless work ethic: as was his wont, he threw himself back into his work within a few months of Harry's death. In the spring he registered several more inventions and late in the summer organized a charity benefit, its enormous size, royal and aristocratic patronage, and the quality of its guest stars a tribute to his position in the entertainment world.

It was called The Fete of the Season, and was for the benefit of the British Home for Incurables at Crown Lane, Streatham, a suburb of London just a few miles west of Forest Hill. Farini confidently told a reporter it would be "one of the biggest things ever seen." About 350 artists, many well known, responded to his call and promised to perform at his three-day program. The Prince and Princess of Wales were to open proceedings, accompanied by two of their daughters, and dozens of titled aristocrats were to be involved. The Archbishop of Canterbury would participate and Princess Louise (Queen Victoria's daughter and wife of the former Governor-General of Canada) would preside on the second day. Among the performers were actors George Alexander and Charles Warner, and variety artistes the Griffiths Brothers, Fannie Leslie and Sam Redfern. Farini supplemented things with his own flower show and "Farini's Merman." But the merman was the only presentation even vaguely like his early amusements—the program was dominated by classical music, elegant mandolin and guitar orchestras, and refined vocalists. About 5,000 pounds was expected to be raised so the Home could be opened without debt. This was not the first time Farini had done something for charity, but the hard work and commitment needed to bring off something of this size indicated how important it was to him; an example of the changes he was going through on the heels of his son's death.

On June 30th, just three days before the big show, *The Era* published a long interview with him under the headline "A Chat With G.A. Farini." The reporter seemed a little intimidated by him and ran through his life's accomplishments without passing much judgement on some of his exaggerations, like the "fact" that he had taken out a thousand patents or that he had performed over Niagara for two seasons. He also made interesting claims that are difficult to substantiate, for example, that he dove two hundred feet into shallow water in his younger days. The reporter was a bit taken aback by Farini's confidence, appearing as it did in blunt, yet matter-of-fact boasts: "Mr. Farini declares that he has never in his life known fear. He has an iron frame, and he has never abused his strength. For drink and tobacco he has the utmost distaste. He does not, he tells you, claim as a virtue what is actually a physical peculiarity—but there is the fact." (These comments about his physical condition were not entirely empty boasts: his lifelong belief in exercising and proper nutrition had made him exceptionally fit.)

On the opening day of the Fete the streets and homes of the suburbs within miles of the Home for Incurables were decorated and people came out to watch the Prince and Princess come down Brixton Hill Road in a carriage

drawn by four horses and led by a military procession.
When the ceremonies were over, Farini and Sir Augustus
Harris took the Prince and Princess on a tour of the
grounds. They were shown the huge set-up of tents in the
adjacent meadow and treated to entertainment by some of
the leading artists. Their Royal Highnesses stopped for a
considerable time at the flower show, a presentation dominated by Farini's well-known collection and augmented
by flowers he had received from the Queen, Princess
Alexandra herself and various other royal family members. A couple of his most beautiful hybrid begonias were
named after the Princess on the spot, at her request; and
then she, the patroness of the Home and the real star of
the show, gave him a beautiful crystal bowl, which he
always cherished.

After the success of the Fete at Streatham he felt ready for
another challenge. In autumn he agreed to become the
manager of what was arguably the world's most famous
singing group: The Moore and Burgess Minstrels. They
were a black-faced or burnt-cork minstrel group that had
been at the top of their profession for many years. In those
days groups of white men dressed up as black men, wearing plantation clothes, playing banjos, tambourines, fid-
dles and bones, and singing traditional negro songs with
accents, were extremely popular and not considered to be
detrimental to the black man's reputation and general
well-being, so much as any consideration was given to that
problem. Some of the greatest singers and performers of
Farini's generation were of this genre, and an evening
with the Moore and Burgess Minstrels as they played fast,
and sang with beautiful voices, and spun around in
dances, was considered to be about the best entertainment
around: foot-stomping, thrilling and family-oriented. They
had been the resident show at St. James's Hall for three
decades, appearing downstairs in its nine-hundred-seat
theatre, revving up the place so much some nights that
the more elegant entertainments upstairs, like (in their
earlier days) lectures by Charles Dickens, were nearly

drowned out by the stamping of feet. Even respectable women went to see them, something which was not common at most music halls; they were said to be not given to "questionable dialogue or double entendre."

In September 1894, after Burgess had died and Pony Moore, a once-flamboyant star on the London scene, retired, a new company was formed, and the distinguished directors asked G.A. Farini to assume the manager's post. During his six-month reign they produced short musical plays like "Uncle Tom's Cabin" and "The Yaller Gal," and continued with the fare that had made them famous. Among their songs were "Irene, Good-night," "Johnny, Get Your Gun," "Little Boy Blue" and "Rock-a-bye Baby," as well as "Happy Little Niggers," "The Popping Coon" and "The Darkey's Jubilee." Farini inaugurated the group's very successful Thirtieth Anniversary Year, and delighted in playing the prestigious role of their manager.

One of the songs they sang that year was "Play the Tunes I Love So Well," words by G.A. Farini and music by Anna Farini. It was a mournful piece about a man who asks his love, in a tearful farewell, to play his favourite songs while he is away. He subsequently disappears, presumed dead. She is left to forever play those songs, dreaming that he might some day return. It gave full vent to both Farini's desire to write poetry and the pain he was feeling from his recent losses. His melancholy was evident. The chorus went:

> O'er the harp my fingers wander,
> The bygone melodies I play,
> As upon the past I ponder,
> Thinking of him who's far away.

Music seemed to be another of his many interests: Lulu was taught to play several instruments and Anna's skill on the piano was likely one of the things which drew him to her. "Play the Tunes I Love So Well" was later published by well-respected Francis, Day and Hunter in London and New York.

At the end of March 1895 Farini quit as manager of
Moore and Burgess. This, coupled with his decision to
leave the Warner agency just a month earlier, amounted
to a retirement from show business. After nearly forty
years he had finally given it up. His transformation from
impresario to gentleman author, inventor, businessman
and horticulturalist was almost complete.

The prodigious rate of invention he had maintained since
the mid-1880s was beginning to slow by the mid-'90s. In
1894 he registered ten inventions with the British Patent
Office, but in '95 there were just two, and in 1896 three.
After that most of his creations, which appeared only spo-
radically, were registered in Canada. Mostly he was working on three or four sorts of ideas: different devices for
making doors spring shut; inventions concerning furniture pieces, including one which strengthened them and
yet did not increase their weight and made them easier to
take apart and move; different plans for machines which
would pack cans and bottles into boxes (for mass production); and numerous ideas for improved watering cans.
    He and Anna also began buying stocks. This was in
keeping with his view of himself as a sort of budding
financier. Their first venture was with the Rhea Fibre
Treatment Company and involved three purchases of a
total of 3,000 shares for 3,000 pounds, a substantial
investment and an indication of the kind of liquid capital
they had. Over the following two decades they would
invest a great deal more money on the stock market.

But, as Farini's interest in inventing an efficient watering
can attests, his great interest had become horticulture.
During the previous few years he became a Fellow of the
Royal Horticultural Society, his flower collection had been
referred to as "famous" by a journal, and in May 1895 he
and his gardener would plant an astounding 60,000 begonias on his estate (he once said that he eventually planted
a half-million a year). Some time either just before or after
Baldwin's jumps he had made another trip to Australia

and New Zealand, this time to test parachutes. While there, his interest in the flora of those two countries, particularly their ferns, increased, and he studied them thoroughly. He collected and pressed several thousand ferns, brought them back to England and slowly classified each and every one, and staked a claim to having the most complete (and valuable) collection of this kind in the world. He also collected ocean sea weeds in Australasia and added them to his collection of marine plants. He already had a background in agriculture, a collection of Kalahari plants and friendships with people like Jenner Weir. But he was most fascinated with begonias and by 1894 he had decided to write a book about them. The idea percolated for a few years and then in 1896 he got at it full time.

He had begun growing begonias about 1890, and of course, had thrown himself into it and become an expert. He grew the tuberous variety, fitting because they produced big, boldly colourful flowers, could be experimented with and were immensely popular throughout flower-show-loving England. He tried hybridizing immediately, but at first had little success. This despite the fact that his connections in the begonia-horticultural world, as in other walks of life, were impeccable. Many of his flowers were acquired from nurserymen who are today considered pioneers in their fields. He ordered seeds from growers in France and Belgium, and in England from men like Cannell, Veitch and Davis who in turn, purchased some of his varieties. But his closest associate was a neighbour: John Laing of Forest Hill, a man at the very forefront of flower experimentation, who had started hybridizing tuberous begonias as early as 1875 and three years later had, in the words of an historian, "startled the horticultural world" with his gold-medal-winning exhibition before the Royal Horticultural Society.

Just like the days when his first attempts on a trapeze landed him a foot deep in manure, Farini refused to give up after his initial failures. He built a seventy-foot greenhouse with his gardener, cut out the glass on Anna's

kitchen table, and then he began cultivating at full speed.
By the time he wrote his book he had dozens of his own
varieties and was winning awards at prestigious shows
throughout the country.

The book was published some time late in 1896 or early
1897, again by Sampson, Low and Marsten. It was a slim,
hard-cover volume, 135 pages long, with a red spine with
gold lettering, and a cover that had at its centre a huge
white-and-red begonia (which he may have painted) that
looked like a cross between a rose and a carnation. It was
strangely like a beautiful human head. *How To Grow
Begonias: A Handbook for Amateurs* apparently sold well.

It was exactly what its title claimed, and very different
in style and attitude from the Kalahari book. Amateur
horticulturalists, often wealthy individuals, had in the
past been well behind professional growers when it came
to flower experimentation and some of this may have
been, as Farini insinuates, because of the growers' reluctance to reveal secrets. But in the 1890s amateurs began
catching up to the professionals and some of the credit
goes to him. His book set out to show amateurs how to do
everything concerning begonias: it told the history of the
flower, the state of begonia politics, the ways to start
growing them, how to hybridize them, how to build a
greenhouse and design boilers and pipes for heating it (his
own invention, of course), how to make a better sprinkler
(another invention, his pneumatic watering can), how to
keep disease away, and on and on, even including a suggestion for the creation of a Begonia Society, complete
with the sorts of prizes that should be awarded. And at
the end he described the numerous begonias he had created, many now blessed with his own name or those of his
friends or family.

Self-reliance and pride, two salient Farini characteristics (which one might not have associated with growing
begonias), found their way into the book. On page after
page he insisted that anyone could grow any sort of begonia (or do anything under the sun it seemed) if they just
applied themselves.

The text was for the most part quite technical, full of his exhaustive dilations (and sentences) about the begonia, but also had its lighter moments; he could never be entirely dry. He told of button-holing one of his own varieties, one which he had cultivated to look like a carnation, and presenting himself to John Laing with the information that this boutonniere actually was a carnation. The learned horticulturalist looked at it closely and then pronounced it "a very good one."

His botanical abilities were remarkable, certainly for an amateur whose calling in life is supposed to be show business. It is obvious that he spent a good deal of time studying. At one point he mentioned that he had made "microscopic examinations" of the pollenated stigma of his begonias and spent an extended time on the effect of London fogs, even referring the reader to a paper written by a university professor and a scientific study of air quality in London. His concern about pollution was prescient, revealing an early awareness of acid rain. Calling the fogs "heavy, filth-laden," he wrote, "I have noticed the kind of fog which makes your eyes smart is no friend of the begonia when in flower. It is a laid down fact that pure white land or sea fogs do not injure plants of any kind. But the real London fog is full of sulphuric acid, and this acid, being soluble in the water that condenses on the plant leaf, attacks...the leaf (etc.)..." For this however, he also had a solution, suggesting that the leaves be syringed with pure rain water.

With the publication of *How To Grow Begonias* he took another stab at respectability and another step away from show business. The move was so complete now that that same year, when an extensive biography of him was published in promotional material for a gold mining company of which he was second vice-president, no direct mention was made of his entire show-business career—he was deemed an explorer, financier, author, world traveller, linguist, land owner and mining expert, a personage of "world-wide reputation." And just a few years later his

own son listed him on his marriage certificate as an
author and inventor.

Things had changed so much for him by 1897 that he
began considering leaving England, the country in which
he had built his great impresario's reputation. Perhaps he
was beginning to feel his age and wanted to go somewhere
to settle down, or maybe he had just been sitting still for
too long in Forest Hill. He was thinking of returning to
Canada, where he had had no permanent residence since
his early twenties. He was patenting more and more
inventions in Canada and the gold mining company which
he joined had its mines in British Columbia.

The Rossland Gold Mining, Development and
Investment Company was formed about 1896 with an
impressive roster of directors. The president was J.E.
Ellis, owner of a huge jewellery business in the heart of
downtown Toronto, member of the Royal Canadian Yacht
Club, the Granite Club and the Toronto Board of Trade, in
other words, someone extremely well placed in Canadian
society. His first vice-president was the Honourable
William Pugsley, Q.C., former Speaker of the House and
Solicitor-General of the province of New Brunswick; the
solicitor was an important Toronto corporate lawyer and
their secretary was the treasurer of Dominion Telegraph.
Their list of 600 subscribers included financiers from
Europe and the U.S., as well as a dentist from Hamilton
named Rennsalaer W. "Mannie" Hunt. Third in the company behind Ellis and Pugsley was G.A. Farini Esq.,
Capitalist, of London, England.

In his photograph in the company's eight-page promotional brochure he looked out at the camera from under a
white felt hat, adorned in a luxurious tie and diamond
stick-pin. His moustache was snow-white, and his hair
was grey. "He is known on the other side of the ocean as a
shrewd financier and a successful promoter of successful
companies; in fact, whether by good luck or management,
or perhaps a little of both, everything he has been connected with has made money both for himself and the
shareholders." They were careful to point out that he was

a Canadian and spoke of his extraordinary personality
and presence, "... (he) is in every way a substantial man,
with quick perception, great force of character and a
suavity of manner that has greatly contributed to his
business successes."

Rossland, British Columbia sits in a basin at the bottom
of Red Mountain in the Rocky Mountains just a few miles
south-west of Trail and a few miles north of the American
border. There was essentially no population there until
the late 1880s when a few prospectors, drawn by gold discoveries nearby, began seeing signs of possible strikes. By
1893 a ramshackle little town had grown out of the mountains as gold-rush settlers headed to this nearly inaccessible area. Within five years more than 7,000 people lived
there, fortified by forty-two saloons. Railway lines were
run in, a smelter was built and in 1897 nearly one-quarter of a million dollars in dividends was realized. During
the five years following 1894, nearly 400,000 ounces of
gold was mined at a value of over seven million dollars. In
the mid-'90s large outside interests became involved in
some of the better mines there and many of them were
based in England. Farini, with connections both in
Canada and England, and his ear to the ground for financial investments and excitement like a gold rush, picked
up on Rossland as it approached its great boom. It has
been said that after he left England he went to the
Klondike Gold Rush in the Yukon (1897-98), the
grandaddy of all rushes; his involvement in the Rossland
ventures may be the source of that story. A number of people made money from Rossland and the town's prosperity
lasted for a couple of decades, but it is doubtful that
Farini's company, as well-heeled as it was, with a pur-
ported capital stock of $2,500,000, became particularly
rich. It does not appear to have made him fabulously
wealthy, nor did it do him in. It was just another adventure in his new business career.

By the time Farini reached his sixtieth birthday in the
summer of 1898, he and Anna had made up their minds to

move to Toronto. In August they reached an agreement to
sell many of their household possessions and some time
between that autumn and spring of 1899 they vacated
Dartmouth Lodge and England for good. He left what
must have seemed like an entire lifetime behind. But
despite his advancing age and the fact that his reputation
had been made in the time of swinging trapezes, human
cannonballs and lost cities, Farini would not be left
behind with it. In every decade of his life he made
changes. And now, coming to Toronto, he changed again
and found new fields to conquer.

When he sailed from London one of the most popular
novels (and plays) of the day was George Du Maurier's
Trilby, starring the dark, bearded Svengali, who deviously
manipulated a young female performer from behind the
scenes.

CHAPTER 25

Inexhaustible

*"Perhaps the most exotic Canadian invention
ever conceived..."*
J.J. Brown, *Ideas in Exile*

*"Friend, you don't know how good some of
your pictures are and how bad others are."*
F.M. Bell Smith to G.A. Farini

Toronto at the end of the nineteenth century was a very different place from the colonial town the swashbuckling young Signor Farini visited in the winter of 1864. For one thing its population had more than quadrupled, reaching beyond 200,000. Now it was a sprawling young metropolis with suburbs stretching out in all directions, stone and steel buildings reaching as high as ten storeys, electric street cars and asphalt-paved roads. Its huge department stores, like Eaton's and Simpson's on Yonge Street, had electric elevators and thick mail-order catalogues that went nationwide. The city was no longer just a consumer centre for the surrounding countryside; now it made things, mass-produced them in fact, and had become the money-capital of central Canada, growing half-a-dozen major banks and sprouting three stock exchanges (to some degree a response to gold rushes). And yet in many ways it was still an old-fashioned place, constantly returning Conservative members at election time, dubbed "Toronto the Good" for its many churches, and able to only narrowly defeat an 1897 plebiscite to disallow the use of streetcars on Sundays. Careful British ways and morals still prevailed.

But despite that particularly unFarini-like ethic,
Toronto's increased cultural activities and its financial-
world boom made it a liveable city for him and Anna. Now
there were art societies, world-renowned choirs, and the
beginnings of a Conservatory of Music; there were new
venues for legitimate theatre and vaudeville, a growing
literary network, and a whole society centred around the
expanding University of Toronto. Finally Farini could live
near home and still do what he wanted: speculate on stock
exchanges, search for financial opportunities, take art
classes with good teachers, test his inventions, and watch
over his gold mining company; and Anna would not feel
too much among the philistines: teaching music, joining
the Conservatory, being involved in ladies' clubs, and circulating in Toronto's increasing German population.

G.A. Farini was almost a different person in Toronto.
Hector Charlesworth, a noted Canadian journalist whose
father had lived in Port Hope, ran across him one day in
1910 in the lobby of a Toronto hotel and, knowing of
Signor Farini by legend, was stunned by his appearance:

...a fine looking, dapper stranger, hearing the clerk
address me by name, accosted me and asked me if I were
a relative of H.G. Charlesworth. On being told that I was
his son, he asked me whether I had ever heard him mention Signor Farini, the wire walker, and revealed his identity with that once famous being. His real name was
William Hunt. He gave the suggestion of a retired manufacturer rather than of one who had thrilled thousands in
many parts of the world by his feats...

During their eleven-year stay in Toronto, Farini aged
from sixty-one to seventy-two. His hair, always carefully
parted and slicked off his forehead, turned greyish white,
and he grew his beard again, though this time it came in
completely white and was judiciously pruned. Wrinkles
and creases appeared on his face for the first time. He still
loved to dress well, though not quite as loudly, showing a
fondness for vests and high collars. Now his spectacles

hung from a string and were tucked into his coat pocket, giving him a sort of intellectual look. He was as active as ever, a man of quick movements and thoughts, exuding an air of health and vitality. His was now an outgoing, expansive personality, impressing people as someone who was hard to keep up with, someone who was always pushing himself to learn more, about everything.

And one of the things he wanted to know more about was boats. To be more specific, a particular boat: a huge, cigar-shaped steel monstrosity once called "the most exotic Canadian invention ever conceived."

Though there is some debate about who first came up with the idea for Knapp's Roller Boat, and Farini's own claim will be duly examined, it would be unfair to not give the lion's share of the credit to the man whose name the bizarre steam ship bore, Frederick Augustus Knapp.

Knapp was a descendant of a distinguished family of United Empire Loyalists. Born in 1854 in Prescott, Ontario, a little town halfway between Montreal and Kingston on the St. Lawrence River, he was educated in private schools, may have spent some of his youth in Port Hope and in 1877 graduated with a law degree from McGill University in Montreal. He practised in that city for a few years but eventually brought his firm home to Prescott. An active, muscular man, his determination evident on his strong, clean-shaven face, he was creative by nature, and like many men in the age of Edison, was obsessed with the idea of inventing something that would change the world. In the early 1890s he thought he found it.

Being a successful solicitor with international clients, Knapp frequently crossed the Atlantic. Inherently impatient, he started thinking about how the long trip could be accomplished quicker. It occurred to him that if a boat were invented which went over the waves rather than ploughing through them it would be much more efficient than anything then in use. This idea slowly evolved into his plan for a "roller boat," a steam-powered ship with a revolving outer shell, which would be borne over the waves at high speed. He constructed a nine-foot-long, three-foot-diameter model in the shape of a cylinder and took it to Glasgow to demonstrate it to naval architects. As a model it worked well, so well that at a proportionate rate a full-scale boat would achieve a speed of 200 miles per hour! Such a vessel would change the world as it was known in the 1890s, allowing passage of the Atlantic in less than a single day; it would also make its inventor fabulously wealthy. But Scottish industrialists were reluctant to back him and it wasn't until 1897 that he secured the support of Ottawa financier George Goodwin, who gave him $25,000 to build his first boat. In the spring of that year construction began at Polson's Iron Works near a wharf in Lake Ontario, at the foot of Frederick and Sherbourne streets in Toronto. The press soon got wind of what was happening and speculation was rife throughout that summer about the huge tube of steel taking shape in the shipyards. By the first week of September they were ready to unveil it and at 6:30 on the evening of the 8th, in front of a large crowd that had been gathering throughout the day, it was lowered on a soapy slide and rolled into the bay, sending up a great wave that splashed the cheering spectators. Many expected it to sink immediately, but it rolled over and stayed afloat, drawing two feet into the water.

The Toronto papers gave the roller boat extensive coverage: printing drawings of the boat as it was dropped into the water, explanations of its design and biographies of Knapp. Soon papers throughout the country joined in, some presenting the boat as Canada's first great contribution to the world of technology, something which would boost her international prestige and help effect a kind of coming of age. But many scientists and naval men expressed the belief that it would never do what its inventor claimed it could.

Knapp's Roller Boat was 110 feet long and 22 feet in diameter, tapering at either end to a 12-foot width. It was an annular cylinder, in other words one made out of (steel) rings; it was to roll over the waves sideways and had flanges or paddles riveted to its exterior to aid the rolling action. At each end was a steam engine with a boiler, set on a weighted (15-ton) platform. The engines powered a huge driving wheel, which in turn powered a system of intersecting cogs that caused the shell of the boat to revolve. To keep the engines horizontal and prevent them from revolving with the boat, the weighted platforms under the engines were placed on four driving wheels. Knapp was fond of saying that the principle of the boat and its movement was the same as the "squirrel in the cage." It was his feeling that the shape of the boat and its buoyancy would cause it to pick up speed as it moved over the waves, and when its rolling motion was aided by great steam power and paddles it would reach unprecedented speeds. Knapp's original design had an inner shell which remained stationary and a single engine in the centre, but several engineers persuaded him to make alterations.

When it was first dropped into the water the platforms and engines had not been installed. It took over a month to do this, get everything operating satisfactorily, and find fitting weather for a trial. By mid-October there were constant rumours that the boat was about to make its maiden voyage and crowds often gathered in anticipation of the great event. A well-dressed, eccentric-looking man in a white beard was often seen conferring with Knapp: author, adventurer, financier and inventor, G.A. Farini. He may have been the co-inventor of the roller boat, though how much he had to do with it prior to 1897 is unclear. It was certainly his sort of thing: a bold, hair-brained idea about water, power and steam engines. If Knapp used a principle first conceived by Farini, Farini did not seem to challenge him on it (at least at first), and stayed so much in the background that his name was only briefly mentioned by the press (and then often misspelled). Knapp needed efficient steam engines to make his invention work and Farini's were exceptionally powerful.

The engines were started on the 16th and the commotion caused by their hissing and steam and smoke belching out led many to believe that a trial run was beginning, but it wasn't until two days later that the boat made its first test run, a tentative little trip before a large crowd, within the slip between two docks. Only ten passengers were allowed on board, and there was speculation about their safety. "Mr. G.A. Farina," the only one without an obvious reason to be there, was seen standing his ground on one deck. That same day he gave Knapp $500 for a half per cent share in any prospective company, his first investment, their agreement hastily written on Toronto College of Music stationery.

Though the shell revolved on the first try and the boat moved, it wasn't until the 21st, on a clear day with temperatures in the mid-50s that the boat was towed out into the bay by a little steamer to give a real performance on the calm water. What followed was a smashing debut. The Toronto *Evening Telegram*, like all the other papers, thought they were witnessing history.

> In the presence of thousands of spectators and surrounded by a flotilla of small craft, the famous roller boat yesterday afternoon demonstrated its claim to be classed among steamships. It rolled up and down the centre of the bay several times, and was cheered on all sides. Every available vantage point along the wharves from Berkeley to Bay street was occupied, and the roofs of the factories along the Esplanade were black with crowds who had gathered, anxious to see the roller boat make its first trip. All day thousands of persons had fairly besieged the Polson shipyards and clamoured to know when the boat was going out.

What an amazing sight it must have been! A huge steel cylinder looking like something from another age, a monster of some sort (called "a gigantic stovepipe" by the *Globe*), rolling about in Toronto harbour for over an hour, groaning loudly as it revolved and surrounded by a navy of little ships saluting it with their whistles like little siblings in awe of their big brother. But despite the acclaim, it never achieved more than seven revolutions per minute (less than 10 miles per hour), one of its paddles snapped off, and when its frolicking was over it was towed back to the dock. Knapp pronounced himself pleased, insisting that his principle had been proven. And it had. But the problem of increasing its speed and making it manageable loomed on the horizon. Knapp acted as though these things were merely the next steps. They were mountains he would never climb.

The following week the *Evening Telegram* featured a political cartoon on its front page depicting the Premier of Ontario, A.S. Hardy, holding his sides with laughter as he watched his Conservative opponent James Whitney in "Whitney's Roller Boat," trying to make good speed on political waters. "Roll along, Jim," taunts Hardy, "but you'll never make the port of Office on that craft."

But Knapp, and Farini, kept trying, insisting that they were taking things easy with the boat and everything was according to schedule. Many others also believed things were going well, as evidenced by the number of people who wrote to the papers claiming that the principle on which the boat was based was actually their invention. One man even put his small tin model in the bay and demonstrated it. On the 27th Knapp sent the big boat out for its final trial of the season. He equipped it with more paddles and flanges and it made better speed, and the addition of a rudder made it much easier to steer. In fact, it out-performed the supposedly efficient little steam cruiser which towed it, to such a degree that the big ship was eventually untied and sent out into the bay on its own and later returned to dock without assistance. It seemed like a step forward. But afterward Knapp as much as admitted to reporters that this boat looked like a failure, not due to any fault in its main principles but because he had allowed others to persuade him to put two engines at the ends rather than one in the centre. He announced that he would build another roller boat, more than twice the size of the first, place the engine in the centre and take it across the Atlantic at high speed. Where he would get the money was another question. But G.A. Farini was a staunch ally, and he had capital to burn.

On October 30th *Scientific American* featured the boat under the headline "The Roller Boat Problem," expressing doubts about it. In November they published another article, complete with a large drawing of the boat in Toronto harbour, but still maintaining their reservations. And their scepticism continued, despite a long letter from a Knapp ally which appeared in the December issue claiming that the boat would not be bogged down by carrying water along its surface ("skin friction") the way the journal's writers had insisted, but would reach such speeds that it would not draw into the water at all. The editor, though fascinated by the idea, was unconvinced. (The magazine erred when they presumed "skin friction" was a fatal defect, but many of their other concerns, like their belief that it functioned like a wall against the wind, proved valid.)

After the first trials Knapp set up a joint stock company called the Knapp Ocean Navigation Company Limited and had a lavish photographic portrait taken of himself and his boat. On January 10, 1898 he wrote to Farini in England, anxious to know when they could meet in New York, full of optimism about larger ocean vessels, and detailing why *Scientific American* was wrong. He seemed nearly desperate to keep "Mr. Farini" on his side, and told him, "Now this will beat any gold mining schemes and is worth a 'big' push on your part." That spring the roller boat was eased into Toronto harbour again and even taken through the Eastern Gap out into Lake Ontario. It seemed to perform satisfactorily and received more attention, including a front-page article in the Toronto *Evening Star*. But really it showed no improvement over the previous year. Knapp again made it clear that he considered this boat just a beginning. He intended to take it to Prescott immediately and start building his gigantic new ocean vessel according to his own plans. But the boat was left in Toronto all year.

By the spring of 1899 the Farinis were well settled in Toronto at 631 Church Street. This north-central part of the city was neither particularly upper crust nor working class. Anna taught piano and Farini pursued various interests, getting involved with more gold-mining companies (he invested $1,000 in New Deer Park Gold Mining Company of Rossland that year) and working on the roller boat. At census time he listed himself as a "mining engineer."

His father, who had been in failing health for some time (and had experienced some mental problems) died on April 10th. He was in his eighty-fifth year and his death did not come as a great surprise. Farini no longer bore deep grudges against him, and his passing was an unpleasant welcome home. Though Thomas Hunt's finances were not in the best of shape, he had done reasonably well for himself, fathering a mostly successful family, and leaving behind two small brick homes on Baldwin Street in Port Hope for his young widow. The family made sure he had a large funeral, conducted at the house by the rector of venerable St. John's Anglican. The casket was borne to Canton and he was buried near Hannah, across the road from the spot where little Willie had been the scourge of the log school house in the woods.

But Farini's fast-paced life didn't slow. When Knapp returned from Chicago in May, after trying to convince investors there of the efficacy of his scheme, he found Farini waiting for him, ready to get on with things both financially and otherwise. They decided to go for broke and make the long trip to Prescott on the roller boat. There would be four passengers: an engineer, a fireman, Knapp manning one engine and Farini the other. At 7:20 a.m. June 9th they left Polson's on their dangerous journey. The *Evening Star* said it "will be watched with more than ordinary interest." Little did the passengers know what awaited them.

Their vessel set out at a lumbering pace and several hours later was spotted only a few miles east of the docks. Then its pace picked up a little, not anything near the rate that Knapp had predicted (he thought it would cover the 200-plus miles in less than forty-eight hours), but it made some progress, rolling along as loud as fifty trains, a huge steel rolling-pin crashing over the waves. By late in the afternoon they were twenty-five miles east of Toronto, approaching Frenchman's Bay near the town of Whitby. Here things started to unravel, and the crew never recovered.

G.A. Farini,
Toronto businessman.

Mechanical problems stalled the boat and brought about a need for more coal, forcing Farini and Knapp to make a dangerous three-hour, seven-mile dash for shore in a little rowboat. But even with repairs and more coal, it still made little headway the next day and they decided to ground it near Bowmanville. They tied it to a tree and headed into town, past places where Willie Hunt had lived and played. Eventually a tugboat towed it down river to Prescott, but in the meantime fascinated crowds gathered at Mann's Point to stare at this futuristic ship. Farini headed off to Port Hope where he informed the press the boat was superb, far superior to any other in existence, and with adjustments would revolutionize shipping. Knapp told the same story in Prescott. *Scientific American* published a fourth and final piece about it, this one much shorter, and more decisive in its criticism.

It stayed at Prescott for the next few years while Knapp had it refitted, placing his engine in the centre, adding a stationary interior area which could accommodate passengers, and running paddles along the full length. But when Knapp took it out for a few tests runs its improvement was minimal. Two great drawbacks remained: it was terribly slow and nearly unmanageable.

In February 1901 Knapp was interviewed by the
Montreal Star. He told them that even with his changes
he did not expect the boat to attain more than six to eight
miles per hour, but insisted that it would use much less
power than regular steam boats and could even accommodate four hundred passengers. It would be employed to
ferry people across the St. Lawrence from Prescott to
Ogdensburg, New York and back, a distance of about a
mile, or a ten-minute ride. But the main thrust of his
interview was that this boat was just a preliminary—his
future plans called for a mammoth ocean roller boat, perhaps as large as 800 by 200 feet! It was to travel at twelve
knots per hour and would carry four million bushels of
grain! The cargo, or huge numbers of passengers, would
sit on three large platforms in the stationary interior.
With it he intended to "divert the trade of the whole North
American continent through Canadian channels, and so,
secure the greater portion of the trade of China and Japan
for the Canadian route." He envisioned a fleet of enormous roller boats traversing the world's oceans.

The original, modified boat saw service as a ferry, but
the larger boat, projected to cost a half million dollars,
remained a dream. By 1904 the original was brought back
to Toronto and had part of its outer shell removed and the
engine refitted in the stern so it could function as a sort of
cylindrical barge. For a few years it conveyed freight on
the lake, notably for the Eastern Coal Company and even
crossed the Lachine Rapids near Montreal.

Farini remained very much involved with the boat
despite its ups and downs, and purchased stocks in the
various companies directly involved with the project: in
1904 he bought into both the Knapp Ocean Navigation
Company and the Lakes Transportation Company, and in
1906 he invested in Eastern Coal. But there seemed to be
trouble brewing in the Knapp-Farini relationship. In June
1905 Knapp unaccountably gave Farini 100,000 shares in
the Canadian Tubular S.S. Oil Company, in November he
allowed him to build his own "tubular boat" and in
December he transferred 3,000 one-hundred-dollar shares

to him. All of these moves, and contractual phrases like
"to concede to Guillermo Antonio Farini the privilege of
building," "for services rendered" reflect a pattern of con-
cession to Farini on Knapp's part. There were also conditions attached to their contracts, like Farini's agreeing to
not operate his boat above the Welland Canal and not
carry freight on it at a rate less than Knapp's. But why
were they splitting apart like this, and what was Knapp
compensating Farini for? The answer came late in 1905.

In December Farini applied for a British patent for
"Improvements in and connected with the Hulls of Ships."
In his specifications he described his invention as "a boat
of a single tube from stem to stern." This invention was
not strictly a roller boat—it concerned the strengthening
of a tubular-shaped boat by the use of interior beams. In
1907 he took out two Canadian patents and one in the
U.S. Though Knapp outwardly insisted that Farini's
patents were invalid, he continued to try to appease him
by handing over parts of the companies. Farini's record as
an inventor, his almost day-to-day involvement in the project from its early days and the possibility that they had
known each other prior to the construction of the first
roller boat, when combined with these patents and
Knapp's eagerness to solve the problem, indicate that
Farini may have suggested at least the shape of the boat,
and possibly more. It is important to note that Knapp's
Roller Boat, according to design, could not have worked
without a cylindrical shape.

In 1907 Knapp officially agreed that Farini held valid
patents and they signed a contract to have some of them
assigned to Knapp in exchange for "seventy-five one thousand dollar shares" in the invention (he also agreed to
give Farini $1,000 per season of the earnings brought in
by another roller boat). The following year Knapp received
$75,000 from Farini for another 75/1,000 share in the
invention, giving Farini a total of 15 per cent, plus whatever holdings he had in the companies. The solution to
their differences, at least publicly, was that the roller boat
was Knapp's invention, with a little help from Farini.

But all the machinations were for nought. The life of
the once-famous roller boat was drawing to a close. Late
in 1908 it collided with a steamer and was severely dam-
aged. The minor cost of repairs seemed too much for this
inferior version of the boat, so they sold it for $595, appar-
ently to someone who intended to use it for scrap metal.
And the costly dream of the big roller vessel, even too
costly for Farini, was never realized, leaving just speculation as to whether it ever would have worked.

The prime minister at the time, Sir Wilfrid Laurier,
had said that the twentieth century belonged to Canada.
The roller boat, conceived near the beginning of the century, might have been a symbol of that hope. But instead
it lay near a wharf at the foot of Parliament Street in
Toronto after 1908, never collected by its buyer, slowly
rusting, until it sank several feet to the bottom of the lake;
it sat there for decades, a little better than half visible, a
symbol of an idea never realized. In the late 1920s, when
city workers came with a dredge to fill in the harbour
lands southward, it was completely covered over and by
the end of the twentieth century it was buried under rail
or concrete, perhaps fittingly deep beneath the Gardiner
Expressway. Frederick Knapp died at age eighty-eight in
1942 at Prescott, still convinced of the usefulness of his
roller boat; in 1923 he tried to invent an automobile based
on the same principle.

Many were the estimates of how much money was sunk
into this bizarre scheme. It was said for example, after
Farini's death, that he invested $125,000, an extraordi-
nary sum in those days. Friends commented at that time
that he cared nothing for money and could have been a
"multi-millionaire," except that he gave "numerous fortunes" away on weird and wonderful schemes. The roller
boat idea thrilled him, so the investment, whatever the
cost, was worth it. It has been implied by some that Farini
essentially lost his life's fortune on Knapp's Roller Boat.

During his first years back in Canada, Farini also had his
son to worry about. In the spring of 1899 Corporal William

Leonard Farini was called into active service with the
Durham Light Infantry on the central-western coast of
Africa. He landed at Burutu, Nigeria and soon saw duty in
the Ashanti region of present-day Ghana. Before he
returned in 1900 he was awarded the Ashanti Medal for
bravery. His exploits were such that they were mentioned
in the London papers and an English friend of Farini's
called his attention to it. Not long afterward, Farini apparently feeling his son had redeemed himself (bravery
always impressed him), a reconciliation occurred. In
December William was married in London and returned to
northern Nigeria. Farini continued in close contact with
him, so close that William's momentary disappearance a
short while later caused him considerable distress and
moved him to write urgent letters to the Colonial Office,
afraid that he had been killed. William would retire from
the army and Africa in 1909 at age thirty-eight, due to
temporary health problems exacerbated by tropical
weather. He then moved to the south-eastern Irish countryside, where Farini's first grandchild, Henry, was born in
1901, followed by another, William, in 1904 and a granddaughter in 1911, whose name, Anna, was a sure sign that
all was well between the two Farini families. William
would later move to Ormskirk, just north of Liverpool,
where he worked for years for the Royal Army Ordnance
Depot. It is interesting that he chose to live in such far-off
places, perhaps shielding himself from the glare of his
father's life and expectations. He is remembered by his
descendants as a kind man with a strict moral code.

Throughout Farini's eleven years in Toronto he continued
to buy into various companies, concentrating his interest
on mining concerns. In this he was not unique: this was
the age of mining fever and news about gold, silver, coal,
etc. filled the Toronto papers; but the amount of money he
speculated with was not ordinary. He invested, at the very
least, $35,000, and purchased well over 15,000 shares in
Moss Empires, Ashnola Smelter, Gowganda Mines Ltd,
Elk Valley Coal and Coke, Twin City Coal, Laurie Silver

Mines and others. When these investments are added to the money he spent on the roller boat, it becomes obvious that money was not a concern for him in those days. It is also evident that none of his investments returned huge profits.

He did more in Toronto than pursue inventions, investments and mining speculation. One of his other interests began in 1903 and lasted for two years: he managed a firm which manufactured whips, first called the Standard Whip Company and then the Toronto Whip Company. It is hard to know why he took up such a profession—perhaps he found there was one hour out of twenty-four when he had nothing to do.

In 1903 the Farinis moved to 50 Churchill Avenue, in the new western suburbs of the city, just north of Dundas Street and a few blocks east of Dufferin. It was a three-storey, semi-detached brick home, not particularly large, but certainly sufficient for the two of them. The neighbourhood was full of middle- and upper-middle-class people, many in the manufacturing trades. Anna continued to teach music here and seemed to be getting on in Edwardian Toronto society: she had joined the Conservatory of Music and was a founding member of the Heliconian Club (in 1909), a ladies' arts group. Their friends were generally from the professional classes: engineers, doctors, professors, financiers, and eccentrics like Knapp, Lu and Edith from Bridgeport, the Hunts from Hope Township, and especially Mannie Hunt, a dentist in Hamilton. The Farinis were people of refined, continental tastes, or at least they tried to give that impression, and their home, their conversation and their activities were full of music and art.

When Farini moved to Toronto he had been interested in painting for over a decade, although he had not done a great deal to cultivate the interest. Almost as soon as he arrived he started studying and by the time he left in late 1910 had virtually set aside all his other occupations. He was consumed by a desire to become the best artist he could possibly be, and that desire never waned for the rest of his life.

In a way, Farini was always an artist. He was an
exhibitor: a man with an aesthetic eye, given to displaying himself and his protégés in colourful costumes and
spectacular settings; he painted fantastic images with creations like Krao the Missing Link or Zazel the Human
Cannonball; it was no accident that Lulu chose photography as a profession, and was skilled both as a musician
and an artist. Proof that Farini's scientific, mechanical
mind was by no means bereft of aesthetic sensitivity was
borne out by his interest in begonias. "...No one knows but
those who have tried it," he wrote in his book, "the pleasure it is to watch the formation and opening of the first
flower of a seedling!"

He always claimed that he essentially couldn't draw
until late in life and only took up art when someone else
spotted his innate abilities and encouraged him.
Apparently he was on board an ocean liner coming back
from Australia and New Zealand, some time in the 1880s,
bearing his collection of ferns and seaweed which he had
mounted, when the wife of an English captain saw his creations and asked if he were an artist. He was flabber-
gasted at such a suggestion but the woman was so
convinced of her instinct about him that she asked him to
make a wood carving for her. This he endeavoured to do,
failing at first, but keeping at it with typical indefatiga-
bility until, using just his pocket knife, he created a
rooster and owl which delighted the Captain and his wife.
Although Farini likely could have made nearly anything
he put his mind to, somehow that experience stayed with
him and slowly the desire to paint grew. He started painting regularly in the late 1890s (often using begonias for
subjects) and may have taken a few lessons.

But his real education began in Toronto. At first he went
to a technical school to get a grounding in drawing, following his meticulous method of beginning with the funda-
mentals. In 1901 he enrolled in classes with well-known
Toronto artist F. McGillivray Knowles, and later studied
with another famous Canadian painter, Owen Staples.
Knowles had apprenticed in Europe under several masters,

before returning to Toronto in the late 1890s to open his
school, an enchanting place full of antiques, paintings and
well-known citizens and artists, who constantly popped in
to the "open-house" studio. Knowles was interested in
music, literature, travel, yachting and shooting, and many
in his wide circle of friends were similarly cultured. The
school, which offered design, ceramics and life classes as
well as painting, quickly acquired an enviable reputation.
His wife was also a good artist and a musician and they
were certainly a couple with whom to be seen in Toronto.
Knowles, who specialized in marine landscapes and portraits was said to be a kind and decent man, but with a
quick temper which he could suddenly unleash on a student. Farini once wrote that art instructors should encourage their students, not constantly criticize them, and may
have been referring to Knowles when he recalled that he
once nearly struck a teacher for a critical outburst.

Knowles, and Staples after him, were part of the dominant school of Canadian art of the time, the realists
(artists identified with this school were not always strict
realists). An extraordinary amount of experimentation
was occurring in Europe, but Canadians, perhaps typi-
cally, stayed the conservative course and kept away from
abstraction. Nearing seventy, this suited Farini perfectly.
His many theories about art, recorded in notes, were cat-
egorical. "All art is a visible expression of nature," he
declared, "...as seen, felt and imagined by the artist.
Fortunately all artists do not feel, see or imagine alike."

In addition to drawing nature as he saw it, his second
preoccupation as an artist was with colour. Because of his
scientific nature he was fascinated by the physical reality
of colour and loved to write about light waves and their
absorption and reflection in objects (which allows us to see
colour). "Colour is a power," he wrote, "a sovereign source
of charm, and one may say that without it nothing can be
completely represented." He also liked to theorize about
the symbolism of various colours, and felt strongly about
contrasting and juxtaposing them, maintaining there was
a wrong and a right way to do it, and the right way was

the one that clashed the least, or most resembled nature. He even went so far as to write at length about the colours of hats women should wear to complement their hair, eyes, etc. Farini was a supremely colourful man, and this fascination was apropos.

Part of his criticism of modernists grew from his feeling that they practised an unnatural use of colour, but Farini's art is marked by unusual colours (often reds and purples), at times loud and bold, and strange colour juxtapositions, like his painting of a pure white cat on a startling purple background.

He once wrote that "[The imagination] is the power that rules the world, without which science would be useless and history have no meaning." But his sense of how one acquired that creativity was decidedly scientific: he insisted there were no "royal roads" in art nor such intangible ideas as "inspiration and atmosphere"; instead, as always, he believed in hard work, practice and a developed sense of imagination. "Artists," he scoffed, "have talked more nonsense about art than any class of men."

Many of his opinions betrayed his Victorianism, at odds with the modern views of the twentieth century. But this was not always true. Farini, the student of life, remained always more a student than a master of art. He learned as the years went past and by the time he died had progressed in his opinions (though he hadn't entirely changed them). Given the hysteria that erupted from critics during early post-impressionist exhibitions in France, it is extraordinary that an artist nearing his eighties, born the year after Victoria came to the throne, could learn tolerance. He often wrote about the importance of being open-minded as an artist, cautioning people to respect the fact that one generation usually rejects the next, ad infinitum, and bristled at the practice of expelling rebels from art associations. His own paintings reflected a slow, though not radical, change over time. The earliest ones tended to be mostly landscapes, often of quaint subjects, colours conservatively juxtaposed, while the later ones had bolder colours, and more exotic subjects, like foreign scenes with

"Waiting for the Sultan" by G.A. Farini.

Photo: W. Edward Hunt

unusual people, including one large painting of a voluptuous nude in a harem.

Farini was decidedly not a great painter. His drawing was often crude, possibly a reflection of the fact that he worked quickly, producing an enormous number of canvases over a short career. Occasionally he created an intriguing picture, as though by accident, or because he lingered long enough over it. At a time when most Canadians had never been outside their country, he could paint from memory the face of a peasant from the mountains of Peru or a white slave from Africa. This gave his work whatever power it possessed: imagine a row of paintings of trees or Toronto streets disturbed by a picture of a naked harem girl in a gaudy red and purple tent. The Canadian preoccupation with its landscape sometimes appeared in his work but he was too much a citizen of the world to be bound by the confines of his birthplace. There was also an air of mystery in some of his paintings, like his depiction of a woman on an ox cart, her head turned away from the viewer. The paintings that achieve this are usually the ones that seem almost impressionistic, with a hint of modernism, where one feels the force of his imagination. Often even a bad Farini painting (in other words, quite a few) stands out as somewhat unusual.

In his early days as an artist he learned quickly. By 1902 he had his first exhibition, in association with the Ontario School of Art. In 1905 he presented 105 of his paintings at an art gallery on King Street East, to be auctioned off for the benefit of the Home for Incurable Children and received good reviews from the Toronto press. By 1908 he was in the big leagues.

In that year a "Thumb-Box Exhibition" was held by fifty-eight Canadian artists at Messrs. W. Scott and Sons Galleries on Yonge Street. It was a unique show, presenting only canvases less than a foot square (it was then fashionable to paint on a much larger scale), and free to the public. Reasonable price tags also made it attractive as did its sense of bringing art to the average person, a somewhat novel concept. It was lauded in the press, called by *Saturday Night* magazine "A splendid little art show" and by the *Evening Star* "Something New in the Line of Art Shows." It was also received well by the public, who jammed the gallery from November 5th to 18th and made it an important event. But it wasn't only because of accessibility that the show was a success—the quality of art was exceptional. The greatest Canadian artists of the day exhibited, and there, amongst the notables, were two paintings by "G.A. Farini FRHS, African Explorer, Author, etc." Important painters like Knowles, Staples, F.M. Bell Smith, J.W. Beatty, and E. Wyly Grier showed, as did three Canadian legends, C.W. Jeffreys, G.A. Reid and J.E.H. Macdonald. Jeffreys was to become the great Canadian historical painter and Reid a master of sympathetic realism. Macdonald, just thirty-five, was the most important artist in the exhibition, though it was not evident at the time. Twelve years later, he helped to form the Group of Seven, the most influential school of painting in Canadian history. The fact that Farini was included in the Thumb-Box Exhibition (and it seems a number of artists were rejected) speaks volumes about his acceptance in the art world of Toronto, despite his age and late start.

Though he painted essentially in one style he worked with many different materials, dividing his paints almost equally between oils, water colours and raffaelli. He also learned to sculpt and would produce a number of competent and interesting, though not masterful, sculptures during his lifetime, creating large standing pieces as well as busts and profiles. Old photographs showed him in cluttered studios, surrounded by his prolific work, among which paintings, sculptures and profiles of Anna abounded.

In 1908 he took a studio at 93 Yonge Street just south of King. Here, between Matthews Art Gallery on one side and Shea's (vaudeville) Theatre on the other, he painted, displayed and sold his work. By this time he listed himself in the commercial pages solely as an artist. In fact, so thorough was his obsession with painting that a major motivation for the Farinis' departure from Toronto in December 1910 was so he could study with masters in Europe.

During their time in Toronto Farini appears to have continued his wandering ways. He may have gone to British Columbia at one point (and possibly to other places in the north and north-west in his capacity as a "mining engineer") and certainly went up into unpopulated regions of northern Ontario on sketching trips with Knowles's classes. It was while on one of those class sojourns that he met Charles Trick Currelly, a notable Canadian who would one day found the world-renowned Royal Ontario Museum and become a father of Canadian archaeology. C.T. was still a young man when they met, but his bright, inquisitive mind and aggressive (often liberal) views appealed to Farini. They shared a Port Hope heritage and would continue as good friends until Farini's death, spending many hours together locked in discussions about exotic topics. Currelly's son later said that his father did not suffer fools gladly nor did he like to be wrong, but in Farini he found someone whose intellect and extraordinary experiences he respected. And Farini, in a small way, actually helped the young man's career. About 1902 he gave Currelly some Roman coins he had purchased from peasants in an Italian market years earlier, a rather generous action which seems typical of him. Currelly took these coins to the British Museum in London and their authenticity and the enthusiasm with which they were received helped his reputation with academics there.

Years later Currelly remembered his first impressions of
Farini. He recalled "a small, agile, white-bearded man
who was learning to paint in what seemed to me his old
age... His stories were endless and his descriptions of foreign countries most vivid."

When the Farinis departed Toronto they left behind a
large circle of good friends. A neighbour wrote to them as
they were leaving, expressing her love for them and her
thanks for various gifts they had given her family, including a small painting of a Muskoka scene and some ferns.
She ended by saying that these things would always
remind her of their "bright, treasure-filled room." But sen-
timent was never strong enough to keep Farini anywhere.
He had made up his mind to make himself a better artist
and Anna wanted to live near her family, so by New Year's
Day 1911 they were in Germany. Frau Farini didn't need
to worry about her beloved seventy-two-year-old "Willy":
at home with European languages and manners, his tran-
sition would be smooth.

How long they planned to stay is not known. But it is
certain they did not bargain on war. Farini had been
touched by it before, but the one which would soon encir-
cle him would be fought on a much grander scale; this
now inoffensive old man would soon find himself a pris-
oner behind enemy lines.

CHAPTER 26

Behind Enemy Lines Again

*"During World War I Farini was interned in Germany
so instead of sitting idle he busied himself by writing
a history of the war."*
Sentinel-Star (Cobourg), September 1, 1965

The Germany which the Farinis settled in at
Christmas 1910 was a thriving, confident place,
unaware that disaster was just four years away. Its famous
Prussian-centred army was the world's most feared, and
industry was still growing throughout the Empire (in 1900
it had produced more steel than France and Great Britain
combined). Already known as a place of great philosophers
and thinkers, it was gaining a reputation for its rigorous
educational system. And the arts were flourishing: Berlin,
because of its size and the presence of the court, was still
the cultural centre, but the beautiful city of Dresden, where
the Farinis came to live, continued to grow in stature.

Dresden was the capital of Saxony and the Müllers
were either Saxon or from nearby Silesia. Called the
"Florence on the Elbe," it possessed a fabulous collection
of art treasures, its platzes boasted some of Europe's
finest statuary and its strasses beautiful cultural buildings. It was a city of music, celebrated for its opera house
and company, and the giants of classical music who had
lived there. Outside the city the famed Meissen China
works, controlled by the King of Saxony, added to the
area's artistic reputation. Obviously this magnificent city

of architectural and cultural wonder suited Anna, not only because her family was there (her sister Ottilie and her three children—her parents were now deceased) but because of the music, almost in the very air around them. It was a far cry from the emerging cultural struggles of Toronto. Farini was well suited here too, as the art of painting was not left out in Dresden's pantheon of cultural assets. The city provided excellent art schools, and a great deal of private tutoring, and the opportunity to see examples of almost any sort of art, some of it by masters, was just a short walk from Farini's door. He had several teachers while living here, among them the eminent landscape artist Berthold Paul Forster, who spoke highly of his progress and encouraged him.

Ironically, a few years before he came to Dresden it became known as a major cradle of German Expressionism, one of the new styles he disliked. A group called *Die Brücke* (The Bridge), was formed there in 1905; other ground-breaking young painters like Otto Dix and George Grosz trained in Dresden during Farini's early years in town. Farini was influenced by German painting, but most affected by older artists like Max Liebermann, the greatest German Impressionist, and Heinrich Zugel, whose slightly adventurous paintings of farm animals was perhaps the closest in style to his. These artists, and the excitement in the air about modernism are what edged him away from the highly conservative landscape style he had learned in Toronto. His many paintings of Germany's countryside and its architecture have a less strictly realistic look, appearing a bit dream-like, without strong lines and the minute attention to detail he had previously been taught to maintain. While the younger schools' emphasis on the need for more feeling and subjectivity appealed to him, and his unique tastes in colours had actually leaned in their direction from the outset, his style would remain objective throughout his career, trying for an essential if not exact imitation of nature; he never ventured into anything even remotely abstract. But he did become a sort of conservative Impressionist.

He was fortunate to be in Europe as its art world exploded: Expressionism, Post-Impressionism, Fauvism, Cubism, Futurism and even Dadaïsm were all thrown into the cultural pot and vigorously debated. The fact that his adventurous nature pushed him to visit the galleries to explore these movements at the moment in history when they were having their greatest effect enriched his already rich life.

The first four years the Farinis spent in Germany were happy ones. Willy was free of financial care or business distractions and could spend his time painting, sculpting, and investigating the cultural scene. Anna loved being with her family and because they were well placed and interested in the arts they mixed well with her eccentric husband, and came to feel genuine affection for him. Photographs from that period often show Anna and Willy smiling: in one she is standing in front of a mansion next to a carriage full of elegantly dressed ladies; in another he is posing in the countryside with his paints and easel, snow-white beard trimmed, peering out from under a straw hat, almost comically attired in an aristocratic pin-striped suit and painter's apron; and in another they are together, happy in each other's company. Their great friendship was enhanced by their ability to be independent, as they often went alone on jaunts across Germany.

The circus and the variety stage were no longer a part of his life and he left no evidence of having even attended such shows after the 1890s. Now his tastes, obviously influenced by the Müllers, were more refined, and when they went to hear music it was always classical. In August 1911 they travelled to Bayreuth to hear a production of Wagner's "Parsifal," perhaps conducted by his son Siegfried. In March 1913 they were in Leipzig to see the legendary Polish pianist and composer (and soon to be Premier) Paderewski play, and two months later were in Vevey, Switzerland to hear him again, this time in a tribute to Camille Saint-Saëns, with Saint-Saëns himself wielding the baton. The great French composer and renowned organist had been championed by Liszt many years before, no doubt one reason why Anna was interested in him.

They were constantly on the move during their early German years. Besides concerts, they frequented the theatre and the cinema, and had a great fondness for hiking, often spending hours in the beautiful forests and hills of the region, Anna keeping up with her septuagenarian husband as he picked flowers or wild fruit or stopped to sketch, ever conscious of the salubrious effect of bracing outdoor exercise. They had a few favourite destinations: one was Vevey, a beautiful place at the foot of the alps next to a lake near Lausanne (Anna may have had relatives or a summer home here—Farini had mentioned it in his Kalahari book so he and Anna must have been going there since their courting days). Bad Warmbrunn (Cieplice Slaskie) in German Silesia (now in Poland), ninety miles east of Dresden, was another place they often visited; it was a resort town with a spa and had Müller family connections (her father and sister were buried in the village cemetery); they spent a number of consecutive months there in 1911 and further time in 1912. Berlin, Leipzig, Hartha and Halle were other frequent travel spots.

Their home base was always Dresden. Over the years they had several addresses there, but for the most part lived south of the Elbe in the old part of the city, amongst its beautiful narrow old streets and art treasures. When they were in town Anna devoutly attended services and functions at the city's many Lutheran churches. Farini, no churchgoer, was often on his own, living in Dresden as if he had been a lifelong citizen, playing billiards with relatives and friends at the Café Central, conversing at high speed in German, and attending his art lessons. He was also sculpting much more than in Canada. He once said he found it easier than painting, and may have considered it his most accomplished art. On March 6th, 1914 he wrote to Canadian Prime Minister Robert L. Borden offering a sculpture for display at the San Francisco World Exhibition: it depicted Canada as a "Female Figure" kneeling at the top of the world, pouring wheat. The globe and the figure sat high above a crudely sculpted platform, complete with further carvings and stairs. Borden replied in two weeks saying that the offer was "worthy of consideration."

But three months later a Serbian revolutionary assassinated Archduke Franz Ferdinand, heir to the throne of the Austro-Hungarian Empire, and effectively smashed hopes of anything as trivial as sending a sculpture from Germany to Canada or as significant as the general well-being of the lives of European people. The once-great friendship of the Germans and the English, which had been souring for more than a decade, was brought to complete destruction in a few months and all of Europe, as well as Canada, and later the United States, plunged into the First World War. Like most wars it was confidently entered into by all sides, but became so brutal and lengthy that it would eventually be called a war to end all wars.

And there was Farini, seventy-six years of age, a Canadian of American birth who had lived much of his life in England, trapped behind German lines. There has been much speculation about what he did during the war and how he was treated by German authorities. He was deliberately vague about his activities after he returned home, a not unreasonable approach for a man who had married one of the enemy and stayed with her during the war.

Though Anna's angry April 19, 1917 entry in her diary declared "...we are *interned*!" after the Farinis were instructed to turn in their passports and report regularly to the Dresden police station, German officials never treated them harshly. In some ways Anna was worse off. She had become a U.S. citizen during her stay in North America and was initially ordered to report on a daily basis while Farini, due to his age, only appeared weekly. But before long these restrictions were eased, Anna was allowed to report weekly, and they were even given permission to travel limited distances outside of Dresden, something Farini (still unable to sit still for extended periods) deeply appreciated.

The war didn't really get going until the first week of

August 1914. At first problems just simmered in the
Balkan area, but soon a huge domino effect of war decla-
rations began, caused by alliances that had been formed
over the preceding years. Germany declared war on
France; France, Russia and England declared war on
Germany and on and on it went, until it seemed half the
world was preparing to fight.

The war began auspiciously for Germany as their well-
prepared army charged through Belgium, swept over its
southern border into northern France, and moved forward
until they came almost to the banks of the Marne River.
Plans were even made for how they would divide up
Europe when the war ended, a scant few months in the
future. The Farinis were able to function normally, but
soon, as the Russians stirred on the eastern front, forcing
Germany to take some of its strength away from the west,
things changed. The French, aided more and more by the
English, regrouped, held the line firmly, and the armies
settled into a horrific, bloody stalemate that characterized
the entire war. The two sides dug into trenches hundreds
of miles long, eventually infested with rats and disease,
and slugged it out for four years, butchering each other in
appalling numbers, in useless attempts to gain significant
ground. Rationing started and things became difficult
throughout Europe. Germany, its access to both the seas
and its bread-basket neighbours severely limited, was hit
hard. Shows of wealth, unduly profiting from anything or
giving the impression of having ample amounts of food
were all frowned upon as the nation tried to pull together,
rich and poor. Fairly soon Farini gave up painting lessons.
He and Anna did not suffer from anything remotely like
malnutrition, but their lifestyles changed. Gone were the
trips to Switzerland, and caught within a narrow existence, the death of Anna's dear sister Ottilie in 1916 was
even more difficult to bear. In 1917 when they were
allowed a brief out-of-town holiday in a country pension,
they revelled in eating fresh eggs and cheese. Everything
in their life was more humble—they went to fewer concerts and art gallery openings.

Farini switched his energy to translating. And he proceeded to do so much of it during the war that it was speculated the German government forced him to do it. It was
his practice to write a great deal anyway, probably on a
daily basis. By late September 1914 he was recording
German newspaper accounts of the war in a small black
notebook he used for art notes and the ideas which constantly came in and out of his mind; and by the end of the
year he was spending part of every day translating into
one-hundred-page notepads, and adding a few personal
comments. He also pasted in photographs of prominent
German military people and troops and couldn't resist
translating correspondents' observations about customs
and scenery in foreign lands. He recorded the war on all
its fronts and involving all participants, all the way from
"Turkish Warfare" to Romanian or Russian. Over four
years he filled thirty-seven books, comprising an incredible four-thousand-page account of the First World War
from a German perspective. The pages of these books,
brought back from Germany after the war, tell an intriguing tale. For one thing, they call into question where his
sympathies lay.

It would have been difficult for him truly to take a side,
though it was easy to decide whom he must give the
appearance of supporting. Anna was the love of his life
and the Müller family had been associated with people
who now ran the war. And the robust, no-nonsense
German approach to life and their constant straining to be
intellectual and cultured, suited him. It has been said that
Germany suffered from an inferiority complex: their
efforts to make themselves important, respected, and even
feared were not unlike Farini's own struggles in life. And
Anna's relatives and friends were going off to war, and
some were not coming back, laid low by English or
Canadian bullets. So he had reasons to desire German victory. And yet to do so he had to turn his back on Canada
and on England and the United States, his homeland, his
adopted home and his birthplace. But his translations and
his personal comments show no sympathy for the Allies.

England is blamed for the war and is accused throughout of stupidity, cruelty and all things evil. They are seldom accorded a single victory, while the brave German troops win battle after battle, displaying heroic courage, intelligence, and decency in war. It is hard to know whether he wrote this because he believed it, or because the consequences of being discovered writing even a single word of praise for the enemy would have been fatal. Deep down he likely had no side. His rebellious, wandering nature made him a sort of permanent foreigner; his side had always been the side of adventure, and he had never been overtly political. So he kept busy recording the conflict, waiting for it to end, keeping his mind fit. The war killed his freedom, but couldn't kill his spirit.

Propaganda was honed to a fine art during World War I and nowhere was this more evident than in German newspapers. "The World's War by G.A. Farini" or "Episodes of the World's War, from a German Point of View" reveals that citizens were allowed almost no bad news, but were fed a great deal that was good, and false. In 1914, after three months of war, he reported that even though it had gone on much longer than expected, German losses were just half of their enemies' and their coffers were much fuller; at this rate the "war cannot last more than a half a year." Employing the pronoun "we" for Germany and "enemy newspapers" when quoting Allied presses, he wrote of England spilling blood simply for their trade advantage, illegal agreements they made, the cruelty of their blockade, their selling out the white race to side with Japan; and of the cruel treatment of German prisoners at the hands of the French, Belgians and Russians: having their ears and noses cut off, their throats slit and their eyes put out. One day Farini wrote this rather ironic statement, "The Times (of London) blames the government for their censoring the German accounts, and thereby prevented the English to know the truth, while other countries publish the news intact. Why don't they tell the public the truth?"

The fact that he often quoted foreign newspapers (even

Russian and Serbian) indicates that either the German press used damning enemy comments as a tool to raise patriotism, or that he translated directly from foreign sources.

In 1915, with things at a standstill in the west, the Germans tried to defeat Russia. They made progress but could not finish their sturdy opponents. Two million Russians were killed and yet they still fought back. On June 10th Farini wrote in his book "my birthday—nice and cool—had first strawberries," and in another he pressed an extraordinary fern, beautifully delicate and curving in the shape of a green rainbow.

In 1916 attention shifted back to the bloody western front, where soldiers from both sides fell in staggering numbers in horrific battles at places like Verdun and the Somme. The Allied world, whether it be in London or Port Hope, heard of English, French and Canadian gallantry, but behind German lines Farini found German newspapers declaring that the English sought only political gains in such tragedies and cared little for peace. In another entry a British officer was criticized for a stupid, vainglorious attack that resulted in the slaughter of his own men. "As sportsman the English commander made a success—but as a general who is responsible for the lives of his men he ought to be brought before a court marshall and tried for the murder of thousands." Pools of blood and "heaps of bodies," he reported, resulted from the Englishman's vanity.

Britain's blockade of Germany caused great suffering and Farini often wrote about its cruelty. Only German U-boats could break it but they were held back as too risky for over a year after they sank the ocean liner the *Lusitania*, causing a number of (non-belligerent) American deaths. Early in 1917 the U-boats were unleashed again, the Allies staggered, and Farini dealt in detail with naval successes. But inevitably more American ships were sunk and on April 6th the U.S. declared war on Germany. Their participation would eventually put the final nails in the fatherland's coffin.

In March 1917 Czar Nicholas abdicated the Russian

throne. Farini wrote, "The Russian Czar was captured on his way from Petersburg..." In November a shaky provisional government was brought down by Bolshevik communists. Farini had a much closer view of the revolution than North Americans: "In Russia chaos reigns everywhere, they are broiling in their own fat—no one knows what the next hour will bring forth. No one knows the truth as all the statements are contradictory—But it seems certain that Lenin is master of the situation in Petersburg and his power is hourly increasing." At the time there was little concern in Germany over the policies of the communists, instead, as Farini's notebooks recorded, there was joy because it would hasten that country's withdrawal from the war. "In Petersburg," he wrote, "the Labour and soldier revolution has won the day and Russia is freed from English and French influence."

The Central Powers turned with full force on the Allies on the western front, hoping to smash their exhausted armies before the Americans could arrive; 1917 was the year of Canadian glory, as they fought valiant, horrific battles at places like Vimy Ridge and Passchendaele. Farini reported nothing of his homeland's bravery and anguish. Much of 1918 was merely a race to see if the American military machine could get to Europe before Germany finished off the battered Allies with one final push. On June 10th, as Farini sat down to record more German victories in his books he noted at the top of the page "My birthday—bright sunshine hot—eighty years old." By late summer, with one-quarter of a million American troops landing in Europe every day, it was only a matter of time before Germany saw the futility of continuing. Now almost all of Farini's entries spoke of Allied attacks, repelled time and time again by heroic Germans. On November 9th the Kaiser abdicated and two days later an armistice was signed. In the preceding four years literally millions of men had been killed and wounded.

Defeat and the resulting conditions of the Treaty of Versailles, in which Germany lost land and much capital and felt humiliated by their opponents (who insisted that

they officially claim full responsibility for the war), must
have been terrible for Anna, her family and her friends. In
Dresden, far from the western front and with Poland
between themselves and Russia, the war had never been
on their doorsteps, but the deprivation of mobility, lack of
quality and quantity of food, and reports of the deaths of
friends and loved ones had been with them daily. And
then to have it all end in inglorious defeat! Farini could
not have helped but be hurt, at the very least for his wife
and her family.

But now that the war was over what was he to do? The
war books, which he carefully preserved, no longer took
up his time. Early in 1918 he had started taking art
lessons again. But due to a lack of materials, teachers, etc.
it is doubtful that they were anything like the studies he
had pursued before the war. Now things may very well
have been worse. The Farinis still lived under conditions
of rationing and were not yet allowed to leave the country,
though they were able to move about more freely. Farini,
as always, wanted to *do*, and the Germany which had so
stimulated him ten years earlier now offered very little.
They struggled on through 1919 and into 1920. During
these years a communist revolution was put down, and
shortly thereafter the Weimar Republic was established.
Political uncertainty (lead from the right by people like
young Adolf Hitler) and financial instability hovered over
the Müllers and their relatives daily.
   The Farinis had invested substantial money in stocks
in Germany and it has been speculated that when ruin
came after the end of the war their investments became
almost worthless overnight. The Müllers' wealth would
have also been reduced by the financial instability. Farini
seemed to have less money when he returned home from
Germany, though he was by no means "broke" as some
have said: in fact, the crippling inflation that besieged the
Weimar Republic did not begin until just after he left. One
of Anna's relatives wrote to Willy in 1919, speaking of the
lack of quality food and the "dreadful" value of the mark.

She ended with this comment: "Germany is simply crushed as never country was before."

The Farinis had every reason to want to leave Germany from the moment the ink dried on the Treaty of Versailles. Finally, after applying to the American Commission in Berlin in 1920, they were granted "safe passage" out of the country. Certificates of Identity, which had to accompany each of them on their journey, were issued on September 7th, good for two months. But "G.A. Farini, artist, address Dresden, Date of Birth June 10, 1838, birthplace Lockport NY, stature 5'8", hair white, eyes blue, face oval," did not waste his time. He and Anna fled to Switzerland within weeks. On October 1st they were in Berne, on the 4th his certificate was stamped at the British Consulate in Lausanne where he had to report, and on the 7th they gained passage over the French border into the Doubs region. They crossed France in a day, speeding over the ravaged areas of the country and coming to Calais on the English Channel. Farini had often been to these places, but he must have been fascinated to see them now, after writing about the devastation that had taken place here during the preceding years. Late on October 8th they crossed the Channel and landed in Dover. Though Germany had been home to him, and he had not considered it solely enemy territory, it was probably only then, on English soil, that he felt safe. He was free to move, and free to *do*, and that, to him, was everything. He was eighty-two years old.

CHAPTER 27

Return to Exile

"Oh isn't it awful!"
Evening Guide (Port Hope), January 18, 1929

Though Farini's transit visa indicated that he was to
proceed from Calais to Southampton and from there
across the Atlantic to New York, he did not do this immediately, and instead went north, via his beloved London,
to the little town of Ormskirk near Liverpool to stay with
his son. In London the Royal Aquarium was long gone,
replaced by the Wesleyan Methodist Hall of all things.
Here the League of Nations, the institution which was to
forever prevent another world's war, would soon have its
first meeting, on the very ground where Zazel had been
shot into space.

His stay with William and his wife Harriet was probably not an extended visit, and despite his well-practised
imperturbability it must have been a wrenching time.
Both he and Anna had aged noticeably and his son
(employed at the Royal Army Ordnance Depot in
Burscough, North Ormskirk) was approaching fifty. There
were three grandchildren at home, Henry age nineteen,
William about to turn sixteen and Anna just nine, and he
may have never seen them before. He had certainly never
seen Anna, though when she was born in 1911 he had sent
her a silver egg cup with a spoon and serviette ring. For

nearly a decade he had been out of touch, behind the lines of the enemy, perhaps supporting Germany as it tried to destroy what was precious to his son. Anna likely spent little time out of the house, especially in any situation where she might have to speak and reveal her nationality. She must have felt nearly as imprisoned as Farini had just a short while earlier.

In old age, members of the Farini family in Ormskirk did not retain vivid memories of meeting their strange grandfather. But one story persisted. Early in the visit William took his father to an engineering workshop in Ormskirk to see a friend who was a professional engineer. The work done there, of course, fascinated the old man and instantly he and his son's friend were deep in conversation. Throughout his stay Farini made almost daily trips to offer his new friend suggestions about various engineering problems. Later the engineer told William that he had been disappointed when it came time for Farini to leave, because he sometimes wondered if the old man knew more about engineering than he did himself.

Late in 1920 they boarded an ocean liner for New York. But when they arrived they headed south rather than north to spend the winter in the sunny luxury of Florida, an indication that they were far from broke. Even when it came to holidaying Farini was a pioneer of sorts: he was one of Canada's earliest "snowbirds." Over the next few years he and Anna would several times head south when the snow began to fall. He painted and explored, in what was now a booming state, several Ringling brothers and other circus people among its winter residents.

In the early summer of 1921 they arrived in Hope Township, homeless. And yet they were rich in possessions: valuable Meissen and Berlin china, antiques, expensive furniture, African hunting trophies, and so on. They were two vagabond aristocrats, citizens of the world, who had been in the courts of kings, friends of famous people, and on stage before thousands. Now they came to the Canadian countryside. It must have been strange for Farini to return to the simple, beautiful and still parochial

place of his childhood, more than six decades after he left
in anger, vowing he would make something spectacular of
himself. So much had happened since the moment that
train had chugged out of the little Port Hope station, his
dear mother tearfully waving goodbye. It hardly seemed
that that arrogant young tough with a soul yearning for
adventure was the same man.

In the interim he had done it: he had lived the life of his
dreams.

Now it was back to reality. But where would the elegant, conquering hero live?

At one time Farini had owned great stretches of the
land in the vicinity of Kingston Road in Hope Township.
Two acres short of 800 to be exact, and the five or six
houses and many buildings (including his factories, barns
etc.) that came with it. During a time when one hundred
acres constituted a respectable farm, Farini had had the
equivalent of eight. And as recently as the turn of the century he had also owned urban property (and apparently
an American ranch). But by the time he returned to Hope
he had divested himself of everything but 350 acres, all
within the confines of the township. It was rumoured that
he sold his property while in Germany, in a desperate
attempt to buy his way out of the country, but records
indicate that he let go of his holdings in several transac-
tions in 1888, 1909 and 1913. It was also said that the
Canadian government used some of his land during the
war and he came home to collect the rent due. Both of
these stories make him sound like a patriot imprisoned
behind German lines and when it is considered that he
was returning with a German wife, and that Port Hope
Armistice day the very next year featured the parading of
the Kaiser's effigy and its incineration near Town Hall, it
would be hard to blame him for arming himself with a
good story or two.

By 1921 he did not own any land at the original Hunt
farm on Kingston Road. Since his childhood this area had
seen the erection of a church and a slight clustering of
homes, and was now called Morrish (after a resident). He

still owned 100 acres just north of there, a country stroll
away. In fact the Marshes had built a beautiful brick
house there near a spot known as Bunker Hill and Farini
had considered it a home-away-from-home during his hal-
cyon London days. But the house was occupied and the
Farinis could hardly ask the family to leave, so they
looked to their other holdings. There was a 100-acre package east of Bunker Hill, but here too there were residents.
Further along Kingston Road toward Port Hope was the
last tract of their land: the 150-acre farm known as Locust
Lawn, now sadly without William Marsh, Jr. and Farini's
sister Ann. Its big brick house was occupied solely by
William and Ann's unmarried daughter and son, Lucia
and Tom. The Farinis decided to move in.

Lucia Marsh was sixty years old and Tom fifty-eight.
The offspring of a farmer, they were not filled with the
bold spirit of their great-grandfather Samuel or the entre-
preneurial drive of their grandfather William; they did not
seek fame or glory or want to imprint the Marsh stamp on
the entire countryside, and were content with life on their
quiet farm. Suddenly Farini descended upon them, bringing his aristocratic German wife, his elegant tastes, his
palette and paints, and the stories of his noisy life. From
the moment they arrived, Lucia was concerned. Knowing
something about Anna, she was worried that she and her
brother would overnight be turned into servants in their
own home. While she did not harbour any dislike of her
strange aunt and uncle, she was reluctant to set them up
as royalty in one of her bedrooms. She said little about her
concerns during their first stay, which lasted about five or
six months and swallowed Anna's ignorance of housework
with good grace. Farini himself was little trouble, so anxious was he to be active. He did farmwork, painted, exercised, wrote, and visited friends.

In November the Signor and Madame left for another
stay in Florida, but when they reappeared on Lucia's
doorstep during the last week of April 1922 she decided to
lay down the law. She told them that, regrettably, they
could not continue to make themselves at home for

another extended stay. This created some friction between them but, perhaps surprising, no lasting bitterness (a few years later Farini would rent Locust Lawn to someone else, forcing Tom and Lucia to move into Port Hope). Farini, ever capable and flexible even at 83, merely purchased a huge tent, and set it up in the orchard, and by mid-summer that was where they were living. To say the least it was a strange situation.

The elderly couple also stayed for a while with the Uglow family nearby, on a farm Farini had once owned (for many years operated by his brother Jim). The house and barn overlooked a beautiful little creek on which Farini had built his long-deceased dams and factories. (Miraculously, just a stone's throw away on the old Hunt farm, stood the ancient little brick barn where young Bill Hunt had erected his first high wire.) Here Farini liked to set up his easel outdoors and paint, straw hat and suit on, producing images of the old creek; and late into the night he would tell Billy Uglow incredible stories that made him shake his head in disbelief.

Signor Farini was a legend from another time, and yet here he was, returning in the roaring twenties from deep in the Victorian age. Almost no one could remember seeing him on the rope, and yet they saw him now, striding up Walton Street, chest puffed out, eyes lit up, as agile and full of bounce as a thirty-year-old. When he first reappeared the *Evening Guide* printed an article about him on their front page. "Famous Tight Rope Walker Returns To Home After Many Years Absence" it read, "Although eighty-four years of age [he was eighty-three] he is enjoying excellent health and says he wouldn't mind in the least trying a turn on the rope again."

About the time the Farinis were returning to Hope after their second stay in Florida, 4,000 miles away in London the letters page of the *Sunday Times* was full of speculation about Lulu and Zazel. On March 5th T.P. O'Connor (MP) made casual reference to Lulu and confused "her" with both Zazel and Zaeo, writing of her "...pink blouse and pink tights and a certain fascinating beauty of face" and discussing the attempts to censor her and her costumes. What a deluge he unwittingly let loose! Letters came pouring in from all over the British Isles, not only informing him of his errors, but adding facts, legend and more errors. "Better I had never been born than have written the paragraph last week in which I mentioned 'Lulu,'" he cried. Slowly, over a period of eight weeks the correspondents solved (almost) the identities of all the performers in question and participated in a lively debate about Nellie Farren's burlesque of Zazel's performance. Farini and his role in the "Lulu imposture," the human cannonball act, and the burlesque were much discussed. Even Baldwin was thrown in, one writer insisting that he and Lulu were one and the same. A knighted gentleman felt compelled to take a crack at sorting things out, poems about Farini's protégés were recited, and an Admiral fondly recalled military "bloods" trying to leap into the net to catch Lulu without stumbling, saying he once saw a sub-lieutenant from a naval college tear off his boots and do it to rapturous applause. Finally, at the end of April, opinions still flooding in, the editor put a stop to things by writing emphatically across the bottom of the last letter, "THIS CORRESPONDENCE IS NOW CLOSED." (Some of the letters

Caricature of Nellie Farren as Zazel, 1877.

Mander and Mitchenson

speculated that Zazel was long dead. Nothing was further from the truth. The very next year English author Sir John Squire met the redoubtable Mrs. Rosa Richter Starr in Monte Carlo and found her to be a "dear little old woman" very proud of being the first real human cannonball and having been painted by George Frederick Watts.)

But Farini had turned those pages long ago. He was now a retired gentleman and artist, looking for a proper place to live. Camping on the Marsh farm was great fun for him and offered the challenge of inventing from the moment he cooked his meals in the morning until he made his bed at night, but he knew this was not the place for his elegant, though obviously game wife. And besides, they couldn't go to Florida every winter and he needed a studio. The mere fact that an eighty-four-year-old should not live in a tent likely never crossed his mind. Before long he was looking for a home in Port Hope. His father had lived there for many years and John Hunt was still there, but Farini's residences had always been in the country. Now, as old people traditionally did in Hope Township, he and Anna moved into town. Their first house was an attractive, squarish brick home on the corner of North and Seymour streets, a pretty area near the churches and schools in Englishtown, and not far from the spot where other Hunts had lived and still lived. It had a good-sized back yard and was large for two; there was room for Farini's studio.

Though Port Hope was certainly not the same place Bill Hunt had known as a teenager, it had not grown at the prodigious rate predicted for it in those heady days. Despite being situated at a good spot on a lake harbour and serviced by the railways, it lost out to other centres in the race for a large population and industry. Since Confederation in 1867 most Canadian cities had been thriving. While places to the west like Toronto zoomed up past the half-million mark, Hamilton surpassed 100,000, and to the east Kingston and Belleville grew substantially, Port Hope had added just a thousand citizens after Confederation and almost none since the 1870s. Even arch-rival Cobourg, to their immediate east, kept slightly ahead of them. Why this happened is difficult to pinpoint, but Port Hopers were certainly not aggressive people. They were a self-satisfied lot, many of their upper crust self-conscious about position, "big fish" in their little pond, and not anxious to test the waters of growth. To be the descendant of a United Empire Loyalist or the scion of some nouveau-riche family from the early years was important in little Port Hope. And so the people who might be expected to push them forward just sat there, almost unconcerned about "progress," in their mansions on the hills on either side of the Ganaraska. They smugly enjoyed being "someone" where they told themselves it counted most. There were two newspapers now, the *Port Hope Times* and the *Evening Guide*, suburbs had appeared, some to the east, but most further up Walton, and north from there along Toronto Road toward the township. The stores, many looking much as they did in 1859, still clustered along Walton west of the bridge. The town hall was still there too, just as Signor Farini had left it after he performed his strong-man routine so long ago. And though motor cars dominated the streets, it was not uncommon to see an old farmer in a horse and buggy, or an elderly Port Hoper in a more elegant hansom. It was a quaint little town, as opinionated as it had always been, and just as English and as Protestant as ever.

In other words the attitude Bill Hunt had battled as a young man, the small-minded, "croaking, grumbling" approach to life, was still alive and well. A world where showmen, boast and adventure were frowned upon. But little did Farini care now. He had a sort of amused approach to life in his final years. He had been an energetic little boy, opposed because of his passions; he had ventured into the world to prove that those opponents had been wrong and he had been honest. At times he had taken things too far, and he had been ruthless, and eventually cynical. He had tried to connect Victorians to their emotions and their opposition had been ferocious. Now, at the end of his adventures he had given up fighting them—they were welcome to their lives. He had turned his own life into a wonderful story, and that to him was enough. And in Port Hope of the 1920s, for every old-fashioned croaker who still judged him there was someone who was fascinated: many had not even been alive when he had been the rascal of the county. He drew his close friends from all ranks, though many were close to the Hunt family, or educated individuals and professionals who could engage his mind. His brothers Jim and Jack were there, the latter well settled in Port Hope and a local legend in the horse world, and the former, who lived in Toronto, in the midst of several marriages that would bring him wealth and headaches. Closest was Dr. Mannie Hunt, now in his sixties and located in Toronto, divorced and on his own, a man with a bit of the rascal in him too, a sport who loved to shoot skeet and speculate a little with stocks.

Old Farini was a friendly man, quick to speak to people, often smiling; a consummate gentleman, polite to a fault and possessed of almost courtly manners. But no one ever doubted he thought highly of himself and could be fast and loose with the truth.

So much of his life had been extraordinary, so expert was he at telling tall tales, and so respected by most of his listeners, that he could spin the most outrageous yarns and have them believed. He took great joy in making up fictions and telling them with the utmost seriousness. He once told a doctor friend that he had lost a wife while performing on a high wire over the Thames River, when a boat's mast caught the rope and sent everyone tumbling. And these were the days when he told others he had been the first human being to walk over Niagara Falls on a tightrope, had killed people with a six-gun in the wild west and invented the trick of levitation. Reflecting on his story-book life, he may have sometimes genuinely lost track of the difference between fact and fiction. Or perhaps he didn't care any more: his many adventures had taught him to value attitude and spirit more than facts.

Anna and Willy were looked upon as unusual people. In contrast to his outgoing geniality she seemed almost dour. She was quiet and withdrawn in Port Hope, hindered by her Kaiser connection, accented English, and uneasiness with commoners; but she certainly was not paralyzed by her circumstances, since she had lived in Canada before and was accustomed to life outside of Germany. Those who knew her remember her as a "nice lady" as aware of social graces as her husband; but she was not given to rolling up her sleeves and working in a small-town kitchen and she let that be known, so to those at a distance she acquired the reputation of a snob. She was often indoors, playing the piano and fretting about this or that, a *hausfrau* as someone described her. Out on the streets Port Hopers saw a small, elegant woman, attired in beautiful dresses, keeping to herself, apparently constantly worried about life, while her husband embraced it with an energetic hug.

Perhaps she was concerned about money. Though a sale of their things would have brought them instant wealth they did not have a great deal of ready cash and Farini sold his remaining farms during the 1920s to keep them afloat. But they always had more than enough to live on, a fact borne out by their trips to Florida and the large sum of money Farini would soon spend on stocks. However, a number of their friends thought they were constantly approaching bankruptcy, an impression created by Anna's frequent comments about her financial concerns, her listeners not realizing that her concept of "broke" was much different than their own.

Anna may have continued to visit music friends in Toronto and she certainly kept in contact with relatives at home, most notably her two nieces. Germany, now in the midst of the Weimar Republic, was in terrible shape. The country's currency was in shambles—inflation ballooning upward. The first Christmas the Farinis spent at their beautiful home on North Street they received a letter from their nieces with $40 worth of postage on it, and a Christmas goose was said to cost $450. Farini sent them money, but their plight gave Anna more to worry about.

He was acquainted with painters during these years, though he did not mix with them as much as he had in Toronto or Dresden. In 1923 the Ontario College of Art established a summer school in Port Hope after its principal, G.A. Reid, was encouraged to do so by C.T. Currelly. The school continued for several years and brought such notables as Reid and Arthur Lismer to town to teach.

Farini knew Reid both through their mutual friendship
with Currelly and their association with the Ontario
Society of Artists, and if he was not a student, must have
at the very least walked down the street to visit the school
from time to time.

Two weeks before the May 20th, 1923 opening of the
summer school, an interview with Farini appeared on the
front page of the *Evening Guide*. Entitled "A Visit With Mr.
Farini," it began with a paragraph about how remarkably
young he seemed (they claimed he strode up Walton
Street hill as though he were forty when he was really
eighty-three—an interesting comment when it is considered that he was actually nearly eighty-five), how he
"couldn't be quiet if you paid him" and how he was a man
of self-sufficiency, not only working his farm but also acting as his own carpenter. He told the reporter that one of
his mottoes was: whenever anything needs to be done
"Farini does it." But most of the article was about the
paintings in his studio and the hours he devoted to their
creation. Much was made of his versatility: he painted
everything from landscapes to portraits and still lifes,
chose subjects from all over the world and was proficient
with oils, water colours and even sculptures. The reporter
wrote that he was impressed by his art, particularly by
his use of colour. Farini launched into his theories, lecturing the poor man about the importance of painting nature
as it is seen. And before the reporter left, the huge
"Canada" sculpture was displayed (he was then adding
tablets with inscribed names of fallen Canadian soldiers),
as were the staggeringly numerous "costume pictures" he
was working on, showing the native dress of peasant
women from around the world.

But the *coup de grâce* was something he called "Waiting
For the Sultan," a six-foot nude of a voluptuous young
woman in the luxurious, purple-and-red harem of her
master, awaiting his call. Farini considered it his masterpiece. A huge, boldly erotic painting, it depicted a pale
woman standing in front of a red couch, casting her eyes
down toward a small hand-mirror. She wears only a thin

gold belt. A piece of clothing hangs from her hand, slippers sit next to her and a robe lies nearby, as if she has just undressed. Her features seem almost mulatto, her hair curiously matted and almost green, to match the robe and the potted palm trees nearby; her feet and hands are large, her arms and legs long and strong, and she stands with her weight on one leg, pushing out her hip, emphasizing its shape—her waist is slim and her breasts large and shapely. Everything about the painting: the colours, her act of gazing at herself, her forceful nudity, and the sense that she is ready to favour her master, exudes sexuality. The *Guide* reporter, choosing his words carefully, noted the "lurid" lighting in the painting that brought the woman's shape forward, and thought her "so life-like you would not be surprised to see her step out from the canvas." It likely would have scandalized many Port Hopers, but it was obviously not meant for them. Later that year it was awarded a commendation at the Canadian National Exhibition in Toronto, a not inconsiderable achievement. It remains the crowning work of his art, and one of his few pictures of merit. A womanizer in his youth, a voluptuary (whose favourite colour was red), and a man given to startling others' senses, his whole life was meant to arouse, both himself and his spectators, and the fact that this painting was his masterpiece seems fitting.

In September, after just a year on North Street, they moved across town to a smaller place, in row housing on the south side of the slope of Dorset Street West, not far from the lake. It was just a minute's walk from the town hall and five minutes from the foot of Walton, where he had debuted on the high wire.

The following autumn they were off to Florida again, but just before they left, Farini gave Currelly another collection of old coins, this time for his Royal Ontario Museum, just beginning its reign as a major cultural institution. They were readily accepted. Such were the treasures in his home.

He was still obsessed with physical fitness. In the

mornings he rose early, rotated his scalp, chinned himself ten times and ate according to a careful diet. One of his favourite foods was yogurt, which Russians and east Europeans had eaten for many years but few North Americans had even heard of. Farini valued its nutritional merits to such a degree that he wrote about it, not only encouraging others to give it a try, but explaining how to make it. This was fifty years before it became one of the staples of Western health food. Once he finished breakfast his normal routine was to hop onto his bike, perhaps dressed in his Sherlock Holmes cap, tweed suit and ribbon tie, with plus-fours at the calves, and cycle seven miles out of town to the Marsh farm on the other side of Welcome. His bicycle trips were most frequent during harvest time, when he worked the Marsh place or helped friends on other farms. He would operate the hay rake, pitch hay, and even climb up onto the wagon to build loads. Lloyd Marvin, whose parents ran one of the old Farini farms in the 1920s could still recall, sixty years later, his amazement when he saw this old man, well into his eighties, grab the side of the hay wagon and flip himself up onto the load. He delighted the hired men and boys with his stories and during pauses would try to get them to walk a tightrope—if they failed he would step onto it himself. The newspapers began noticing his long treks to the farms (on roads that weren't paved until 1925), and one printed the astonishing fact that he could make the whole trip home from the country in twenty-six minutes. They thought this "pretty fair" for an eighty-four-year-old (they were just one year off this time). "Our friend, Mr. Farini," wrote the *Guide* later, "is working in the hay fields these days and he says it is splendid exercise."

The newspapers loved to quote him (*The Times* even published his poem "The Hero" in late 1924) and record his amusing activities, but seldom did he tell them much about his amazing past. This was the subject of rumours, and to many people he wasn't an energetic, kindly old man, but a mysterious person of dark secrets, with a history so strange they wouldn't dare ask about it. They heard bits and pieces of his life, fragments of stories that acquaintances would recount when they saw his elegant form moving past them on the street. He did not seem like one of them. They heard that he had killed his wife by letting her fall off his back at Niagara and that someone had burnt his Hope Township butter factory to the ground. Some understood that even at his advanced age he was still unrepentant in his belief that human passions were not to be controlled, but should be explored regardless of the consequences. And the consequences, they had heard, had been substantial in his life.

In the second week of December 1925, the *Port Hope Times* decided to set the record straight about him. They sent a reporter to his house on Dorset Street to hear his life story in detail. But the things he said, published in a two-part article, only added to the legend.

From 1926 to 1928 Farini aged from eighty-eight to ninety, and yet showed no signs of slowing down (though he suffered from poor circulation in his hands and always wore gloves to keep his fingers warm). He became slightly thinner, his face a little more wrinkled, but his step retained its bounce, and his active mind continued to surprise his friends. Surely death was closing in—but he seemed undaunted.

He even began speculating on the stock market again. In the late twenties he purchased more than 35,000 shares in various companies, the vast majority in his beloved gold industry. Though most weren't bad investments, and some even turned a small profit, one was so disastrous that it rendered the good choices nearly insignificant. By the end of 1928 he had bought 25,700 shares in Skead Consolidated, the first company he invested in and the one into which he would pour by far the greatest amount of money. Most of the shares were purchased for a dollar a piece...by January 1929 they were worth one-quarter of a cent each: $25,000 had been turned into $64.25.

Farini had a rather cavalier attitude about money. He loved to acquire it, and something like gold sparkled in his mind like the spangles on Joe Pentland's costumes, but ultimately it was unimportant to him. He had confidence in his ability to make great amounts of it, and didn't worry about speculating. But this became a dangerous habit in his late eighties when he had no way of recouping his losses. Thus the Farinis' worth continued to dwindle. By the late 1920s his land sales, Anna's money, and the little he gained from the stocks kept them afloat in their little semi-detached house. Its interior, packed to the rafters with an incredible array of Farini's mementos and Anna's possessions, gave the appearance of wealth.

On March 31st, 1926 Ringling Brothers Barnum and Bailey, the colossal "big one," opened at the new Madison Square Garden in New York. Among the performers in Clyde Ingalls' sideshow was the one and only Krao Farini, the Missing Link. It was an extraordinary show, five rings, featuring some of the most famous names in circus history. Never before or since has such stunning talent been seen on the same show; even the Ringling brothers themselves, up from Florida estates, were sights to be seen. *Billboard* magazine, in a front-page article, reported that attendance during the first week was an all-time record for any circus or theatrical enterprise. Krao, who first toured with Barnum and Bailey in 1896 had developed her act to the point where she now appeared as a refined, educated lady capable of speaking five languages. She was forty-nine years old, healthy and happy. But during that momentous first week at the Garden, she suddenly became seriously ill and had to retire to a home owned by friends who cared for her whenever she was in New York. She contracted a severe case of influenza, declined rapidly, and died on April 16th. A few days later she was buried at St. Michael's Cemetery, Astoria. She was held in high regard by her fellow freaks and at her funeral they spoke of her kindness and wonderful disposition. "If any one has gone to heaven that woman has," said Carrie Holt, the fat woman. Others, like the giant who had to bring his own chair, and the "leopard skin girl" who wept openly, called her "the best liked of freaks" and "the peace maker of the side show." She had asked to be cremated in order to avoid being viewed in the casket (Krao had been terrified of being stared at when not in the sideshow and had always worn a veil in public), but because she had not written the request it was denied.

Obituaries appeared in the *New York Times* and *Billboard*, the former running two large columns, telling of her origins in "jungles of Siam," her flexible hands and cheek pouches; other articles mentioned the hair on her back, said to be as thick as a horse's mane. All accounts spoke of Farini, who had "found" her and made her famous. The comments about her education, personality and the fact that her last name was Farini right up until death spoke volumes about his treatment of her. The Port Hope *Evening Guide* ran a story on their front page ("Krao 'The Missing Link' First Found in Siam by Port Hoper"), and a reporter went around to Dorset Street and got some facts and a few good tales. Krao's "papa" reported that he had gone to Siam to find her and had become her legal guardian, and spoke of her abilities with languages, her skill as a contortionist, and about being thrown out of Italy for exhibiting a "missing link." He had recently visited her and had been pleased to discover that good contracts had made her well off.

As Farini Hunt's years stretched out toward ninety perhaps his greatest friends were children. They had heard the story-book legends about him, and they adored this wiry old man with the billowing white beard who rode a bicycle with the seat pulled up a foot higher than the handlebars. He was like a combination Santa Claus and P.T. Barnum and knew instinctively what they liked. When he walked down the street children would sometimes call out "Freeny! Freeny!" as he passed. In those days the dictum that children were to be seen and not heard was almost law in Port Hope, never questioned by the little people who were thus declared unimportant. But Farini Hunt was different, unlike any adult the children had ever known. He gave them things, told them stories, and charmed their young souls. Seventy years later, elderly people who were children in Port Hope in the 1920s, break into smiles when recalling him. C.T. Currelly's son (who grew up to be a judge) remembered him as a friendly old man, always optimistic and given to laughter. He specifically recalled how Farini would pay attention to children and thought of them as "nice little people," not mere nuisances. He treasured the time when the old man climbed to the top of the barn at Locust Lawn to capture a couple of young pigeon squabs because he thought the boy might like to have them. His niece (Mannie's daughter) Thelma can remember his habit of bending over and stretching his arms out to her in greeting and getting a kick out of hearing him rattle on in Italian to a neighbourhood grocer in Hamilton. And Jack Hunt's grandson Ted recalls Uncle Farini giving him and his brother presents: like season's tickets for ice skating at the local rink, a weird hard-tire bicycle and, of all things, a musket, a present considered a little strange not only by their parents but by the boys themselves. Ted also recalled a painting that hung in his great-uncle's house on Dorset Street: of a ferocious Newfoundland dog which seemed to leap at visitors the minute they opened the door.

The old man told the kids wild things about walking over Niagara Falls, about The Greatest Show on Earth, and killing a lion with a revolver as it dragged him along the desert sand. No one else could match him.

His conversations with adults equally intrigued his listeners. C.T. Currelly remembered hearing not only eloquent tales of extraordinary experiences, but also hundreds of new approaches to complex mechanical problems: "Now, why wouldn't this work?" Farini Hunt would ask enthusiastically. He didn't appear overly boastful and his well-modulated voice never rose appreciably; he merely exuded self-confidence and took pride in his achievements. His friends were astounded at the breadth of his knowledge, but above all were charmed. The man who had seemed such a terror so often during his life was now a charismatic old gentleman dressed elegantly, kissing good friends on both cheeks in greeting, and often seen gathering flowers. But there were others who heard his loud stories and smooth talk and considered him a charlatan. He was not to be trusted—a not entirely ill-advised opinion.

Despite the bluster, and his apparent youth, his mortality began creeping into his mind. On October 29, 1926 he made up his will, an unremarkable document which left various moneys, stocks and possessions to Anna, William Farini in Ormskirk, and Mrs. Lulu Farini in Brooklyn, and a few paintings and artifacts to Currelly. In 1927 one of his grandchildren married in England and the following year his first great-grandchild was born. And then he turned ninety. Anna made her feelings known in English lines.

> To my dearest Willie, June 10th 1928
> It is 90 years ago today
> that in this world you came to stay,
> A lucky star brought you to me,
> Your loving wife I'm proud to be....
> I send my prayers to him above,
> To guard you ever, dearest love.

But even Anna's love could not guard against death.

On January 1st, 1929 Emma Neill Hunt, Farini's stepmother, died at the Hospital for Incurables in Toronto. Now that Emma (several years Farini's junior) and sister Ann and brother Tom, and many of his friends and protégés and even wives had fallen by the wayside, he seemed to be living beyond his time. And the circumstances of Emma's death were frightening.

Though old age contributed to her passing, something else was the deciding factor. December 1928 and January 1929 was a frightening time for the elderly in southern Ontario. A killer was passing through their midst, as virulent as the "spotted fever" that had taken Mary Soper and Sam Marsh in 1813. It was nothing more than

influenza, but it brought with it complications, most
notably a pneumonia that could kill, and old people were
its favourite victim. So pervasive was the epidemic that it
produced headlines, daily articles and death tallies in Port
Hope and Toronto newspapers. On January 12th the
Evening Guide reported that 474 people had died from the
flu in the previous three months—and the toll was rising.

That winter had been a strange one, as if things were
not quite right with the world. It would snow for a while
and be briskly cold and then a thaw would come. Again
the snow would come and melt again. The streets were
filled with slush, the river rose to dangerous heights, and
ice was everywhere. The *Guide* began to worry that this
horrible weather was contributing to the mounting number of deaths of Port Hope's elderly citizens.

Farini was now in his ninety-first year. He considered
himself invulnerable, just as he had nearly eighty years
earlier when he danced on the breaking dam in
Bowmanville. The perils he had survived and his incredible physical fitness made him think he would live past one
hundred, and his friends and acquaintances didn't doubt
him. He kept exercising, watching his diet, and maintaining a positive attitude. It was said that he expected to out-
live Anna, though she was well over a decade younger.

On January 11th a blizzard went through Port Hope
and everything froze, but within a few days it was melt-
ing again. On the 15th another storm came, depositing
more than six inches of snow on the ground. In the midst
of this, Farini suddenly became ill. Then came the terrifying news: it was influenza.

He stayed home for as long as he could, apparently as
calm as ever in the face of another hurdle. Throughout his
life people had remarked at the coolness of his nerve, and
in illness this bravery did not desert him. But on the 15th
he was so sick that he had to be taken from his home and
brought to the hospital on Ward Street. "Our old friend,"
said the *Guide* the following day, "was removed from his
home on Dorset Street to Port Hope Hospital suffering
from the flu. He is doing as well as can be expected." Anna

was devastated. She thought so much of him and depended on him so thoroughly that the thought of losing him was inconceivable. She never thought she would see the day when it was the unconquerable Willy, and not herself, who was slipping away. But perhaps he could hold on. Perhaps he could, like the conjuror he was, extricate himself from another tight squeeze.

One wonders what he thought about, confined to a hospital bed. Perhaps of Mary spiralling downward away from him and crashing into the seats in Havana, of slipping on the high wire inside the sack over the gorge at Niagara, of seeing Lulu miss the net in Dublin, of moments of desperation in the Kalahari, or missing his moment at the Royal Geographical Society. Perhaps it was of the sound and colour of The Greatest Show on Earth, the explosion when Zazel shot through the Aquarium, of striding down Broadway dressed to the nines with Lu and his flowing hair, of his many meetings with King Edward; or maybe it was of simpler things, like walking through the woods to school in Canton. Or did he think of the secret he kept of the Lost City of the Kalahari, and all the other mysteries he might soon be leaving behind.

Or perhaps, he dreamt of flying.

On the 16th young Ted Hunt, age ten, was told to go to the hospital to see his Uncle Farini. There was the sense that he might never see him again. The boy entered the hospital room shyly and approached the bed. He expected to see a frail, beaten old man. But instead he saw his greatuncle sitting bolt upright in bed, reading the paper; he held it firmly in front of his face, informing himself, and his arms didn't shake an inch.

The boy doffed his cap and asked the great man tentatively, "Uncle Farini...are you going to die?"

Farini fixed him with a theatrical stare. "Nonsense!" he said, "A fortune-teller came to see me the other day, and she told me I would live for another twenty years!"

The next day, January 17th, 1929, William Leonard Hunt, the Great Farini, was dead.

EPILOGUE

It is said that if someone dies on a rainy day their spirit will live forever. The day Farini died, in the midst of a Canadian winter, there was sleet and rain in Port Hope and the Ganaraska River began to swell and kept on swelling. He had loved water from the time he was a child and now it exploded in his home town: it ran over the banks and up Walton Street, and three stores were completely washed away. There were reports of injuries, large chunks of ice lay on the street and a Toronto paper sent an airplane, a flying machine, to photograph the destruction from above. They put Port Hope's flood on their front page.

"Most Remarkable Man Passes Away" read a headline in the *Guide*: "...everyone was surprised to learn that he had succumbed... Had we time and space his life would make a most interesting account but we can only touch on some of the salient points about which we know from personal contact with this most remarkable man."

Then, perhaps surprisingly, came an avalanche of obituaries, in the *New York Times, Montreal Gazette, Toronto Daily Star, Niagara Falls Gazette* and local papers in places like Oshawa and Peterborough. The Canadian Press sent out a story which was picked up all over, though curiously, there was little notice in England. Many of the obituaries made errors, calling him Gilarma Farini, saying he had walked Niagara in 1864, that his wife had fallen from his back there. But he was nearly as much to blame for this as the passing of time; his stories had been gathered up and put together in a pastiche of tall tales.

The most spectacular record of his life was published in the Toronto *Evening Telegram*. They printed three accounts, the last nearly a full page long with seven photographs: "Farini the Great" as Svengali with a long black beard, Lulu in various incarnations, and the adventurer sitting on a dead giraffe in the Kalahari. The article made an array of claims. Among them: that Guillermo Antonio Farini was the name of an heroic Italian athlete, gladiator and hero; that Lulu was believed to be supernatural; that Farini once ran Cole Brothers Circus, climbed part of Mount Everest and travelled in China. There was also an interesting story about a well-known saying.

...Farini, too, coined the famous epigram credited to Barnum, "the people like to be humbugged." Barnum had advertised that the circus had a horse with its head where its tail ought to be. Paying their money to see this freak in a sideshow, patrons saw a horse backed in a stall instead of standing in head first. There was a howl of "humbug." Barnum was worried, but Farini suggested that he answer the newspapers merely by saying: "The people like to be humbugged." And—perhaps because they do—the answer more than satisfied.

Historians have found other sources for the "humbug" saying, and it appears to have been first uttered before Farini and Barnum were associated. But it fits him better than the American: he believed, almost as a fundamental principle, that people desperately wanted to be told there were fantastic things in life.

The funeral took place on Saturday the 19th, from the chapel of Port Hope undertaker A.W. George on Walton Street, and the service was conducted by a local Anglican rector (apparently Farini's conversion to Catholicism had not lasted). It is not known who attended the "solemnly impressive" occasion, though the pallbearers were all from Hope Township, and Anna was there, almost paralyzed with sorrow. The procession moved slowly up Walton Street (which was treacherously icy) to the burial spot at St. John's Cemetery on Toronto Road, a fitting route that leads into the township. As the cortege edged along it passed many people and a remarkable thing happened: children removed their caps and stood silently beside their elders, aware that this was "Freeny" being honoured.

Anna passed two more unhappy years in Port Hope, far from her home, pining for the incomparable Willy. His small estate, which was divided up between William Farini, Edith and C.T. Currelly (who received "African and other trophies", some Etruscan vases, etc.), left her little on the surface (even his two diamond studs and his precious silver punch bowl from Queen Alexandra went to William), but she owned Locust Lawn farm, had some cash of her own and, most importantly the invaluable contents of their home. But when Farini died, worldly goods, like everything else, meant nothing to her.

Either out of kindness or for less charitable reasons Farini's friends Margaret and Alex Brown adopted the lonely and mentally deteriorating old German lady in 1929 and kept her in their home on Sherbourne Street. She signed legal agreements giving up her possessions, income and Locust Lawn in exchange for their care. On June 7, 1931 she died, age seventy-seven, and was buried next to Farini, lowered beside him the day before his birthday. Margaret was named executrix of her will. Its execution was a little problematic, as evidenced by Currelly's enquiries as late as Christmas 1933 (with his solicitors hovering in the background) about a Bushman's cape, some horns, elephant's remains and Sevres china. These items finally came into the museum's possession in 1941, supplemented by a giraffe's head, an albatross's head, a boomerang and a bull whip.

Margaret Brown, described as "a real character" by a fellow Port Hoper of her day, perhaps a fitting personality to
possess the Farinis' unusual worldly goods, died in 1938.
Seven years later, at a public auction, Alex divested himself of the enormous collection of old-world valuables he
had inherited. It drew a great deal of press coverage,
notably from the *Toronto Daily Star* who focused their
attention on a little box containing a cigar which Anna
claimed Liszt had smoked. "You would hardly believe all
the things Bill Hunt did," Brown told a big-city reporter,
"...he used to bring some of his friends back here and we
used to wonder what he'd be up to next." Dealers were
stunned by the array of things that had been hidden in the
Brown's little Port Hope home: Farini's steel drums, his
world-weary travelling trunks, and bound volumes of nineteenth-century entertainment papers, but also near price-
less pieces like Napoleon III's china teapot, and Marie
Antoinette's sewing cabinet which Anna claimed her father
had taken from Paris in 1871; a Bechstein of Berlin concert
grand piano, presented to Anna by the Kaiser; a German
silver tea service for eighteen, Meissen china and Royal
Dresden figurines. There were also precious personal
things: a court jacket Liszt had worn, the portrait he had
autographed to Anna, and the letter he wrote to her not
long before he died; and to many, the least of the valuable
items, Farini's favourite painting, Waiting for the Sultan.

By 1931 the search for Farini's legendary Lost City was
well underway in southern Africa. In 1933 *The Radio
Times* of England featured Zazel, who died four years
later and was immortalized in 1940 in the W. Somerset
Maugham short story "Gigolo and Gigolette." In 1936 the
Royal Alhambra Palace was torn down and a movie house
was built on the site. Farini's remaining brothers and sisters died in the thirties and forties, Mannie passing away
at age ninety in 1948.

In the beautiful countryside of upper New York State
just over the Massachusetts border near the village of
Hillsdale, another kindly old man with a white beard

spent his final years. Retiring there from photography and motion-picture work in Brooklyn, Lulu outlived Edith, who died in 1934. His daughter became an artist and his granddaughter a professor and novelist, who fondly remembered him as the best of grandfathers, but understood from her grandmother that "circus" was not a topic fit for discussion. Lulu passed away in 1939 and was buried in the Hillsdale cemetery; his simple stone reads "Louis Farini."

Occasionally articles were published about Signor Farini: they appeared in *Reader's Digest*, various smaller publications and sporadic pieces in the Port Hope *Evening Guide*. They contained many errors. In 1956 the appropriately titled American magazine *True*, in a glowing piece about Blondin, reported that Farini, humiliated at Niagara, had gone to Europe and died there young and penniless as the result of a fall from the wire. Though an indignant article appeared in the *Guide* in response, and in 1963 they published a piece about him entitled "Hope's Man of the Century," they too made errors, and for the most part even Port Hope forgot him. A photograph of Farini in leotards became possibly his best-known image in the region, though it was actually a snapshot of Lulu. From time to time interest was shown in writing a book about him, but the task seemed too daunting and the evidence for his feats too skimpy. He was relegated to brief mentions and footnotes. And besides, he hadn't really done anything: he hadn't discovered a cure for a terrible disease, he hadn't led a country to victory in war, he wrote no classic book and no streets or buildings or cities were named for him. His life had merely been an adventure, and a less than respectable one at that. It had been useless.

His grave remained unmarked for sixty years, and was then covered with a small, flat stone. It goes unseen in the winter, buried beneath blankets of snow. Thus the great illusionist vanished, slipping between the pages of popular history like a rabbit back into a hat.

ACKNOWLEDGEMENTS

During the course of researching and writing this book I visited, and wrote to, many countries on several continents, met a great many intriguing people and made some lasting friends. It seems a lifetime since I began. Farini lived in many worlds: following him has made me inhabit them and enriched my life. First among those who must be thanked is my family who, seeing my resolve, supported me throughout many years of work, and my wife, Sophie, whose hours of toil on my behalf seem innumerable. I also want to thank Dr. John Turner of Formby, England, circus historian extraordinaire and friend; Dr. Gordon Brown, another extraordinary (this time North American) circus historian and friend; Leon Warmski, Senior Reference Archivist at the Archives of Ontario, who encouraged me through the years and offered his consummate skills whenever they were needed; and Donald Loker of the Local History Department of the Niagara Falls NY Public Library for his enthusiasm and guidance.

Farini relatives have also been helpful. Lulu's granddaughter (also Farini's grand-niece) Edith Taylor has been a joy to correspond with; Farini's niece Thelma Saunders graciously took the time to talk to me on several occasions;

Farini's great-granddaughter Ann Hindley, her husband, Sam, Joe Robinson and the whole Robinson clan of Skelmersdale, England treated me like a veritable family member every time I visited them; Dennis and Hazel Farini and Margaret Farini of Ormskirk did likewise. In Canada, Ted and Doreen Hunt, the younger Ted Hunt, Robert Saunders, Phyllis (Hunt) Pearson and Lynda (Hunt) Baird also spoke to me freely about their memories; also Larry Minck and Maude S. Deemer.

In Port Hope and vicinity: Michael Wladyka readily opened his vast archives to me and gave unstintingly of his time whenever asked; others in the area include Wolfgang and Anne Arnold, Edna Barrowclough, Cal Clayton, Judge J.C.N. Currelly, Aleda Dickinson and her son Clarke, Belle and Rudolf Eyman, Peggy Foster, Richard Gardiner, Mrs. Mac Irwin, Rolf and Marjorie Kenton, Robin Long, Grace Marsh, Lloyd and Marian Marvin, Mrs. Harold Reeve and Norm Strong. Also the East Durham Historical Society and the 4th Line Theatre company. In the Bowmanville area there was Bill Bagnall, Stuart Candler, Phyllis Dewell, Forrest Dilling, Jack Gordon, Norman and Joan James, Elsie Lunney, Garfield Shaw and the Bowmanville Museum.

While researching I joined the Circus Historical Society of America and the Circus Friends' Association of Great Britain. Many of their members and other circus people contributed to my research. Among them were: Robert Bogdan, whose freak-show expertise I leaned on, Fred Dahlinger, Steve Gossard, Orin C. King, Bernth Lindfors, Don Marcks, Robert Parkinson, Rick and Fred Pfening, John Polacsek, A.H. Saxon, George Speaight, Mark St. Leon and Stuart Thayer.

Others who must be thanked for their contributions include: Cynthia Good for her confidence in me and her enthusiasm, Pierre Berton, Lee Davis Creal, Robertson Davies, Dr. Robert Gidney, Scott Haldeman, Wyn Haldeman, Tasso Komossa, Ricardo Martinez, Michael Mitchell, Maye Musk, Dean Owen, Charles Pachter, Dennis Reid, Lloyd Scott, Barbara Sears, George Seibel,

Bruce Stinson, Phillip V. Tobias, Dr. Alan Walker and Don Withrow.

Most important of the many libraries, archives and other institutions I consulted were: the Archives of Ontario in Toronto, where the extensive "The Farini Papers" are housed; the Niagara Falls NY Public Library; the Library of Congress; the British Museum Library and its affiliated music, patent and newspaper libraries, all in London; the Theatre Museum in London (and Claire Hudson); and the Circus World Museum in Baraboo, Wisconsin.

I have drawn on the standard sources of books, censuses, directories, land records, newspapers, periodicals, etc. of Farini's time and today, and interviewed many people who either knew Farini, or something about him. My bibliography, had it been included here, would have stretched over dozens of pages.

For scholars seeking further detailed information: a full bibliography, notes and much of the research material for *The Great Farini* can be found at the Ganaraska Region Archives in Port Hope, Ontario under the care of the East Durham Historical Society.

The author appreciates the support of the Explorations Program of the Canada Council: without its financial assistance this book would not have been possible.

Shane Peacock
Toronto, Ontario